FLORIDA STATE
UNIVERSITY LIBRARIES

MAY 17 1995

TALLAHASSEE, FLORIDA

Lord Lyndhurst

Lord Lyndhurst. Used by permission of the Master and Fellows of Trinity College, Cambridge.

Lord Lyndhurst
The Flexible Tory

Dennis Lee

UNIVERSITY PRESS OF COLORADO

© by the University Press of Colorado
P.O. Box 849
Niwot, Colorado 80544

All rights reserved.

Cover: Lord Lyndhurst, from a drawing by George Richmond.
Used by permission of the Master and Fellows of Trinity College, Cambridge.

The University Press of Colorado is a cooperative publishing enterprise supported, in part, by Adams State College, Colorado State University, Fort Lewis College, Mesa State College, Metropolitan State College of Denver, University of Colorado, University of Northern Colorado, University of Southern Colorado, and Western State College of Colorado.

The paper used in this publication meets the minimum requirements of the American National Standard for Information Sciences—Permanenece of Paper for Printed Library Materials. ANSZI Z39.48–1984
∞

Library of Congress Cataloging-in-Publication Data

Lee, Dennis, 1943–
    Lord Lyndhurst: the flexible Tory / Dennis Lee.
      p. cm.
    Includes bibliographical references and index.
    ISBN 0-87081-358-7
    1. Lyndhurst, John Singleton Copley, Baron 1772–1863.
2. Great Britain—Politics and government—19th century.
3. Politicians—Great Britain—Biography. 4. Tories, English.
I. Title.
DA536.L9L44   1994
941.081'092—dc20
[B]
                                            94-26518
                                            CIP

10 9 8 7 6 5 4 3 2 1

My greatest debt is to my wife, Esther, and children, Elliot and Alexandra, without whose patience and helpfulness this work would not have beem possible.

CONTENTS

Illustrations		vii
Introduction		ix
Acknowledgments		xvii
1.	From the New World to the Old World	1
2.	Copley's American Tour	13
3.	Launching a Career	23
4.	Upon a Larger Stage	35
5.	A Reward for Perseverance	47
6.	Keeping Afloat	60
7.	Setting up the Duke	69
8.	Concession Over Consistency	77
9.	Lady Lyndhurst's Adventure	89
10.	Expediter of Justice?	104
11.	A Sinking Ship	111
12.	Rescued by the Whigs	117
13.	Throw Open the Floodgates	128
14.	This Fatal Bill	139
15.	The Most Splendid Moment	148
16.	Dolly's Exit and Peel's Hour	159
17.	Disraeli's Staunch Friend	180
18.	Breathing Life Into the Party	191
19.	New Queen, New Wife, New Ministry	209
20.	His Last Chancellorship	219
21.	A Living Link	233
22.	The Nestor of His Party	244
23.	Ever Resilient	256
Notes		271
Bibliography		307
Index		313

ILLUSTRATIONS

Frontispiece: Lord Lyndhurst

1.1   Lord Lyndhurst
4.1   Sarah Baroness Lyndhurst
5.1   Lord Lyndhurst as Lord High Chancellor of England
6.1   The Chancellor portrayed as a timeserving careerist
8.1   Dressing for the House
9.1   Scene painter and property man
9.2   The affidavit
9.3   Lyndhurst's shadow appears to bear horns
11.1 God save the King
12.1 Wants a situation
12.2 The chameleon
16.1 Coplinda Lindhursta the cook
16.2 Lyndhurst in his parliamentary robes
17.1 Benjamin Disraeli
19.1 Drawing of Lyndhurst seated, bearing his signature and the words: Author of "Summary of the Session"
21.1 Lyndhurst
23.1 Bust of Lyndhurst

Introduction

There is something in human nature that likes to discover a villain. Although John Singleton Copley, Jr., Baron Lyndhurst, has not attained the distinction of true villainy, he has been portrayed by many historians in an unsavory fashion. This three times Lord Chancellor of England is one of the very few politicians of his era not to have a modern biography. Lyndhurst played a significant role in nineteenth-century British politics, participating in the efforts of Britain's governing elite as it struggled with the constitutional crises of the 1820s and 1830s. Later, he helped to transform the Tory party into the Conservative party. He also gained importance as the patron of Benjamin Disraeli. The perception of Lyndhurst is a clouded one because, initially, two biographers arguing opposite viewpoints wrote about him. The first was Lord Campbell in his *Lives of Lord Lyndhurst and Lord Brougham* published in 1869.[1] It is a harsh partisan indictment, which has been accepted by most subsequent writers. The other biography, *A Life of Lord Lyndhurst*, by Sir Theodore Martin, appeared in 1884 and is an apotheosis commissioned by the widowed Lady Lyndhurst.[2]

Lady Lyndhurst certainly received her money's worth from Martin's portrayal of a "very remarkable man." Lyndhurst emerges as a great lawyer and statesman, one of the greatest of England's judges, who missed supreme power by the accidents of fortune rather than any fault of his own. Martin claims for Lord Lyndhurst a place in line just behind the foremost Tory leaders of his day: "In all measures of importance the Duke of Wellington and Sir Robert Peel leant so greatly upon the counsels of Lord Lyndhurst that his voice may be said to have been next to theirs the most potential in the Cabinet."[3] Martin's glowing biography abounds with references to Lyndhurst's excellent qualities: "Indeed, by sheer superiority of intellect, and by his intuitive tact and judgment in situations of difficulty, he had acquired such an influence in the councils of his party, that his presence among them was indispensable."[4]

Lyndhurst's feats of oratory supplied a clear, eloquent, penetrating voice that in his later years won him the title of England's Nestor. When he died at age ninety-one, full of years and honors, even the critics of his political career were ready, in the words of Martin, "to give credit to him for wise and generous and patriotic impulses in his public life." Such is the shining image that unfolds in the biography that Lady Lyndhurst sanctioned. It is an image of a great man who wielded great power "without meanness or self-seeking."[5] By way of contrast, Lord Campbell outlines a career that *was* founded on meanness and self-seeking. Campbell had applied to Lyndhurst for materials to use in the preparation of his biography. The latter replied without candor, "Materials you shall have none from me; I have already burnt every letter and paper which could be useful to my biographer, therefore he is at liberty to follow his own inclinations."[6] Obviously, Lyndhurst didn't want Campbell to write about him.

Lyndhurst's papers do exist. The materials Sir Theodore Martin used have been divided. The greater portion is kept in the Glamorgan Record Office in the County Hall in Cardiff, Wales, where the papers were deposited by Lyndhurst's descendant, the Earl of Aberdare, in 1967. A smaller but politically more significant collection of papers was given by Lady Lyndhurst to Trinity College sometime after 1884. There is also the family correspondence that was published in 1882 by Lyndhurst's American niece, Martha Babcock Amory.[7] The collections at Cardiff and Cambridge give an impression that someone, whether Lyndhurst himself or his loyal widow or her agent, did comb through his papers. No material present suggests a less than sterling statesman. These sanitized collections can be supplemented by letters from, to, and about Lyndhurst that survive in the Wellington Papers at Southampton University, the Disraeli Papers in the Bodleian Library, University of Oxford, and the subsequent publication of memoirs, journals, and letters since Martin's and Campbell's works.

Unfortunately, when Lord Campbell was left to his own devices, he followed a malign inclination fed by decades of bitterness and envy. His hostility stemmed from both political disharmony and Lyndhurst's rejection of Campbell's desire for social intimacy. Campbell's initial admiration for his colleague is suggested in his boast of the new cabriolet he had ordered: "Copley is the only other legal man with a carriage of this sort."[8] The scorned Campbell built an image of a parvenu lawyer "very unreasonably ashamed of his family" and of the fact that he was born in America.[9] He also charged that Lyndhurst held republican, even Jacobin opinions until he attained middle age, whereupon he jettisoned those opinions for fame and fortune with England's Tory rulers. Allegedly, he exchanged his hopes for a democratic revolution and a republic for office and, eventually, elevation to the highest councils of government. Campbell was adamant: "He was a Whig and something more, or in one word a Jacobin."[10]

In addition to being a turncoat and a shameless apostate, Lyndhurst was a reckless and licentious talker. He squandered his income and lived extravagantly. Even as a judge he faltered, for "he would not heartily give his mind to his judicial business."[11] Even his appearance signaled his wicked ways: "His features were strongly marked and his whole countenance well chiselled — with some fine lines of thought in it — nevertheless, occasionally with a sinister smile of great cunning and some malignity, which obtained for him the sobriquet of Mephistophiles."[12] Indeed, Campbell's Lyndhurst took on the shape of a villain.

Historians, for the most part, have taken their cue from Campbell. Lyndhurst has done service as a "bad Tory," whereas laurels have been heaped on such "good Tories" as Peel and the Duke of Wellington. In the pages of history books, Lyndhurst is "the distinctly mediocre lawyer"[13] who became "the skillful and unscrupulous Lord Lyndhurst."[14] Even his heart was interpreted as made of sinister stuff, for example, at Victoria's accession: "The little Queen's first appearance in council conquered all hearts (except the cast-iron organ of Lord Lyndhurst, who remained perfectly calm while his fellows dissolved into tears and ecstacies)."[15] There is consensus that he was "unprincipled," and we are assured that "Peel did not like Lyndhurst, whom he thought unscrupulous and untrustworthy."[16] Norman Gash, in his biography of Sir Robert Peel, acknowledged Lyndhurst's professionalism in leading his party "more as a brilliant advocate speaking to a brief than as a committed statesman."[17] Gash referred to "the wayward Lyndhurst"[18] as one "to whom both enmities and principles were largely foreign."[19] Gash minimized Lyndhurst's role, sacrificing it in his emphasis on Peel.

Lyndhurst's unfavorable image did not begin with the publication of Campbell's book. It took root during his lifetime — in fact, early in his political career. He was both a combatant in and a casualty of the political wars in which he participated with such enthusiasm. He was perceived by some contemporaries as an opportunistic careerist. During the years when he served as Lord Chancellor in the Cabinet or led opposition forces in the House of Lords, he was censured in debate by political opponents as an erstwhile republican, even a former Jacobin, who had abandoned his ideals for government favor. A persistent theme runs through the criticism leveled at Lord Lyndhurst: that he had abandoned the reform or republican principles of his early manhood for those principles he later held.

Lyndhurst railed against the statement that he had been "a Whig, or something more than a Whig" by noting that he had never belonged to any political party until he entered Parliament. He also stated that he had never belonged to any political society, and he challenged his colleagues in the House of Lords to cite any statement or act of his that supported the characterization."[20] When Lord Melbourne took up this line of attack, Lyndhurst declared that the charge was "a base calumny, and I give it the most unqualified contradiction."[21] Yet it was a calumny that would not cease. Lord Denman, a prominent Whig who had ridden the circuit with Lyndhurst in the early years of their legal careers, adopted the refrain that Lyndhurst had "entertained extreme opinions." He added that such was "the perfect conviction of all who knew that noble and learned Lord." Lyndhurst challenged his accuser to "adduce a single fact in support of his charge"; otherwise, he could not respond in specific terms to unspecific charges. In exasperation, the former Lord Chancellor concluded that against him who "throws his arrows in the dark, I know not what to combat."[22] No evidence was ever brought forward to substantiate these frequently repeated charges, nor has any evidence ever been discovered. However, the perennial charge of political apostasy was too useful a cudgel for Lyndhurst's opponents to lay down.

In his *Biographical Studies*, Walter Bagehot alleged that Lyndhurst joined the Tory party "under circumstances of great suspicion. He had held — loosely, we apprehend — some sort of ultra-Liberal opinions. . . . He was a Liberal, if he was anything; and charges continued to be made against him for many years of having deserted his principles."[23] Bagehot argued that Lyndhurst, reputed to possess "an intellect of the highest cultivation" and "a first-rate judicial mind," could never have sincerely believed in Toryism and the narrow-minded policies it embraced. It is absurd to say that the greatest political intellect of his time — and some such claim as this might justly be made for Lord Lyndhurst — truly believed that the Catholics should not be emancipated, that the Corn Laws should be maintained, that there should be no reform in Parliament, that the narrow system of 1818 was a perfect or even an endurable system. I do not mean to charge him with acting contrary to his principles — that charge was made years ago but as the exaggerated charge of political opponents who saw that there was something to blame but who, in their eagerness and haste, overdid their accusation. The true charge is that he had no principles, that he did not care to have opinions.[24] Bagehot reflected the inability of liberals to believe in the possibility of intelligent conservatism. He concluded that if Lyndhurst "had paid fair attention to the subjects of his time, he would have been on what all parties now admit to be the right side. If he had had a sincere wish to improve and benefit mankind, he would have been forward in the ranks of the Liberal party, who were then employed in doing so."[25]

Thus, allegedly, Lyndhurst chose the wrong side. The Whig interpretation of history allows a right and a wrong side to great political questions.[26] Those who choose the wrong side are scorned, but special revilement is saved for those who abandon the side of rectitude and progress to serve the backward-glancing opponents of what is good and true. There is a seductive symmetry in interpretations of history that range good against evil and present history as an unfolding pageant in which heroes, while pursuing worthy goals, triumph over villains. Lyndhurst may have been as bad as or even worse than his detractors claim, or perhaps he is a victim of distortion. Caricature offered as historical interpretation ill serves both its victims and those who would understand not only events but the people and the motives these events encompassed. Bagehot entitled his essay "What Lord Lyndhurst Really Was," and he offered his own explanation. However, a more accurate explanation may go farther afield than Sir Theodore Martin or Lord Campbell or Walter Bagehot pursued it. Lyndhurst may have been more than the hero or villain they separately discovered.

Instead of assigning praise or blame, my account examines Lyndhurst as an important part of the process whereby England's ruling elite responded to demands for change. Lyndhurst was a young man studying at Cambridge when the French Revolution swept across Europe. Some were inspired by what they perceived as the dawning of a new and better day. Others saw with horror the uprooting of the twin linchpins of civilization: property and religion. These latter individuals, residing in England, feared — in fact, awaited with certainty — a similar convulsion that would shake their land and their lives. Although there was to be no parallel in England to the French experience, expectations of upheaval were genuine and shaped men's motives and behavior.[27] A great deal of violence reinforced these fears of revolution. It is important to keep in mind that violence or the threat of violence was an important force until 1848. Although the much dreaded cataclysm never arrived, the specter of social and political disorder cast a very real shadow. And it was under the burden of this lengthening shadow that the Tory leadership found it necessary to adapt to an emerging process of responsible government. Simultaneously, Tories were able to adapt this process to their own specifications to make it palatable. Lyndhurst's strong suit was adaptation because his personal need was always to adapt. The skills that had carried him to political eminence were ideally suited to fostering the adaptability of an aristocracy to govern the people. He could be a shepherd in this distasteful but necessary undertaking.

Although, as I attempt to prove, Lyndhurst was philosophically a conservative throughout his career, he displayed an inclination to be moderate by supporting concessions and reforms when he felt they were justified. His accommodation to change fitted the requirements of Peel's Tamworth Manifesto. Lyndhurst was, in fact, a moderate during most of his career. This consistent pattern has been obscured by his rather splashy leadership of the House of Lords in its opposition to reform during the 1830s, a flamboyant undertaking that was an aberration from his usual moderate course. His conduct, he believed, was justified by a need for the Lords to reassert themselves in their traditional role as a balancing element of the Constitution after they had caved in on Reform in 1832. Lyndhurst is open to criticism for his role as a mischief maker in the House of Lords during the 1830s. Yet it is important to note that public support for further reform was running out at the time, and, in this sense, he was moving with a shifting tide.[28] Yet this period detracts from his classification as a statesman in the Tamworth tradition. Lyndhurst was in step with Peel's outlook during the remainder of his public life.

Lyndhurst, pilloried as a political chameleon, showed consistency in two important areas. First, he remained conservative throughout his political career on the major issues of defending and preserving the balanced Constitution and the Established Church. Second, he was a moderate who showed a willingness to support reforms when he believed they were justified. His early life reveals indications of his conservatism and his moderation. These values are evident in letters he wrote while traveling in America; they are also reflected in a prize-winning essay he wrote while a student at Cambridge. Interestingly, his father played a role in promoting moderation between U.S. patriots and Tories in Boston prior to the outbreak of the American Revolution.

In respect to Lyndhurst's conservatism, his participation in some early controversial court cases sends mixed signals. Early in his legal career, he had successfully defended a Luddite and later secured an acquittal for Dr. James Watson, a radical agitator, on a charge of high treason. His role did not alienate the Tory government. Instead, the ministry was so impressed by his skill as an advocate that it resolved that he should never again argue against the Crown. When he was retained by the ministry in the treason trial of Jeremiah Brandreth and his fellow conspirators, some denounced him for changing sides. After the Cato Street conspiracy was uncovered, Copley's participation as a prosecutor in the trials of Arthur Thistlewood and his confederates demonstrated his concern for law and order, the first principle of a Tory government. As far as defending the Constitution and the Church are concerned, his opposition to changes affecting the House of Commons, the House of Lords, and the Church in Ireland placed him squarely in the mainstream of traditional conservatism. In 1856, when he was well into his eighties, he opposed a measure to create life peers because it would have altered the fundamental character of the House of Lords. In attempting to detect consistent aspects of Lyndhurst's career, it is easy to be distracted by the chronological phases of his public life: rising rapidly in the 1820s, making mischief in the thirties, and adopting the role of a patriotic elder statesman in the forties, fifties, and early sixties.

Lyndhurst was a self-made man. Here lies the key to his flexibility and moderation. It was a tremendous accomplishment and simultaneous burden for him to rise by dint of his own hard work and then to keep afloat politically. Charles Greville, who observed Lyndhurst at close range over a long period, described him as a "soldier of fortune" and added the label "lawyer of fortune."[29] This is reminiscent and, in fact, an anticipation of Disraeli, whose patron Lyndhurst was. On this shifting ground, Lyndhurst was extremely vulnerable, and the wire-pulling of the first Lady Lyndhurst rounded out the story. His financial instability was compounded by his spendthrift and flamboyant lifestyle, in which his wife was a keen partner. His Tory colleagues could rationalize his acceptance of Whig patronage because "they knew his deplorable state in point of money."[30] Greville was right when he observed that "his example is a lesson to statesmen to be frugal, for if he had been rich he would have had a better game before him."[31] Lyndhurst often treated politics as a game and exhibited a detachment that invited censure for an apparent lack of commitment to deeply held principles. Frequently, he seemed to be purely a brilliant lawyer speaking from a brief — supremely eloquent but with an eloquence that cloaked an underlying flexibility that was distasteful to stubborn people who wore the heavy garments of principle, people who reflected the changing standards of political behavior the Victorian era produced.

Was Lyndhurst's pliability a useful element in the game of high politics he played? Certainly it served his own self-interest, and this is what many found so offensive. Was it also useful for the dual tasks of governing his country and serving his party in his time? These are larger and more lasting questions that are considered in these pages. Let us approach them with

Lyndhurst's own exhortation in mind. The words are taken from his prize-winning essay, "A Dissertation Upon the Character and Memory of William III," which was written while he was a student at Cambridge University: "The time hath at length arrived when passion and prejudice ought to subside, and the revolution of a century should leave us capable of examining without partiality his motives and his actions, and of assigning to each their proper portion of censure or applause."[32]

ACKNOWLEDGMENTS

I wish to express my thanks to the following individuals and institutions for their courtesy in allowing me to read and quote from papers in their possession or to which they hold the copyright: the Controller of Her Majesty's Stationery Office; the Master and Fellows of Trinity College, Cambridge; the Glamorgan Record Office, County Hall, Cardiff, Wales; the British Library; the University of Southampton; the National Trust; the Institute for Historical Research; London University; and the National Register of Archives. I am most grateful to Dr. Peter Marsh for his support, advice, and kindness, which contributed immeasurably to my effort. I am indebted to Dr. Vernon Snow, who read my work and enabled me to profit from his excellent suggestions. I acknowledge with gratitude grants from the Roscoe Martin Fund and the Syracuse University Senate Committee on Research.

Lord Lyndhurst

1
From the New World to the Old World

The life of John Singleton Copley, Jr., had two beginnings. He was born in Boston in the British colony of Massachusetts on May 21, 1772. His life began anew when he arrived in England with his mother on June 28, 1775. The little party, which included young Copley, his mother, and two sisters, had quit America on May 27, six days after the boy's third birthday. In his own words, it was a journey made "in consequence of the state of political affairs."[1]

Turbulent events brought Susannah Copley and her children from the new world to the old. Incidents leading to America's revolution had made life in Boston not only unpleasant but even dangerous. The children's maternal grandfather, Richard Clarke, was a tea merchant and one of the consignees of the tea that American patriots dumped into Boston Harbor during their notorious tea party. Controversy whirled around the elder Clarke and pursued his family, forcing them to flee, victims of political upheaval.

On his mother's side, John Singleton Copley, Jr., could trace his lineage to Mary Chilton, who came to New England aboard the *Mayflower* in 1620. Copley's father's family consisted of comparative newcomers. His paternal grandparents, Richard Copley and Mary Singleton, met and married in County Clare, Ireland, immigrating to Boston in 1735. Richard Copley died one year later. He was survived by his wife and one son, John Singleton Copley.

On November 16, 1769, John Singleton Copley married Susannah Farnum Clarke, the daughter of Richard Clarke. Clarke, together with two of his sons, Jonathan and Issac, was a principal importer of tea in Boston during the decade preceding the revolution. The Clarkes were well connected. One of Richard Clarke's daughters was married to the son and namesake of Thomas Hutchinson, the Lieutenant Governor of the colony. Hutchinson became Acting Governor upon the departure of Francis Bernard in 1769. In this role he encouraged tea merchants' defiance toward patriot restrictions on importation of that commodity. Two of his sons, Thomas and Elisha, were among the merchants who refused to support the boycott of British goods, which Americans attempted to mount as a response to the Townshend Act in 1768. Richard Clarke & Sons was also among the mercantile firms that declined to adhere to a nonimportation agreement. Together the Clarkes and the Hutchinsons faced the fury of public opinion, but they thought the game was worth the candle. The Clarkes had amassed a large inventory of English tea and continued to add to it during the year of the boycott. They anticipated that the nonimportation agreement would create a shortage and that they could reap a large profit as a consequence. They miscalculated, underestimating the success of the nonimportation agreement. Fearing the consequences of public disapproval, the tea merchants were forced to halt the sale of tea in August 1768.

By 1771 the Clarkes were back in the tea business, importing dutied tea. During that one year they imported fifteen thousand pounds.[2] Their business venture placed them on a collision course with American patriots. The East India Company hovered on the brink of bankruptcy with an eighteen-million-pound surplus of tea in its warehouses.[3] Mindful of the company's important presence in India, the House of Commons passed a Tea Act in May 1773. This Act provided for full remission of all British duties on tea exported to the American colonies, but, significantly, an import tax of three pence per pound was retained in America. The measure allowed the East India Company to sell tea directly to consignees in America. The absence of British duties enabled the company to sell its tea at a lower price than colonial merchants who obeyed the law and purchased their tea through middlemen at higher prices. The company shipped half a million pounds of tea to four American ports: Boston, New York, Philadelphia, and Charleston. In each city a group of merchants was designated to be consignees of the shipment arriving at that port. In Boston three firms were chosen: Faneuil & Winslow, Thomas & Elisha Hutchinson, and Richard Clarke & Sons.

American opponents of the Tea Act vented their fury on the consignees. In both Philadelphia and New York the consignees were branded public enemies at mass meetings and capitulated to demands that they resign their commissions. In Boston the consignees refused to cave in. Richard

Clarke, using the pseudonym "Z," wrote a newspaper article in which he defended the plan for the disposal of the tea and described its advantages for American merchants.[4] Clarke and his fellow consignees received a summons to appear at Liberty Tree to publicly resign their commissions. When the designated time passed and they failed to appear, a delegation accompanied by a large crowd marched to Clarke's store, where the consignees had gathered. When the latter spurned the crowd's demands, the mob rushed the building, breaking down the door. The Clarkes and their associates fled to a second-floor counting room, where they found refuge for an hour and a half until the crowd dispersed. This unnerving episode signaled to the consignees that resistance would entail some rigors.

This incident of mob violence took place on November 3, 1773, and was followed by a formal town meeting held in Faneuil Hall on November 5. A committee was deputized to demand the resignation of the commissions. The consignees' refusal was characterized as "Daringly Affrontive to the Town."[5] Nearly two weeks later, Jonathan Clarke arrived in Boston aboard a ship from London. He was believed by many to be bringing orders from the East India Company. A town meeting was called for the next day. Before that meeting could take place, a menacing crowd gathered in front of the Clarke home, where the family had assembled to welcome its returning member. As the crowd grew more threatening, a shot was fired from within the house. No one was hurt, but this action so infuriated the mob that its members hurled whatever missiles they could seize through the broken windows, harming both occupants and furnishings. The Clarkes stubbornly refused to give an inch, and, at length, the crowd dispersed.

Once again the town meeting appointed a committee to secure the consignees' resignation, and once more they refused to resign. An attempt was made to reach a compromise with the Boston selectmen, who demanded that the tea be returned to England. Nothing less would appease the aroused citizenry. Clarke found this solution unacceptable because English law prohibited reimportation of tea, and both ships and cargo would be vulnerable to confiscation when they reached England. On the other hand, the tea could not be landed. If it were taken ashore and the duties paid, the patriots' protest would have failed.

Amid this deadlock, the senior Clarke migrated to the relative safety of Salem and his two sons fled to Castle William, a military outpost on an island in Boston Harbor. Richard Clarke's son-in-law, John Singleton Copley, stepped forward in the role of peacemaker. He was respected as a native son who had gained recognition as a successful artist. His painting *The Boy With the Squirrel* had been exhibited in London in 1766. This work, together with successive paintings, had won him critical praise within the London art world. He had been elected a Fellow of the Society of Incorporated Artists of Great Britain and had painted several of New England's leading citizens.

Clearly, Copley was an ambitious man. He had married into one of the most prominent families in the colony of Massachusetts, and his own accomplishments had won the respect of his fellow citizens. Copley had a reputation as a political moderate on the issues that were dividing Americans. Now he was called upon to act as a go-between to persuade his brothers-in-law to abandon the safety of isolation at Castle William and attend a town meeting. Boston's selectmen gave him two hours in which to bring the agents of the East India Company from the castle; they would not budge. Having failed in his mission, Copley made a strong appeal to the townspeople to follow a course of moderation. He pointed out that the consignees faced certain financial ruin if they sent the tea back but that they would not intervene if the people acted to return it. On behalf of the consignees, Copley pledged that they would not try to unload the disputed cargo. He denied the charge that they were merely tools of Governor Hutchinson. The meeting broke up after it was resolved that the consignees' response was inadequate. The tea must be sent back to England without payment of any duty.

Governor Hutchinson would not allow this to happen. The ships bearing the tea were not allowed to sail out of Boston Harbor without permits attesting that the required duties had been paid. On December 17, a twenty-day waiting period stipulated by customs regulations was due to expire, and the tea would be liable to confiscation for nonpayment of customs duties. On the evening of December 16, in response to the Governor's reiteration of his stand against permitting the ships to leave, a group of colonists disguised as Mohawk Indians boarded the ships. As eight thousand people watched approvingly, they broke open 342 chests of tea and dumped their contents into the harbor. This act of defiance stirred British rage. In 1774 Parliament passed the Coercive Acts, which ended self-government in Massachusetts and closed Boston's port. Americans had moved a step closer to independence.

At this perilous moment John Singleton Copley acted on a plan he had held in abeyance for several years: he set out to travel to Europe to view the works of the masters. Copley was a self-taught artist who had received his early instruction from his stepfather, Peter Pelham, a painter and engraver. Copley had begun his career as a professional portrait painter when he was eighteen. In 1766 Benjamin West, a native U.S. artist, viewed Copley's *The Boy With the Squirrel* in London. He was so impressed that he arranged to have the painting shown at the Exhibition of the Society of Incorporated Artists. The work earned critical praise, and members of London's artistic community marveled that this painting was the effort of a self-taught artist who had never left the colony of Massachusetts.

The following year, Copley was admitted as a member of the Exhibition of the Society of Incorporated Artists. He entered in the group's annual exhibit a portrait of a young lady with a bird and a dog, which, like the one he had sent the year before, aroused great interest. Copley began to consider whether his career might better prosper in the more lucrative London art world. However, he felt some ambivalence, which he expressed when he wrote, "Were I sure of doing as well in Europe as here, I would not hesitate a moment in my choice; but I might in the experiment waste a thousand pounds and two years of my time, and have to return baffled to America. . . . My ambition whispers me to run this risk; and I think the time draws nigh that must determine my future fortune."[6]

The option of foreign travel was postponed by Copley's marriage to Susannah Clarke in 1769. The birth of children further delayed any departure, and Copley had to support not only his fledgling family but also his ailing mother and his younger half brother. Throughout 1771 and 1772 he held sittings in New York to earn the means to pay for a tour of Europe and to support his family during his absence. In 1774 the time seemed ripe, and Copley prepared for his long-delayed journey. He departed from Boston in June 1774 and on July 10 arrived in London, where his fellow artists welcomed him. With the help of Benjamin West and Sir Joshua Reynolds, he was able to paint the Prime Minister, Lord North. Copley's stay in London was brief, but it suggested to him the possibility — in light of the rapid deterioration of events in Boston — of bringing his family to England, where the chance for greater professional fulfillment and reward loomed.

For the moment, Italy and its treasure trove of artworks beckoned to him. Lord Lyndhurst in later years described his father's tour: "He remained there (in Italy) about a year studying the works of the Italian school of art. He afterwards visited Holland and the Low Countries — in pursuit of the same studies."[7] While in Italy, Copley made copies of the works of the masters, including Correggio's *Madonna* and *St. Jerome*. During his Italian tour he received news from his wife of the worsening political crisis in Boston. Revolution was in the air, and woe to Tory sympathizers. Clarke had escaped to Canada disguised as an Indian. Copley's option of moving himself and his family to England was pressing in upon him. In answer to her alarming reports, the artist wrote to his wife from Rome on October 26, 1774: "I find you will not regret leaving Boston. I am sorry that it has become so disagreeable. I think this will determine me to stay in England, where, I have no doubt, I shall meet with as much to do as in Boston, and on better terms."[8]

A considerable sacrifice was made, however. Copley risked abandoning a twelve-acre tract of land he owned. It was farmland at the time; today it is Beacon Hill, one of Boston's most valuable pieces of real estate. The expatriate lamented the possibility of this loss: "As for my property in Boston, I cannot count it anything now. I believe I shall sink it all; it is very hard, but it must be submitted to. . . . I wish I had sold my whole place; I should then have been worth something; I do not know now that I have a shilling in the world."[9] Money was always to be a cause of worry for Copley, as it was to be for the son to whom he would one day leave his unpaid debts. The loss of the Beacon Hill property was a major blow to the family's financial security. Twenty years later, John Singleton Copley, Jr., would journey to America and attempt to secure some measure of compensation for his father's abandoned property.

Additional letters from Boston painted an increasingly gloomy picture of inevitable war. Susannah Copley's bleak accounts of life in Boston drew the following response from her absent husband: "Your situation must be very unpleasant; the daily expectation of bloodshed must render thoughtful persons unhappy. You have answered a question asked in my last, namely, 'Whether you wished me to go to Boston, or if you should come to England.' You seem desirous of the latter. This makes me very happy. . . . Should I now return to America, I should have nothing to do, and I cannot think of going back to starve with my family."[10]

The small party of mother, son, and two daughters reached Dover on June 24, 1775.[11] Their voyage had lasted twenty-eight days, considered a speedy passage at that time. Copley believed his wife and children had remained in Boston and did not know that they had already landed in England when he wrote two letters that expressed his thoughts on America's prospects in its flight from British hegemony. In the first letter, addressed to his wife and dated July 2, 1775, he accurately foretold the outcome of the conflict.

> By a letter from London, I was informed, since I wrote you, that what I greatly feared has at last taken place. The war has begun, and, if I am not mistaken, the country, which was once the happiest on the globe, will be deluged with blood for many years to come. It seems as if no plan of reconciliation could now be formed; as the sword is drawn all must be finally settled by the sword. I cannot think that the power of Great Britain will subdue the country, if the people are united, as they appear to be at present. I know it may seem strange to some men of great understanding that I should hold such an opinion, but it is very evident to me that America will have the power of resistance until grown strong to conquer, and that victory and independence will go hand in hand.[12]

Copley echoed these views in a second letter to his wife written on July 22, 1775: "Whoever thinks the Americans can be easily subdued is greatly mistaken; they will keep their enthusiasm alive till they are victorious. You know, years ago, I was right in my opinion that war would be the result of the attempt to tax the colony. It is now my settled conviction that all the power of Great Britain will not reduce them to obedience."[13] Thus, Copley put himself on record as dissenting from the noxious opinions that had so alienated his in-laws from their neighbors. He had left America without bitterness, and he passed on his goodwill toward that country to his son, who in later years always felt an affection for his native land.

When the news that his family had found refuge in England reached him, Copley had mixed feelings of relief and regret. He acknowledged his hope that they would come but lamented the fact that his mother and half brother had remained behind in "that miserable place."[14] If Boston had become a scene of strife, London was a place of sanctuary, a safe harbor. Susannah and her children were sheltered in the home of a brother-in-law. Her father arrived from his exile in Canada and took up permanent residence in England. The group awaited the return of Copley, who had not yet completed his foreign tour. At last the family was reunited when he arrived in London in December 1775. The separation had involved great emotional sacrifice, but it had enabled Copley to complete his education by studying Europe's masterpieces. Now he could go forward to use his profession to earn money for himself and his family. They could all commence living their lives.

A few years after the family was reunited, Copley painted a picture that symbolized the reestablished domestic life of the little group. Sir Theodore Martin described it in his book:

> By this time a boy and a girl had been added to the family. The four children, with their mother, her father Mr. Clarke, and Copley himself, are all introduced into the picture. The central point of interest is Mrs. Copley, who is seated on a couch with her then youngest daughter lying across her lap, while she bends towards her eldest boy, the future Chancellor, who is standing by her side, and looking up to claim a share of her caresses with a tender, smiling earnestness, that speaks volumes for the depth of the attachment between the mother and her boy.[15]

Called *The Family Picture*, it hung in a place of honor in Lord Lyndhurst's home throughout his life.

The success of Copley's historical paintings, together with the revenue from commissions for portraits, afforded him some economic security during his initial years in England. His success as an artist was confirmed by his election to the prestigious Royal Academy, a singular honor for members of his profession. Initially, after being reunited in London, Copley and his family resided in Leicester Fields, but they later moved to a larger house at Number 25 George Street in Hanover Square. This house, where Copley set up his studio, remained the family home throughout his life; upon his death it passed into the hands of his son. Eventually, Lord Lyndhurst purchased a house next door and connected the two dwellings, creating a more commodious establishment. Three more children were born, two girls and a boy. Scarlet fever claimed the elder girl and the boy in 1785. Richard Clarke, a pensioner of the Crown, lived with his daughter, son-in-law, and grandchildren until he died in 1795.

Within the family circle, which was marked by a special closeness that may have been a consequence of the family's previous separation, the future Lord Chancellor grew to be a genial lad. His cheerfulness and taste for fun caused one American relative to note, "Friends from this side of the Atlantic have carried back to him the tales they had heard of his boyish pranks and how his father would reprove him, and exclaim, 'You will be a boy, Jack, all your life!' At which the aged statesman would gently smile, as the memories of his youth rushed on his mind, and answer, 'Well, I believe my father was right, there.'"[16]

John Singleton Copley, Jr., was son to a father who was ambitious not only for himself but also for his only male offspring to survive childhood. The senior Copley gained success and fame as an artist at a time when his fellows in that profession sought a status above that of craftspeople whose betters hired their talents. These contemporaries of Sir Joshua Reynolds — knighted for his skill — aspired to be gentlemen and, more significantly for the future of the young Copley, for their sons to be gentlemen. The vision of an expanded horizon was evident in the plans Copley made for his son, and the young man was a willing and able entry in the race for honors and emoluments.

Early in his life, there were signals that the boy was meant for big things. He was a serious student who mastered his lessons with a fervor that never left him. The boy's first exposure to formal education was at Clapham, a school in south London. Later, Copley enrolled at a private school in Chiswick, maintained by the Rev. Dr. Horne. Lyndhurst, in an autobiographical sketch written near the end of his life, recalled that Horne "was a good classical scholar, and infused into us a fairly good proportion of Latin and Greek."[17] Copley benefited from this instruction by applying himself with great discipline. To his elder sister, who served as his sounding board as he drilled himself in the classics, he admonished, "No matter whether you understand the text or not, be sure I make no mistake in a single word, or even in an accent."[18]

While at Chiswick, young Copley displayed the facility for precise retention and retrieval of information that distinguished his later career. He also showed considerable talent in the fields of mathematics and mechanical science. Dr. Horne wrote a glowing report of the boy's progress: "Young Copley improves very much; he is a very promising youth."[19] This promise marked him out among the other students. As his departure neared, Dr. Horne wrote to a friend at Trinity College, Oxford, "Copley is on the point of leaving us and entering at the University as he believes, but whether Oxford or Cambridge I know not. He is a prodigiously improved young man."[20] Copley was eighteen years old when he matriculated at Trinity College, Cambridge, as a pensioner on July 8, 1790.

When he passed through the Great Gate of Trinity, Copley entered a world in which his abilities could catch the attention of people who could significantly promote his success. In these years, although he showed an aptitude for mathematics, chemistry, and physical science, his enthusiasm for classical literature continued, and he was able to indulge his enjoyment of the Greek and Latin poets and philosophers. His great memory, always his most formidable talent, enhanced his reputation. He applied himself rigorously to his studies and noted in a letter home that "I have been so closely occupied the whole of this term that I have scarcely had a moment for my own amusement and for the gratification of my friends."[21]

He described his room and his routine after he had moved from the attic to the middle story of his lodging place: "My room contains eight chairs and two tables commodiously. Not so extremely small. . . . Here, according as my inclination prompts, I either turn over the pages of science, or wander through the flowery and less rugged paths of poetry and polite literature." Despite his commitment to a regimen of toil, the youth cautioned his mother lest she conclude "that I am so enveloped in these pursuits as to neglect amusements of a lighter nature; they are in their turn, perhaps, equally important. I am naturally a friend to gayety; I love to see what is to be seen."[22]

A warm family bond is evident in letters sent home during his Cambridge days. Copley wrote of "that affection and filial regard which glow in my heart, and which no distance, no time can ever impair." Even allowing for the extravagant language of the age, this declaration gives an indication of the emotional attachment he felt for his parents and his sisters. Recurring echoes of the strength of the family unit marked Copley's life during this period when he was dependent on that source for his needs, both monetary and emotional. He was eager to know of and share in what he described as "those various and complex concerns which at present engage and agitate the minds and bosoms of our circle in George Street."[23] Copley possessed a fierce desire to please that circle. His ambition to make his family proud of his accomplishments complemented their great expectations of him.

Lyndhurst's academic path was paved with distinctions. A letter to John Singleton Copley, Sr., from the Rev. T. Jones told of "the very great credit which your son has gained in the late examinations."[24] Young Copley received a prize of £25 for his efforts. His performance had been judged the second highest in the field of mathematics for the entire University of Cambridge during the Tripos examinations and ranked first at Trinity College.

In 1794 Copley won a prize awarded annually at Trinity for an essay on the life and achievements of King William III. In this essay, which suggested his own future motivation, Copley cited a "gloomy truth" that the pure motive of promoting the public good "is but a cold principle of exertion" and counseled that "we must look to some more selfish and efficient springs of action."[25] He concluded that self-interest operated in William's case, for although "a warm desire to establish the general independence of Europe was a first and noble principle of exertion . . . this honourable motive was sharpened by the powerful workings of ambition."[26] The essay also contained statements regarding the young scholar's political outlook. He censured the "rigid republicans" who had rendered Holland defenseless.[27] He despaired that "the ardour of reform should hurry men to too great extremes" and endorsed approvingly "the gradual operation of time."[28] Finally, he lauded William III for his moderation when success crowned his efforts.[29]

Copley, facing his examination for his bachelor's degree, felt he had to distinguish himself against formidable competitors. He explained the rigors of preparation to his father, who had chided him for his laxness in writing: "I have been so closely occupied the whole of this term that I have scarcely had a moment for my own amusement, and for the gratification of my friends. . . . The first part of this term I was busily employed in preparing for examination, which was to qualify me for the dignity of a scholar of the college." He labored under the burden of what he believed to be an underdog position, and he gave his reasons: "The candidates were numerous, and as seniority was generally very much regarded in the election (I being the last entered of my year), I was obliged to supply by some degree of superior merit this deficiency. The result was successful."[30]

In 1795 Copley was elected a Fellow of Trinity College. The position carried a stipend as well as academic recognition. This financial gain removed some economic pressure from the senior Copley, whose artistic reputation had begun to decline, opening a period of financial stress that continued throughout the remainder of his life. Rev. Jones sped the welcome news to the residents of George Street, adding that, with no further examination, young Copley was "at liberty to devote the whole of his attention to the study of the law."[31] He had, in fact, made an initial effort toward this objective on May 19, 1794, when he was admitted to the Honorable Society of Lincoln's Inn. He remained there during the Easter term but later returned to Cambridge, where he took on a new project that postponed the immediate pursuit of a law career. Even before he was designated a Fellow of Trinity College, Copley had been appointed a Traveling Bachelor by the university. The appointment brought a stipend of £100 a year for three years and required that the recipient forward periodic accounts, in Latin, of his foreign travels to the university's Vice Chancellor.

Copley's destination was the United States, the land of his birth. This opportunity allowed him to serve as a surrogate for his parents in making contact with the relatives and friends from whom they had parted two decades earlier. More important, the journey enabled Copley to attempt to regain his family's lost Beacon Hill property.

2
Copley's American Tour

Copley's journey got off to a rocky start with what the voyager called "stiffish weather," but he was able to report that he had "not yet felt the least symptom of sea-sickness," and he hoped to avoid it entirely. The winds blew with such force that the ship was driven from its moorings before it could weigh anchor. In drifting, the vessel caught the anchor of a Danish ship. This development threatened a collision, which was averted. Despite these mishaps, Copley delightedly wrote to his mother that "I am a great sailor already."[1] His seaworthiness was severely tested in the course of a stormy passage that lasted more than eight weeks.

Upon disembarking in Boston on January 2, 1796, young Copley immediately set out to accomplish his mission of recouping the family fortunes. The Beacon Hill estate, consisting of twelve acres with three houses, had been occupied by British troops at the beginning of the American Revolution. During their encampment the troops fortified the area but also destroyed the fences that had marked off the property. When the British forces vacated Boston, Copley's land was occupied by U.S. soldiers. When the war ended, Copley placed his interest in the property in the hands of an agent in Boston. This decision proved to be a blunder. Without authorization from the absent owner, the agent disposed of the property for a price, the amount of which was in doubt. Copley's assignment in the United States was to unravel this complex state of affairs. He might at best regain the property or at the least recover compensation equal to the value of the estate.

Upon his arrival in Boston, Copley learned that a vessel was to sail for London momentarily. He scribbled a few sentences informing his family that in his first hours ashore, he had already contacted General Hull, into whose hands the property had passed. Copley immediately grasped the problems he faced. A man named Scott had made an affidavit that no verbal agreement, such as the one the senior Copley claimed, had ever taken place. Delay was also certain because the issue could not be dealt with before May. Copley's analysis was this: "If you can make yourself a subject of the United States you are clear. If otherwise, I am not yet sufficiently informed to say what may be the result if you are decreed an alien." His parting counsel was "take courage."[2]

On February 27, Copley wrote to tell his father that his dream of regaining his lost property was not to be realized. On the advice of the lawyers the young Copley had retained, he had agreed to accept on his father's behalf a settlement of £4,000. He felt anxiety about his father's reaction: "how you will be affected by the result, whether it will give you dissatisfaction or pleasure, I cannot determine. I have acted for the best, as I thought at the time, and still continue to think."[3] It had been obvious to Copley that should the case be argued in court, a successful outcome was unlikely, and a delay of at least two and a half years loomed. A compromise was acceptable to both parties. Young Copley assured his father of his own diligence in the matter: "I do not believe any person could have obtained from them one shilling more."[4] He proposed that he retain £500 after forwarding the rest of the settlement to his father. He would hold this money in the event that during his tour of the United States he discover a promising investment.

In his mind, Copley was turning over the possibility of his family's permanent return to the United States. Originally, this plan had hinged on a successful outcome of the suit over the Beacon Hill property. Now he began to consider another piece of land further west of Boston in central New York State. He was at a stage in his life when to a young, ambitious man, anything seemed possible, including a new life in a new land. John Singleton Copley, Jr., stood at a crossroads, and he could choose his future. He discussed this option in the February 27 letter to his father:

> I have thought ever since I set foot in this country that it was possible you might think of returning hither. That you would find your profession more profitable than in England I have no doubt; the state of society and of government would be more congenial to your inclinations, and nothing but the difficulty of moving seems to stand in the opposite scale. If I had a tract of good land, perhaps 5,000 acres, which may be purchased for no very considerable sum, I would in four or five years, if it should please God to bless me with health and strength, not only render it a very valuable and productive estate, but also a delightful retreat to you and my dear mother whenever you should choose

to enjoy it. Land of this kind is to be had in a good climate, and within two hundred or two hundred and fifty miles from Boston and New York, a distance which will continually diminish as the facility of communication, owing to the rapid improvement of the country, increases.[5]

The tour of the United States was for Copley, as it would have been for almost any young man his age, a great adventure, and he alluded to it frequently during the remainder of his life. He wrote to his family, who was eager for news of developments pertaining to his progress, of his awareness that "every subject that I can start relative to this country may afford interesting matter to you." He knew, too, that as the only son and brother in a close-knit family, every morsel of information about his well-being would be hungrily devoured. "Even were I to talk about myself," he glowed, "I trust you would not deem it entirely stupid. Well, then I *will* talk about myself." He described what he saw in his looking glass. The circle in George Street would find it difficult to recognize him. Instead of a "pale, thin, helpless-looking dog," they would feast their eyes upon a "lusty, rosy, stupid-looking fellow." As for good spirits, he declared himself "actually crazy" with them. He had never enjoyed "three more pleasant . . . weeks since I was born."[6]

Well he might relish the hospitality and fuss made over him. His family had maintained its ties with U.S. relatives and friends since its departure twenty years earlier. Furthermore, he was the son of a noted American-born artist, a fact certain to gain a favorable response from the fiercely nationalistic Americans of that day. Doors were opened to him. Boston's leading families welcomed him into their homes. He entertained his family with reports of who was pretty or sensible or homely or lively or agreeable or ridiculous. The Lieutenant Governor had entertained him at "two handsome, alderman-like dinners; I never saw such a collection of food, except in Leadenhall Market, during my whole life." He saw the new State House, in the process of being built, and judged the rooms "extremely lofty and spacious, and upon the whole it had a striking effect."[7]

He had a special message to pass on to his father. He whispered into his sisters' ears: "The *better* people are all aristocrats. My father is too rank a Jacobin to live among them." One republican who received young Copley's scorn was the legendary patriot and Governor of the Commonwealth of Massachusetts, Samuel Adams. He pronounced him "superannuated, unpopular, and fast decaying in every respect; in addition to this, and perhaps on this account he has taken no notice of me."[8]

Copley set out to explore a United States that was in the initial throes of nation-building. He was present during the first decade of the republic, when people still held their breaths over the fate of a fledgling system of government. The Federal Constitution established the bone and sinew of governmental structure. The political infighting during the early years of the republic gave blood and flesh to the basic structure. Suspicion and hostility were the daily bread of political life. The elitist Federalists, followers of George Washington and Alexander Hamilton, were seen by their opponents as the leaders of a conspiracy to undermine the fragile fabric of government to open the way for a stronger regimen based on the British model. In turn, the Federalists saw the Democratic-Republican adherents of Thomas Jefferson and James Madison as a band of levelers who would subvert the new order of things to appease the mob, the very underbelly of society. In this acrimonious debate, each camp attempted to surpass the other in professions of loyalty to the Constitution and the nationalistic values of the day. The harshest censure Americans could level against one another was that they were not loyal to the new system of government and that they plotted secretly for its downfall.

Such were the parameters of the U.S. political struggle as John Singleton Copley, Jr., set out for the seat of government, Philadelphia. The nation's capital had been moved from New York City in 1791 as part of a sectional compromise. The government remained in Philadelphia for a decade before being moved to the new city of Washington, which the President modestly referred to as the Federal City. Copley journeyed to this site of new beginnings along the Potomac River. Since his arrival in his native land, he had sought to understand the currents of U.S. politics. He had immediately picked up the outlook of the Federalists and wrote to his mother that "the opposition here are a set of villains. Their object is to overset the government, and all good men are apprehensive lest they should on the present occasion be successful."[9] Copley was referring to the debate over the Jay Treaty, which had been signed on November 19, 1794, as an attempt to head off an Anglo-American war. Tensions had been building because of British refusal to evacuate the northwest military outposts along the Great Lakes that were within U.S. territory as stipulated in the Treaty of Paris in 1783. The British justified their failure to carry out this treaty provision on the ground that legal obstacles had been raised to prevent the recovery of prerevolutionary debts owed to British merchants and of Loyalist property appropriated by the states.

A second issue had arisen to compound hostile feelings between the two nations. In 1793 the British government, pursuing its war against revolutionary France, had issued orders in council that interfered with neutral shipping. The vigorous enforcement of these orders had led to the seizure of U.S. vessels and sailors. The situation threatened to erupt into open warfare, and the treaty was designed to preclude this threatened disaster. Under the articles of the agreement, the British pledged to withdraw their forces from the northwest outposts on or before June 1, 1796. They would also pay compensation for seizures of U.S. ships. In turn, the United States agreed to guarantee the payment of prerevolutionary debts owed to British merchants. A joint commission would determine the amount. Joint commissions would then take up the Canadian boundary issue and the amount of compensation for illegal maritime seizures. The Mississippi River was declared open to navigation by both countries. Although some concessions were made for U.S. shipping in the British West Indies, they were so meager that the U.S. Senate eventually rejected this provision of the treaty.

When the articles of the agreement were revealed, a storm of protest ensued. Jefferson's Democratic-Republicans headed the opposition. Copley followed the conflict with interest and forwarded an account of the struggle to his family:

> The President and Senate, in whom is vested, by the Constitution, the power of making treaties, have ratified the treaty with Great Britain. But the Lower House seem inclined to refuse the appropriation necessary for carrying it into effect. They are now debating the question, and I fear a great majority will be against the execution. The Middle and New England States are strongly in favor of the treaty; the Southern States, in particular Virginia, who will be called upon for the payment of her debts in case the treaty takes effect, are in violent opposition to the treaty. A great schism seems to be forming, and they already begin to talk of a separation of the States north of the Potomac from those on the southern side of the river. The underwriters refuse to insure; produce has already fallen, and every person is alarmed. A war with England, perhaps a civil war, will be the consequence of success in the present opposition. These are the sentiments of the people here. They are not, however, my sentiments. Depend upon it all will end well. I even entertain some doubt whether the executive will not have a majority in the

> House of Representatives. But if not, I do not apprehend such serious consequences as people in general look for.[10]

Copley's analysis of the U.S. political scene was astute. The Senate had already ratified the treaty on June 24, 1795, with the exclusion of the article relating to West Indian trade. The controversy shifted to the House of Representatives, where the Democratic-Republicans were mustering their forces in a last-ditch effort to undermine the treaty by defeating the appropriation for enforcing its provisions. After much heated debate, the appropriation was approved by one vote on April 30, 1796 — just ten days after the Traveling Bachelor had committed his views to paper.

Throughout his life Copley maintained his interest in U.S. developments. His sister, Elizabeth, married an American in 1800 and left England to live once more in Boston. Many letters were exchanged between brother and sister and their families, which helped to keep alive Lord Lyndhurst's U.S. connection. It is noteworthy that he felt the U.S. situation to be so congenial that he considered returning permanently to the land of his birth. Copley's lifelong empathy for the United States and Americans was an indication of his cosmopolitan and flexible outlook.

In addition to his correspondence with his family, Copley supplied reports to the Vice Chancellor of Cambridge University, Dr. Richard Bellward, as the university required of all Traveling Bachelors.[11] He began his first report with a geographical description of "that city which is destined to be the chief seat of the American government." After relating details of the Potomac River's flow, Copley described the new city Americans were creating as a symbol of their faith in their country's future:

> The place chosen for the site of Washington is a rising ground advantageously situated; almost in the center stands the Capitol, from whence you have an extensive view over the river, and the far-off plains of Virginia in the distance. This building will be about three hundred feet in length, with columns of the Corinthian order. As yet the foundations only are laid, the building only partly showing itself. At about a mile distant is the residence reserved for the use of the President; this building is composed of square blocks of stone (dug out of the quarries of Aquia, as are the stones of the Capitol) so placed as to produce an appearance of considerable magnificence.[12]

Copley also visited nearby Alexandria, which had four thousand to five thousand inhabitants, some of whom extended their hospitality to the visitor from England. He described attending a commemoration of American independence on July 4, "which is everywhere celebrated by sports and rejoicings."[13] The highlight of the occasion was the presence of President George Washington, whom the Alexandrians invited to a dinner at which Copley was also present. As the son of a famous artist and a representative of a distinguished university, Copley enjoyed entrée into the privileged circles of the U.S. political and social world. The clearest evidence of this advantage was the fact that President Washington received him at his home, Mount Vernon. Copley always remembered this encounter and singled it out as the most interesting day of his life. The English visitor sensed the unique place Washington occupied in the affairs of the young Republic. His natural dignity and taste for simplicity were most apparent when one found him at his ease at Mount Vernon. Copley correctly recognized that the house and its situation were representative of the man, and he sent a detailed description to Dr. Bellward:

> We went to Mount Vernon for the purpose of paying our respects to the President of the Republic. Between that place and Alexandria are open fields not remarkable for any particular beauty; the soil is barren, the roads rough and hilly; the gardens even of the presidential residence display neither culture nor beauty. The house, however, built of stone, much worn by time, situated on high ground, is large, and commands a view of the mighty Potomac, stretched out at no great distance, and of the ships sailing to and fro between Alexandria and the ocean. We found the President courteous, hospitable, and facetious. He freely discoursed on many subjects, such as the house, the gardens, and the circumjacent country. The house presents no appearance of luxury — the simple, honest character of Washington is alone conspicuous.[14]

The young man encountered some chiefs of the Catawba tribe who were calling at the President's house. These Native Americans were leaders of a dwindling tribe that had turned to agriculture, abandoning their former occupation as warriors. The Native Americans held a fascination for Copley, reflecting a European preoccupation with the savages whose dignified simplicity marked them as being among nature's noblemen. After leaving Virginia, he and his party crossed the Ohio River and visited

Native American villages between Kentucky and Upper Canada. Copley made an observation about the Native Americans that anticipated his future sense of values: "If they perceive no chance of victory, they think it prudent to retreat."[15]

Copley's decision to visit the Native American villages considerably lengthened his stay in the United States. He explained his expanded stay in a letter to his mother from Philadelphia on December 2, 1796. He had arrived in the United States with the priority of settling his family's claim to the Beacon Hill estate. Second, he sought to rekindle family ties and old friendships on behalf of "the circle in George Street." These purposes he could accomplish in the "principal cities" of the United States. However, "when I was desirous of ascertaining the advantages which America might hold out to myself, a more enlarged view became expedient." New York, Philadelphia, and Boston — hubs of commerce and the professions — did not offer the inducements to persuade him "to a change of situation." Instead, it was the West, with its advancing frontier, that beckoned this young Englishman. He wrote that he had been advised that "a settlement in the western parts of the United States could not fail of leading a young man of prudence and of education to wealth and honor."[16]

Copley explained to his family that "as the result of affairs in Europe was uncertain," he had decided that failure to investigate possible sites for future settlement "would be highly indiscrete."[17] This reference to "affairs in Europe" was an allusion to the French Revolution. However, at the same time, financial and personal problems had beset Copley's father, and these developments caused the son to consider a move that would bring his family back to the United States. Early in his career, the senior Copley had basked in the approval of those whose opinion carried weight in the art community. This initial approval had turned to censure when his paintings failed to duplicate the success of his earlier work. Numerous lawsuits filed against engravers of his paintings were also sapping away his emotional and financial resources.

Copley's relationship with his mentor, Benjamin West, had soured, and admiration had given way to jealousy, which had intensified when West had been elected president of the Royal Academy. An obsessive hostility toward West involved Copley in intrigues and caused him to jockey for advantage in Academy affairs. His peevishness and growing surliness turned friends into critics. This emotional degeneration was reflected in his painting: his technique had begun to deteriorate. Emotionally, artistically, financially, even physically, he was drained — too drained to undertake so taxing a project as establishing a new life in America. The senior Copley's money would have financed the purchase of land in the United States, and, therefore, young Copley was unable to relocate when his father's interest in such a move waned.

Unaware of the futility of his hopes, the son pursued the possibility of a new life for himself and his family in the United States. Diplomatically, he avoided mention of the advantages that might come to his father if he abandoned the arena of his torment and humiliation. These considerations must have been among his priorities when he decided that "the sacrifice of time would be more than compensated by an accession of very interesting information." He added a further assurance that "curiosity also to become acquainted with a country which is, at present so much a subject of conversation, and which is extolled as the garden of the world, [was an] additional and powerful inducement."[18]

"Garden of the world" — the United States might be that in the eyes of foreign visitors and of her own people. But there were serpents in the garden in 1796. In his Farewell Address, President Washington advised his fellow citizens to avoid permanent alliances that might pull them into Europe's quarrels, and he deplored the dangers of a party system. Relations with France had deteriorated further when the French Directory, in retaliation of the Jay Treaty, interfered with U.S. shipping. The relationship between the two former allies continued on a downhill path when the Directory refused to receive Charles Cotesworth Pinckney, the U.S. Minister to France, when he arrived in Paris in December 1796. A few weeks before this rebuke, Copley had written to his mother "that the public mind is much agitated here from an apprehension of a war with France." He added, "My judgement, such as it is, would persuade me to believe that such an event is not probable."[19]

Copley's observations about current events extended to domestic affairs as well as foreign relations. His attention focused on the presidential contest, only the third under the Federal Constitution and the first that was not simply a ritualistic endorsement of the great George Washington. He reported that "the elections for President interest very strongly both parties. They are nearly equal, the *Aristocrats* and the *Democrats*, in number. The result is, therefore, uncertain." The Englishman wrongly predicted the outcome of the race. He said, "The returns that are made persuade me that the republican, Jefferson, will succeed. The bets are in his favor."[20] These proved to be losing bets, but only for the moment. The close outcome of the selection process was an indication of things to come. The poll in the

Electoral College reflected the growing strength of the Democratic-Republican party, which was a by-product of public dissatisfaction with the Jay Treaty. Vice President John Adams, the Federalist candidate, garnered seventy-one votes, which was sufficient to elect him President. Thomas Jefferson, the Democratic-Republican nominee, drew sixty-eight votes and gained the Vice Presidency as a consolation prize under the rules governing the process. Four years later, in a rematch, Jefferson would best Adams in the presidential election. For the time being, however, both Federalists and Republicans continued to regard their political adversaries as illegitimate phenomena who were disloyal to the Constitution.

In a letter to his aunt, Mrs. Charles Startin, Copley revealed his sensitivity to the enormous significance of the undertaking that commanded the efforts of Americans: "The moderate but spirited and energetic conduct of the American Government has exalted the character of the nation in the opinion of the haughty inhabitants of Europe, who were accustomed to regard with too supercilious an eye a people just risen from the subordinate rank of colonists."[21] Copley's choice of the United States for his travels was remarkable in itself. Most Traveling Bachelors took the Grand Tour, a year spent traveling through Europe to complete their educations. Copley returned to Europe a rare man. How many Europeans had walked and broken bread and slept among America's savages? How many had trod the narrow streets of Boston or New York or Philadelphia or the fledgling Detroit? How many had enjoyed the hospitality and attention of the exalted George Washington at Mount Vernon? Copley bore the stamp of his U.S. journey, and it made him a marked man in the eyes of some contemporaries — touched, if not tainted, by his experience of dwelling amid republicans.

3
Launching a Career

His U.S. tour behind him, Copley faced the necessity of beginning his deferred legal training. He had been admitted as a member of Lincoln's Inn on May 19, 1794, and remained there during the Easter term. However, he had detoured from his path to the legal profession when he traveled to the United States. Upon his return to England, he did not settle down immediately to study law but returned to Cambridge, where, upon the payment of a fee, he was routinely awarded a Master of Arts degree on July 5, 1797. Although his annual allowance of £100 as a Traveling Bachelor ended when he returned, Copley continued to receive a larger yearly stipend as a Fellow of Trinity College. This support continued until 1804 and served as a financial cushion throughout the critical years during which he was completing his legal training and making a tentative start on his career.

After completing some preliminary studies, Copley entered the chambers of Mr. Tidd, whose reputation as a special pleader singled him out as a mentor for ambitious novices. J. B. Atlay, in *The Victorian Chancellors*, described Tidd's influence when he noted that "three of the Victorian Chancellors, Lords Lyndhurst, Cottenham, and Campbell, as well as Lord Chief Justice Denman, were among his pupils, and the dingy chambers of King's Bench Walk are famed as a veritable nest of legal singing birds."[1]

Copley's initiation into the legal profession was a struggle. The first years of a special pleader were always difficult. Sir Theodore Martin's definition sheds some light on Copley's early position in the legal profession: "Special pleaders in general are not at the Bar. One or two who remain pleaders permanently are considered as something between attorneys and barristers, but the common way is for a young man to plead a few years *under the Bar,* as they call it, before being called. It is easier to get this kind of business than briefs in the Court, and you thus gradually form and extend your connections."[2] This was a time for patience, of waiting for clients and opportunities. During this period young Copley had to shoulder an increasing share of the family expenses. The income from his fellowship stipend ceased in 1804. The elder Copley worked steadily at his art, but his income decreased. The war with France drained that portion of the national income that in better times had supported the arts. It was primarily Copley's failing skill as a painter that dimmed his last years, yet he struggled to recapture his earlier critical and financial success.

The new century brought a fortuitous turn in events when Copley's elder daughter, Elizabeth, known affectionately within the family as Betsy, married in 1800. Her husband, Gardiner Greene, was a prosperous Boston merchant and a widower with three children, a girl and two boys, ranging in age from ten to fourteen. Elizabeth Copley was thirty years of age at the time of her marriage, which took her back to the city of her birth, where she would reside for the remainder of her ninety-five years.

The marriage was a significant watershed for the Copley family. It produced an abundance of letters that passed in both directions over the Atlantic and that chronicled the progress of the aspiring John Singleton Copley, Jr. More important for the young man's future, this new family connection produced a loan that enabled him to pass on to the next stage of his legal career. He now sought to escape the limbo of a special pleader through admission to the Bar, a step that required some financial backing to tide him over while he established a reputation sufficient to bring in at least a minimal income to support himself.

Copley found himself in serious financial straits. His allowance as a Fellow of Trinity College had brought him about £150 each year since 1795. Unfortunately, he could retain this stipend after 1804 only if he took Holy Orders. He rejected this alternative after slight consideration, so the income ended. His father was too hard-pressed to contribute any funds directly, but he did perform an essential service that filled young Copley's need: he turned to his new son-in-law on the other side of the Atlantic for assistance. In him he found an able and willing agent of deliverance. On November 23, 1803, the senior Copley requested a loan of £1,000.

An affirmative answer, together with the loan, arrived in the return mail. Financial salvation from his brother-in-law enabled Copley to launch his career at the Bar. He would never be free from economic worry during his long life; however, this generous backing proved a major turning point for him, and he remained deeply obligated to Gardiner Greene. He wrote a forthright letter that not only conveyed his gratitude but also summarized his situation:

> I am to thank you for a very serious obligation, and I *do* thank you with my whole heart. It is now considerably more than a year that I have been waiting for an opportunity to be called to the bar; but my father, from various unforeseen circumstances, has not been able to afford me the pecuniary assistance which was absolutely necessary for this purpose. Your friendship has supplied the deficiency, and I cannot sufficiently express the sense which I entertain of your kindness. It will not be improper, and it may be a duty, under these circumstances, to state to you the nature of my prospects. After five years of regular application and study, I hope I may venture to say, at least to so near a friend, that I am moderately conversant with the system of our laws; and by continual and repeated practice at the societies of mock debate, I think I have also acquired, what is not less essential than a knowledge of the laws, some degree of ease and fluency of expression. I have also, during my practice as a special pleader under the bar, formed some professional connections which, I hope, may materially tend to facilitate my progress and to promote my future interests. Under these auspices, and assisted by your friendship, I am now to launch my bark into a wider sea; I am not insensible of the dangers with which it abounds. But, while to some it proves disastrous and fatal, to others it affords a passage to wealth, or, what is of more value than wealth, to reputation and honours.[3]

Less than three weeks after he wrote his letter of gratitude to his benefactor, John Singleton Copley, Jr., was called to the Bar on June 18, 1804. He was thirty-two years of age.

So little information exists, outside of family correspondence, about these early days that a small clipping is of particular interest. Taken from the *Stamford Mercury* and captioned "Lord Lyndhurst's First Brief," the article relates that:

> At Kesteven sessions, held at Falkingham in 1804, there was an appeal case entered, in which Messrs. Wyche and Torkington, attorneys of Stamford, were engaged. On their arrival in that town they learned that their opponents had secured the services of Mr. D'Ewes Coke, barrister, who went the Midland circuit. Mr. Coke had a travelling companion who had that year been called to the Bar. The Stamford attorneys, not wishing to throw a chance away, resolved upon giving a brief to Mr. Coke's friend. The case was argued on both sides, and it resulted in Messrs.

> Wyche and Torkington proving victorious by the aid of the young barrister — John Singleton Copley, who for many years afterwards went the Midland circuit, also practicing in the Lindsey sessions Courts.[4]

John Lord Campbell described this initial period of Copley's career in less than glowing terms: "He took to Quarter Sessions very cordially, and had success in poor-law cases, as well as in defending prisoners charged with petty larcenies, but this did not extend his fame beyond the limits of a single county, and even here, when the assizes came round, he found himself postponed to juniors who had won reputation as successful special pleaders in London."[5]

A sense of indebtedness to Greene brought forth repeated letters from young Copley's mother, his sister, Mary, and his father testifying to his hard work and promise of success. These partisan letters constitute a litany as they attest to the unrelenting efforts of the son and brother: "He is making all possible exertion to get forward in his profession."[6] "He is pressing on with all his might."[7] "He has every prospect of getting forward in his profession."[8] "He is indefatigable in his attention to business."[9] But a cautionary note recurs: "It is a work of time, and at present the expenses . . . greatly exceed the profits."[10] "It must necessarily be slow, from the nature of the thing."[11] "The law is a terrible up-hill profession; nobody knows the difficulty till he tries."[12]

There was an underlying, sometimes unconscious, sometimes conscious plan behind all of this "exertion." Always close to the surface was the goal of advancing, of pressing ahead. The family's hopes and needs rode on Copley's success. The "friends in George Street" were the great constant in his life during this period, as they had been during his earlier life. They "are all very sanguine in the expectations they have formed of his success." They "trust he will meet with that success which will produce happiness for himself and friends."[13]

The cause was so important, Copley's family assured one another again and again. When an acquaintance obtained a place as an under-secretary of state with a salary of £2,000 a year, Copley's sister lamented, "It is a great thing for so young a man, and I cannot help thinking John would fill the place just as well. . . . I wish my brother could meet with some good friend to give him something."[14] To be granted a handsome appointment, a political plum, was essentially the key to Copley's future success, as events proved. Yet it was a winning formula that would not soon work its magic.

Many bleak years of riding the circuit preceded any breakthrough in Copley's career. It was on the Midland circuit that he attracted his first public notice by defending a Luddite at Nottingham in 1812. Between 1811 and 1816, workers in the lace and stocking weaving trades vented their anger on the improved looms they believed were responsible for their misery. A widespread rash of machine breaking occurred in Nottinghamshire, Derbyshire, and Leicestershire. Threatening letters to employers were signed "Ned Ludd." The name was derived from a tale of a one-time village idiot who pursued his hecklers into a house. Unable to apprehend those who had mocked him, he vented his fury on some stocking frames that were on the premises. Subsequently, when frames were broken, their destruction was attributed to Ned Ludd. Thus, the name *Luddites* was applied to those who engaged in any form of machine breaking.

E. P. Thompson, in *The Making of the English Working Class*, attempted to trace the cause of Luddism:

> Both war and successive bad harvests had contributed to raising the price of provisions to "famine" heights. But this will not do as an explanation of Luddism; it may help to explain its occasion, but not its character. These years of distress, 1811 and 1812, added the supreme grievance of continuous hunger to existing grievances. It made each device by which the least scrupulous masters sought to economise on labour, and cheapen its value (power-looms, shearing-frames, or "cut-ups"), seem more offensive.[15]

These acts of industrial sabotage even gained public sympathy in the Midlands and the West Riding of Yorkshire. Hence, as Thompson noted, "The trials of accused Luddites at Nottingham took place amidst threats, demonstrations, and on one occasion in a packed court-room which was supposed to contain armed men."[16]

It was in Nottingham that Copley defended John Ingham, who was charged with writing two threatening letters to a Mr. Nunn, owner of a lace factory. The letters pledged that "fifty of his frames should be destroyed, his premises burnt, and himself and one of his leading assistants should be made personal examples of." The letters promised as well "that atonement should be had, atonement which will make human nature shudder."[17] There was little doubt that Copley's client had penned the ultimatum and had signed it with the sobriquet "Ned Ludd & Co." Conviction for this offense required the death penalty, but local feeling ran high in favor of the defendant.

Copley pointed out that the indictment contained a serious flaw. It stated that the intended victims were the "proprietors of a silk and cotton lace manufactory." Under cross-examination, the manager of Nunn & Co. revealed that both a separate silk lace manufactory and a separate cotton lace manufactory existed. Copley objected that these were not described correctly in the indictment. His objection was sustained, and he won an acquittal for his client. Copley instantly became a popular hero and was borne back to his lodgings on the shoulders of his admirers. From this victory, won without passion and hinging on a technicality, some concluded that Copley shared the radical goals of the followers of the ubiquitous Captain Ludd.

In 1813 Copley decided to take the status of Sergeant-at-Law, a position open to any barrister with seven years' experience at the Bar. In keeping with custom, he was "rung out" of the Society of Lincoln's Inn. A footnote in Martin's biography explains the significance of this ritual: "It is customary on a member of this inn being made sergeant-at-law, to eject him in the most amicable manner from the society, ringing the chapel bell, and at the same time presenting him with an embroidered purse, with a substantial enclosure as a retaining fee for his future services as a sergeant, if the society should need them."[18] Copley's mother wrote to her daughter in the United States about her son's "advance in his profession," noting his good prospects and adding that "his character is high in his profession."[19]

At the same time, the family correspondence during this period chronicled the declining fortunes of the elder Copley and the family's growing and ultimately total dependence upon its struggling son and brother. The artist's pictures had no buyers, and stopgap loans from his son-in-law in America were sought and acknowledged in pitiful letters. A request to borrow "six hundred pounds more" expressed the father's anxiety that his financial distress would overwhelm his son: "My son will be bound for the six hundred pounds, but circumstanced as he now is, I find that I cannot perplex him farther with my concerns at present."[20]

Upon the beleaguered artist's death at age seventy-eight on August 9, 1815, his debts devolved on his son. It was a lamentable legacy, and Copley became the only means of support for his widowed mother and spinster sister. The widow wrote of her late husband's faith in their son: "He blessed God, at the close of his life, that he left the best of sons for my comfort, and for that of my dear Mary the best of brothers. I pray that his cares may not overpower him."[21] And pray she well might. Young Copley had in recent years advanced whatever money he could spare to his family. He kept only what he needed for his own subsistence, and he could save nothing. Now he took on his father's debts and the establishment in George Street. Eventually, the debts were paid, and the entire house was reclaimed from boarders who had supplemented the family income temporarily.

Copley might be the focus of his family's hopes, but their satisfaction with his efforts was mingled with regret at the loss of his company and attentions. The lament recurred in his mother's letters to his sister in America: "I have not seen your brother for some days; his whole time is so occupied . . . we only see him just at dinner, — very often not then, — and directly he is off."[22] On another occasion the mother wrote, "We drank tea yesterday with your brother at his pleasant chambers. . . . We visit the counselor, as he cannot come to us in term time; he is to leave us again in a few days for the sessions and circuits."[23] Again: "He is now upon the circuit, and when in town we are obliged to make ourselves as content as we can without his society, for he is very little with us."[24] And still again: "A short dinner with us . . . the only time we have his converse."[25]

His mother's accounts of his disciplined application were punctuated with references to his partaking of pleasure. In August 1809 he had been at Brighton for a week "to take a few dips in the sea."[26] In autumn 1811 "he has taken a week or two at the seaside."[27] Copley had a strong taste for pleasure, and Paris was an ideal locale in which to indulge this taste. He had gone there with friends to spend a week when his father suffered his fatal attack in 1815. Letters calling him back did not catch up with him until after the senior Copley's death. Three years later, in 1818, he toured the Continent for two months in a summer excursion that took him through France, Switzerland, and as far as Turin. He was accompanied by a party of friends. His mother and sister stayed behind; nonetheless, they took satisfaction in his widening horizons and in their conviction that "if his health continues, there is no doubt of his rising to one of the first situations in the profession."[28]

In dealing with this early stage in Copley's career, Campbell, in his critical biography, assessed the young lawyer's political beliefs:

> He remained, however, for a considerable time unchanged, particularly in his devoted attachment to republican doctrines. Strange to say, his hero was Napoleon the Great. . . . He loudly deplored the disasters of the Russian campaign in 1812, and felt deep sympathy with the fallen conqueror, whose dominions had

afterwards shrunk within the narrow limits of Elba. What then must have been his raptures when he heard that Napoleon had escaped, had landed at Cannes, and was marching triumphantly to Paris! It is said that Copley, hearing this news while walking in the street, enthusiastically tossed his hat in the air, and exclaimed, "Europe is free!"[29]

Campbell's Copley does not square with the Copley who sarcastically noted Napoleon's assumption of imperial status: "The cidevant consul has prevailed upon himself to accede to the wishes and prayers of the senate."[30] When the threat of invasion grew more ominous, he drilled as a soldier in the ranks of volunteers. Copley described the mood of his fellow citizens, extolling their singleness of purpose as they awaited the foreign foe: "Never, upon any occasion, was there a greater display of loyalty, zeal, and unanimity, and before the lapse of a twelve-month you may expect to hear of events highly honorable to the British character." He lauded the "energy, firmness, and constancy of temper which have ever distinguished the people of this country."[31] So much for the charge that Copley cheered the rising fortunes of the French Emperor.

Campbell, writing four decades after the events he described had allegedly occurred, recalled a young Copley who had sympathized with radical opinions:

> The Tory leaders he utterly eschewed. He did make acquaintance with some eminent Whigs, but thought poorly of them, as their notions of reform were so limited. Although he would not mix with the Radicals of the day, who were men of low education and vulgar manners, he thought they might be made useful, and by rumour he was so far known to them that they looked forward to his patronage should they be prosecuted by the Crown for sedition or treason.[32]

Fear of revolution had been a continuing source of anxiety for more than two decades in England. A sense of danger lingered during the stretch of years in which John Singleton Copley, Jr., attained political maturity and rose to assume a place at England's helm. Even after the Thermidore Reaction and the Napoleonic Wars had created disillusionment with France, a fear of violent revolution gripped people's minds. Real suffering among the poor and the exposure of desperate plots to establish a new social order kept this fear alive. Copley was drawn into this vortex when he helped defend Dr. James Watson, who was brought to trial for high treason along with a number of cohorts who included Arthur Thistlewood, destined to lead the ill-fated Cato Street conspiracy. It was not Dr. Watson who selected Copley for his defense but Charles Wetherell, who had been retained as counsel.[33] According to Martin, he "stipulated as the condition of his undertaking their defense, that Sergeant Copley should be associated with him."[34] The trial, held at Westminster, lasted from June 9 through June 17, 1817. Lord Ellenborough presided. He was assisted on the bench by Justice Bayley, Justice Abbott, and Justice Holroyd. The four prisoners — Watson, Thistlewood, Thomas Preston, and John Hooper — had gained their request to be tried separately. Dr. Watson stood trial first.

The charge against him — that he had "levied war against the King" — stemmed from a riot that had occurred on the previous December 2. After a meeting at Spa Fields, during which several inflammatory speeches had been delivered, the crowd marched with its leaders through Clerkenwell and Smithfield. At Snow Hill Watson's son entered a gunsmith's shop and demanded arms. In the course of a scuffle, a pistol he was holding discharged, seriously injuring a bystander. A mob plundered the shop, carrying off its contents of firearms and ammunition. This armed body made its way through Cheapside to the Stock Exchange, where the Lord Mayor and a few soldiers confronted it and arrested three participants. By this time the mob was decreasing in numbers, but the remainder pressed on to the Tower. Confronted by soldiers and the looming bulk of that fortress, the rebels' enthusiasm abated.

Three months passed before the government decided that treason had been committed, and then it determined to proceed with a series of state trials. The *Times* carried reports of the trials, along with alarming accounts under the heading "Disturbances." On June 10 the newspaper reported rumors of threatened insurrection, "a general rising of the people . . . for the purpose of overturning the Government." The news available on June 12 confirmed these rumors: "The wretches . . . had determined, in the madness of their hearts, on hoisting the signal for a general rebellion." Details were supplied: "Some were armed with firearms, the rest with pikes. The disaffected have proceeded to acts of outrage and pillage." By June 13 the *Times* could assure its readers "that the insurrection in Derbyshire and Nottinghamshire has been checked. . . . Forty-eight of the insurgents have been made prisoners." A number of muskets, pistols, and pikes had been seized. There was no question but that "the cry of the disaffected was for a complete change — for Revolution!" The next day, the declaration was repeated: "Their object was a redress of grievances and a revolution."[35]

The government was clearly on edge, but did the Spa Fields rioters threaten the State? Sergeant Copley argued "no" in his address to the jury, which he described as "an English jury, the best guardians of the liberties of the country."[36] Copley spoke of accuracy and precision, the same conditions that had enabled him to secure the release of John Ingham in the Luddite trial five years earlier. Once again he was directing the attention of the court to the accuracy of the indictment. This time the flaw was no technicality. He argued that the indictment was too extravagant in its charges. Watson was charged, first, with intent to put the King to death; second, with intending to depose the King; third, with levying war against the King; and last, with conspiring to levy war in order to compel the King to change his measures. Copley declared that the Crown lawyers showed little confidence of gaining a conviction on any one of these charges. Should the first fail, they would fall back on the second or the third or the fourth. "By throwing the net as widely as possible," the prosecutors had revealed their hope to "give themselves some chance at least of catching a verdict."[37]

Sergeant Copley urged the jurors to consider what had actually happened and what had been the defendant's objective. Was war actually levied; was this, in truth, an occasion of "flagrant civil war?"[38] No doubt inflammatory speeches were addressed to the crowd at Spa Fields. They were indiscreet; they were improper. Yet that was not the issue. The jurors must decide not whether the defendant had acted indiscreetly or improperly but whether he had been guilty of high treason; whether he had formed and attempted to carry out a plan to subvert the government.

Copley traced the developments that followed the breakup of the meeting, when the marchers were joined by "a number of spectators, women, and idle boys." Copley told the jurors that "this revolutionary army, of which we have heard so much, and which seems to have filled my learned friends with dismay, consisted of nothing but a rabble of an hundred men."[39] The prosecution had asserted that part of the plan had been to attack and take possession of the Bank of England. However, the crowd passed its gates and made no effort to seize the funds that would alleviate their greatest lack. At the Stock Exchange, where they were alleged to have levied war, there was a skirmish in which the mob was attacked by eight unarmed men and the Lord Mayor. The Lord Mayor had not been called as a witness, and this omission, Copley declared, occurred because that magistrate "would have laughed at the idea of this being civil war."

The only opposition the rioters met was at the Stock Exchange. They met no additional challenge. No civil or military power was mounted against them. Copley posed the question, "Armed and unchallenged, what did they do?" He gave the answer: "They wandered about without aim or object, and they fired into the air to celebrate their assertion of their existence."[40] Having sketched this aimless scene, Copley inquired, "Does this look like a settled intention, a fixed design to overturn the Government? What is their purpose and design?" He answered: "Clearly nothing."[41]

Finally, Copley focused his attention on the Crown's principal witness, John Castle. His testimony was the sole proof submitted for the charge of conspiracy to overturn the State. Copley admonished the jurors to remember Castle's testimony "as a salutary caution, as a light and guide to you in this inquiry; let it be the pillar of fire by night, and the cloud by day, to direct your course through this long and interminable wasteland of evidence."[42] During cross-examination Copley revealed that Castle had saved himself from the gallows on two previous occasions by giving testimony against his confederates, who met their deaths as a result. Copley declared that Castle was a person of disreputable character, and he expressed his conviction that the informer, "from the beginning to the end, intended to make these men his prey, and that with this view he endeavored to draw and seduce them into the commission of crimes. He appears on every occasion to have been the most forward and the most active. I believe this to have been the malignant principle of his mind and conduct, to endeavor to entrap and ensnare his associates." Copley was by implication attacking the use of informers, a long-standing practice of the Tory government. Having discredited Castle, the Sergeant-at-Law expressed his confidence that the jurors would view the aftermath of Spa Fields "in its true light, as a mere riot, a mischievous riot."[43] It was not a crime of a more weighty character, and its object was not the overthrow of the government. The jury took an hour and a half to return a verdict of not guilty.

Once again Copley was a hero. From the walls of London placards were hung proclaiming "Copley and Liberty." The populace wore ribbons bearing the same slogan. Campbell alleged that Sergeant Copley was "generally understood to entertain pretty much the opinions professed by the prisoner, though with prudence sufficient not to act upon them till there should be a fair prospect of their success."[44] Campbell had also claimed that the dissidents had "looked forward to (Copley's) patronage should they be prosecuted by the Crown for sedition or treason."[45]

The radicals' expectation, if it existed, might have been sobered by consideration of the successful defense Copley offered. He had portrayed his client as part of a misguided and pathetic band that preached Thomas Spence's basic ideas: an end to the monarchy, the confiscation of private property by the propertyless, and the holding of all land in trust for the public good. The government, Copley demonstrated, had overshot the mark in characterizing the inflammatory speeches delivered at Spa Fields and the subsequent random violence as treason. Watson and his fellows were blatantly inadequate for the roles in which the prosecution portrayed them. And Copley had revealed them in all their lunacy. Lord Castlereagh, Secretary of State for Foreign Affairs in Liverpool's cabinet, had attended the trial, and he noted that "if Sergeant Copley had been for the Crown, the prosecution would have succeeded."[46] Copley was retained by the ministry in the next state trial — a ministry that was hungry for a conviction.

4
Upon a Larger Stage

On June 9, 1817, the day Sergeant Copley had begun his defense of Watson, five hundred people heeded the call of Jeremiah Brandreth to "turn out and fight for bread" in Derbyshire. In what became known as the Pentridge Rising, Brandreth and his followers coerced many of their fellow citizens to contribute firearms, and Brandreth fatally shot one man who refused to give over his weapon. Supplementing their firearms with pikes, the ragtag band marched to Nottingham. The volunteer cavalry and militia that awaited them there scattered their forces and dashed their naive dreams of setting up a provisional government and sending relief to their wives and children.

When Brandreth, William Turner, Isaac Ludlam, George Weightman, and their co-conspirators stood trial in October 1817, they faced a battery of ten of the foremost representatives of the legal community.[1] This team was headed by the Attorney General and the Solicitor General. Copley's role was very limited. His participation was confined to the cross-examination of witnesses, establishing that the marchers forcibly entered homes, demanded arms, and insisted that the male householders join the rebels. He led his witnesses through accounts that established the use of threats and force. He elicited testimony that recounted the revolutionary objectives of the rebels: they would cancel the national debt and begin anew; they would burn the houses of Parliament and establish a new government.

During the trial of Jeremiah Brandreth, which lasted three days, Copley examined only one witness, William Roper, who had refused the demand for firearms. This examination was brief, lasting under five minutes. At the next trial, that of William Turner, Copley examined two witnesses, Henry Tomlison and George Goodwin. He briefly reexamined Goodwin. Again, the testimony reinforced the tale of coerced marches and appropriated pikes and guns. There were no significant revelations from the witnesses or oratorical flourishes from Copley. It was standard courtroom procedure.

Copley's limited role drew fire from Thomas Denman, counsel for the accused in both the Brandreth and Turner trials. He marveled that the government had deemed it necessary to summon the leading legal talent of the circuit into action. Foremost, he inquired, "on what principle of fairness these unfortunate prisoners were deprived of the bulwark which they would have found in the talents, the zeal, the eloquence, and the useful experience of my learned and excellent friend Mr. Sergeant Copley?" Denman laid bare his charge that the administration had been able to silence the eloquent and effective voice of an erstwhile champion of the victims of government suppression: "Why was he to be brought for the first time into the service of the Treasury, for the prosecution of persons so insignificant? — why but because he had been the victorious champion of the rights and liberties of the subject upon a former occasion, and therefore was now to be silenced, and prevented from rendering the same services to those who stood so peculiarly in need of his assistance."[2] Denman pointed out that the prosecution had not enlisted Copley "to avail themselves of his commanding eloquence." He told the jury, "You have scarcely heard his voice — he has sat a mute spectator — he has hardly examined a witness — he has not said a single word in the way of speech." Although he did not express the charges in words, Denman was, in effect, censuring Copley for abandoning his principles in exchange for a climb up a rung on the ladder of success. He implied that Copley was or would be the recipient of the government's largesse. Copley had no more extensive role during the subsequent trials of Isaac Ludlam and George Weightman. He examined witnesses and continued to establish the coercive search for arms and the attempt to forcibly recruit householders that had occurred along the march to Nottingham.

Lord Campbell echoed Denman's implied allegation, proclaiming: "At last arrived the crisis of Copley's fate, when a new and brilliant career was opened to him, which he entered upon, throwing aside the 'Burden of his Principles' as joyfully as Christian, in the *Pilgrim's Progress*, got rid of the 'Burden of his Sins.'"[3] Walter Bagehot made it all very clear in his *Biographical Studies*. Copley opted for personal profit and self-interest: "This was the explanation of his joining the Tories. Not to join them was poverty then; to join was wealth. They were firmly fixed in office. As the satirist then sang — Naught's constant in the human race, Except the Whigs not getting into place."[4] For accepting the attention and patronage of the ruling party, Copley was damned in the annals of Whiggery. Bagehot's chilling verdict was "he played the game of life for low and selfish objects."[5]

At the conclusion of the trials, the ministry secured what it had sought desperately: convictions. Eleven of the convicted were transported for life. Three were exiled for fourteen years. Six others were imprisoned for terms varying from two years to one year to six months. The most severe fate was saved for the leaders. On November 7, 1817, Jeremiah Brandreth, William Turner, and Isaac Ludlam were "hanged until they were dead; when they were cut down, and their heads were severed from their bodies."[6] The Prince Regent, acting on behalf of the King, graciously remitted the remainder of their sentence — namely, that their bodies be divided into four quarters.

The trial of Watson had brought Copley to the notice of the government. Brandreth's trial inspired the government to invite him into Parliament. Sir Theodore Martin explained that Copley had received a message from Lord Liverpool, "through a common friend," conveying this suggestion.[7] In later years Lord Lyndhurst declared that "no pledge, promise or condition of any sort was required, offered, suggested or imposed."[8] He was returned for Yarmouth in the Isle of Wight, a Treasury borough. This rotten borough was one of two that formed the parliamentary interest of Leonard Thomas Worsley Holmes who, like his father and grandfather before him, had put his boroughs at the disposal of ministries in return for patronage for family members.[9] Copley assumed his seat in the House of Commons in March 1818.

Campbell declared flatly that Copley's seat was awarded to him "with the clear reciprocal understanding that the *convertite* was thenceforth to be a thick and thin supporter of the Government, and that everything in the law which the Government had to bestow should be within his reach."[10] Susannah Copley's projection for her son sounded a similar note: she "was rather anxious for this new occupation, but [with] much hope that it is all right, especially as he is to be one of the great men of the country."[11] Copley was an ambitious man blessed with great intellectual powers and professional skill. The government's promotion of his career was the turning point for him. Parliament was a large stage upon which he could display his talents, and, indeed, he became one of the country's great men. But, for his political enemies, Copley's entry into Parliament was always to be "a very flagrant case of ratting."[12] Yet, he had climbed the first rung on the ladder of success.

Copley made his parliamentary bow in debate on May 4, 1818, when he supported a government measure to permit judges to limit the reward given to witnesses on whose evidence criminals were convicted. His position was not incompatible with his stand on government informers at the Watson trial.[13] Two weeks later, on May 19, Copley addressed the issue of revolutionary ferment, the same Copley whom Campbell later described as "the professed admirer and eulogist of the French Revolution."[14] The House of Commons was debating a renewal of the Alien Bill, dating from 1793, which empowered the ministry to deport aliens suspected of plotting against the peace of the kingdom. Copley denounced the targets of this legislation as "a set of persons from the Continent who were educated in and who had supported the French Revolution; persons who were likely to extend in this country that inflamed and turbulent spirit by which they themselves were actuated; persons who did not possess either morality or principle, and who could not be expected to respect these qualities in this country."[15]

Copley's remarks were intended to be an answer to the charge that he was a political turncoat. But instead, they triggered a baptism of fire, as the opposition regaled him with hoots and catcalls. He declared in the face of the uproar that "I will repeat that I express myself as I feel, and in doing so, I shall not be disturbed by any clamour which may be raised in the other side of the House, as there is not one who knows me but is aware that the observations which I have made are the result of my conviction as to the line of conduct which ought to be pursued on the present occasion."[16]

Copley offered his assessment of the political state of the nation. He announced his belief that the great mass of Englishmen and women were attached to the Constitution and the laws. At the same time, there still existed in England "a sufficient number of disaffected persons to disturb its quiet — a set of persons who, possessing the will to disturb the public peace, might, by such a junction as that of a set of disaffected foreigners, be stimulated to acts of outrage and disturbance."[17] Solemnly, the Member for Yarmouth warned against throwing

> an additional quantity of combustible matter into the country, in order to see how much we can bear without exploding. I do not wish to make the experiment as to the quantity of fresh poison which may be inhaled without destroying the Constitution. In 1793 similar arguments . . . to those of the honourable gentlemen opposite had been used, but the country, by not acting on these arguments, had avoided all the horrors into which they

would otherwise have been plunged, as a neighboring country has been.[18]

Copley had confronted the charge of political apostasy in the most forceful manner and in the most important public forum in the kingdom. The criticism would surface again and again across the years; it was too useful a club for the opposition to lay down. Parliament dissolved at the conclusion of the 1818 session, and Copley was returned to the new Parliament for Ashburton, a rotten borough under the patronage of Lord Clinton. The government's lawyer stood unopposed when he replaced Richard Preston, who had proved too independent in the House of Commons to suit Liverpool's ministry.[19]

Copley had entered Parliament in middle age, which was later than usual. Many young men first came to the House of Commons after taking a degree. Copley was now forty-six. A contemporary described him at this midpoint:

> I hardly know a man at the Bar who avails himself so often of the advantage afforded by a liberal education, and by reading which has not been confined to law. He is more than a lawyer, and apparently well read not only in the historians, but in the poets of his country, so that at Nisi Prius he shines with peculiar brightness. He seldom offers anything that is frivolous or unnecessary, or that does not mainly conduce to the point at which he is aiming. His periods are formed not only with correctness, but with great nicety and exactness. His sentences are frequently long, but they are not involved in parentheses, and are always complete, well constructed, with due relation and proportion of parts, and not by any means deficient in variety.[20]

This tribute to Copley's oratorical skill heralded him as a speaker in Parliament.

Susannah Copley described the earliest stage of her son's parliamentary career: "He was offered a seat in the late Parliament, free of expense, which he did not think it wise to refuse; and in the late change he was requested to stand for Ashburton, in Dorsetshire, from which he is returned with Sir Lawrence Polk, the other member. There was no contest, but of course some expense which attends these matters, — such as dinners to the constituents, etc."[21] His mother's understanding of the terms on which Copley entered Parliament was soon borne out. Early in 1819 he was promoted to the rank of King's Sergeant and named Chief Justice of Chester. The post allowed him to retain his law practice, and his mother, ever attuned to the financial implications of change, noted that "the pecuniary returns are rather more favorable, with less fatigue, than that of attending the circuit as barrister."[22] Campbell's sour comment on Copley's new post was to recall Lord Castlereagh's remark, after the Watson acquittal, that "if Sergeant Copley had been for the Crown the prosecution would have succeeded." Campbell alleged that Castlereagh's observation elicited this rejoinder: "Bait your rat-trap with Cheshire cheese, and he will soon be caught."[23] Because of his appointment, Copley had to go through the formality of reelection as the Member for Ashburton. His tenure as Chief Justice of Chester was brief. Soon he was again the recipient of ministerial favor. He was appointed Solicitor General in the summer of 1819, replacing Sir Robert Gifford who had been made Attorney General. A knighthood accompanied the appointment. Sir John Copley was now part of the Liverpool ministry. He had climbed the second rung on the ladder.

These changes in Copley's career paralleled a significant change in his personal life. His mother had long lamented his unmarried state. In 1807 she regretted that "as yet it has not been marrying time with him; I certainly should be glad to see him happy in that way."[24] She was disappointed in her hope as year after year her son remained a bachelor. She wrote to her daughter in 1810 that she could not report that "your brother is in the road to domestic happiness."[25] Five years later, when Copley was forty-three, his mother addressed her daughter in the United States once more on the subject: "I begin to fear whether I shall see him married. I wish I might: I think it is better that this should not be deferred to a late period of life."[26] The following year Copley's sister, Mary, wrote to their sister, Elizabeth: "I wish he was married, but he cannot afford it at present, and indeed I fear he will not be able to till it is too late."[27]

Finally, on March 13, 1819, Copley took a political wife: Sarah Garay Brunsden, a widow of Waterloo. Her husband, Lieutenant Colonel Charles Thomas of the Coldstream Guards, had fallen at Waterloo after only six weeks of marriage. More significantly, she was a niece of Copley's close friend, Sir Samuel Sheperd, one-time Solicitor General and the current Chief Baron of Scotland. Susannah Copley wrote to her daughter that the marriage had "taken all his friends by surprise," but "like many others, when this important event has been delayed, he has made a quick transit." Copley's mother, though not acquainted with her new daughter-in-law, noted that Sarah Garay "has the appearance of possessing everything estimable and interesting in character. . . . The Lady is between twenty and thirty, very pleasing and elegant in appearance."[28] Susannah Copley reported that her son and his bride set out immediately upon the circuit, where he took up his duties as Chief Justice of Chester. They returned to live in the family home on George Street. Copley's mother and unmarried sister moved to a house that he provided for them in Hanwell, eight miles outside of London.

Campbell noted that "Lady Copley was exceedingly handsome, with extraordinary enterprise and cleverness. She took the citadel of fashion by storm, and her concerts and balls, attended by all the most distinguished persons who could gain the honour of being presented to her, reflected back new credit and influence on her enraptured husband."[29] Together, Copley and his new wife made a dashing couple. He was always described as a handsome, charming, and vivacious man. Now he had as a partner a woman whose beauty was the subject of much comment. She was described as resembling a painting by Leonardo da Vinci.[30] She sat for the foremost portrait painter of her day, Thomas Lawrence. Her lovely face in Lawrence's work remains the best available insight into the impact she made on her husband's life and career. She took a fierce interest in both politics and her husband's advancement. Two things were said of Sarah Garay Copley: that she was very ambitious and that she was very beautiful.

A handsome wife and a knighthood graced Copley's life in 1819. In a year when all should have been bliss, Sir John Copley believed there was a real danger of revolution in England. In 1817 the government had suppressed an uprising in the Midlands and then suspended the writ of habeas corpus and restricted public meetings. A good harvest later that year brought calm. In 1819 discontent was again on the rise, as protest meetings assembled in Birmingham in July and in Manchester in August. The Manchester meeting brought as many as sixty thousand people together at St. Peter's Fields to hear the popular demagogue, Henry Hunt. The meeting ended in a rout as the magistrates, frustrated in their attempt to arrest Hunt, set the ill-disciplined militia to the task of dispersing the crowd. In turn, the terrified militia was rescued from the crowd and the crowd from the militia by regular troops. In the panic that followed, nine men and two women were killed, and four hundred others were wounded. The ministry, after congratulating the magistrates for their effective response, proposed Six Acts. Two of the Six Acts were aimed at the press: eliminating loopholes in the tax laws that encouraged a cheap press, and clarifying libel

Sarah Baroness Lyndhurst. After Sir Thomas Lawrence in the British Museum. Used by permission of the British Museum.

laws. Other Acts prohibited military drilling by civilians, limited public meetings, and restricted the right to bear arms. The sixth Act sped up trials of journalists. Peterloo, as it was dubbed, became a bitter sarcasm in the English consciousness. In contrast to the glory of Waterloo, it symbolized the government's callousness when confronted with the sufferings of the poor. Waterloo had been an occasion for pride and celebration; Peterloo caused only outrage and division.

Copley had once drawn a pathetic picture of Watson and his revolutionary followers. These were men, he pointed out, who had only the vaguest notion of what the overthrow of the Constitution would bring. They were men of limited goals and unsophisticated dreams that centered on free beer. In his role as Solicitor General, Copley was responsible for presenting the Six Acts to the House of Commons — which required a reversal of his role in the defense of Watson. Now he expressed a far different outlook, one that suggested to his critics an opportunistic change of mind. Characterizing the threat of revolution as genuine and widespread, he called for the adoption of the Six Acts to meet the extraordinary dangers that menaced the country. He added that many on the opposition benches were prone to underrate these perils when they protested that the alleged dangers were confined to only two counties.

Copley dismissed this optimistic conclusion with an enumeration of additional locales of upheaval: not only Cheshire and Lancashire but also the counties of Northumberland, Cumberland, and Durham as well as the western parts of Scotland. He noted tensions in London and its vicinity, in Coventry and other parts of Warwickshire, and, finally, in the county of Stafford.

Changing tack, the new Solicitor General invoked the specter of the French Revolution, which, he argued, had at its outset been dismissed as merely local. He attributed the conflagration that followed to the inertness of the friends of the monarchy in the other parts of that kingdom, for "who did not know that, at the commencement of that revolution, a large part of France was not alienated from the existing government?" Copley always underscored the trauma of France's revolution. He did so in a manner that was calculated to summon two varieties of fear — fear fed by recollection and fear fed by anticipation. France's watershed was never far from his thoughts, and he labored to ensure that it would not elude those to whose hearts and minds he appealed. He challenged the House of Commons with the query: "Is all the experience derived from the course and progress of the French revolution to be lost to the world?"[31]

Measure by measure, the Solicitor General enumerated the remedies proposed by the government. Coolly, he ran through the infamous Six Acts. The ministry demanded severe punishment for persons who participated in drilling for revolutionary purposes, possessed firearms illegally, engaged in seditious libel, or disseminated blasphemous publications. Additional stamp duties were placed on newspapers and periodicals, a measure directed not at the regular press but at "the cheap and low press." Copley's expansion of this point revealed his view of the distinctions among people. He described the targeted publications as those that "were sold at such a price as afforded the lowest orders an opportunity of perusing them." Furthermore, "the persons who sold them were men of no property or character."[32]

Most significant was the measure that required that all meetings called for the purpose of drawing up petitions be limited to participation by the inhabitants of the parish in which the meeting was held. Copley charged that these were assemblies "collected under the pretence of petitioning for parliamentary reform, but with the purpose of exhibiting the strength of the disaffected, encouraging their friends, and intimidating their opponents." This variety of intimidation was, Copley warned, "a most formidable engine in advancing the plans" of the fomenters of discontent.[33] The Solicitor General assured the Commons that the danger of revolution was real, propelled by a "combined system" that the Commons was now called upon to counteract; it could do so only with the adoption of "another system equally combined in its nature; and therefore the bearing of one measure upon another, as if one evil upon another, could not be lost sight of."[34]

The Seditious Meetings Bill was the most controversial of the Six Acts. Copley agreed that the people had a right to meet for the purposes of deliberation, petition, or redress of grievances. But when tumultuous meetings held under the cloak of professed legal and constitutional objects were in reality pursuing illegal purposes, it was the duty of the legislature to intervene — not to prevent free discussion but "to place public meetings under such regulations that they might be held without injury to the constitution."[35] Copley concluded his address arguing for adoption of the Six Acts by declaring that a policy of firmness was urgently needed. The government had no alternative, for "how are Ministers to conciliate these reformers who are drawing the sword against them? It would be weakness to attempt it. They are not men to be conciliated. To offer conciliation would be to succumb — would be to give a triumph to the disaffected, and an encouragement to them to rally round the banners of sedition."[36]

His strong defense of the government's repressive program made Copley a target for opposition rancor. Three weeks later the Whig artillery focused on the Solicitor General. Henry Grey Bennet, a Member for Shrewsbury, urged that Copley "consider well before he threw out insinuations against men who were distinguished both for the purity and integrity of their private life, and the consistency of their political character."[37] This hint that Copley was inconsistent in his politics and impure in his private life previewed the charges that were to dog him throughout his career. Copley replied to the charge that he was a political renegade: "I have never before the time of my entrance into this House belonged to any political society, or been in any way connected with politics; and even if I had intended to connect myself with any party, I confess that, during my short Parliamentary experience, I have seen nothing in the views, the policy or the conduct of the gentlemen opposite to induce me, as a true friend of the Constitution, to join them."[38]

James Scarlett, a Whig destined to cross one day over to the Tory side, joined the fray and sarcastically agreed that he had never heard that Copley had been a member of any political society or belonged to any political body. He added:

> All that could be said is, perhaps, that my honourable and learned friend now entertains opinions different from those he had formerly expressed respecting his present associates; but there is nothing wonderful in this; it is natural that we should like people better the more we become acquainted with them. The very apprehension of being thought inconsistent will excuse some warmth — a warmth which seems to verify the old proverb that proselytes are generally enthusiasts.[39]

This type of needling might have drawn a hearty laugh along the opposition benches, but it sheds light on the climate of abuse that surrounded Copley. He had chosen to be a political partisan and could take solace in the fact that he was a partisan unmistakably on the rise. He might dismiss these attacks as political jealousy, but the warmth with which he rose to meet them betrayed the deep annoyance they caused him. When Campbell said to Copley, "Had you come into the House on the popular side, what a firebrand you would have been!" Scarlett added, "He would have retained his name of Jacobin Copley." To this the Solicitor General rejoined, "That is a calumny lately invented."[40]

Copley had to deal with these allegations of apostasy for several decades, and he always did so in a spirited and aggressive manner. Yet even Atlay, in his sympathetic *The Victorian Chancellors*, concluded, "There is no smoke without fire."[41] Copley had probably indulged in some loose talk. His political opinions were vague when he entered Parliament. He could as objectively make the case for the government as he had the case for Watson. No deep and long-felt convictions drove him. The aptitude of a lawyer to argue either side of an issue underlay his entry into politics, which he viewed as an adjunct to his legal career. Whigs rejected Copley's calculating approach to his roles in the courtroom and the House of Commons. They could not forgive his allegiance to Tory policies after they had mistakenly counted him as one of their own. In the opinion of his Whig contemporaries, Copley was the supreme careerist — and a renegade.

5
A Reward for Perseverance

After a reign of sixty years, King George III died on January 29, 1820, old and blind and mad. Among those who took note of his death was a desperate and daring band of men led by Arthur Thistlewood. They plotted nothing less than the slaughter of the King's Ministers. The plan was to murder the Cabinet members at one of their weekly dinners. When these occasions were suspended in consequence of the King's death, the conspirators postponed their designs temporarily. When the dinners were resumed, Thistlewood and his fellow conspirators learned from the newspapers that the Ministers planned to dine at Lord Harrowby's house on February 23. They set about to carry out their mission.

> Some of their number, it was arranged, should watch the house; another of them was to call at the door, on the pretext of delivering a dispatch-box; hand-grenades were then to be thrown in at the dining-room window, while the body of the conspirators rushed into the house, and, having secured the servants, were to assassinate the Ministers, bringing away with them as trophies the heads of Lord Sidmouth and Lord Castlereagh in bags provided for the purpose. This done, the conspirators were then to set fire to the cavalry barracks. They hoped by this time to be joined by the "people," and with their aid to storm the Bank of England and the Tower, and to establish a provisional government, with the Mansion House as its headquarters.[1]

As luck would have it, one of the conspirators had second thoughts about the venture and revealed what was afoot to Lord Harrowby. All outward signs of preparation for the dinner went forward, but the targets for death were alerted that the dinner was canceled. The potential assassins, about twenty-five in all, were overtaken by the authorities in a loft over a stable on Cato Street just as they were preparing to depart and to make themselves immortal. In the fracas that followed, gunfire was exchanged, resulting in the death of one police officer. Nine suspects were arrested, but Thistlewood and several of his confederates escaped — briefly. At daybreak Thistlewood was captured as he lay in bed.

The defendants requested to be tried separately. As a consequence, a series of treason trials slowly unfolded. The trial of arch-conspirator Thistlewood began on April 17 when Attorney General Sir Robert Gifford opened the case. Copley, as Solicitor General, examined the government's chief witness, a man named Adams, who had been one of the conspirators and turned state's evidence. At the conclusion of three days of argument, Copley delivered the Crown's summation. The defense counsel had argued that the projected crime had no political design. Copley attacked this stratagem. Thistlewood's language and conduct belied this interpretation, for he had repeatedly warned his followers of the danger of retreating. Copley also asserted that if the criminal design lacked any political motive and had been framed solely with a view to creating confusion and amassing plunder, then why prepare so large a quantity of ammunition? No less than twelve hundred rounds of ball-cartridges were available. Surely, an even greater objective than to assassinate His Majesty's Ministers was sought. It was intended to be mass murder as the springboard to insurrection "in which it was hoped and expected that the great body of the people would instantly join. . . . All that they conceived to be necessary for the attainment of their object was to strike one great blow, — to exhibit an appearance of force; and they confidently expected that this would be followed by a general revolt they might lead and conduct at their pleasure."[2]

This was no plan of assassination to be followed by plunder. Instead it was a design for assassination to be followed by revolution. The English had lived with the specter of revolution hanging over them since the last decade of the previous century. And here it was before them, "an atrocious design against the laws and Constitution of their country, and which was to commence by the sacrifice of some of the best blood of the nation — by the murder, among others, of that distinguished individual who had led our armies to victory, and exalted among the nations of the earth the name and character of Englishmen."[3] This was a reference to the Duke of Wellington, Master General of the Ordnance. It took the jury only fifteen minutes of deliberation to find Arthur Thistlewood guilty of high treason.

Two days after Thistlewood's conviction, Copley opened the case for the prosecution of James Ings, one of Thistlewood's principal lieutenants. Again he reviewed the sequence of events that would have followed the assassinations. Once more he demolished the defense plea that because the plan was so improbable, so absurd, and so extravagant, it could not have truly sought to overturn the system of government. The jury again returned a verdict of guilty. Three more trials followed, those of John Brunt, William Davidson, and Richard Tidd.

Of these three, Copley participated only in the trial of Brunt, delivering the Crown's summation. He referred to "the pernicious writings of Paine," which had done so much to foment a thirst for revolution.[4] He acknowledged a proper avenue for reform. "God forbid," he declared, "that a man should be considered as an enemy of his country because he is a friend to reform — to reform to be effected by lawful means."[5] Again he paid homage to Wellington, extolling him as a hero who "has so raised and exalted the name and character of our country, who has thrown into the shade the glorious deeds of past times, and realized whatever of glory our wishes or our fancies had conceived."[6]

Finally, Copley emphasized how genuine he believed the menace of revolution had been. Thistlewood and his fellow conspirators did not rely upon their own strength, resources, and numbers to accomplish the work of insurrection; rather, they believed "the people are everywhere desirous of a change."[7] They looked to the discontent and bitterness of the laboring classes to fuel the fires of rebellion that they believed, once ignited in the capital, would race across the kingdom like a sheet of flame.

It may be erroneous to conclude that there was no genuine threat of revolution simply because no revolution ever occurred. English citizens, including English politicians, did not know what would happen next, and consequently they were always on their guard. The Thistlewood plot had revolutionary aspirations, and Copley proved this. He expressed this conviction when he said, "I cannot bring myself to believe, that a number of men could unite together, to murder in cold blood, for no object that can even be suggested, but from malignant feelings alone, such a body of distinguished individuals. As a means to accomplish revolutionary designs, I can understand it."[8] The government always had to stand on watch for a revolution; the fact that it waited in vain may be proof of the effectiveness of its vigilance.

This preoccupation with revolution was a grim business. Some comic, if awkward, relief resulted when the Prince Regent became King George IV. He had long waited to mount the throne, and he took great pleasure in his new rank. Only one flaw marred this King's accession: the existence of his Queen. He had married Caroline of Brunswick in 1795 in a loveless match contracted to produce an heir. Once that purpose was speedily accomplished, the two lived apart, pursuing separate pleasures. As the Prince dallied with successive mistresses, his future Queen led a wandering existence, traveling about Europe in the company of adventurers. This had all of the appearance of impropriety and, almost certainly, the substance, too.

In 1805 the ministry had set in motion the Delicate Investigation, an inconclusive inquiry that sorted through rumors of the Princess's infidelities. Many who opposed the government saw political profit in championing the unhappy Caroline's cause. Taunts of "George, where's your wife!" plagued the Prince Regent when he appeared in public. This distasteful state continued until the death of the old King brought the Prince to the throne and simultaneously raised his spouse to the rank of Queen Consort. Upon hearing the news of her husband's accession, Queen Caroline hurried back to England, where many indignities awaited her.

King George IV would have no part of Caroline. He rejected her role as Queen. Against the advice of his Ministers, he sought to divorce this woman who was so loathsome to him. The government, recognizing a politically explosive issue, introduced a Bill of Pains and Penalties that would strip the Queen of her title and rights and, at the same time, dissolve the marriage between the warring spouses.[9] It was a messy affair in which Sir John Copley, as Solicitor General, had to conduct the prosecution of Queen Caroline before the House of Lords.

As the trial unfolded through seventy days, stretching from August 17 to November 6, passions soared on both sides. Upholding a double standard that prosecuted Caroline while her libertine husband was freed of accountability for his behavior, Copley, as was his habit, went about his work methodically and without emotion. He did not hesitate in depicting the pattern of intimacies that encompassed Her Royal Highness and her servant, Bartolomeo Pergami. The Princess and Pergami "were constantly conducting themselves like lovers, or like man and wife during the day, while every preparation was made to prevent the interruption of their intercourse during the night."[10]

Copley recounted the familiarities at the Villa d'Este, the retreat where the Princess was staying in Italy: "Walking arm in arm in the gardens, alone in a canoe upon the lake, embracing and kissing each other; where such intimacies were proved, even between persons in an equal rank of life, accompanied by a constant anxiety for access to the bed-chamber of each other, no court could refuse to draw the inference that adultery had been committed."[11] In Italy a portrait of the Princess was painted that portrayed her as a "Penitent Magdalen," a questionable choice of character, Copley pointed out. The painting was in the possession of Pergami. At the same time, a portrait of Pergami was painted for Her Royal Highness. As her servant posed for the portrait, the Princess rearranged his open shirt, commenting, "*Je l'aime comme ça.*" The Princess's lady-in-waiting admitted that Pergami had seen Her Royal Highness in her pantaloons while she was at her toilet. At the time, her neck and breasts were uncovered, and the alleged lothario observed, "How pretty you are. I like you much better so."[12]

Copley urged the House of Lords to consider Pergami's promotion, which was "as rapid as it was extraordinary." What was the nature of the handsome Italian's services that would justify his advance in the esteem of the Princess? Copley had listened, together with their Lordships, in vain "for the smallest proof of these extraordinary services that were to justify this promotion." All that had been tendered in explanation was a reference to his "respectful obedience," an obedience so "respectful" as to secure for him the reward of being created a Knight of Malta, a Sicilian Baron, and Grand Master of the Order of the Holy Sepulchre.[13]

The provocative garb of both the Princess and Pergami was a recurring point of inquiry throughout the long trial. Copley, a man of the world, warmed to this subject and alerted the Lords to the fact that even clothed bodies could not pose a barrier to the consummation of shared passions. The Princess, attired in a loose and gauzy morning gown, was observed lying side by side with this "singular looking stout-built man" who wore a Grecian robe. The Solicitor General averred that this was the usual sleeping attire in the East and had proved no insurmountable barrier to the increase of the population of that region. Copley concluded by urging their Lordships to consider in their collective mind's eye "the embrace of a woman of high fortune, of high character, to a man low in situation, compared with hers," and only the Queen's gauzy gown stood barrier.[14]

One of the trial's most dramatic moments came during Copley's cross-examination of Lieutenant John Flinn of the Royal Navy, a witness for the defense. He had been in command of a small vessel on which the Princess sailed to the Holy Land in company with Pergami. He testified that to the best of his knowledge, Pergami had never slept in a second bed provided in the deck tent in which the Princess slept. Copley challenged Flinn's assertion that although the voyage spanned several weeks, he did not know where Pergami slept. At one point the witness, under Copley's unrelenting questioning, fainted. "I knew that he was lying, and I looked hard at him.

He fainted away and was taken out of court," Copley would reminisce later.[15]

Finally, the aggressive Solicitor General cited the public turmoil the case had created, a turmoil that raged beyond the chamber in which the Lords deliberated. Threats had been brought to bear in attempts to overawe their Lordships. Even the name of the Queen had been invoked for this purpose and had been appropriated for attacks "against all that is sacred and venerable in this empire — against the Constitution — against the Sovereign — against the hierarchy — against all orders of the State." Copley acquitted the Queen of any responsibility in this manipulation of her cause, for otherwise they "must imagine that Her Majesty was aiming at the overthrow of the government of the country, to be replaced by revolutionary anarchy."[16] Copley had invoked the chilling specter that was never far from people's minds: the specter of revolution.

The government was never able to produce an actual witness to an act of "licentious, disgraceful, and adulterous intercourse" between the Queen and Bartolomeo Pergami. Instead it assembled an extensive account establishing the fact that the two had mingled "with indecent and offensive familiarity and freedom." The prosecution had proved a flagrant appearance of impropriety if not the impropriety itself. In the law this had always been sufficient to establish the commission of adultery. Yet when the vote was taken on the second reading, the bill to deprive Caroline of "the exalted rank and station of Queen Consort" was adopted by only 123 to 95 — a majority of 28 — not an encouraging victory. At the third reading, on November 10, the Lords voted 108 in favor and 99 against the measure, producing a thin 9-vote margin of victory for the government. So narrow a majority convinced the ministry to withdraw the bill.[17]

The Queen had won. The crowds acclaimed her when, on November 29, she proceeded in state to St. Paul's to give public thanks to God for her triumph over those who had tried to bring her down. When the King was crowned on July 19 in Westminster Abbey, she resolved to attend to claim her own crown. The government, anticipating an embarrassing contretemps, submitted to Attorney General Gifford and Solicitor General Copley a query as to what precisely constituted the Queen's rights on this momentous day. Gifford and Copley issued a joint opinion that "Her Majesty is not entitled, as of Right, to be admitted into the Abbey on the day of the Coronation before the Doors are opened for the entrance of His Majesty and the Procession, but that afterwards, and during the performance of the Ceremony of the Coronation, Her Majesty, as well as all other Persons, will be entitled to admission indiscriminately, as far as the space will allow."[18]

Thus, the Queen possessed no right to admission to the abbey as a consequence of her regal station. She was lumped together with "all other Persons" and was entitled to admission "as far as the space will allow." These circumstances did not suit Caroline's purposes. On Coronation Day she set out at 5 A.M. in what state she could muster, and, arriving at the abbey, she attempted to gain admission at each of the principal entrances, only to be turned away. This aggressive display of bravado only amused the fickle public, which hooted at her frustration. It was the King's day; that of the Queen had passed. Some said the humiliation broke her heart, for a fortnight later it gave way, and Caroline's turbulent life ended. Her doctor diagnosed a less romantic cause of death: an obstruction of the bowel.[19] She found rest among her family in the cathedral at Brunswick. Her coffin bears a plate inscribed with her own epitaph: "Here lies Caroline of Brunswick, the injured Queen of England."[20]

People soon forgot the royal sideshow and turned their attention to other matters. But years later, when the career of Lord Lyndhurst was reviewed, it was acknowledged that although his task was an unpopular one, "it is highly to his honor, and speaks volumes to the moderation and fairness with which his part of the case was conducted, that this part of his career was not then and has never since been remembered to his disadvantage."[21] A similar assessment appeared in a memorial tribute to him: "such was the dignity of his demeanor, and such were his calmness and moderation, that *he* escaped the obloquy which the managers of that unpopular and damaging trial generally incurred."[22]

As Copley's public career prospered, his domestic life moved in a new direction. The passing years brought children into the circle on George Street. In January 1820 a daughter was born to Copley and his wife. The baby lived only three weeks. Another daughter was born in March 1821, causing her paternal grandmother to observe, "Very different from the last; a fine baby, though not a son."[23] A second healthy daughter followed to add to the growing family. Copley acquired a country house at Hanwell and retreated to its relative quiet when he could get away from his work in London. When able to take a holiday, he would go to Paris with his wife to enjoy the sophisticated pleasures of that city.

Copley's professional advancement continued. In 1824 he succeeded Sir Robert Gifford as Attorney General. His proud mother wrote to her daughter, relaying news of this appointment: "he is now Attorney-General, which situation, of course, brings additional responsibility, and demands attention, with its rewards."[24] The twin themes of reward and a lament for his lost presence in the family circle recur in the letters of his mother and sister. He was "entirely occupied," so that "the sight of him is a great favor."[25] Again, "It is quite in vain to expect anything from him." And when he did steal a few hours to join his mother and sister, "He always brings his work with him."[26] Lament they might, but his family saw in his preferment the crowning of the long and intense effort to propel him forward in his career.

When the Master of the Rolls died unexpectedly and that position fell vacant, Copley was the choice of the Prime Minister, Lord Liverpool, and, on September 14, 1826, was given the appointment. The Mastership of the Rolls was a customary springboard to the Chancellorship. Lord Eldon, the current occupant of that high office, observed upon Copley's appointment, "He goes to school in the lower form (the Rolls) to qualify him to remove into the higher, if he takes the Chancellorship."[27] His rise was nearly complete.

Parliament was dissolved in 1825, and during the election campaign, the issue of Catholic Emancipation pressed to the forefront of political debate. It was an issue that divided people both inside and outside the government. The debate over the right of Roman Catholics to sit in Parliament was treated as an open question in the ministry, a decision that had brought George Canning into the Cabinet. At a time when the Catholic question polarized people and Ministers, Copley decided to stand for one of the two seats for Cambridge University, which was staunchly anti-Catholic. Copley himself took the position that the inclusion of Roman Catholics at Westminster would undermine the union of the Protestant Church and the political nation — a pillar essential, in his view, for upholding the English Constitution.

The two incumbent members for Cambridge were Lord Palmerston and George Bankes. Palmerston had represented the university since 1812 and was Secretary of War, whereas Bankes had served only since 1822. Copley's intention was to contest Bankes's seat, bowing to Palmerston's seniority. However, when the poll was taken, he took first place, edging out Palmerston who ranked second and won the other seat. Palmerston, a strong supporter of Catholics, attributed his second-place showing to treachery from the anti-Catholic portion of Liverpool's Cabinet, which he believed had maneuvered against his election.[28] The result underscored the division among colleagues in the Tory party and also signaled that Copley's political fortunes might be tied to this divisive issue. This lesson could not be lost on so astute a politician as Sir John Copley.

Copley chose to participate in the debate on Catholic relief when Sir Francis Burdett's resolution for considering the Roman Catholic claims came before the House of Commons on March 5, 1827. This occasion precipitated an ugly clash between Copley and George Canning, who had succeeded Castlereagh as Foreign Secretary and leader of the House of Commons. When Lord Liverpool, the Prime Minister, was incapacitated by a stroke on February 17, Canning moved closer to the helm. His eventual assumption of the premiership also heralded the departure of Eldon, who, as the most rigid of ultra-Tories, would not tolerate subordination to Canning, a symbol of Catholic relief. With Eldon gone Copley could occupy the Woolsack, the seat on which England's Lord High Chancellor sits when presiding over the House of Lords. It was no time for a conflict. Copley spoke out, however, in a move designed to establish and display his anti-Catholic credentials. His expression of strong opposition to concessions to the Catholics was calculated to inform others, particularly the King, that he was a suitable Protestant candidate for the Chancellorship.

Copley began by disclaiming any bigoted motives and assuring his listeners that if he could be satisfied that concessions could be made safely, "no one would go to greater lengths in obtaining them," even though he now felt it his duty to oppose them.[29] But, "The Roman Catholic religion is a religion of encroachment. . . . The Roman Catholics of Ireland believe that they have been supplanted by the Protestants, and that it is not less their duty than their interest to supplant them in turn; and from the immense influence exercised over them by their hierarchy, it is not to be supposed that they will desist from making claim after claim until Catholic ascendancy is finally established."[30] Copley's speech on March 6, 1827, was an argument for strong securities for the Protestant Church of Ireland to accompany any concessions to Catholic demands for participation in the political nation. If securities were proposed to which Catholics would accede and with which Protestants would be satisfied, Copley pledged that he, "for one, shall be ready to make concessions."[31] Yet his reference to securities was vague; he offered nothing specific to his listeners. But he had voiced strong views, citing the aggressive nature of the Roman Catholic Church, long the preoccupation of both British Protestant opinion and Copley's Cambridge constituents. He had cautioned against concessions that would undermine the Protestant Church as well as drive a fatal wedge between Ireland and Great Britain. Copley opposed Catholic Emancipation on pragmatic grounds, not on principle — a position from which it was easier to retreat.

Canning took umbrage at what he interpreted as a suggestion that those who had advocated securities in the past had abandoned their principles. In a surprise move, Canning introduced an opinion, signed by Copley as Solicitor General, asserting that to correspond with the Pope or his representative was to incur a penalty of praemunire. Canning was referring to the offense of resorting to a foreign authority and, thus, calling into question the supremacy of the English Crown. Copley's opinion had been issued in response to Canning's inquiry as to the proper response he should give to a letter he had received from Cardinal Gonsalvi, the papal Foreign Minister. Citing this opinion, Canning underscored the contradiction in the requirement for securities: England would not communicate with the only agent able to pledge and maintain securities, a consideration that destroyed the viability of any approach requiring securities. He concluded by denouncing the Master of the Rolls for impeaching his honor and honesty.[32] Canning's attack took Copley by surprise, but Canning soon regretted his virulence. Within days the two parliamentarians repaired their relationship, a relationship that would draw them closer when, after Liverpool's resignation, Canning formed his own government a month later. Eldon, unwilling to serve under Canning, promptly relinquished the Chancellorship, and Canning offered the post to Copley.

On April 25, 1827, Sir John Singleton Copley was created Lord High Chancellor of England with a peerage that raised him to the rank of Baron. The motto on his coat of arms was Ultra Pergere: to proceed further.[33] It spoke volumes about his career of advancement. Susannah Copley declared that her son had been "appointed to the high station of Lord Chancellor by the particular wish of the King."[34] She noted, too, that his title, Lord Lyndhurst, "is one of choice, not derived in any way."[35] Copley had pondered the title he should take. He had no ancestral estate to provide him with a locational title. Initially, he had considered Lord Ashbourne, an allusion to his former parliamentary district, and the choice appeared settled, for Palmerston wrote on April 19 that "Copley is Chancellor as Lord Ashbourne." But there was one cause for reservation. Copley was disconcerted by a reference to "romantic Ashbourne" in a poem about the "Derby Dilly."[36] The reference was to one of Canning's poems published in the *Anti-Jacobin*.

Why Copley settled on the designation Lyndhurst remains something of a mystery. Sir Theodore Martin concentrated in his biography on the

A Reward for Perseverance 57

Lord Lyndhurst as Lord High Chancellor of England. Thomas Phillips, R.A., 1830, in the National Portrait Gallery. Used by permission of the National Portrait Gallery.

apprehension caused by Ashbourne and gave no explanation for the actual selection. Campbell merely noted that "Copley was raised to the peerage by the title of Baron Lyndhurst of Lyndhurst in the county of Southampton."[37] The most reasonable explanation appeared in the *Standard* upon the ex-Chancellor's death: "It was at Lyndhurst, in the New Forest, that he first met the lady who afterwards became his wife . . . and, as an enduring memorial of the happiness that had sprung from that casual meeting, he chose Lyndhurst for his title, and, as he might then hope, for the perpetuation of his family."[38] It was a romantic story, and, whether accurate or apocryphal, Lord Lyndhurst it was to be.

The transfer of the Great Seal from Eldon to Lyndhurst was effected without acrimony and with expressions of goodwill on both sides. The new Chancellor advised his predecessor to "consult your own convenience" on the transition but suggested that it should take place before the meeting of the House of Lords on May 2.[39] On April 30 Eldon relinquished the Seal to the King, who gave it immediately to Lord Lyndhurst. George IV expressed his pleasure at being able to consign it to the custody of one who enjoyed his complete confidence. On May 2, the day when the Lords reassembled, Lyndhurst publicly assumed his new distinction. At noon he received well-wishers at a levee at his home on George Street. These friends and colleagues escorted him to Westminister Hall, where he put on his robes, took his oath, and assumed his place on the Woolsack. Observers agreed that he conducted himself with "seriousness and dignity."[40]

More than preeminence and a peerage were Lyndhurst's reward: his post represented enormous economic gain. The new Lord Lyndhurst was keenly aware of the financial implications of his changed circumstances. In fact, he discussed his prospects with Charles Greville, Clerk of the Privy Council, who confided to his diary that he had dined with the new Chancellor:

> (He) talked to me a great deal about his acceptance of the Great Seal and of the speculation it was. He was Master of the Rolls with 7,000 [pounds] a year for life when it was offered to him; he debated whether it was worth while to give this up to be Chancellor for perhaps only one year, with a peerage and the pension. He talked the matter over with his wife, and they agreed that if it only lasted one year (which he evidently thought probable) it was worth while, besides the contingency of a long Chancellorship.[41]

When asked by Lyndhurst whether he thought the government was popular and regarded as strong, Greville responded that he thought it was solid on both counts and assured him that "he had a good chance of being Chancellor as long as his predecessor had been, there being so few candidates for the office." This inquiry was indicative of Lyndhurst's continuing preoccupation with keeping his place. It would have been a great disappointment to have lost it after a fleeting tenure. Greville made the following observation: "In talking of the speculation he had made, political opinions and political consistency seemed never to occur to him, and he considered the whole matter in a light so business-like and professional as to be quite amusing."[42] Lyndhurst approached his elevation as he had everything else up to this point: mainly as a lawyer, concerned, as most lawyers were, for income and professional advancement. No one mistook Lyndhurst for an individual overly addicted to a political creed. He was flexible, and his desire to keep his place made him a good political barometer.

6
Keeping Afloat

When a stroke removed Lord Liverpool from active political leadership, the ultra-Tories could no longer block George Canning's claim to the premiership. His star had risen to such a height in the political firmament as to make choosing him unavoidable. Although George IV was unenthusiastic about accepting so vocal a pro-Catholic as his First Minister, he realized that a thoroughly Protestant[1] ministry would not succeed. He reached this conclusion after the Protestants found themselves with a majority of only four when the House of Commons divided over the Catholic issue in early March 1827. Thus the stubborn monarch, facing the inevitable, invited Canning to lead a government that retained the incumbent Ministers, with one stipulation: Canning must not commit the Cabinet to Catholic Emancipation. The issue was to remain an open one in the ministry.

When Charles Greville had assured Lord Lyndhurst that the new government was on solid ground, he was unrealistically optimistic. As Canning attempted to keep together Liverpool's administration, a large number of Tories left the Cabinet: Sir Robert Peel and Wellington, followed by the Earl of Westmoreland, Lord Bexley, Viscount Melville, Lord Eldon, Earl Bathurst, and several junior members. The total reached forty-one. This mass exit constituted a dramatic rejection of Canning's leadership and symbolized his loss of support among a large sector of the Tory party. Canning was Prime Minister, but the Tory party was falling into pieces.

Eldon's departure was no surprise because he was well into his seventies and he had spoken frequently of his desire to retire. More significantly, he was a militant Protestant, and he would have refused to serve under Canning. Lyndhurst's appointment as his successor was part of the new Prime Minister's attempt to construct his government in a way that attained both the appearance and the substance of balance between Catholics and

Protestants. He had more difficulty convincing staunch Protestants to join him than he did in persuading Catholic sympathizers.

With Copley as Chancellor, Canning had acquired another Protestant for his Cabinet, bringing the number to three out of twelve Ministers. However, Lord Grey, a leading Whig who was unfriendly to Canning's efforts, thought that in view of Copley's recent statements in the House of Commons, the new Chancellor brought too strong an infusion of Protestantism into the government. Grey confided to Lord Lansdowne, a fellow Whig, that Copley's appointment "speaks a language too plain to be misunderstood."[2] Grey's chilly assessment coincided with Canning's overtures to the Whigs. Canning succeeded in fashioning a coalition that enabled him to be Prime Minister with Whig support. In return, the Whigs gained very little for their role in a Whig-Canningite coalition. Initially, they assumed three Cabinet posts, which were followed by three more posts within a month's time.[3] However, they received no official endorsement of Catholic Emancipation.

Lord Lyndhurst indicated his approach to religious questions when Parliament debated a bill to make a concession to Protestant Dissenters. This was a government measure to allow Dissenters to have their marriages performed by their own clergy and in their own chapels. When Lord Eldon mounted a vigorous opposition, the new Chancellor crossed swords with his predecessor by proclaiming that it was insensitive to force individuals who were not members of the Church of England to participate in its marriage service. Lyndhurst cited the Unitarians, whose doctrinal beliefs were inconsistent with the orthodoxy of the Anglican rite. He spoke of "this solemn mockery," which he urged "ought to be got rid of for the sake both of Dissenters and of the church . . . for it would be a relief almost as much to the church as to the Dissenters."[4] He concluded by declaring that the government's interest in regard to the marriage ceremony should be limited to a concern that the valid occurrence of that ceremony be easily verified. The bill was sent to a committee where it languished, thus postponing the repeal of this remnant of religious discrimination until a later day.

This calm approach, without impassioned commitment, became Lord Lyndhurst's trademark. Although he expressed conventional anti-Catholic sentiment in debate, he was personally untainted by religious bigotry. His outlook regarding religious issues was foreshadowed in the essays he had produced as a Cambridge undergraduate. In "A Sketch of the Reign of Elizabeth," he denounced the "unrelenting bigotry"[5] of Queen Mary's reign while recognizing Mary of Scotland's plight when she was engulfed by "the fanaticism and fury . . . the bigoted rage of her subjects."[6] In his prize-winning analysis of William III, the young Copley had alluded to the religious strife during England's Civil War as a time when the country was "tainted by the infusion of a deadly poison." It was an era in which "there had grown up a wild and destructive fanaticism."[7] Lyndhurst was mindful throughout his life of the lengths to which a militant religious faith could drive his fellows.

Events moved quickly as the Canning ministry lived out its short and beleaguered existence, fighting off attacks from both the right and the left. The end came with surprising suddenness: "It was while sitting out in the garden of Lord Lyndhurst's house at Wimbledon, on the 10th of July, that Canning got the chill which was the proximate cause of his death."[8] He died on August 8, 1827, and Lyndhurst had to reassess his future prospects. Would he prove himself a man for all seasons in the uncertain political season ahead? Lyndhurst was soon assured of continuance as Lord Chancellor in any new government, because King George IV stipulated that the Cabinet would retain its existing membership. There would be no new faces, particularly no new Whig faces. His choice for the new leader was Viscount Goderich, who would accept the King's requirements without a murmur. Goderich's weakness was his most attractive quality from the royal perspective. The new Premier could not manage the King.

Lyndhurst sensed that Goderich's days were numbered. The vacillating Prime Minister could not last. Lyndhurst saw proof of this in Goderich's desperate attempt to present the King with an ultimatum. When George IV devised a plan to bring the Marquess Wellesley into the Cabinet as President of the Council, a ploy designed to please the Tories, Goderich insisted that Lord Holland be brought in at the same time — a development that would both satisfy the Whigs and compel the King to redeem a pledge he had made to Lord Lansdowne that the first vacancy would be filled by Holland. The nice balance of the simultaneous appointments was calculated to please both Tories and Whigs. Writing to the King of the necessity of additional strength for the tottering regime, Lord Goderich declared that "strength cannot be obtained from one side only, for such an attempt would infallibly cause the immediate dissolution of the Administration." The solution was paired appointments, whereby both Wellesley and Holland would enter the Cabinet. Only an arrangement of this kind would enable Goderich to continue in his post.

Such an ultimatum was out of character for the First Minister, and, in the final paragraph of his decisive letter, he reverted to bumbling. He wrote of "how deeply he feels his own inadequacy to discharge the great duties of the situation." His health was enfeebled, and he felt anxiety for the uncertain prospects of his wife, whose health had deteriorated as well.[9] In his reply the King agreed to Holland's admission if it were coupled with the inclusion of the Duke of Wellington as head of the Ordnance. He then seized upon Goderich's confession of "inadequacy" and expressed his regret that "Lord Goderich's domestic calamities unfit him for his present situation," adding coolly, "over this the King unhappily has no control."[10]

Goderich had once again played the fool to his King. William Huskisson recognized the changed situation immediately when Goderich reported the King's reply to him. He noted that "the premier is the depository of the king's general confidence, and that from the moment the king understands from him that he is no longer adequate to fill that situation, the administration over which he presided is virtually dissolved."[11] Huskisson pronounced the situation "a very pretty kettle of fish."[12] The King immediately showed what he regarded as Goderich's letter of resignation to Lord Lyndhurst, requesting that he keep the contents confidential. He felt he must find another Prime Minister, and he wished to enlist the aid of the Chancellor in that undertaking. He summoned Lyndhurst to the Royal Lodge at Windsor. George IV placed great reliance in his Lord Chancellor, and, after seeing Huskisson, he sent him to the Chancellor, "referring the whole to his better judgment."[13]

Lyndhurst sensed that the resolution of the crisis might well determine his own fate, so he resolved that when the Ministers fell, he would fall standing up. He continually conferred with John Herries, Chancellor of the Exchequer, and informed Sir William Knighton, the King's private secretary and a Tory sympathizer, that Herries and Lord Bexley would leave the Cabinet if Lord Holland were brought in. Lyndhurst thought the King should be prepared for this. He had already mentioned to the monarch that Holland's appointment would probably compel Herries to resign. Now he added an ominous warning for Knighton's consideration: "Should they determine to adopt this course my situation will be most *painful*. I shall be left, with the exception of Ld. Anglesea, alone in the Cabinet as to questions connected with the support of the Church and the Protestant interest."[14] Lyndhurst anticipated that such a desertion would leave him a lonely and ineffective pillar of Protestantism. His own ambitions inspired him to form some design to protect his position while Goderich's government tottered.

Both Knighton and Herries sought the return of the ultra-Tories to the Cabinet, and Lyndhurst had concluded that this was the most probable outcome. But it was an outcome that was postponed for the time being. A rumor, which was not based on truth but was plausible, circulated that the ultra-Tories were conspiring to join with Grey to defeat the government and force the King to take them back. Grey had felt isolated when his Whig colleagues supported Canning's ministry, and, as Goderich clung to his brief premiership, the Whig leader was awaiting an opportunity to reassert his political leadership.[15] The King detested Grey and would not submit to having any ministry forced upon him. This rumor bought time for Goderich, but the respite was short. Knighton and Herries prepared a new plan to undermine the government. Herries raised an objection to the nomination of Viscount Althorpe, a Whig, as Chair of the Finance Committee of the House of Commons. Huskisson's prestige as leader of the Commons was bound up in Althorpe's selection; if it failed, he would have left the government in protest. Neither Herries nor Huskisson would back down, and the beleaguered Goderich faced a new crisis in his ministry. In supporting either of his Ministers, he would alienate the other and thereby destroy his government. Goderich did nothing. He refused to throw his support to either camp, and he refused to go to the King and inform him of the deadlock.

Lyndhurst decided it was time to act. He had been preparing his stand all along. Arthur Aspinall analyzed the Lord Chancellor's maneuvering and concluded: "There is . . . no doubt that Lyndhurst, as well as Knighton and Herries, was deeply immersed in intrigue and was playing a deep game of his own. He had decided that, whoever else might lose, he would be the gainer by the impending dissolution of the government. He decided, too, that in view of Goderich's extreme unwillingness to exercise the functions of his office, he must act as prime minister himself."[16] What a revelation of Lyndhurst's considerable political as well as professional ambition! Within a few months of his elevation to Chancellor, he was acting almost as Prime Minister.

Lyndhurst planned to go to Windsor Castle and inform His Majesty that the government was at the end of its tether. He had written on the last day of 1827 to request that Knighton prepare the King for an imminent debacle. He felt it was his duty "in some way to communicate to the King that I was convinced the Government could not go on in its present form."[17]

The Chancellor portrayed as a timeserving careerist, 1829.
Used by permission of the British Museum.

Lyndhurst's resolution forced Goderich to play out the final scene of his troubled tenure. The hapless Premier went to Windsor on January 8, 1828, to tell the King that his government had foundered over the conflict between Herries and Huskisson, which was precipitated by Althorpe's appointment to chair the Commons Finance Committee. The King asked Goderich to send Lyndhurst to him.

The Lord Chancellor arrived at Windsor and advised the King to invite the Duke of Wellington to form a ministry. On January 9 Wellington received the royal summons through the Lord Chancellor. He sent an account to his confidante, Harriet Arbuthnot: "I was awoke this morning before 8 by a note from Lord Lyndhurst to tell me that he must see me immediately, as he had a Message to deliver from the King. He came shortly afterwards, before I was dressed, and told me that the Government was dissolved, and that the King desired I would attend him at Windsor to receive H. M.'s commands respecting the formation of another."[18] Wellington, escorted by Lyndhurst, departed for Windsor, where the King told him he wished him to form a government. The monarch wanted the Cabinet "to consist of persons holding both opinions on the R. C. [Roman

Catholic] Question . . . he has no objection to any of His late or former Servants, or to anybody excepting one Person whom he named. . . . But he gave me Carte blanche in respect to everything and everybody excepting that one Person, who is Lord Grey!"[19]

Wellington sought time to confer with his friends and immediately contacted Sir Robert Peel, entreating him to come to London for consultation. He noted in his letter to Peel that "excepting Lord Lyndhurst, who it must be understood, is in office, everything else is open to all mankind except for one person Lord Grey."[20] Lord Grey was the bugbear of the King, whereas Lord Lyndhurst was his sine qua non. Grey had gained the King's everlasting dislike because of his public support for Queen Caroline at her trial.[21]

Thus Lyndhurst not only survived the dissolution of Goderich's feeble ministry but also secured a central place in the King's confidence and, consequently, in the new government. Wellington insisted upon talking to "Publick Men" before forming a ministry. In the aftermath of his summons to Windsor, his consultations continued to involve the Lord Chancellor, who was deputized to communicate the progress to the King. On January 11 Lyndhurst notified the monarch's private secretary that "Peel and Bathurst and Huskisson and Goulburn have consented to serve under the Duke. Dudley *will* accept and he and Wm Lambe are proposed by *Huskisson*, and to this proposition no objection has been made."[22] The principle issue, Lyndhurst pointed out, was what to do in regard to Lansdowne and the Whigs, a ticklish matter. Huskisson was convinced that Lansdowne would decline to serve under an anti-Catholic Prime Minister. Wellington believed it would be harmful to make any offer, for it could only, in Lyndhurst's words, "cool the zeal if not weaken the support of our Tory friends, who are at present very warm and active in favour of the embryo Government."[23]

The Lord Chancellor recounted the reasoning that had prevailed in the high councils of the Tory party:

> It would be a poor compliment, it is said, to offer to an able and tried friend an office which had been refused by Lansdowne. It is also considered that to give Lansdowne the opportunity of refusing place, might have the effect of setting him up again with his ultra Whig friends and render his future opposition more effective than it might otherwise prove. On the other hand if Lansdowne should consent to remain in office it must of course be in connection with S(pring-) Rice, Macdonald and perhaps

Abercrombie etc. which would be offensive to our friends and very troublesome to the Government, exposing us to perpetual annoyance by communicating our counsels, views etc.[24]

He was arguing against the inclusion of any Whigs and he was now more concerned about the zeal of "our friends," the Tories. He thus had departed from Liverpool's tradition, let alone Canning's, of a broad-based coalition. His determination to keep his place precluded the luxury of consistency. The Whigs would go, and the Canningites, as the liberal Tories were called, would remain in Wellington's government, which was not the ultra-Tory ministry some had hoped for. Lyndhurst was secure — for the time being.

Wellington, after apprising Mrs. Arbuthnot of the King's commands, concluded that "the Case cannot stand better."[25] He was wrong. The most serious pitfall awaiting his ministry was expressed in his message to Peel that "the King said it was to be understood that the Roman Catholic question was not to be made a Cabinet question."[26] In other words, the ministry would propose no solution. However, pressure to place the Catholic issue on the political agenda would continue to dog Wellington. Catholic Emancipation would prove to be the dominant issue of his stewardship. The press of events in Ireland had constantly prodded British rulers. William Pitt's plan for Ireland's political union with Great Britain in 1801 had promised Catholic Emancipation as an inducement for Ireland's participation. The proposal, however, had stumbled because of George III's stubborn refusal to allow any concession to his Catholic subjects, and Pitt had resigned. The King's intransigence symbolized the political kernel upon which the British Tories chewed. They would tolerate no measure they believed might endanger the politically sanctioned religious monopoly of the state Church.

The campaign for Catholic Emancipation had continued since the failure of Pitt's proposal for union in 1801. By 1825 the Catholic Association, founded two years earlier, had mushroomed in importance. Its might sprang from the Catholic rent, a weekly assessment collected by the priest in every parish. These contributions fueled the propaganda of the Irish nationalist movement, and Daniel O'Connell's fiery leadership gave direction to the awakening surge for unity among his fellow citizens. Tension mounted on May 10, 1826, when a bill for Catholic Relief passed the Commons by thirteen votes only to perish at the hands of the Lords, who rejected it with forty-eight votes to spare. In the general election of 1826, the issue was brought before the electorate. The newly elected House of Commons rejected another Emancipation bill by a majority of four.

In a Waterford by-election, the Catholic peasantry, led by the parish priest, united to reject the candidate of the Marquis of Waterford, an outspoken critic of Emancipation. It was a bold and effective departure from the politics of deference. A more shocking display of impertinent solidarity lay in store for Ireland's alien masters: the County Clare by-election, which turned Wellington's Catholic policy upside down. Although that crisis was several months away, time was running out for Wellington and those surrounding him, all of whom preferred to postpone a final resolution of the Catholic issue.

7
Setting up the Duke

From start to finish, the Duke of Wellington's task was an impossible one. He wanted to keep the ultra-Tories out of his government while retaining their support. He continually denied any plan to make concessions to Catholics, and he agreed to the King's stipulation that Catholic Emancipation must remain an open question. The Canningites, for whom William Huskisson was the spokesperson, were pleased by the large inclusion of pro-Catholics in the Cabinet. Four Canningites held office: Charles Grant, Lord Dudley, Lord Palmerston, and Huskisson. Four other pro-Catholics sat in Wellington's Cabinet: Lords Ellenborough, Melville, and Aberdeen, and William Lamb. The pro-Catholic majority was eight to six.

Despite its narrow Catholic majority, Wellington's Cabinet was more Protestant than its two predecessors had been. Although both previous ministries had been officially neutral on the Catholic issue, Canning's government had contained only three Protestants out of twelve members, and Goderich's Cabinet had included only four Protestants among its fifteen participants. By comparison, the Wellington government was perceived as anti-Catholic. Thus Sir Robert Peel, whose strong Protestant views had led him to decline to serve under Canning, agreed to join Wellington's Cabinet. Peel believed, as did many others, that the new Prime Minister's well-known opposition to Catholic Emancipation was a surety. Wellington was attempting to retain broad Tory support. His soldier's nature was too relaxed on religious matters to replicate the overheated sentiments of such ultras as Lord Eldon, the Duke of Newcastle, and the King's brother, Ernest, Duke of Cumberland. His constant objective was to keep his government afloat.

The relief of Dissenters from the statutory prohibition against their serving in municipal corporations or in Crown offices without first taking communion according to the Anglican prayerbook, accomplished by the repeal of the Test and Corporation Acts on May 9, 1828, caused Catholics and their supporters to take heart. The government had not introduced its own measure but had simply submitted amendments to Lord John Russell's proposal to remove the disability. The legislation legitimized the idea of changing constitutional practice regarding religious matters. As well, it announced Wellington's willingness to introduce and carry through a change that reversed one of his previous positions. No immutable constitutional dictates were barriers to his adaptability. The same applied to Lyndhurst's behavior. In the debate over repeal in the House of Lords, the Chancellor urged his colleagues to consider the changes "calmly and temperately."[1] Referring to the practice whereby nonmembers received the Church of England's sacrament of communion in order to take office, he explained his view that repealing the sacramental test but retaining the necessity of taking the Oath of Supremacy was a sufficient bar against the intrusion of Roman Catholics into the government of the corporations. In taking this position he collided with Lord Eldon, his predecessor, who expressed his customary anxiety that the Church might be left vulnerable to those who traveled different paths in seeking God. Lyndhurst hoped their Lordships would send the measure before them "out to the world accompanied with such a spirit of conciliation as would be highly advantageous to the country."[2]

Although the repeal of the Test and Corporation Acts gave an enormous, but unintended, boost to the chances for the passage of Catholic Emancipation, relief for Dissenters was not the wrenching concession it would be for Catholics. Dissenters did not embody the unsettling specter of Irish nationalism coupled with loyalty to a religious orthodoxy that flouted national borders. Catholics carried the heavy liability of fealty to Rome, yet they had one great advantage in resolving their predicament: the increasing deterioration of Irish affairs. This urgency forced Wellington to act, loath as he was to do so.

Before he had to come to grips with Catholic demands, Wellington had to reshuffle his Cabinet. This necessity arose when two parliamentary seats were detached from East Retford as a result of electoral corruption. They were reassigned to the Hundred of Bassetlaw, which was dominated by Newcastle, the ultra-Tory Duke. Huskisson wanted the seats to be given to manufacturing centers and offered his resignation in protest. He had intended this as a gesture and was surprised by Wellington's unhesitating acceptance. His followers in the ministry — Grant, Dudley, Palmerston, and Lamb — also left. The departure of the Canningites did not ruffle Lyndhurst, who found the reconstituted Cabinet compatible with his Protestant outlook. Although two Catholic sympathizers, Sir George Murray and William Vesey Fitzgerald, were brought into the Cabinet, an anti-Catholic majority now prevailed, and the ultra-Tories savored their gain. As the storm cloud of Catholic relief grew larger, the Prime Minister considered his priorities and his options. In *The Catholic Question in English Politics, 1820 to 1830*, G.I.T. Machin suggested that "Wellington must have foreseen that adoption of Catholic relief would, unless handled with extreme delicacy, shatter the Tory party. Anxious as he was to prevent this he may have thought that by dispensing with the Huskissonites he would regain enough of the ultras' confidence to win their neutrality, if not their support, for the measure which he contemplated."[3]

However, events marched faster than Wellington anticipated. On May 12, 1828, the House of Commons passed by a majority of six votes Sir Francis Burdett's perennial resolution requiring the consideration of "the state of the laws affecting His Majesty's Roman Catholic subjects . . . with a view to . . . a final and conciliatory adjustment."[4] This action was a reversal of the year before. When the resolution of the Commons came before the peers on June 10, Lord Lyndhurst rose from the Woolsack and spoke out firmly against the measure.

The Chancellor reaffirmed his opposition to any concession, and he challenged the position that a surrender to Catholic demands would calm Ireland. He cited, as he had in the past, the influence of the Catholic priesthood and hierarchy, arguing that concessions would merely strengthen their influence. Lyndhurst sounded a theme of securities for the Protestant Church of Ireland, despairing of their attainment because he claimed he possessed documents that proved that the Catholic clergy and laity wanted "no less than absolute, unqualified, and unconditional emancipation."[5] Lyndhurst did not produce these documents for his fellow peers, an action that might have impressed some in his audience. However, he did harry the advocates of Emancipation by declaring that even Pitt, Charles James Fox, and Canning — all friends of Catholic relief — were on the side of securities. Lyndhurst confessed that he saw the difficulties of the issue, but he could see no way out of them. In concluding he took refuge in the issue's emotional impact, declaring that "because I love the Protestant Church of Ireland . . . because I think it the bulwark of the Church of England, I am not willing to forego my support to it, and I do not see my way out of the difficulty. I wish to God I did, but I am satisfied that to comply with what is required, instead of diminishing that difficulty, would increase it."[6]

From Lyndhurst's mouth to God's ear. His prayer for "a way out of the difficulty" would be answered within the year. He might see no resolution at the moment, but events forced him and many like him to take a harder look. The outcome of the County Clare by-election on July 5 convinced him that change must come because Ireland was on the cutting edge of rebellion. The defiance expressed in Daniel O'Connell's victory ended the luxury of a policy of drift. Political practice dictated that all new Cabinet members must stand for reelection to Parliament upon their elevation. As the newly appointed President of the Board of Trade, William Vesey Fitzgerald, a pro-Catholic, submitted to the election process. O'Connell, who was a Roman Catholic, entered the race and was elected. Although the law prevented him from taking his seat, his election carried a harrowing promise of repeated elections in which Roman Catholics were the victors even though they could never take their seats at Westminster. Other O'Connells would be elected over and over again to parliamentary seats, seats they could never occupy because of their Catholic faith. These victors in limbo might one day even assemble in a separatist Irish Parliament, spearheading a nationalist revolution.

Wellington understood the message from Ireland: concession must be made. The Clare by-election result was the trigger event that persuaded the Premier that Catholic Emancipation must immediately be placed at the top of the public agenda in order to preclude a political upheaval that would bring down his government and, more significantly, repeal the Union.[7] None of this was lost on Lyndhurst. He saw both the necessity of a resolution for the conflict and Wellington's growing inclination to produce his own measure. But he was not yet certain that the Duke had adopted a decisive plan of action. As the King's man, Lyndhurst was in a better, safer position than anyone else in the Cabinet to push Wellington toward concession. In early July, during the polling in the County Clare election, the Lord Chancellor told Lord Ellenborough that "we must try [to see] if we cannot set up the Duke during the vacation to end the Catholic question."[8] On August 1 the Duke broached the subject with the King, a critical first foray because of the monarch's antipathy toward any change in the condition of Roman Catholics. The Prime Minister's memorandum to the King stated bluntly that "we have a rebellion impending over us in Ireland, excited, organized, and this organization directed by the leaders of the Roman Catholick Association and their directions carried into execution by the Roman Catholick priests." Wellington added that "we have in England a Parliament . . . the majority of which is of opinion . . . that the remedy is to be found in Roman Catholic Emancipation." He proposed the legal suppression of the Catholic Association and the disenfranchisement of the forty-shilling freeholders. However, he stipulated that these potentially explosive measures must be coupled with the granting of Catholic Emancipation. He concluded that "it is the duty of all to look our difficulties in the face, and to lay the ground for getting the better of them."[9]

Wellington requested the King's permission to explore the issue and its resolution with two individuals: Sir Robert Peel and Lord Lyndhurst. Peel, as leader of the House of Commons, would bear the responsibility for steering any remedial measure through that chamber. Lyndhurst, as Lord Chancellor, would assume the role of defending the ministry's new policy in his capacity as presiding officer of the upper house. Both men carried the burden of renouncing their past opposition to Catholic relief. Whereas Peel contemplated resignation in view of his strong opposition to concession in the past, Lyndhurst saw no need to sacrifice himself in a similar fashion. Yet he questioned whether the government could reverse its position and survive the outrage the ultras were certain to feel.

Lyndhurst's concern for the consequences of the risk involved must have made a strong impression on Wellington, who commented on the Lord Chancellor's preoccupation with the pitfalls involved in granting Catholic relief. The Tory leader wrote on August 10 to his friend and confidante, Mrs. Arbuthnot, that "I don't make much progress with the Chancellor respecting the Roman Catholick question. He is afraid of it. He is very sensible that something must be done, and very ready to do anything that will go down and will not occasion confusion in which he may lose His Place."[10] Wellington's statement must be considered in the light of Lyndhurst's desire, expressed to Ellenborough on July 3, to "end the Catholic question." The two statements underscore Lyndhurst's conviction that the issue had to be solved and his anxiety that the government might fall, causing him to lose the Chancellorship. Hard-won, the culmination of long years of toil and no little privation, his office was the glittering prize that crowned the efforts of a self-made man and realized his family's hopes.

George IV was in need of reassurance. He had led a life of dissipation but clung to a rigid observance of external forms of religion. When his father, King George III, protested that Emancipation went against his conscience, his subjects believed in his sincerity. But, as J. H. Hexter noted in his article "The Protestant Revival and the Catholic Question in England," "No one seriously believed that George IV had a conscience."[11] Lyndhurst's strength and self-confidence had earned him the King's respect, trust, and favor. Yet the monarch was a troublesome master, who on one occasion had caused Lyndhurst to exclaim to Greville, "The fact is, he is mad."[12]

Mad or sane, the King had to be dealt with. On August 3 George IV informed his Prime Minister that he granted his "full permission to go into the question of Ireland with the Lord Chancellor and Mr. Peel and we have this settled understanding that I pledge myself to nothing with respect to the cabinet or any future proceeding until I am in possession of your plan."[13] The King continued to drag his feet all along the way, but his opposition was only one of the many obstacles blocking the way to concession. First, the three ministers, Wellington, Peel, and Lyndhurst, had to achieve some measure of agreement among themselves before facing the King again. They had to unite their collective wisdom and determination to produce a plan. Then and only then could they gain their sovereign's permission to consult with the full Cabinet. With these hurdles behind them, they could submit their proposals to the test of parliamentary and public opinion, girding themselves for the political firestorm that would rain down upon their efforts.

Wellington sent a letter to Lyndhurst suggesting the licensing of the Roman Catholic clergy. He described this plan as an amendment to his earlier proposal for Emancipation. Those priests who took an oath of allegiance would be paid by the Crown, and their licenses would be subject to annual renewal. An unlicensed priest who performed any religious function was liable to penalties.[14] The Lord Chancellor thought the arrangement might be a genuine option, but he anticipated religious objections by Catholics to the licenses. He believed this was a probable pitfall. He suggested that certain high officials, who oversaw the dispensing of Church patronage, be exempted from the Catholic relief measure. These included the Lord Chancellors of both England and Ireland, the Lord Lieutenant of Ireland, and the First Lord of the Treasury. Lyndhurst thought the number of seats available in Parliament for Irish Catholic members should be limited. Finally, he proposed that the entire package dealing with a Catholic settlement be passed for the duration of seven years, thus assuring a scheduled opportunity to revise it.[15] Lyndhurst's position was more generous than Wellington's suggestion that Catholic disabilities should not be repealed flatly but should merely be suspended in an annual gesture.

Peel saw the difficulty involved with annual suspension. It would give a member of Parliament, by legislative enactment, a term of office different from the usual tenure, which was the duration of a Parliament, thus at least theoretically shortchanging Catholic parliamentarians. Peel also agreed with Lyndhurst that a limitation on the number of Catholic members of the House of Commons might be "very useful as a security." He concurred, too, with the Lord Chancellor's stipulation that Catholics be excluded from a handful of offices in the gift of the Crown. Concerning the question of licenses for clergy to perform their priestly functions, Peel feared the same objections from Catholics that Lyndhurst had cited.[16] Peel essentially agreed with Lyndhurst's plan rather than Wellington's.

Although Wellington had talked with Lyndhurst personally, he had had only written communication with Peel. He sought a face-to-face meeting with both men so that the three individuals privy to the secret could exchange their views more fully. He proposed a day in the first week in September for a meeting with his two confidants.[17] After this initial meeting Wellington, Peel, and Lyndhurst continued to deliberate and to keep their secret. This policy of secrecy was not without its costs, for the Catholics in Ireland railed against the government's seeming indifference and took to the streets, staging huge demonstrations. These gestures in turn kept the anti-Catholics in England in a continuing state of agitation. Their network of militantly Protestant Brunswick Clubs paralleled the efforts of Ireland's Catholic Association.

Ernest, Duke of Cumberland and brother of King George IV, had helped to initiate the Brunswick Clubs. Cumberland, who lived in Hanover, subjected the King to a constant barrage of letters pressing him to stand firm against any concession. He strongly urged him to bring back Eldon "whose Protestant principles are decidedly known." This was no criticism of Lyndhurst's less-than-fanatical defense of the Protestant position, because the Royal Duke wanted Eldon made President of the Council, not Lord Chancellor. In fact, he envisioned that "that great pillar of Protestantism" would "be of great assistance to Lord Lyndhurst."[18] Cumberland apparently believed the Lord Chancellor would welcome this "great assistance" from his predecessor.

Wellington chafed under the pressure of the situation, exclaiming in exasperation that "whatever they may say in Ireland, the Brunswick Clubs in this Country are unpardonable."[19] Although the Irish agitation was still the greater source of anxiety for him, the Protestant militants in England were making Wellington's task of carrying a measure for a Catholic settlement more difficult. The ministry also faced the opening of a new Parliament on February 5. This occasion required the preparation of the King's speech, which would have to address the Catholic challenge. As this deadline neared, Lord Lyndhurst was preoccupied with the amount of risk to the government that would accompany a complete turnaround on the issue of Catholic disabilities.

On December 27, 1828, Lyndhurst unburdened himself to Lord Ellenborough. He confided his belief that "the Duke must see the King soon, and tell him what he wishes to do." Lyndhurst revealed the counsel he himself would give his sovereign: "The Chancellor will tell His Majesty it is much better to concede quietly and with good terms what cannot be prevented. That if the Ministers meet the question and are beat, as they would be, they must go out, and His Majesty would only be able to find Ministers resolved to carry the measure in any manner."[20] Consistently, Lyndhurst argued a course of action that would keep both his faction and himself in office.

8
Concession Over Consistency

In mid-January 1829 the Duke of Wellington was prepared to bite the bullet. The Archbishop of Canterbury, together with the Bishops of London and Durham, had repeatedly rejected his attempts to secure their support for conciliation. Sir Robert Peel's decision not to resign counterbalanced this setback. Wellington recognized that the time had come to end his policy of drift and to play a bold hand against the King's stubbornness. On January 15 the entire Cabinet waited for their sovereign at Windsor Castle. All six Ministers who had previously adhered to an anti-Catholic position confronted the King; they included Wellington, Lord Lyndhurst, Earl Bathurst, Peel, Henry Goulburn, and John Herries. Like a solid wall they stood before their monarch and declared the undeniable necessity of immediately framing a policy of concession. The King surrendered and gave the entire Cabinet his permission to consider the whole state of Ireland. It was a momentous turning point. The Ministers had stormed the King's closet and wrung from him grudging consent to press on.

Two days later the Duke of Wellington gave a complete report on his progress to the full Cabinet. He held to his original plan for licenses, and Lyndhurst countered with an arrangement that required registration instead of licenses. The Chancellor wanted the Crown to have the power to strike a priest's name from the register. He added a penalty of imprisonment on summary process before two magistrates. Peel suggested that the power to inspect all communications from the Pope be dropped. Wellington objected, but the Cabinet generally was against continuing inspection of papal missives. Because some Catholics had expressed their willingness to take the Oath of Supremacy, the Cabinet discussed the validity of such pledges of fealty.

The Ministers looked to the Chancellor for clarification. He gave his opinion that the term *jurisdiction* meant *legal jurisdiction*. He believed any Catholic might take the oath and suggested that it was originally intended that Catholics should be eligible to do so.[1] Lyndhurst, believing that the system of licensing priests was insufficient to reassure the public, approached Lord Ellenborough to devise some alternative. The licensing proposal was not the only source of anxiety for the Chancellor. He was also uneasy about the method of implementing his own proposal for registration of the Roman Catholic clergy. Striking a priest from the register might be interpreted as persecution and could spawn a troublesome class of martyrs. Ultimately, the Cabinet decided against giving the government the power to strike priests from the register. The Duke was reluctant to agree to this, but he relented.[2]

Lyndhurst wrote the final memorandum for the King, summarizing the Cabinet's work. It was the result of a week's deliberation and endorsed full equality for Roman Catholics in the holding of civil offices with only a few exceptions, principally offices responsible for dispensing Church patronage. All of the Cabinet's discussion had been an exercise in drifting, for none of the stipulations thrashed about were included in the final settlement. No plan for the registration or licensing of clergy, together with their payment by the state, was included. Wellington's colleagues rejected any form of control over the Irish clergy, regarding it as an entanglement with the Catholic Church. Instead, the government settled on two very different forms of security: the suppression of the Catholic Association and the repeal of the enfranchisement of the forty-shilling freehold — as discussed by Wellington the previous August. Thus, in a two-pronged thrust, an electorate of the Irish poor would be eliminated as well as the militant organization that had fomented its rage. In exchange, Ireland would achieve the very real, as well as symbolic, gain of parliamentary participation.

When George IV received the recommendations, he did not hide his repugnance. He was either genuinely befuddled by or feigned his surprise at the sweep of the concession. When Wellington noted that Catholics would continue to be excluded from those judicial offices linked to the Church, the King marveled that a Catholic might hold any other judicial post. When the Prime Minister alluded to the inclusion of Catholics in Parliament, the King was incredulous, declaring, "Damn it . . . you mean to let them into Parliament."[3]

On February 5 Lyndhurst, sitting on the Woolsack, peered through his lorgnette and read the King's speech to Parliament. The Catholic Association was described as "dangerous to the public peace and inconsistent with the spirit of the Constitution." Parliament must grant the necessary powers to suppress it. Once this policy was adopted, Parliament should "take into its deliberate consideration the whole condition of Ireland, and review the laws which imposed civil disabilities on His Majesty's Roman Catholic subjects."[4] The speech sought to calm the fears of the ultra-Tories by counseling the peers to "consider whether the removal of those disabilities can be effected consistently with the full and permanent security of our establishments in Church and State . . . which it is the duty of His Majesty to preserve inviolate."[5] The scene was tense. Ellenborough noted that "the Chancellor was so nervous on reading the passage relating to Ireland that he did not give it its full effect."[6] Another observer recorded that "the cunning Chancellor, who is known to be anything but a Bigot, affected to read that part of the Royal Speech which referred to the Catholic Question with intense feeling — he almost cried — lest he should be suspected of having given way easily."[7]

Daniel O'Connell immediately left Ireland to hasten to London to lobby for Emancipation. He was both acclaimed and reviled along the way. Reaching London, he met with Whig leaders, who counseled him to disband the Catholic Association at once as a gesture to smooth the course of the relief measure. He adopted their suggestion and relayed a directive to disperse the organization. The mighty arm of Catholic resistance was quietly demobilized on the eve of its victory.

O'Connell's appearance in London was paralleled by the arrival of the Duke of Cumberland. The King's arch-Tory brother had rushed over from Hanover when he learned of the government's plan to admit Catholics to Parliament. This development ignited his strong sense of the necessity to defend the Protestant Constitution, which he set about doing immediately. He arrived at Dover on Saint Valentine's Day and rode to London amid the cheers of enthusiastic Protestant supporters. After a night's sleep, he went directly to Windsor Castle. The King was surprised at both his arrival in England and his allegation that the government had pledged the sovereign to Catholic Emancipation. George IV repeated his protest that he had promised nothing, stating "that he *never* would give his consent to such a measure . . . and added that Lord Lyndhurst, the Lord Chancellor, whom he looked upon as a pillar of Protestantism, had promised the King that he might rely upon him to stand by *him* should there occur any unpleasantness with the Duke of Wellington."[8]

As the Duke of Cumberland attempted to steel his brother's courage, Lord Lyndhurst arrived. As the Duke departed and just before the Chancellor entered the royal presence, the two men had a brief encounter that foretold of the approaching struggle. Lyndhurst had been unaware of the Duke's presence in England and, after expressing his surprise, voiced a hope that Cumberland would support the government in its efforts to extract itself from the Catholic quagmire. The Duke abruptly dispelled any such expectation Lyndhurst might have had. Declaring that he could never abandon his past position, he said he found it incredible that the Lord Chancellor could do so. According to the Duke, the following exchange ensued. "Lyndhurst: 'A political man must learn to forget today what he has said yesterday.' Cumberland: 'Your Lordship's opinion upon the character of a politician differs so widely from mine that I must suppose that we shall now differ *entirely*.'"[9] This confrontation laid the foundation for an estrangement between Lyndhurst and Cumberland that would soon expand into a bizarre triangle encompassing the beautiful and politically ambitious Lady Lyndhurst. For the time being, Cumberland's opposition was not only a potential obstacle to the government's plan but was also a public embarrassment.

The Duke of Cumberland's presence in England wrought a dangerous change in the King's attitude. His distaste for Catholic relief was hardening into open opposition. On February 25 the monarch indicated to Wellington that he desired to revoke his consent. Two days later, in a five-hour interview, the King recited the obligation sealed by his coronation oath and the legacy of his father's unshakable position on the issue. Marathon interviews with the King, Wellington, Lyndhurst, and Peel continued; and the Prime Minister indicated his readiness to resign to make way for a Premier whose policies might be more to his sovereign's liking. The King wept and declared that the Duke was the only Minister who possessed his confidence. George IV gave way but later assured his brother that he had "not given up one point."[10]

Wellington pressed the monarch to get Cumberland out of the country. The King was like a cornered animal and summoned Lyndhurst to carry out this unsavory work. Expressing the confidence he had always shown in the Chancellor, he said, "You are the proper person to go to my brother and state this to him, as coming from me."[11] Lyndhurst demurred at carrying out this mission without consulting the Prime Minister. He rode through the night, reaching Wellington's country seat at Stratfield Saye at three o'clock in the morning. The Duke was displeased to be awakened and to learn that the King had contrived to put the onus of Cumberland's departure on the government by insisting that the request come from within the Cabinet. Nothing further was done, and Cumberland stayed.

The King and his Ministers met in a dramatic showdown on March 3. George IV faced Wellington, Lyndhurst, and Peel in a six-hour session. It was a tearful encounter during which the King protested repeatedly that he had never understood the full import of the change in policy. He could not permit any meddling with the language of the Oath of Supremacy. He had no choice but to withdraw his consent. He threatened to abdicate. Instead, the Ministers resigned. The trio returned to London to tell the other Ministers of this development. Ellenborough recorded Wellington's account of the King's behavior in his diary:

> The Duke says he never witnessed a more painful scene. He was evidently insane. He had taken some brandy-and-water before he joined them, and sent for some more, which he continued to drink during the Conference. During six hours they did not speak 15 minutes. The King objected to every part of the Bill. He would not hear it. The Duke most earnestly entreated him to avoid all reference to his Coronation oath. . . . It seems that he really does not know what his Coronation oath is. He has confused it with the oath of Supremacy.[12]

Wellington shared with the Cabinet his belief that the King would have to recall him when he found he could not form a new government. He suspected that George IV knew this and had only let the ministry go temporarily to make it appear he had been forced to capitulate against his will, thus freeing him from public censure.

In less than twenty-four hours the King did as expected. He could not do without his Ministers. The King's mistress, Lady Conyngham, and his private secretary, Sir William Knighton, helped him to arrive at this realization. The Ministers withdrew their resignations, and, to prevent any further backsliding, they secured the King's consent in writing. George IV dispatched a letter informing Wellington that he would not prevent his Ministers from going forward with their plans for Catholic relief. He added the plaintive commentary: "God knows what pain it costs me to write these words."[13] The Duke insisted that the unhappy sovereign write "approved" across his letter of March 2, which set forth the government's change in policy. He acquiesced, and the Ministers withdrew their resignations. There was no further retraction from the King.

Peel, in a turnabout that was more dramatic than those of Wellington and Lyndhurst, steered the Catholic Relief Bill through the House of Commons. He had previously, as proof of his respect for the wishes of his constituents, submitted to the humiliation of electoral rejection by the Oxford electors. He was immediately returned from the pocket borough of Westbury, where the incumbent, Sir Manesseh Lopez, stepped down to create a vacancy for him. On March 30 the measure was carried by a majority of 320 to 142. On the following day Peel, accompanied by almost a hundred members of the Commons, marched to the House of Lords and placed the Catholic Relief Bill into the accepting hands of the Lord Chancellor.

The contest shifted to the Lords. In this arena both Wellington and Lyndhurst faced accusations of inconsistency. Lyndhurst had already made a brief statement on February 19 to account for the turn their proceedings had taken since the King's speech two weeks earlier. In that speech he assured the Lords that the measure of relief contemplated by the government would contain no proposition that would be inconsistent with the Constitution. He added that he should "ill deserve the high situation in which I have been placed by the kindness of his Gracious Majesty, if I could join in advising any measure, which could endanger the interests or well-being of this Protestant Constitution."[14] Lyndhurst alluded to the passage in the King's speech that had recommended that members of Parliament consider the Catholic measure "with the temper and the moderation" that would best contribute to a successful outcome for their deliberations. Acknowledging the tremendous public agitation by groups on both sides of the issue, the Lord Chancellor observed that "since that day, every possible attempt has been made to excite the public mind, so as to render it impossible to discuss it in the proper spirit."[15]

The government's decision to grant concessions to the Catholics broke open a wellspring of Protestant emotion that engulfed the principal Ministers who were perceived as the authors of a treacherous measure. The Duke was hooted at by mobs as he journeyed to and from Westminster. The intense feeling his change in policy had ignited culminated in a duel he fought with the arch-Protestant George Finch-Hatton, Earl of Winchilsea, on March 21. Peel had been turned out by the Oxford electors and savaged for ratting on a cause he had pledged to defend. Lyndhurst, too, was excoriated for ratting. The obloquy heaped upon him reached a climax when the Attorney General, Sir Charles Wetherell, although a member of the same government, denounced the Lord Chancellor for "such apostasy — such contradiction — such unexplainable conversion — such miserable, such contemptible apostasy."[16] This shocked the government, and there were demands for Wetherell's dismissal.

Wetherell had been piqued because Peel had told him of the Catholic relief measure only seven days before Parliament reassembled.[17] Peel answered his obstreperous colleague in the House of Commons. He charged him with breach of confidence for revealing information he had obtained in his official capacity as Attorney General. Wetherell denied that he had committed any breach of confidence, but he had given the government an excuse to dismiss him. Lord Ellenborough noted that the miscreant had "attacked the Chancellor in the most violent and vulgar manner." He was glad, because Wetherell "was a discredit to the Government, and I am delighted at our prospect of getting rid of him."[18] On March 20 the Cabinet determined that he must go: "His dismissal is to be placed, not distinctly upon the Catholic question, but upon his conduct in abusing the Chancellor, betraying confidence, etc."[19]

Wetherell's attack had been delivered in the House of Commons where Lyndhurst was not present. In the House of Lords, where he presided, the Chancellor also encountered accusations of inconsistency. On April 3 he announced that he would "vindicate my own consistency," and he declared that "I am ready to accept the challenge."[20] Lyndhurst began by citing two occasions when he had addressed either House of Parliament on the subject of Emancipation. He stressed that in these previous statements he had said that "if concessions to the Roman Catholics could be made, consistently with the security of the Protestant Established Church, and consistently with the great interests of the empire, I considered we were bound to make them." So Lyndhurst was arguing that the settlement proposed by the government involved no danger to those cherished institutions of Church and Union. In the end, resist as he might, the conclusion that the only sensible avenue open to the government was one of concession "had forced itself upon my mind." He was claiming that he was an unwilling victim of common sense. Concession had overwhelmed him. Yet he gave no explanation of the essential securities.

Lyndhurst proceeded to invoke the necessity of heeding his own sense of duty. He approached this justification by recounting England's record of failure in Ireland. For years past, a harsh policy that imposed civil disabilities had produced only upheaval and discord. Furthermore, the condition of Ireland had been growing worse year after year. During the past two years it had grown worse still, and there was reason to believe that in two more years it would deteriorate beyond their greatest fears. In view of this steady descent along a hellish path, how could he say England should "persevere" in a hard policy? Lyndhurst defended his volte-face by arguing that the continuing use of force was justified only if it produced some amelioration. This had not happened in Ireland. Coercion had only produced greater intransigence. The time had come to try a different approach, one that granted concession in order to conserve the Protestant interest in Ireland. Conciliation must be tried where severity had failed. Lyndhurst, the Lord High Chancellor and Keeper of the King's Conscience, proclaimed that "this is the ground on which I, for one, give my entire concurrence to the measure now before the House." The volte-face was accomplished.

Then the Chancellor took a detour. He singled out Lord Eldon, his predecessor on the Woolsack, for a special reprimand because Eldon's voice was too powerful to ignore. Lyndhurst invited his colleagues to look at Eldon's twenty-five-year record in the Cabinet. Adopting a line of argument that Whigs found congenial, Lyndhurst pointed out that during Eldon's tenure, the condition of Ireland had steadily worsened, and yet the previous Chancellor had "applied no remedy to the evil." He "did not suggest any line of policy to stem the disorders that had beset Ireland." After compiling a record of neglect, Eldon "now came forward to oppose with his utmost force" a policy of conciliation.[21] Lyndhurst concluded his rejection of Eldon's criticism by pointing out that the Ministers possessed information on the subject that Eldon did not have, and if he had he would have conceded that unless concession were granted, "the Protestants of Ireland would be annihilated — not annihilated by force or violence, but constantly reduced by being compelled to quit the country."[22] Lyndhurst was taking refuge in privileged knowledge.

The Chancellor pointed out that from the time of Elizabeth to that of William III, there had been no exclusion of Catholics from Parliament. If a Roman Catholic took the Oath of Supremacy, there was nothing to prevent him from taking his seat there. Eldon sprang to his feet and challenged Lyndhurst as to whether he had known this fact during the previous year. "I did not," replied Lyndhurst, "but I have since been prosecuting my studies. I have advanced in knowledge, and in my opinion even the noble and learned lord might improve himself in the same way."[23] The Lords tittered at this rejoinder, and no one pointed out that Lyndhurst was wrong. Catholics had been excluded from Parliament by the Test Act of 1678.

At last, Lyndhurst turned to the issue of securities. What was the security on which Lyndhurst relied for the safety of the Protestant Church? He relied, he declared, "mainly and principally on the purity and soundness of its doctrines — on the arguments put forward by those great and good men, who had supported that creed in former days, and on the zeal, learning, and exertions of the present clergy."[24] This statement was truly astounding. Lyndhurst was admitting that after all of the discussion about securities, in the end there would be none. It was a bold performance. In closing, the Chancellor cited the personal attacks that had been directed at him, an acknowledgment that indicated that they had carried some sting. He protested, however, that "I care not for the personal obloquy which might be cast upon me for my advocacy of this measure." He added that he had performed his duty in the truest sense, "fearlessly and conscientiously, and to the best of my ability." Now, as he contemplated his future, he assured his listeners and posterity that "my most anxious desire, as it will be my greatest consolation, is to be associated with their Lordships in carrying this great object into effect."[25]

The next speaker, the Earl of Falmouth, an anti-Catholic, singled Lyndhurst out for special censure. He characterized the Chancellor's speech as "the most marvelous instance of conversion of all those by which the present measures must be forever distinguished."[26] He held a document that he described as the best answer to Lyndhurst's arguments. It was a copy of the Chancellor's speech delivered in the same chamber on the previous June 10. He cited its disclaimer that Lyndhurst would not accede to concession unless he was prepared to grant a Catholic ascendancy in Ireland. Falmouth threw back in the Chancellor's teeth the essence of his about-face: Lyndhurst's former belief that concession would not purchase tranquility. Having underscored the starkness of Lyndhurst's new position, Falmouth characterized the government's new policy as "the death-warrant . . . of our pure Protestant ascendancy."[27] In a final salvo, he declared that "consistency is one of the brightest gems in the character of a British statesman," and he censured him who would, when sinking, "catch at the straw of expediency to save himself from drowning."[28]

Lord Winchilsea declared that he could recall no parallel to Lyndhurst's two conflicting speeches less than a year apart except for the experience of a woman who gave birth to twin babies, one white and one black.[29] In a contemporary political caricature, Lyndhurst was portrayed as a turncoat. He was shown dressing for the House of Lords and putting one hand into the armhole of a coat a footman in livery held out. The footman said: "Your Lordship's coat is become very threadbare for you know you turned it only last year — and it had been turned before that; so I much doubt it will bear turning any more."[30] Lyndhurst was saved from the harsher accusa-

Dressing for the House. Portraying Lord Lyndhurst as a turncoat on Catholic Emancipation, 1829. Used by permission of the British Museum.

tions that assailed Peel because no one expected consistency from the Chancellor.

On April 4 the Duke of Wellington responded to "a charge brought against several of my colleagues, and also against myself . . . of a want of consistency in our conduct."[31] The Duke lectured his detractors by pointing out that a higher consideration than mere consistency had activated his present course. It was duty, pure and simple, that had led him to face the desperate state of affairs in Ireland and to embrace some measure that would calm that troubled nation. The Duke, without hesitation, admitted that the Relief Bill was the result of "the difficulty, nay the impossibility, of finding any other remedy for the state of things in Ireland."[32]

Wellington admitted that he, like many of his colleagues, had voted against a similar measure in the past. He acknowledged that the members of the government were aware that they would be sacrificing their popularity to their sense of duty to King and country. To raise once more the cry of "No Popery" would have secured their popularity but, at the same time, would have thrust a burden on the interests of the country, "a burden, which must end in bearing them down, and . . . we should have deserved the hate and execration of our countrymen."[33] Wellington had forthrightly acknowledged "the difficulty, nay the impossibility, of finding any other remedy." His frank admission of the necessity of the course he had adopted carried a more convincing and dignified tone than Lyndhurst's.

Charles Greville noted that "the Chancellor made a very fine speech last night."[34] Harriet Arbuthnot concurred in this assessment up to a point: "The Chancellor's speech was very clever & ingenious, impudent to the last degree for he owned he had formerly argued the subject in a directly opposite sense, but he said he had since prosecuted his studies & rather gloried in his inconsistency." This woman, who was the intimate confidante of Wellington, added a stinging opinion of the Chancellor: "He is a sad fellow without an atom of dignity."[35]

On its second reading in the House of Lords, the Catholic Relief Bill was carried 217 to 112, a majority of 105 votes. The third reading confirmed its passage with a winning margin of 104 votes. Only one unpleasant hurdle remained: the King must give his grudging consent, something he refused to do in person. Therefore, a commission was appointed to act in his name. Writing to his nephew, the Duke of Buckingham, Thomas Grenville stressed George IV's lack of enthusiasm and the danger it might pose to the ministry: "The royal assent was yesterday given by commission, I believe, with a very reluctant mind, and many rumours are abroad of the King being persuaded by the Duke of Cumberland to look about for the means of forming a new Administration." Grenville noted that "the King, however, is fonder of abusing his Ministers than of changing them; for a few hard words cost him nothing; but a great political change could not be made, if at all, without much more trouble, fatigue, and worry to the King than he will like to expose himself to."[36] In 1829 George IV was a tired King. His tears had not swayed his Ministers in March. Harsh words were no more effective in April.

Lord Lyndhurst, together with Lords Ellenborough and Bathurst, performed his function as a Commissioner and gave the royal assent to the Catholic Relief Bill on April 13. The *Age* declared that the Chancellor's inclusion as a "principal actor in the infamous scene" was appropriate, for he was a turncoat "who had only nine months ago denounced the measure as fatal and perfidious."[37] A month earlier the same newspaper had described a Lord Chancellor "who cares little for any religion, who has so often veered about in his politics, that nobody suspects of any fixed principles."[38] Lyndhurst was no hero in the attainment of Catholic Emancipation, but he was, in the language of the *Age*, a "principal actor." His lack of "any fixed principles" was his greatest asset in this crisis.

9
Lady Lyndhurst's Adventure

If Lord Lyndhurst was not a hero in the Catholic relief crisis, neither was he the villainous accomplice that many perceived him to be. The year 1829 was heavy with reproach, scandal, and rumor of dismissal for the Lord Chancellor. Thomas Fretley, identified in the pages of the *Age* only as a denizen of Lincoln's Inn, conducted a letter-writing campaign denouncing Lyndhurst. In his missive of April 5, Fretley included the substance of the charges Campbell published forty years later. Lyndhurst's first fault in Fretley's eyes was that he had "inverted the ordinary course of things" by his spectacular rise to occupy the Woolsack. The writer alleged that "without the advantages of birth or fortune, with talents never held to be considerable . . . your Lordship has risen to, and maintained a station high in rank, power, and consideration." The rest of Fretley's letter is significant because it recounts what became the standard detractor's version of Lyndhurst's career. Reviewing Lyndhurst's rise to high station, Fretley described the Chancellor's early opinions as those of "a reformer, almost a republican." He noted, too, that Lyndhurst had no compunction about joining George Canning's largely pro-Catholic administration. Viscount Goderich did not displace Lyndhurst as Chancellor, but "his administration fell to pieces, like a child's house built with cards . . . and we often see that in such a calamity one card (say a knave) is supported by some accident and left standing, while the others fall."[1]

In closing his letter of censure, Thomas Fretley pledged to resume his letter writing in the not-too-distant future. One week later, on April 12, Fretley unleashed a second missive whose phrasing evoked the profession of Lyndhurst's artist father, a subject the Chancellor's detractors raised frequently to underscore his nonaristocratic origin: "Your Lordship's moral portrait has for some time been in a state of forwardness, the outline completely formed, and many of the lines drawn. Still the piece was imperfect, but your Lordship is hourly filling up the details with the hand of a master.

Scene painter and property man. Evoking Lyndhurst's father who was a painter, 1829. Used by permission of the British Museum.

Every touch makes some new point of character, or calls forth some expression which before had been too faintly traced." The subject of this second attack was Lyndhurst's clash with Lord Eldon during the debate on Catholic relief. The Chancellor's behavior toward his predecessor was characterized as entailing a confession of Lyndhurst's own sense of inadequacy: "His talents you always feared, his integrity only suggested odious comparisons, and for his learning, it would be absurd to suppose that it should confer any claims to your Lordship's consideration." Fretley concluded his attack by marveling at "the alacrity with which you disclosed how bitter a satire you consider his Lordship's character to be upon your own."[2]

Sir Robert Peel was simultaneously the target of attacks from anti-Emancipation Tories, but to a far greater extent. This was not the first time anyone had accused Lyndhurst of being a timeserver, but Peel had refused to be a part of the administration of the pro-Catholic Canning. His past conduct had recommended him as the ablest leading Protestant. Now Orange Peel had become Lemon Peel. His turnabout on Catholic Emancipation was more to his discredit than Lyndhurst's was to him. The Chancellor was not regarded in any quarters as an individual who would sacrifice himself for principle. He was a self-made man. In the eyes of his critics, he was a careerist, an opportunist, and an unprincipled parvenu. His father had won critical acclaim as an artist early in his career but later had to struggle to earn his living as commissions grew meager. He had died in debt in 1815. His son paid the debts in full over a period of several years, during which he also supported his mother and sister. Both as Copley the lawyer and later as a member of the peerage, Lyndhurst had always had to give attention to earning money. His £14,000 annual salary as Lord Chancellor was a political plum that provoked envy, but it was not sufficient to support his opulent lifestyle. All of London was talking about his financial embarrassments. There was comment about the splendor of his furniture, his plate, and his entertainments.

Political caricatures played up the theme of Lyndhurst's continuing need for money and his lack of pedigree. Often he was portrayed extending a greedy palm or with outstretched arms and greedy fingers. In one print he is shown grasping two purses, one inscribed "Bribes" and the other "Gold."[3] In another print he is contemplating how to "pay my debts and contract new ones."[4] Others deplored his lack of pedigree. Some, like Peel, did not object to the fact that Lyndhurst was a self-made man, as was Peel's own father. But many, often Whigs, were fierce snobs. They were for the most part descended from ancient lineage and regarded Lyndhurst as an upstart. Lord Campbell, in his biography, charged that Lyndhurst was ashamed of his father's profession as a painter, and several political caricatures made reference to his father's work among paint pots and brushes. Lyndhurst's best rejoinder to this criticism was to hang his father's works throughout his home, where England's social and political elite would be reminded of his true pedigree.

Few questioned Lyndhurst's ability as a jurist, and this ability carried him to the forefront of politics. In this respect he was a product of a system of merit, which was always to some extent true of the legal profession. There were many who looked askance at him for this. Lady Salisbury, a Tory who was close to Wellington, expressed this contempt when she recounted a gathering at which Lord Lyndhurst "said something at dinner, before all the servants, strongly reflecting on the King. I forget the words, but there was a silence and the Duke (of Wellington) turned the conversation. I was amazingly struck with the contrast between Lord Lyndhurst and the others, who were all such perfect gentlemen; and he with his acuteness and ability constantly reminded one of his origin."[5] Ability and accomplishment he might have, but he was undeniably an outsider, a parvenu, one in whom the highborn might always detect a strain of vulgarity.

Harriet Arbuthnot, a staunch Tory, encountered Lyndhurst when she dined at the Duke of Wellington's London home. Her verdict echoed that of Lady Salisbury: "The new Chancellor . . . is a shabby fellow and always follows le plus fort, but consequently is a good political barometer . . . he will be quite sure to rat to us the moment he thinks his present house a falling one." Mrs. Arbuthnot's censure extended to the Chancellor's wife: "Lady Lyndhurst is a singularly vulgar woman, who two years ago was trying to get into good society by being rampante & cringing to any body she thought more fashionable than others, and now that she is Mad[me] la Chancelliere she is very grand and means to be dignified which makes her excessively amusing. I understand the real fine ladies protest she shall never go into any of their houses."[6]

Soon charges of corruption whirled around Lyndhurst. The *Atlas* on June 14 singled out Lady Lyndhurst for trafficking in church preferments that were in the gift of the Lord Chancellor. The newspaper alleged that she did so without her husband's knowledge. Lady Lyndhurst made an affidavit denying the charge before Chief Justice Lord Tenterden, and an ex-officio information against the editor, Robert Bell, was filed on June 26, 1829. The editor was convicted, but the charge that Lyndhurst's patronage had been mishandled was part of a widespread whispering campaign that

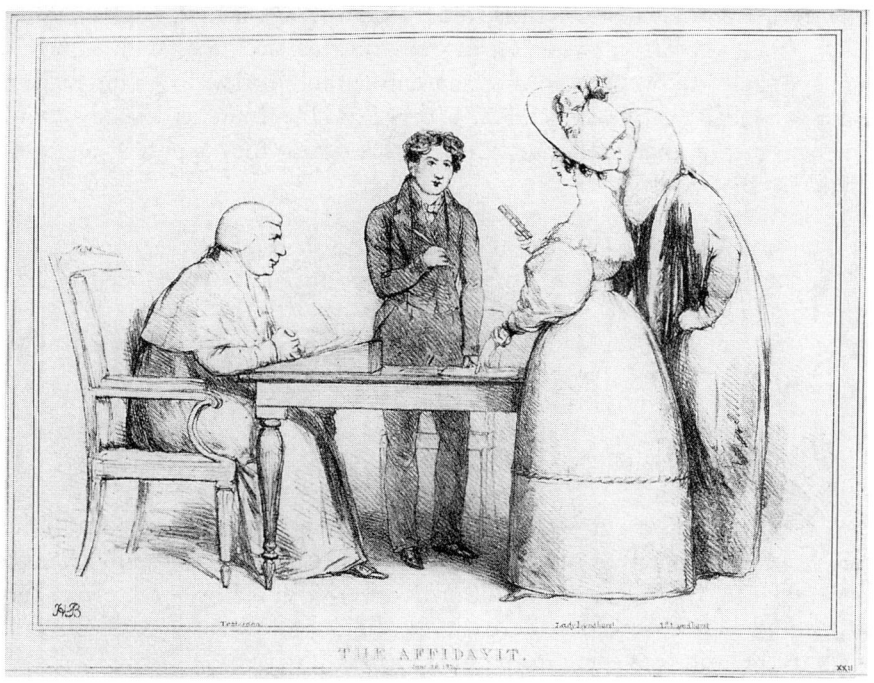

The affidavit. Lady Lyndhurst was charged with being the intermediary in trafficking in ecclesiastical appointments. She made an affidavit denying the allegation in court, 1829. Used by permission of the British Museum.

originated in the camp of the Duke of Cumberland, who was feeling righteous and betrayed after his failure in the Catholic relief struggle. Lord Ellenborough confided to his diary on June 11 that "the world has had imposed on it a story of the Chancellor's selling his Church preferments. This is an arrow from the Cumberland quiver."[7]

On June 20 Ellenborough described another development in the rumor campaign against Lyndhurst: "The Chancellor has prosecuted the *Morning Journal* for a libel accusing him of taking money for Sugden's appointment as Solicitor-General. I heard him tell Lord Bathurst, with reference to another calumny against him, that he had fortunately preserved through his secretary the grounds on which he had given everything he had disposed of."[8] This prosecution for libel had originated after an allegation had appeared in the *Morning Journal* describing the impending appointment of Sir Edward Sugden as Solicitor General. The libel lay in the suggestion that the post was to be awarded in consideration of a loan of £30,000 to the Chancellor. The newspaper, in denying that any libel had occurred, declared that "the utmost inference unfavourable to Lord Lyndhurst that can be deduced from the article . . . is that Lord Lyndhurst is a needy man." The *Morning Journal* challenged Lyndhurst's fitness for his post as a consequence of his poverty:

> It is truth that a poor man who has an exalted rank to support must be a borrower. It is true also that a borrower is not an independent man. It is a proposition as true as either that he who is not an independent man is not fit to be lord chancellor; for, however rigid the integrity of the debt-burthened magistrate may be, his integrity cannot controul the corrupt hopes of creditors; still less can it obviate the public jealousy of an officer who ought to stand in every respect above suspicion.[9]

The case was heard before Lord Tenterden, and a jury returned a guilty verdict on the charge of libel against the author, printer, and publisher on December 22, 1829. Despite Lyndhurst's courtroom victories over his libelers, the general charge that he bartered the public trust for personal gain stuck in the minds of some individuals.

Published reports of Lyndhurst's imminent dismissal or resignation reflected the wishful thinking of his enemies. On June 9 the *Morning Journal* was positive that "there are some complex movements . . . with regard to the Chancellorship and Lord Lyndhurst. His lordship's conduct has not given satisfaction, either to Ministers, the suitors in his court, the lawyers before his bar, or to the country at large. His retirement is, therefore, generally spoken of."[10] Two days later readers of the same publication were reminded of Lyndhurst's impending departure and were acquainted with the reasons for his exit: "Lord Lyndhurst, it is fully understood, resigns the great seal forthwith. His own acknowledgment of incapacity for the office of lord chancellor is assigned as the only reason of his abdication. . . . But incapacity is not the sole cause of this retirement. Lord Lyndhurst's habits and circumstances have long caused the administration to feel the value of character in such a high office."[11]

The public prints were stinging in their censure of public figures, and a flood of abuse engulfed both Lord and Lady Lyndhurst. The *Age* treated its readers to a parody entitled "Mock Morality of the Times." "His Lordship on the Woolsack" was likened to a roué who had "married a woman who was once not so chaste as she ought to have been." The newspaper alleged

Lyndhurst's shadow appears to bear horns. A reference to his relationship with his wife, 1832. Used by permission of the British Museum.

that Her Ladyship was "playing with every man who struck her fancy" while her husband "looked tamely on and countenanced such shameful profligacy." The readers were assured that the Chancellor was "almost as profligate himself."[12]

Lyndhurst's involvements with women were legendary. Charles Greville noted that the Chancellor, obsessed with Lady Fitzroy Somerset, made a fool of himself in pressing his suit.

> Since I have been away, the Chancellor has had a touch of love, and for a person not less immaculate than Lady Fitzroy Somerset. I met her at the Review breakfast the other day, and she told me all about it, Lady Worcester having previously given me an account; he seems to have been *fou, tout-à-fait perdu la tetê,* for he wrote her note after note, and some from the bench telling her he was sitting to lawyers to whom he could not listen, for his thoughts were all occupied with her, pleasant for the Suitors this and would make a pretty paragraph for a speech on Chancery abuses, at least as an *argumentum ad Cancellarium.* The other told me it was all true, that he had exhibited himself very ridiculously, that she had remonstrated with him strongly, had told him she did not care what he did, so that he abstained from being ridiculous. He swore he had not succeeded, to which she replied so much the worse, as success would have been the best excuse for his folly. La Belle would have nothing to say to him, so he has been obliged to give up the pursuit.[13]

Lady Lyndhurst was said to be the mistress of Lord Dudley, who grew increasingly mad under her spell. When his family committed him to a lunatic asylum, they sought the return of family jewels that Dudley was alleged to have given to Lady Lyndhurst. A scandal ensued and harmed Lord Lyndhurst's reputation.[14]

Yet both Lyndhursts had their defenders. Lady Holland, the leading Whig hostess, was foremost among them.[15] She noted in her journal that "the Chancellor & his handsome brunette wife dined here (Holland House). He is very good humoured. She is odd & clever."[16] A year later, Lady Holland had more to say about the wife of the Lord Chancellor and her participation in the social scene at Brighton: "We have enjoyed agreeable society here, many of my own intimates, with the infusion of a few novelties, Lady Lyndhurst, for instance, sparkling & brilliant in beauty, & with odd sallies, not from any affectation of being original or flashy in conversation, but really from coming into the beau monde when her ways were formed for another class. She is good hearted & good natured."[17] Lady Holland's praise of Dolly, the pet name intimates used for Lady

Lyndhurst, continued after a political breach had interrupted their relationship. The diarist recorded that "we always when we meet have a great exchange of civilities with the Lyndhursts. She has called upon me; & he & I chat freely. She is a great beauty."[18]

Beauty, a keen interest in political matters, and scandal were the hallmarks of Lady Lyndhurst's life. "It is very curious the sort of part this woman contrives to play," Charles Greville confided to his diary, "and how she mixes up love and politics, so as to make herself of importance. Detesting her husband *as a husband,* she sticks to him closely *as a Partner,* and labours for his aggrandizement and interests with abundant zeal and success."[19]

"Mixing up love and politics" — if that was Dolly's vocation, she carried it off astutely. She decided that Earl Grey — the leader of the Whig opposition — might be of some use, should the Tory government fall, to prevent or cushion a tumble from the Woolsack. Grey had not liked Lord Lyndhurst originally, but after meeting Lady Lyndhurst he reversed his opinion. Reputed to be a ladies man, Grey was in his mid-sixties when he became infatuated with Dolly. He insisted on being seated next to her at dinner parties. Greville recorded the details of their first meeting: "I well recollect one night at Madame de Lieven's I introduced Lord Grey to Lady Lyndhurst. We had dined together somewhere, and he had been praising her beauty; so when we all met there I presented him, and very soon all his antipathies ceased and he and Lyndhurst became great friends. This was the cause of Lady Lyndhurst's partiality for the Whigs, which enraged the Tory ladies . . . but which served her turn and enabled her to keep two irons in the fire."[20]

The abuse that befell Lord Lyndhurst covered Lady Lyndhurst as well, and she became a principal figure in a new scandal that suggested a sexual dimension. This remarkable episode was noted in numerous letters and journal entries and was the talk of London. It was in no small way linked to the great struggle for Catholic Emancipation, because it included two of the principal protagonists in that recent conflict: the Lord Chancellor and the Duke of Cumberland. Greville noted the onset of this cause célèbre on August 8, 1829: "There is a story current about the Duke of Cumberland and Lady Lyndhurst which is more true than most stories of this kind. The Duke called upon her, and grossly insulted her; on which, after a scramble, she rang the bell. He was obliged to desist and to go away, but before he did he said, 'By God, Madam, I will be the ruin of you and your husband, and will not rest till I have destroyed you both.'"[21]

London learned of the "scramble" and the menacing threat that followed when the *Age*, in tongue-in-cheek fashion in order to avoid libel, reprinted an excerpt from another newspaper on August 2:

> We copy the following absurd paragraph, the falsehood of which it is unnecessary for us to contradict, from the *Dublin Freeman's Journal* of Monday last: — THE DUKE OF CUMBERLAND. — It is stated that *this person* was turned out of Lady Lyndhurst's home some few days ago. Having acted so as to incur her Ladyship's displeasure, she ordered that he should be turned out of her house — and turned out he was. On retiring, it is said that he exclaimed, "*I shall make the Chancellor pay for this!*"
>
> It is well known to every person who has had the honour of Lady Lyndhurst's acquaintance, that there is not in his MAJESTY'S dominions a lady of more polished manners, of more dignified affability, or more amiable disposition, than the Noblewoman alluded to. Had she any feeling of dislike towards his royal Highness, which we do not believe (a Prince of the Blood insulted by a lady!) it would most assuredly not be shown in the way our contemporary alludes to — a way which would belie the whole tenour of her Ladyship's previous life.
>
> We are really astonished how such trash can find its way into what ought to be a respectable paper.[22]

After the item had appeared in print, both Cumberland and Dolly took pains to furnish details of their encounter. The King's brother recounted that he had met the beautiful wife of the Chancellor at a party at Lady Bathurst's London home. This encounter occurred at the height of the Catholic Emancipation crisis and before the vote was taken in either House of Parliament. After dinner, when the gentlemen joined the ladies in the drawing room, Cumberland sat beside Dolly on a sofa. The conversation was to the point. "So sir, you are come to turn us out?" she asked. The Duke replied that he had no such intention. "Oh, I know you are a very wicked man, and as mischievous as the Devil!" she responded. "At least," rejoined the Duke, "give me the credit of being a *bon Diable*." "Very agreeable, I acknowledge," she said. "But pray have pity on my poor husband! Do not turn him out, I beg and beseech you! If not for his sake, at least for mine."

By Cumberland's account, Lady Lyndhurst had encouraged him on this occasion and playfully berated him for his failure to call upon her. He remonstrated that he recollected "a most elegant dinner at your house."

He could not call on her now, he protested. Her rejoinder: "What! Not call upon me! Oh fie! Not when a handsome woman asks you?" Cumberland did not deny that "the temptation is very great, but circumstanced as I am, it would be highly improper for me to enter the enemy's camp." Cumberland's self-serving account underscored his reputation as a womanizer. "I merely mention this conversation," the Duke submitted in his memoirs, "as this conversation led me to expect, from the extraordinary style of it, that an anecdote I had heard a few days before from a particular friend was true: namely, that the Duke of Wellington had said: in case he could not succeed in persuading me to leave England, that they must try to throw some handsome woman in my way, to engage my attention and thus divert it from politics."[23]

Three months later the Duke of Cumberland appeared in Lady Lyndhurst's drawing room. Dolly gave her version of what had happened to Charles Greville when she met him on Wimbledon Common. She invited Greville into her carriage, and the two discussed the notorious "scramble" during a long drive. Dolly was eager to talk, and Greville was eager to listen. Dutifully, the chronologer of events great and small confided Her Ladyship's account to his diary:

> She said that the Duke called upon her, and had been denied, that he had complained, half in jest and half in earnest, to the Chancellor of her not letting him in; that on a subsequent day he had called so early that no orders had been given to the Porter, and he was let in; that he made a violent attack upon her, which she had resisted, that his manner and his language had been equally brutal and indecent, that he was furious at her resistance, and said he would never forgive her for putting him to so much annoyance.[24]

Cumberland's version was entirely plausible, and many chose to believe it. From Dolly's account emerged the unmistakable fact that the Duke had called upon her believing that his attentions would be favorably received. She failed to explain how he might have acquired that impression. Perhaps, as with Grey, she had contemplated an amorous intrigue that was in her husband's interest but had changed her mind. For some reason she had decided to bar him from her home, and when by an oversight he was admitted, an awkward confrontation that had political dimensions followed.

When the report of the alleged incident was printed in the Age, the Duke of Cumberland sent a copy to Lord Lyndhurst and requested that Lady Lyndhurst issue a statement contradicting the libel against his good character. Lord Lyndhurst, unaware of the incident until he read the newspaper account, replied that he counted the report among the many calumnies directed at his wife. Yet he ignored the Duke's request for a refutation. Cumberland would not drop the matter; he persisted in his demand for a denial. Lyndhurst, in turn, would not budge. Perhaps he relished Cumberland's discomfort, although it is odd that he would encourage a scandal involving his wife. Harriet Arbuthnot described what followed as "a most hostile correspondence."[25] It consisted of six salvos traded back and forth. Lyndhurst frostily declined "to annoy Lady Lyndhurst by an inquiry into the details of what passed upon that visit." In a final effort the exasperated Duke cited "loose reports which had passed in conversation" and repeated his declaration that the reports circulating were "utterly false." The last word on the subject came from the Chancellor, who stated firmly that he had no wish to know the content of "the loose reports." He noted that no one who knew his wife could doubt that the reports were "utterly false (to use Your Royal Highness's expression) and basely calumnious."[26]

After receiving Cumberland's demand for a denial from Lady Lyndhurst, the Chancellor consulted the Duke of Wellington. The Prime Minister suggested the language of the rebuff in which Lyndhurst declined to trouble his wife, adding, in the hostile third person, that "with what relates to Your Royal Highness the Lord Chancellor has no concern whatever." Having gained the support of his chief, Lyndhurst took steps to preserve the King's goodwill in this touchy matter. Greville noted this occasion of royal endorsement: "The Chancellor went down to Windsor, and laid the whole correspondence before the King, who received him very well, and approved of what he had done." In his account Greville emphasized George IV's fickleness: "but, of course, when he saw the Duke of Cumberland and had heard his story, he concurred in all his abuse of the Chancellor."[27] Both Lyndhurst and Cumberland passed the letters around their respective circles in self-serving campaigns for vindication. The letters' contents were read and discussed eagerly. Individuals took sides. When Greville met Lyndhurst at Windsor Castle for a council, the latter expressed his wish to show him the correspondence. He related that after the incident, Lady Lyndhurst had told him of the Duke's denunciation of both him and the ministry. She had withheld any reference to the Duke's rough treatment of her because she felt "it would put him in a very embarrassing position." But she would never receive the Duke again.[28]

The matter did not end there. Reports began to drift in from Lord Grey, Lord Durham, and Lord Dudley. The content of these rumors was of an urgent nature. Cumberland was talking about Lady Lyndhurst "in the most gross and impertinent manner." Now Dolly told the Chancellor what she had held back: that the Duke "had been very insolent and made an attack upon her." Lyndhurst was, by his own account, "incensed." He considered what he might do, but "after much consideration he thought it better to let the matter drop." Time passed. The principals in the incident refrained from any communication. Lyndhurst "felt the ridicule and inconvenience of putting himself (holding the high office he did) in personal collision with a Royal Duke."[29] There was also the notoriety that would engulf Lady Lyndhurst should she become the center of a public scandal.

But the matter would not rest. Princess Lieven, wife of the Russian Ambassador, obtained the correspondence and, because of her opposition to the Wellington administration, was receptive to any reports that might tarnish the Chancellor and his wife. She passed the letters on to Lady Cowper, who judged that the Chancellor's letters were "very shuffling and blackguard."[30] Princess Lieven, with the original letters in her hands, promised Lord Grey that she would try to obtain a copy of this "curious correspondence." For the present, she assured Grey that she "could not have imagined that any creature existed so vile and so mean as the Chancellor has shown himself to be." She added, "One of his letters is a perfect model of infamy."[31] Grey, infatuated with Dolly, promptly championed her cause. He informed the Princess that Lady Lyndhurst had told him of "her adventure" with the Duke of Cumberland. He recounted that "she described it as a most brutal attack on his part, followed by the most violent denunciation of revenge."[32] Grey had not heard about the correspondence and entreated Princess Lieven to send it to him if she could obtain it. She promptly delivered a packet containing transcripts of the celebrated letters. She added her own prejudiced judgment: "To my mind, the mere fact that the Duke of Cumberland began the correspondence proves him to be innocent of the charge laid to his account. His first letters are perfect; the answers from the Chancellor are miserable productions — trying to evade the question, and failing therein . . . the whole affair is, after all, a bad piece of business, whichever way you look at it."[33]

Grey argued that Cumberland's initiation of the correspondence was no proof of his innocence. The Chancellor was in a unique position, and because of his high office his options were few. Lady Lyndhurst was a victim of sorts because those who heard the scandalous reports would believe that she must have encouraged the Duke and brought it all on herself — whatever "it all" encompassed. Grey conceded that Lord Lyndhurst's letters were evasive, but he stressed that Cumberland, rather than obtaining the contradiction he sought, had instead evoked "a strong enunciation of the principal part of the charge." Grey concluded that it was *"une fort méchante affaire,* which it is equally the interest of all parties to have consigned to oblivion as soon as possible."[34] Lyndhurst's eagerness to share the correspondence satisfied the curious but also drew their censure. Greville thought the Chancellor acted "with rather too undignified a desire to submit his conduct to the judgement of a parcel of people who only laugh at them both, and are amused with the gossip and malice of the thing."[35] Thomas Creevey regretted his absence from London when the scandal was at its height: "What a pity I was not here when Charles Greville had in his possession the correspondence between Lord Chancellor Lyndhurst and the Duke of Cumberland concerning the attempted *Rape* by the latter of Dear Lady Lyndhurst."[36]

Misfortunes plagued the Lyndhursts when they passed several days as guests of the Duke of Wellington at Walmer Castle at the end of August. Princess Lieven relayed the latest gossip to Lord Grey, announcing that "the Chancellor has been within an ace of drowning himself, and Lady Lyndhurst had a *fausse couche* in consequence."[37] The Prime Minister relayed the details to Harriet Arbuthnot: "Lady Lyndhurst is better this day. But she was very ill yesterday — so ill that the Chancellor sent to London for her Accoucheur. She positively miscarried in my Carriage on the Road up the Hill of Dover. She might have miscarried five Minutes sooner sitting on a Bench in a publick Walk near the Sea or a publick Library at Dover!"[38]

The summer of 1829 brought the Lyndhursts no relief from the stress of the spring. At the core of Dolly's contretemps with the Royal Duke was the continuing and paramount concern lest the Chancellor lose his place. Dolly was never shy about promoting her husband's interests and may have attempted, through sexual intrigue, to neutralize an opponent. Her romantic invitations were, she had discovered, the political coin of the realm. The Cumberland fiasco was a flirtation that went awry, and its reverberations placed both the Chancellor and his beautiful wife in an awkward scandal that delighted the opponents of the government. This stormy episode had grown out of the politics of the Catholic issue, but to many observers it was simply an occasion when Lady Lyndhurst had embarrassed her husband. The Chancellor was part of the Wellington ministry, and whatever degraded him would discomfit his colleagues as well. Years later Lyndhurst shared cordial relations with the Duke of Cumberland, who became the King of Hanover in 1837 when that country's Salic Law placed him instead of his niece, Victoria, on Hanover's throne. Lyndhurst and the King exchanged friendly greetings when the latter's grandson was born.[39] In 1843 Lyndhurst hosted a dinner and reception in honor of the King of Hanover in his home on George Street. This gesture, after the passage of fourteen years, was an unusual postscript to the bizarre scene that had once entangled Lord and Lady Lyndhurst in a web of controversy.

10
Expediter of Justice?

As Chancellor, Lyndhurst had to grapple with the larger issues of his day. At the same time, he was compelled to expend his energies on the less dramatic day-by-day routine connected with his office as Lord Chancellor. Chancery reform was a tedious but insistent legacy of Eldon's incumbency. Lord Eldon had been Chancellor for a long time, from 1801 to 1827, and during his tenure Chancery litigants invariably experienced long delays and great expense. Eldon had not created this problem, but it had grown worse under his rule. His precise methods could not keep pace with the heavy traffic that bogged down the Court of Chancery. Dickens's *Bleak House* reflected truth, not fiction.[1]

The court had been created to countervene the shortcomings of the common law. It dealt with cases involving grants of property, offices, treaties, charters, and commissions. The court could treat each case on its merits and grant a judgment that applied only to the suit without creating binding precedents. In this way the court circumvented the standard procedures of the regular courts. The Court of Chancery was originally conceived as an expediter of justice.

In Eldon's day this original raison d'être was the opposite of reality. The Chancellor presided as the only judge in his court, yet he could not devote his full time to these duties because of the multiple demands of his office. Some of his judicial authority was delegated to the Master of the Rolls, who sat when the Chancellor did not, but his decisions had to pass before the Chancellor for final approval. The Chancery staff functioned on a fee system. The clerks profited from performing the manifold individual tasks a suit in Chancery involved. The clerks thus had an incentive to slow the process and multiply the separate operations: "Litigants were obliged to order, and pay for, copies they did not want and which were sometimes never made. The sixty clerks were paid by the page for drawing documents; and so they developed such large handwriting, and used such wide

104

margins, that it was said a skillful clerk could spread six ordinary pages into forty. Attempts to reform these abuses met with hostility and almost complete failure."[2] To correct these abuses, a commission had been created in 1824. Eldon, in his capacity as Chancellor, chaired it — not the most auspicious beginning for a body that might find it necessary to discredit his methods. According to one contemporary, "Things had reached their lowest ebb. Even a simple matter could take five years to determine, and vast funds — £39 million — mouldered in court, out of human dominion, the remains of undecided cases and wrecked fortunes."[3]

Two years later, in his capacity as Attorney General, Sir John Copley introduced in the House of Commons the measures recommended by the commission. He defended the commission against "insinuations thrown out against them," noting that anyone who believed he or she had been unfairly treated in Chancery proceedings was urged to testify before the commissioners. Copley answered those who had called for ending the Chancery's jurisdiction, begging the House to consider how essential the jurisdiction of the court had become. He pointed out that "almost all personal property is vested in trusts (either expressed or implied) for its preservation."[4] Because courts of common law had no jurisdiction in these matters, a jurisdiction such as that of Chancery had to exist. Copley cited cases involving patents and copyrights in which an immediate injunction might be necessary to prevent ongoing piracy or infringement, something the common law was unprepared to address with alacrity. The performance of specific contracts between partners, the surrender of deeds fraudulently obtained or withheld, and the protection of widows and infants were all areas that required redress from a court of equity — redress that was not forthcoming from a court of common law.

Having made his case for the court's jurisdiction, the Attorney General came to the difficult part of his speech. He acknowledged that there had been delays in the work of the Chancery: in fact there had, he declared, "been instances of gross abuse; but if there has been but one instance, it is the duty of the House to interfere." These were bold words that prefaced an apologist's explanation of "a slight arrears" that the severe illness of the late Master of the Rolls had created in the Vice Chancellor's court. The subsequent illness of the Vice Chancellor himself in 1824 had caused an arrear of about seven terms, which was less than two years.[5] In the previous eighteen months, that arrear had been reduced to four, a delay of just over a year and no greater than was experienced in the Court of King's Bench. In twelve months' time, Copley optimistically predicted, that backlog would be eliminated. Critics of the Court of Chancery had projected that it would take forty years for the backlog in the Lord Chancellor's court to be caught up. Copley denounced these projections as "a mass of misrepresentation and misunderstanding."[6]

Taking the political high road in this debate, the Attorney General stressed to the House that he had "abstained entirely from every personal or party allusion." He argued that the Chancery system alone was the subject in question. Consequently, he stressed that he had taken pains not to allude even once, except incidentally, to Eldon, "who has presided for so many years and with such distinguished zeal, and learning, and ability, over it." Copley had saved if not the best, certainly the touchiest part of the issue until last. Eldon was at the center of the Chancery controversy, and his halting methods symbolized the system that created frustration and anger in litigants who sought to transact business before his court.

Copley mounted a strong defense of the Chancellor. He did so because the charges of judicial sloth at the top could not be ignored. He avoided the pitfall of damning Eldon with faint praise. He quoted Sir Samuel Romilly, whose hostility toward Eldon was well-known, to the effect "that no man he had ever known, or read of, had possessed more talent to qualify him for his place. That he had never met with a judge so anxious to do justice to the suitors in his court; that if he had a fault . . . it was an over nicety and anxiety upon that head."[7]

Critics of Eldon pointed to this "over nicety" as one of the principal causes of delay that had become a byword for the Court of Chancery. Copley concluded with his own tribute to the aged Chancellor. The Attorney General recounted that the venerable jurist had serviced the state for fifty years: "From the moment when he had attracted the public eye, he had been marked out for the high situation which he now holds." Copley himself was mounting, rung by rung, the ladder to "the high situation" Eldon had occupied, and his listeners were not unmindful of his progress in that upward direction. Many among his audience might have dismissed as self-serving his description of Eldon: "not one act has there been in his whole life, which has not affirmed the opinion originally entertained of him." Copley concluded his defense of the Lord Chancellor by insisting that "as a member of the commission his conduct has been most active, candid, and liberal."[8] Copley's speech drew snickers and a quick rejoinder. John Williams responded, "If the individual at the head of that court has fulfilled all the expectations formed of him . . . how happened it, that in so long a period he has not corrected those abuses, which could, at any time, have been done by a simple order of court?" Williams also mentioned Copley when he noted that the Attorney General had casually stated that "the delays which have been so much clamoured about, are fancied grievances, and have no real existence."⁹ The parliamentary session of 1826 ended before passage of the bill was completed.

On September 14, 1826, Copley became Master of the Rolls, an appointment that made him part of the Chancery system. In this capacity he introduced another measure for Chancery reform in February 1827. Once again Copley justified the existence of a court of equity and acknowledged that there was great delay within that tribunal. However, speaking from his own experience, he argued that "the blame of delay rests with the agents of the suitors."¹⁰ He advocated that he, as Master of the Rolls, be armed with the power to coerce recalcitrant solicitors to move more quickly.

Acknowledging that many of the proposed reforms might have been effected by the Lord Chancellor's fiat, Copley offered the lame excuse that "it would have been unwise if he had done so. It was certainly better to call in the authority of Parliament for the whole."¹¹ Copley concluded his defense of Eldon with a declaration that "it is a little too much to expect that the Lord Chancellor of this country, whose occupations are so numerous, and whose whole attention is necessarily taken up by the business of his office, should step in and answer all the purposes of this commission himself." He noted that some people had found fault with the Chancellor because he had failed to do "what it has taken a commission of twelve learned men two years to accomplish."¹² The response, swift and short, singled out Eldon as the culprit. M. A. Taylor portrayed the Lord Chancellor as "the cloven foot" who had repeatedly tripped up all efforts to reform his court. Eldon was "where the real source of the evil they complained of lay." Referring to Copley, Taylor marveled that "any man possessing the acute mind of my right honourable and learned friend can fail to see the difficulties." Eldon had gone so far, Taylor alleged, as to threaten to resign should any change in his court be endorsed by Parliament.¹³

A Chancery reform bill introduced during the 1827 session met the same fate as its predecessor and never became law. But over the next two years, many of the recommendations the commission had proposed in 1825 were adopted as rules of the court, without parliamentary sanction, at Lyndhurst's behest. By 1829 Lyndhurst, now Chancellor, was ready to advance his own program of Chancery reform. He renounced any plan to alter the initial stages of a suit. The forms of bill and answer were serviceable as they stood, and the introduction of oral evidence during the examination of witnesses would afford no advantage. Declaring that the commission had neglected a crucial stage, Lyndhurst concentrated on reforms in the hearing of the cause itself, recommending that a new judge should be appointed as a member of the Court of Chancery. This magistrate should have the authority to hear causes and motions that would normally be channeled exclusively through the Chancellor and the Vice Chancellor. Lyndhurst proposed that this new judge should have jurisdiction over the equity cases from the Court of Exchequer. The Lord Chancellor also proposed a more extensive role for the Master of the Rolls, who sat too briefly as a judge. Lyndhurst's plan called for the Master to sit in the mornings like other judges and break off only when necessary. He concluded by stating that "considering the salary and emoluments of the Master of the Rolls . . . the public have a right to claim at his hands a more extended degree of service than he at present affords."

Lyndhurst took pains to acknowledge that the same evils existed to the same extent in his time as had existed in the time of his predecessor. After extolling Eldon for "his profound sagacity, his great erudition, and his extraordinary attainments," Lyndhurst asserted that he did not ascribe the delays in the Court of Chancery to the former Chancellor but "to the system established in that court."[14] He thus arranged for the support or at least the neutrality of the formidable Eldon. His efforts gained a qualified approval from Eldon on the second reading of the bill in the House of Lords.

On the third reading, however, the former Lord Chancellor took the attack. He reported that the present Master of the Rolls had expressed to him "his determination not to take up himself the new duties he was appointed to perform. . . . The Master of the Rolls has business enough." That very morning the Lord Chief Baron, whose Court of Exchequer was both a court of law and a court of equity, had given Eldon "a most formidable account of what would be the effect of the notion of putting an end to his Equity jurisdiction." In reply, Lyndhurst regretted that his predecessor had not stated his objections to the bill earlier. He restated his goal of ensuring that the Chancellor would hear causes "when they are ripe for hearing." He knew of no other way to accomplish this than by creating an additional judgeship. The measure before the House was for that purpose alone, and the other proposals would be left to the next session.[15] The bill received a third reading in the Lords, but Parliament suspended its deliberations before it could be taken up by the House of Commons.

In the next session, Lyndhurst tried a different approach. On March 22, 1830, he proposed a bill "to facilitate the administration of justice in the Courts of the Country." This effort was much wider in scope than the previous measures, which had focused solely on the Court of Chancery. The introduction of this bill gave Lyndhurst an opportunity to review the government's progress in the area of law reform. He praised the efforts of Sir Robert Peel, who deserved the gratitude of the country for the strides he had made in reconstituting criminal law in his role as the Secretary of State for the Home Department. Peel had abolished the right of Church authorities to try in an ecclesiastical court any member of the clergy accused of a serious crime. He had consolidated laws pertaining to larceny and forgery. The record showed, too, that he had caused the repeal of four hundred statutes and eliminated the death penalty for nearly three hundred offenses.

Currently, the government was preparing bills for simplifying procedure in the common law courts. As he had in his former proposal, Lyndhurst was asking Parliament to reassign equity cases from the Court of Exchequer. He repeated his request for the appointment of an additional judge in equity to relieve the Chancery courts. Future plans included abolishing the Welsh jurisdiction, bringing Wales into the circuit system, and providing an additional judge for each of the courts of common law to take up the growing workload. Finally, the government intended to extend the jury system to Scotland, to streamline the procedure in the ecclesiastical courts, and to bring reform to the offices of the Masters and Clerks in Chancery.[16]

The Lord Chancellor drew criticism in the debates in the House of Commons. Sir Charles Wetherell, the former Tory Attorney General who had taunted Lyndhurst for his turnabout over Catholic Emancipation, flung new taunts at him by charging that this bill "is intended simply for the personal convenience of the Lord Chancellor." He recalled Sir Samuel Romilly's opposition to the creation of the position of Vice Chancellor in 1813 as an unwarranted delegation of the Chancellor's power that would undermine the dignity of that office.[17]

Lyndhurst's efforts were as ambitious as they were doomed. The bill survived a third reading as well as Eldon's attempts to alter it in the House of Lords. But the Commons was to be its graveyard, for the death of King George IV in June 1830 brought the dissolution of Parliament before the ill-fated bill gained a second reading in the lower chamber. For the time being, Chancery reform foundered on partisan division and the chance death of the King. But Lyndhurst's involvement in this issue did not cease. He would participate in future debates on this continuing problem, whose resolution had merely been postponed.

11
A Sinking Ship

The Duke of Wellington's government suddenly faced unrest from both north and south. Strikes disrupted the factories in the north. The Prime Minister sent troops to confront and stop the strikers. Life was no better in the countryside after two successive bad harvests. In Kent, rick burning and machine breaking increased the pace of violence. In October, riots erupted. Wellington appraised the rising terror and dispatched more troops. Popular unrest added to the Duke's larger problem: his ministry was tottering. The death of George IV in June brought his brother, the Duke of Clarence, to the throne as William IV. His accession necessitated a parliamentary election, an inopportune development when viewed from the Tory benches in Parliament. The Whigs garnered an increase of fifty votes in the House of Commons, but Wellington still retained a majority — albeit an undependable one because the country squires were restless.

Against a backdrop of shifting events, elite political games continued to command the attention of Lord Lyndhurst. He knew that both his party's and his own fortunes were uncertain. Harriet Arbuthnot believed the prospect of the Duke of Clarence as King frightened the Chancellor. The Royal Duke had been forced out as Lord High Admiral by the ministry in August 1828 after an awkward struggle. Lyndhurst speculated that "we shall all be turned out as soon as he is King."[1] But it was not only the Duke's possible desire for revenge that troubled Lyndhurst: there were reports that the Duke of Clarence had seen Lord Grey. In the Chancellor's quick and intuitive mind, the elements of a scenario began to fall into place. Grey had been the one individual whom George IV loathed and found singularly unacceptable as a Cabinet Minister. His successor did not share this obsession. Lyndhurst recognized that Grey would become the viable alternative to form a government under the new King.

Consequently, the Chancellor counseled Wellington to preempt this alternative. He urged the Duke repeatedly to shore up the government by taking in Lord Grey and some of his followers. On one occasion he went to Walmer Castle, Wellington's home as Warden of the Cinque Ports, to persuade him of the necessity of making this overture.[2] Reports of Lyndhurst's attempt to sway the Duke were exchanged by Princess Lieven and Lord Grey. The wife of the Russian Ambassador had been visited by the Chancellor at Brighton. She assured Grey that Lyndhurst "agrees with you and with everyone as to the necessity of a modification in the Government."[3] But this omniscient lady had heard that the Duke of Wellington rejected this advice. Grey acknowledged that he had already learned of the Chancellor's conviction that the ministry needed additional strength and had thus counseled his chief, "who, in his usual peremptory way, had at once silenced the proposal." Then Grey added his own measure of Lyndhurst's stature: "If the chancellor was aware of his own power, he would not suffer his opinions to be set aside in this manner."[4] This may have been an indication of Grey's high opinion of Lyndhurst's influence or of Lady Lyndhurst's allure or a combination of the two.

Lyndhurst, often indiscreet in his conversation, was never more so than when he confided in the archintriguer, Princess Lieven. Laboring to undercut the Duke of Wellington, she broadcast Lyndhurst's confidences. She wrote to Lady Cowper that "I tell you this in secret: (the Chancellor) is greatly worried about the position of the Government."[5] Princess Lieven, subscribing to the belief that a secret was something one related to one person at a time, continued to spread Lyndhurst's statements. She wrote to her son in Russia that during a solo visit, the Chancellor had censured "the Duke of Wellington's obstinacy in remaining at the head of the 'poorest administration which England has ever seen' [take note that these are the Chancellor's own words]."[6]

Wellington might well have taken encouragement from an unexpected quarter: the new King himself. William IV held a theory of constitutional monarchy that set him apart from his brother, George IV. He felt a sense of loyalty to his Ministers so long as they represented the will of the nation. This loyalty precluded any political communication with the opposition forces. Surprisingly, the King bore no grudge against Wellington for his dismissal of him as Lord High Admiral. The Iron Duke was his Prime Minister, and he placed his confidence solely in his chief Minister. Greville witnessed an expression of this devotion to Wellington: "He announced to all whom he saw around him, to all the Ambassadors and Ministers of foreign Powers, and to all the Noblemen and Gentlemen present, that as long as he should sit upon the throne he should continue to give him the same confidence."⁷ Encouraging as this pledge of support might be, it suggested the King's political naïveté. He failed to recognize what so many saw: that Wellington's ministry was sinking. Or so it appeared. The facade of naïveté, may have masked a wiser and safer policy than George IV had pursued. William was acting on the principle that the King's duty is to support his Prime Minister until Parliament determines that the First Minister no longer holds the confidence of the nation. So the King would do nothing to undermine Wellington, but he also would do nothing to save him should he fall.

As the public waited for the Duke's fall, Lord Lyndhurst, never one to wait, busied himself with his mission to persuade Wellington to reinforce the government. Princess Lieven informed Lady Cowper that the Chancellor "is very insistent that Palmerston should be approached. He told the Duke so, but does not know if his words have had any effect."⁸ Lyndhurst contemplated a turn in Palmerston's direction because when William Huskisson had perished during the inaugural festivities of the Liverpool-Manchester Railway, his Canningite followers had been set adrift. Palmerston might well channel them back into the Tory camp. The Duke was cool to the plan, but the combined efforts of Sir Robert Peel and Charles Arbuthnot persuaded him that Palmerston should be approached. Lord Clive, a friend to both groups, was the chosen intermediary.

Palmerston was not averse to joining the beleaguered ministry with some Canningites in tow. He regarded the offer of three Cabinet places for Canningites as a beginning. But he wanted more: additional posts in the ministry, not only for Canningites but for Whigs as well. Wellington blanched at the prospect of turning his government into a facade for Whigs and liberal Tories. And an even more objectionable condition was thrust in the face of the Duke of Wellington: Palmerston sought an endorsement of Lord John Russell's bill for parliamentary reform, which had been defeated in February. This was too much for the Duke, who rejected out of hand what he regarded as a form of blackmail. This demand served only to stiffen his resolve to oppose reform.

Wellington's inclination to reject reform had been hardened by the impertinence of the Canningites' attempt to insist on reform as the price for their inclusion in his faltering ministry. The Duke's mind was set: he would resist all efforts to bring about parliamentary reform. His resolution became crystal clear during the debate on the King's speech. After a succession of speakers, it was Lord Grey's turn. He spoke in a conciliatory vein, and it was only toward the close of his remarks that he touched on the subject of reform. Grey hoped the government would not postpone the issue in the same way it had put off responding to the demands for Catholic relief.

When the Duke of Wellington rose to answer Grey, he astonished many of his listeners with the intensity of his rejoinder. Grey had confessed that "he was not prepared with any measure of reform," and now the Prime Minister, too, "could have no scruple in saying that his Majesty's Government is as totally unprepared with any plan as the noble Lord." The Iron Duke stated flatly: "I am not prepared to bring forward any measure of the description alluded to by the noble Lord. And I am not only not prepared to bring forward any measure of this nature, but I will at once declare that as far as I am concerned, as long as I hold any station in the Government of the country, I shall always feel it my duty to resist such measures when proposed by others."[9] The Duke had finished his remarks. Silence followed, then a buzzing, which increased from a murmur to a roar. The Duke was surprised. "He asked a colleague what it meant. 'You have announced the fall of your Government, that is all!' was the reply. The colleague is believed to have been Lord Lyndhurst."[10]

The Duke's mind was as shuttered against reform as the windows of his London home were shuttered against the bricks of the menacing throngs that took to the streets when word of his speech spread. The locked gates and covered windows of Apsley House were only symbols of the unease that overcame the ministry after Wellington's renunciation of further change. A more pressing challenge than broken windows awaited the government and required a decision. November 9 was Lord Mayor's Day in London. King William and Queen Adelaide planned to dine in state with the new Lord Mayor at the Guildhall. The Ministers, led by Wellington, would be in attendance. What had been planned as an occasion of celebration now loomed as a provocation to rioting. The King's presence would provide a rallying point for demands that he dismiss his Ministers. To go on with the royal visit would be to court violence of unknown dimensions. To cancel the scheduled fete would be to admit that the government could not control the situation and protect the sovereign in his own capital, a terrible loss of face for Wellington. The King himself spoke of postponement.

The Cabinet met on November 7, 1830, to resolve the matter. When the Duke announced that he and Peel had agreed that the King's visit must be put off, Lyndhurst "seemed almost to take fire at the idea of this, but the Duke very quietly begged him to hear the letters before he decided." These

God save the King. Lyndhurst singing with the Duke of Wellington and Sir Robert Peel. Portrayed as the arch-timeserver, 1830. Used by permission of the British Museum.

letters were a litany of threats and abuse that pledged the assassination of the Duke. Wellington's concern was the potential for widespread bloodshed rather than his personal safety. Lord Ellenborough recorded in his diary that "the feeling in the Duke's mind was that we should not be justified in giving an occasion for the shedding of blood, by means of a crowd of our own making. The consequences of the collision would be incalculable, and might affect all parts of England."[11]

The Cabinet argued the implications of putting off the King's visit. Public confidence would be shaken, and many would proclaim that the government had weighed down the King with its own unpopularity. By Ellenborough's account, "The Chancellor was most unwilling to postpone the King's visit." He argued that some would say that the Ministers had done it only for their own sakes and had sacrificed the monarch. There would be a violent storm in Parliament, and the mobs would still seek the

Ministers in their homes.[12] Lyndhurst's despair over this latest setback underscored his belief that the government had embraced its own ruin.

The Lord Mayor's banquet was canceled, and only sporadic clashes between roving bands and the police occurred. Wellington and his colleagues had expected a dramatic end, but their finale was of a quieter sort. Their deathblow was dealt not by London's rabble but by an ad hoc union of ultra-Tories with Radical, Whig, and Canningite supporters of parliamentary reform in the House of Commons. The Duke had offended the country wing of his party over the issue of Catholic Emancipation. He had now alienated all those who looked to the government to produce even a modest measure of reform in the same spirit of concession that had removed the Catholic issue from the public agenda. Defeat came on a motion to create a select committee to investigate the civil list accounts. The November 15 vote in favor of the motion was 233 to 204, placing the government in a minority of 29. Wellington was tired and ready to leave. He tendered his resignation the following day.

The Duke had been carried away by an irreversible tide. He did not like change, whereas the nation was hungry for it. What was needed was a masterstroke of constructive statesmanship, which was not the Duke's forte. The Tory party had been on the downswing since Liverpool's stroke, which had been fatal to both him and his party. Lyndhurst's rise had coincided with the decline of the Tories, whose internal discord signaled a lack of united purpose and leadership. The Chancellor, a man committed more to his own career than to principle, had gained and held his place for nearly three years, but, as he told the Duke, "the game was up."[13]

12
Rescued by the Whigs

The end of the Wellington ministry brought personal and financial disaster for Lord Lyndhurst. His annual salary of £14,000 as Lord Chancellor came to an end. Lady Carlisle attended a solemn dinner at the Lyndhursts' London home during the final days before the fall. She observed that "the Chancellor looked black" and "Dolly was in a very stormy state."[1] The women of George Street made no effort to hide their distress, causing the Duke of Devonshire to declare, "I am miserable for the Lyndhursts — and his mother is in a terrible way about it. Lady Lyndhurst says they won't be poor, but of course an immense difference — poor thing."[2] The "immense difference" amounted to £10,000, because the annual pension of an ex–Lord Chancellor was only £4,000 a year.

As far back as 1828 Wellington had predicted that because he lacked great wealth, Lyndhurst "must go with any Government as to politics, for he cannot live without place, as he had no property and he has already expended *three years* beforehand his salary."[3] Soon rumors circulated that Earl Grey would retain Lyndhurst in his post. Lady Holland passed on this information to Sir Denis Le Marchant, a loyal Whig who later became Henry Brougham's secretary. Le Marchant had heard that the Chancellor had betrayed Wellington to the Whigs, and his continuance on the Woolsack would be payment for his treachery. Eagle-eyed observers had seen Grey going in and coming out of Lyndhurst's house on several occasions.[4]

Lord Campbell believed these reports, confiding to his diary that "Copley will try to intrigue and keep the Great Seal."[5] John Wilson Croker, Secretary to the Admiralty, doubted the allegations but observed that "the knowing ones suspect he will *rat*."[6] Lyndhurst's secretary, John Murray, gave grist to the rumor mill when he "went about saying that there was no reason why (the Chancellor) should retire, for he entirely coincided with Lord Grey and could conscientiously support all his measures."[7] It all seemed plausible — for the moment. Lady Lyndhurst proceeded to make use of Grey's infatuation with her. "Lord Grey and Dolly sat together the whole of yesterday evening," Lady Carlisle wrote on November 11.[8] The plan was for Lyndhurst to continue on the Woolsack as he had when Viscount Goderich followed George Canning and when, in turn, Wellington succeeded Goderich. He would be a Chancellor in perpetuity, a Chancellor for all seasons. This arrangement was not unthinkable, given Lyndhurst's attempts to bring Grey into Wellington's ministry.

Only one barrier blocked Lord Lyndhurst's continued presence on the Woolsack: Henry Brougham, Whig firebrand and trumpet of reform, who now asserted his claim to the Chancellorship.[9] Grey was not eager to satisfy this claim. Campbell suggested that "Lord Grey's real motive . . . was that he might avoid handing over the Great Seal to Brougham, of whose temerity and insubordination he had a most distressing anticipation."[10] But Brougham would not budge. When Grey sent him an offer of the Attorney Generalship, he tore it in pieces, tossing them in the air. Brougham's intransigence destroyed any hope that Lyndhurst might remain in office. Croker recorded on November 18 that "after some doubts, the Chancellor's resignation is certain. My Lady was all yesterday begging Lord Durham to use his influence to save her Lord — [I] believe without the least sanction from him. He seems to be quite fair and steady to go with his friends."[11] Charles Greville believed Grey had given way in his plan to keep Lyndhurst as Chancellor because his ministry could not afford to have Brougham playing the maverick in the House of Commons: "Grey, however, was still anxious to serve Lyndhurst and to neutralize his opposition."[12]

Greville recorded the reaction of a Chancellor who had just lost his place: "Lord Lyndhurst, who loses everything by the fall of the late Government, cannot get over it, particularly as he feels that the Duke's obstinacy brought it about, and that by timely concessions and good management he might have had Lord Grey, Palmerston, and all that are worth having."[13] The £4,000 pension on which Lyndhurst now had to live was "quite inadequate to support Lady Lyndhurst's fashionable establishment."[14] But rescue was on its way. Grey went about praising Lyndhurst, professing a fondness for him, and declaring that he should like very much to do anything he could for him. Greville believed "he would not dislike to take in Lyndhurst by-and-by."[15] He could satisfy his sense of obligation to Dolly at the same time.

Grey created a vacancy for Lyndhurst by pushing Sir William Alexander out of his post as Chief Baron of the Exchequer. Alexander, seventy-six

WANTS A SITUATION.

An intelligible, middle-aged man, in the prime of life, who has met with a reverse of fortune. Having been in the habit of keeping large sums of money, he is fitted for the place of Steward. As he has had recently the management of the person and property of a gentleman suffering under imbecility, he would not object to the situation of keeper in an insane establishment. Is married, and his wife (who will be found an accommodating female) will either *go out* with him or separately. Enquire of the Hall Sweeper, near the Court of

Wants a situation. A destitute Lyndhurst sits on the steps of a closed and dilapidated Conservative Club, which bears the placard: "To Let." The same notice appears on his hat. His wife is called an "accommodating female," 1832. Used by permission of the British Museum.

years of age and in failing health, was known to be mulling over retirement. Acting on this premise, Grey offered the Chief Barony to Lyndhurst, who promptly reported this development in a note to his wife. He stressed both the positive and negative aspects of the offer: "The salary is £7,000 a year; but . . . I should be subjected to so much *obloquy* and *abuse* if I accepted it, that I think I had better decline it."[16]

Lyndhurst had much to consider before responding to Grey. The salary, although half that of the Lord Chancellor's, exceeded Lyndhurst's pension by £3,000. The ex-Chancellor's gainful employment would save the treasury the pension altogether. But this was a small point. Aside from the financial implications, there was the political significance of the appointment. Croker thought it would be "best for the Whigs, for it would remove Lyndhurst from politics. In his present position he is always a point d'appui for the formation of a new Government."[17] But it would be a great loss to the Tories because, as Greville stressed, they "counted on him as their great champion in the House of Lords."[18]

Lyndhurst had anticipated the annoyance of his Tory colleagues when he wrote to his wife of the offer. The prospect of exile from the Tory camp was a genuine risk should he accept Grey's largesse. Lyndhurst was never one to burn his bridges, and he hoped to keep open an avenue by which he might return to the Woolsack in a future Tory government. Consequently, he wrote to Wellington, Peel, and Lord Aberdeen, informing them of Grey's assurance that the appointment would be nonpolitical. Lyndhurst would in no way be bound to support the Whig government or its policies.

Wellington replied with a pledge of support for "any arrangement which can tend to your convenience and advantage."[19] He knew well of Lyndhurst's need for a government salary. Peel advised him regarding the offer to "be assured that you will have my warmest wishes that it may promote your happiness."[20] Lord Aberdeen's reply stated more explicitly the ticklishness of Lyndhurst's position. He expressed encouragement but added his regret for "the consequent diminution of your political activity." He agreed that "the explanations to which you refer are calculated to remove many of the difficulties which must naturally have suggested themselves to your mind."[21] The response from the leading Tories was positive, for "they knew his deplorable state in point of money."[22]

Then a difficulty arose. Alexander began to have second thoughts about resigning. Lyndhurst's appointment was stalled, and a flurry of letter writing began in an effort to dislodge the recalcitrant Alexander. In the midst of this awkward business, Grey took time to update Lady Lyndhurst on the progress of his efforts. In a communication headed "Secret and Confidential," he cautioned her not to take alarm at the official character of his letter and alluded to "all the mistakes" that had occurred in the wake of his offer to Lyndhurst. Grey informed Dolly that he had met with Lord Tenterden, Chief Justice of the Court of King's Bench, who was to act as a go-between with the Chief Baron in securing his exit. Alexander's reluctance to resign grew from a concern over a pension; he was stalling to extort a pledge of a financial incentive. Grey's letter underscored his anxiety to reassure Dolly. He wanted to keep her favor and wrote: "I thought it better to wait till I had more positive authority to make a communication to him, before I write to Lord Lyndhurst; but, in the meantime, it appeared to me that there could be no harm in my apprising you of the present state of this business; that you may prepare Lord Lyndhurst for it."[23] Lord Durham, Grey's son-in-law and Lord Privy Seal in the Cabinet, also wrote to Lady Lyndhurst when he learned "how shamefully Alexander has behaved." Declaring his disgust, Durham shared with Dolly his belief that someone must have instigated Alexander's retraction of his resignation. Durham ended his note because he could "not write any more for vexation."[24] The Whig leaders had taken pains to write to "this woman who mixes up love with politics."[25]

Alexander might be, as Greville described him, a wretched judge and very rich, but he wanted to be richer, at least to the extent of being assured a fat pension.[26] Lord Tenterden served as the contact between Grey and Alexander, and it was through his good offices that the recalcitrant Chief Baron communicated to the Prime Minister his renewed resolution to resign "at any time, at which it will suit his Majesty's government to receive my resignation." He coupled this revelation with his "humble request" that the King grant him a pension. Alexander added a postscript: "I beg it as a favour of you, that this step be taken as soon as possible."[27] Within hours, Grey conveyed the glad tidings to Lyndhurst that it was His Majesty's pleasure that he should be appointed to the vacant office. He noted that as Lady Lyndhurst had informed him that the difficulties had made no change in the former Chancellor's willingness to accept the post, he had moved quickly to begin the process of appointment. The Prime Minister concluded his letter with this declaration: "I beg you to be assured that nothing could have given me greater pleasure than the conclusion of an arrangement which I hope will prove as satisfactory to yourself as I am confident it will be advantageous to the public service."[28]

Brougham, in sending his good wishes to Lyndhurst, added the wry comment, "I was very anxious to have it over and fixed, for fear our friend Alexander might change his mind again."[29] Lyndhurst's letter of acceptance to Grey acknowledged the Whig premier as his benefactor by declaring: "There are many circumstances which render this appointment agreeable to me, but there is nothing that will recommend it more than the recollection that I am indebted for it to your friendship."[30] Reports circulated that Lyndhurst was destined to enjoy an even greater share of Whig largesse. "He takes the judicial office upon an understanding . . . that he is to be Chief-Justice on Tenterden's death or retirement," Greville confided to his diary, adding, "This is the secret article of the treaty."[31]

Many believed, as did Greville, that Lyndhurst had not struck a bad bargain given his options. He seemed in a position whereby he might go with either party when it suited his ambitions. Because he did not have a reputation for consistency, little was expected from him in this area. He certainly did not share Peel's genuine distress at charges that he was a turncoat. Greville caught the essence of the situation when he observed that whatever way Lyndhurst might jump, he might do it "without any *additional* loss of Character."[32]

For the time being, the Lyndhursts hoped to keep two irons in the fire. Their success would depend on Tory reaction to the ex-Chancellor's new appointment. Although Wellington was sympathetic to Lyndhurst's financial plight, others were not as understanding. Lord Ellenborough reported that "Arbuthnot and the others seem to consider Ld. Lyndhurst as much fallen, and irrecoverably, by his acceptance of the *Chief Barony*." He added his own judgment: "I feel he is, too, & pity him. His poverty consented and his wife forced him."[33] The Arbuthnots, both husband and wife, were severe in their opinion of Lyndhurst. Harriet Arbuthnot declared to Greville that the Tories "considered themselves released from all obligations to him for the future." But she pointed out that there had been no quarrel, no rupture, and that every Tory had heard that the Lyndhursts were desperate for money.[34]

Lyndhurst served as Chief Baron of the Court of Exchequer for four years. There were three superior courts of common law: the Court of Common Pleas, the Court of King's Bench, and the Court of Exchequer. The Court of Exchequer was both a court of law and a court of equity. As a court of law, it could provide redress in all actions with the exception of the real actions. Its ancient revenue jurisdiction empowered it to determine and enforce the proprietary rights of the Crown against subjects. As a

The chameleon. Lyndhurst accepts the office of Chief Baron, 1832.
Used by permission of the British Museum.

court of equity, the court possessed the original jurisdiction for tithes. It might also grant an injunction to stay a trial.[35] Before the ex-Chancellor's appointment to head the court, its business had slowed to an unsatisfactory pace. Between 1826 and 1830 only five hundred cases had been heard before this court, whereas King's Bench had tried eleven thousand cases during the same period of time. Lyndhurst set the wheels of progress in motion. Brougham had hailed Lyndhurst's elevation as "starting, or rather founding anew, the Exchequer with an éclat and lustre." Brougham was probably considering his own prospects when he noted his pleasure that by becoming Chief Baron, Lyndhurst had ended the "absurd and, in these times, absolute nonsense of a Chancellor, when he leaves office, not taking any other."[36] The popular judge presided over what increasingly became a popular court. Business moved quickly. Sir Theodore Martin concluded that "he entirely changed the character of the Court. It had for many years fallen into disrepute; but it now became a favourite with legal practitioners, and the most busily occupied of all the Courts."[37]

Part of a Chief Baron's duties involved riding the circuit, and Lyndhurst took pleasure in what for some proved an arduous and tedious undertaking. Lady Lyndhurst, frequently accompanying her Lord on his judicial travels, attended the evening dinners at which were assembled the local Bar, the grand jury, both senior and junior counselors, and the country squires. After Lord Lyndhurst visited Beaumaris in North Wales, where he presided over the Anglesea Assizes Court in August 1832, a member of the Irish Bar recorded a colorful impression of the eminent jurist, who was then in his sixtieth year:

> When I met him and Lady Lyndhurst walking up the street to their hotel, he looked more like a cavalry officer than a solemn judge, for he was dressed, according to the fashion of the day, in white Russia duck trousers, strapped under his boots of polished leather, and in a becoming frock coat. His gaiety of air, his handsome, well-cut features, his straight figure, had all a soldierly cast. He was not long at his hotel when he was called on by . . . the foreman of the Grand Jury . . . with the uncommon but chivalrous request that the Grand Jury might be honoured at their dinner by the company of Lady Lyndhurst as well as that of her husband. To this Lord Lyndhurst gaily assented, and in this company of distinguished gentlemen Lady Lyndhurst was the only lady guest.

The writer remembered Dolly for "her brilliant eyes and fashionable bearing."[38]

Campbell's account of Lyndhurst on the Bench of the Court of Exchequer, although offering some words of praise, censured him for failing to give his mind heartily to his judicial task. His attention to his work was limited to the time he spent in court: "The rest of his time he spent in attending the debates of the House of Lords, or in forming cabals with his political partisans or at the festal board."[39] So he didn't steer clear of politics.

Campbell's charge that Lyndhurst was too cavalier in carrying out his judicial duties is best contradicted by his disposal of the celebrated case of *Small v. Attwood*.[40] Martin rhapsodized over the Chief Baron's performance, declaring that it was "regarded at the time as a marvel of intellectual power and of that faculty, which was pre-eminently his, of reducing a chaos of details into luminous order."[41] *Small v. Attwood* raised the question of whether a contract for the sale of coal and iron mines in Staffordshire was valid because of alleged misrepresentations on the part of the seller. The arguments in the case stretched out for twenty-one days, commencing on November 21, 1831; however, almost a full year transpired before Lord Lyndhurst rendered his decision on November 1, 1832. High praise for Lyndhurst's performance on this occasion came from an unlikely source. Campbell, who was present, declared:

> The Chief Baron paid unwearied attention to the evidence and the arguments, and at last delivered (by all accounts) the most wonderful judgment ever heard in Westminster Hall. It was entirely oral, and without even referring to any notes, he employed a long day in stating complicated facts, in entering into complex calculations, and in correcting the misrepresentations of the counsel on both sides. Never once did he falter or hesitate, and never once was he mistaken in a name, a figure, or a date.[42]

Lyndhurst, ruling in favor of the plaintiff — the purchasers — concurred with their contention that they had overpaid for the mines. This decision was eventually appealed and reversed in 1838 by the House of Lords, which decided that the purchasers were responsible for their bad judgment in the event of overpayment.

At the outset of his tenure as Chief Baron, Lord Lyndhurst took little part in the debates in the House of Lords. Grey requested that he continue his efforts to carry a Regency Bill through the upper chamber, an assignment he had undertaken as Lord Chancellor. When William IV became King, his eleven-year-old niece, Princess Alexandrina Victoria, became the heiress presumptive to the throne. Should she become Queen while still a minor, a Regency would be necessary. Lyndhurst secured approval for a measure that designated the Princess's widowed mother, the Duchess of Kent, as potential Regent.

During the initial months of the parliamentary session, Lyndhurst confined his remarks in the Lords to commenting on the efforts of the new Lord Chancellor, Lord Brougham, to reform the Court of Chancery and to establish both new local courts and a new Court of Bankruptcy. Lyndhurst was the soul of moderation and restraint in addressing Brougham's proposals for legal reform. He stated at once those points with which he agreed and reserved his opinion about others until he had had an opportunity to consider details more fully.

In the course of his remarks, Lyndhurst took up a proposal to increase the Lord Chancellor's pension to £6,000 annually. Although he might have been expected to warm to the prospect of this increase, he instead cited a possible difficulty. He suggested that should the ranks of retired Chancellors number three or four, the House of Commons might balk at providing so plump a financial cushion to so many individuals. Lyndhurst suggested that some employment might be found for ex-Chancellors to lessen the drain on the Treasury — for example, as Lord President of the Privy Council. Then an additional stipend might be added to the pension, resulting in a savings to the government on the customary salary for the post the retired Chancellor would fill.[43]

Currently, Lyndhurst explained, the pension ceased when an ex-Chancellor accepted another appointment, as had happened when he became Chief Baron. His words were a frank statement of his own financial experience. His candor risked the censure of those who were contemptuous of his alleged "desperation in point of money." But Lyndhurst showed a lack of embarrassment by openly acknowledging a situation that had required his own rescue by a generous political opponent. His remarks were conciliatory and moderate in tone. Lyndhurst concluded by declaring that he was glad that "so much is now likely to be done of (Chancery reform) which I had attempted to do, though I have unfortunately failed." He stressed that the current Chancellor and he were united in their desire to see "an end of the odium" that had clung to the Court of Chancery.[44]

Behind this friendly facade, Lyndhurst was weighing the options that stretched before him. The former Chancellor was always a man for the main chance, ready to shake off the encumbrance of the past and embrace new developments that might promote his career. As he surveyed the political scene, he concluded that Grey's government did not promise to be strong. It depended upon too many loose votes in the Commons drawn from Radicals, Irish partisans, and ultra-Tories. And because the life of this Whig ministry might not be a long one, the Tories could hope to return. Lyndhurst became convinced that in this eventuality, Peel would be the man of the hour. The Duke was unthinkable as Prime Minister again — "out of the question." Peel would serve with him but never under him. Wellington's circle, his little cabinet, composed of "the women and the toad-eaters," despised Peel, and that precluded any real cordiality between the two men.[45]

And where did this leave Lord Lyndhurst? Lord Bathurst thought Lyndhurst's resignation with his colleagues had kept him in the good graces of his party. Greville correctly predicted that the ex-Chancellor "means now to set to work to gain character, and as he is about the ablest public man going, and nearly the best speaker, he will yet bustle himself into consideration, and play a part once more."[46] With a change in government, a return to the Woolsack, if that were his wish, was not unlikely for Lyndhurst — and Peel was the leader he would likely serve. When he had confided his belief to Greville that Peel would be Prime Minister, he offered no timetable, but he had added one ominous contingency: "if there is not a revolution."[47] The specter of violent upheaval was never far from people's minds. This unnerving prospect loomed more menacingly as the great struggle over the reform of parliamentary representation sifted people's loyalties.

13
Throw Open the Floodgates

Lord Grey entered office amid the expectation that he would carry through some measure of reform. Excepting the ultra-Tories, who were acting out of pique, the union of Whigs, Huskissonites, and Radicals that brought him to power represented a joining of pro-reform views. This coalition now expected him to realize its hopes. The opponents of reform also expected a measure to be brought forward. Many failed to understand that when Grey and the Duke of Wellington had dueled over the need for reform during November 1830, Grey had spoken truthfully: he had no plan. Now, as head of his own government, he had to adopt one and do so quickly. England was waiting.

Within weeks of forming his ministry, Grey set events in motion when he "asked Durham, as they came down the steps of the House of Lords, to 'assist him in drawing up a Reform Bill' and to take Lord John Russell into partnership in the enterprise."[1] By the end of January 1831, Grey was able to inform Princess Lieven that "the King has had our plan to Reform fully explained to him, and he understands it perfectly. The result is that we can now go with it to Parliament with the full concurrence both of the King and the Cabinet."[2] On March 1, 1831, Russell introduced the bill in the House of Commons. It was a bombshell, going much further than the Tories had anticipated. The latter had been prepared for a variety of reform that would not differ too greatly from what they themselves would have introduced had not Wellington made his rigid stand. Grey's Cabinet was committed to framing a measure extensive enough to satisfy public opinion to such an extent that it would serve as a basis to resist demands for further innovation. However, it stipulated that any changes be based on property, reflecting existing franchises and territorial divisions.

"Satisfying public opinion" meant abolishing rotten boroughs. The government proposed to eliminate both Members from sixty boroughs with populations under two thousand (designated the Schedule A boroughs) and one Member from an additional forty-six boroughs with fewer than four thousand inhabitants each (Schedule B boroughs). This enormous number of disfranchisements would permit Grey to enfranchise the large towns with forty-two seats. The membership of the House of Commons would shrink from 658 to 596. The voting qualification was to be set at £10 for all householders in the boroughs and £10 for leaseholders in the counties. A half million new voters would be created from the ranks of the middle class, according them recognition of their political worth from an aristocracy that would now have to weigh them in its political calculations.

As Russell tolled the list of boroughs fated for complete or partial disfranchisement, the opposition Tories reeled at the sweep of the proposed change. Grey justified the bill's far-reaching impact on the ground that it could then more justly be ratified as a final adjustment to settle the reform issue once and for all. Grey was convinced that this measure would shore up aristocratic influence and not be an invitation for further concessions. No Reform Bill or an unsatisfactory one might push the situation into a political abyss from which there would be no return.

Grey believed passage of the bill would be completed swiftly in both Houses. He was too optimistic. Fifteen months of struggle stretched before him. He did not realize how great a stumbling block the Lords would prove to be. Grey had assured the squeamish King that the bill would pass both Houses handily. William IV had no taste for a battle that might require a dissolution of Parliament followed by elections. Grey encouraged the monarch to believe that this would not happen. He believed it himself — but not for long. Even before the battle lines were drawn, Grey had declared, "How much preferable the life of a dog is to that of a Minister!"[3] The Tory Lords would give him numerous occasions on which to feel this sentiment even more keenly in the days and months that lay ahead.

The Tories collected themselves to consider what kinds of difficulties they could create. They began by doing what they were lately accustomed to doing: arguing among themselves. They disputed the correct course for opposing the Reform Bill. Should they declare total war and reject the bill on the second reading, or should they pick it apart bit by bit in committee, where they could more quietly usher it into oblivion? The latter course, its proponents argued, would withhold from the government an excuse for calling an election. Baron Wharncliffe pressed this less dramatic strategy, believing dissolution followed by a polarizing election might likely increase pro-reform forces in the Commons while diminishing the Tory opposition. Finally, the less dramatic alternative would gain time during which public passion might abate.

However, the Tories were a disunited army that lacked agreement on tactics. Sir Robert Peel, sensitive to the charge that he was repeating his turnaround that had made Catholic Emancipation possible, stood firm in his opposition to the bill. He and his supporters would marshal whatever strength they could to halt the bill at its second reading. A moderate group, led by Sir Edward Knatchbull and Sir Richard Vyvyan, leaned in the direction of rejecting the measure at this stage and endorsing a pledge to support a measure for moderate reform. Finally, a remnant of ultras, captained by Charles Wetherell, resolved to fight until the bitter end.

Lyndhurst watched this Tory disunion from the sidelines. Unlike Wellington, he had been no rigid opponent of reform. The King had told Henry Brougham "that except the Duke of Wellington, every one of the last Government, when he saw them on their resigning had stated their belief of some reform being necessary."[4] But Lyndhurst, too, shared the dilemma of the Tories — coping with proposed change. The Tories were not prepared to propose a reform measure of their own. Yet if a Reform Bill were going to pass anyway, could they afford to oppose it to the bitter end? They would have to function in a reformed parliamentary world. How well could they do this if they entered that uncertain world encumbered by the stigma of unrelenting obstruction?

During the second reading debate in the Commons, Vyvyan moved that action on the bill be postponed for six months. He coupled what was in effect a form of rejection with a declaration of support for moderate reform. Vyvyan's attempt failed, and the House took up the principal measure. On March 23, 1831, amid tears and cheers, it gave the bill the slimmest possible endorsement: ayes 302 and noes 301. In the Lords, Wharncliffe pressed his belief in the need for some reform and acknowledged that "an effective and proper measure of Reform was quite necessary."[5] This conciliatory stand — a repudiation of Wellington's rejection of any reform on November 2 — irritated the Duke, who refused to embrace any meaningful reform. In this frame of mind, he wrote to Lyndhurst on March 25, notifying him that the debate in the Lords was about to begin. He advised him of Wharncliffe's intention and of a need for assistance in the debate.[6] Lyndhurst's response must have disappointed the Duke, for it told of the Chief Baron's inability to attend the debate on Wharncliffe's motion because he was detained by business, an obvious excuse. He agreed that "Wharncliffe's motion is unfortunate. He is unmanageable."

Lyndhurst, then on circuit, noted that the Reform Bill, although deriving support among the higher classes, had no active opponents in the districts through which he had traveled. Warwick was an exception. He concluded with a faulty prophecy: "It is reported there will not be a dissolution. The reformers believe it unnecessary."[7]

Avoiding a dissolution was important to those Tories who realized that an appeal to the country would strengthen the Whigs. They took a gamble when General Isaac Gascoyne, an ultra-Tory from Liverpool, proposed to reject the ministry's proposal to reduce the House from 658 to 596 Members. This reduction would entail a significant loss among English constituencies. On April 18 Gascoyne moved that the number of Members for England and Wales not be reduced. Two days later the Tories achieved the union they had been lacking when they defeated the government on Gascoyne's motion by a count of 299 to 291, whereupon Grey demanded a dissolution. The reluctant King agreed, hastily appearing in the House of Lords amid a scene of disorder. His presence prevented action on a motion from Wharncliffe that begged the King not to dissolve Parliament. The Tories had hoped to delay a prorogation, but the ministry had hustled the King — looking splendid in his crown and robes — into attendance. However, what was noticed most was that his crown was on awry, perched at a jaunty and precarious angle. When Lord Durham had summoned the Master of the Horse to ready the royal carriage, that harried official had protested that he must first finish his breakfast. When told there was no time for delay, he exclaimed, "Lord bless me, is there a revolution?" "Not at this moment," Durham replied, "but there will be if you stay to finish your breakfast."[8]

Indeed, a "revolution" was in the making. By going to the country Grey had hoped to secure a mandate for reform so that the Tories would be forced to flout public opinion. The election returns trickled in between April 28 and June 1, giving the Whigs a majority that ranged between 130 and 140 Members — a guarantee of the bill's repassage in the Commons. The Reform Bill was reintroduced in that chamber on June 24. These dramatic events provoked Lord Lyndhurst to emerge from his posture of judicial restraint and assume a more energetic role in halting the bill's progress.

The Duke of Wellington received a letter from Sir Henry Hardinge at the end of May describing the King's most recent reception. Lady Lyndhurst, venting her anger at Brougham, playfully asked Hardinge to be her second in a duel. He wryly observed to the Duke that after having failed to receive anything from the Whigs, Dolly had joined the opposition. He added that Lord Lyndhurst opposed the Reform Bill.[9]

Lady Lyndhurst was sending mixed signals. She might voice disenchantment with her Whig friends, but at the same time she had hot words for the Tories. Charles Greville found her "full of pique and resentment against the Opposition and the Duke, half real and half pretended, and (she) chatters away about Lyndhurst's not being their cat's paw, and that if they choose to abandon him, they must not expect him to sacrifice himself for them."[10] Dolly, who had never made an effort to conceal her Whig leanings, indicated her support for the Reform Bill far and wide. On September 21 Lord Holland wrote in his diary: "Lord Lyndhurst and Lord Grey at dinner. Lady Lyndhurst's conversation would lead one to hope he will not vote against 2d. reading of bill, and betrays much estrangement from the party in opposition."[11] Loquacious Dolly continued to make known her pro-reform views a few days later when she and her husband dined with Greville, who noted a difference of opinion between the two: "the *mari* talks against the Bill, the woman for it. They are like the old divisions of families in the Civil Wars."[12] It is possible that Dolly's expressed support for the Reform Bill when her husband was opposed was a strategic choice arrived at jointly in an effort to keep their options open for as long as possible.

Despite whatever sympathy Dolly may have had for Grey and his cause, Lord Lyndhurst was being forced by events to take a more visible and active role in killing the measure. If, as some had speculated, Grey's motive in appointing Lyndhurst Chief Baron had been to remove him from the political arena, that possibility had been unrealistic, even though it was customary for the Chief Baron to stay out of politics. Lyndhurst was the major oratorical weapon in the Tory arsenal. His voice as well as his vote would be enlisted to battle the hated reform measure in the House of Lords. Given his long association with the Tories, he probably entertained few illusions that the Whigs would satisfy his continuing appetite to occupy high office. Brougham was the Whigs' Chancellor, and the Tories understood Lyndhurst's need for place. He was not too outré an ally in the looming contest. In midsummer Lyndhurst pledged his solidarity at an opposition meeting. On September 20 he advised the Duke of Wellington: "If we have a fair prospect of success we ought to divide upon the second reading."[13] A great change occurred in Lyndhurst's activity when the Reform Bill came before the House of Lords.

The House of Commons passed the Reform Bill 367 to 231 on its second reading on July 7. The bill passed 345 to 236 on a final division on September 22. That same day Russell, followed by an escorting procession of more than a hundred Members of Parliament, carried the bill to the House of Lords. The most potent threat Grey held over the Lords was the creation of peers sufficient to carry reform. Grey had not yet secured a pledge from the King to do this, but the Lords realized the possibility existed. Basically, King William wanted no creation, and, failing that alternative, he did not want a large one — which was the only kind that would have any effectiveness. Five reformers had been raised to the Lords in June. The coronation peerages in September had numbered fifteen, which was not enough to scare anybody. In autumn of 1831 there was still doubt about the genuineness of this variety of leverage.

Ellenborough and Wharncliffe were against an outright struggle, hoping to amend the bill successfully in committee. Their plan had no appeal to Wellington, who believed it might be more difficult to sustain majorities in successive committee votes than to rally his troops for a dramatic showdown on the second reading. He hoped for a majority of forty or possibly more. The Duke believed time would be the reformers' undoing. If the opposition could only gain time, there was no telling what unforeseen turn of events might rescue it from the unpalatable Reform Bill. Wellington's pen expressed this sentiment on the eve of the Lords' debate: "We here think that there is reason to believe that there is a very prevailing change of opinion in the country upon the subject of the bill. At all events, we think that the House of Lords ought to give the country a chance of being saved by affording further time to consider this question."[14] Three weeks later he repeated his wishful speculation: "In this interval, the country may manifest an important change of opinion, or providence may otherwise save us from the misfortunes impending."[15]

The decision for a division on the second reading was made at a dinner at Apsley House on September 21. Wharncliffe urged that this position be coupled with a pledge to support moderate reform. His plea was rejected. It was rejected a second time at another Tory dinner on October 1. Some still objected to endorsing any support for reform as a disloyal repudiation of the Duke's declaration, which had brought down his ministry. Others felt that in rejecting Grey's bill, they must not appear as intransigent opponents of any reform measure whatsoever. Lord Lyndhurst was not present at either of these dinners. He did, however, support the Duke's strategy of opposing on the second reading. At the same time, he took the more moderate position of not wanting to close the door to a less sweeping installment of parliamentary reform. Remarkably, he had been dining with Lord Grey and Lord Holland at Holland House during the first Tory dinner on September 21. It was on this occasion that Lady Lyndhurst had talked favorably of the bill and encouraged Holland to hope that the Chief Baron would not oppose the second reading. However, when the Lords began their debate, his name was on the roster of speakers opposing Grey's version of reform.

The debate on the second reading opened on October 3 and spanned five days. Special galleries had been erected to accommodate the large number of spectators. An imposing battery of speakers included Grey, Lansdowne, Holland, Goderich, Melbourne, and Brougham for the bill and Wellington, Eldon, Lyndhurst, Winchilsea, Dudley, Wharncliffe, and Harrowby against it. Lyndhurst's turn came on the fifth day, October 7. He began by challenging the consistency of the bill's most prominent supporters. In view of his own recent switch on the issue of Catholic Emancipation, this mode of attack must have astonished and irritated many among his listeners. He cited earlier statements favoring more gradual and less sweeping reform made by Grey, Russell, Melbourne, and Brougham over the past fifteen years. He contrasted their past declarations with the content of the current bill and laid a charge of inconsistency at their feet. Knowing his own vulnerability in this area, the Chief Baron pointed out that he cited these changed views of his colleagues only for the purpose of "contrasting the opinions dispassionately formed by men of high talent with the opinions embodied in the Bill, and formed in a time of intense excitement."[16]

After his startling beginning, Lyndhurst addressed the principal objections the Tories had raised against the Reform Bill. It would destroy the balanced Constitution of King, Lords, and Commons; it would unleash social revolution; and, regardless of what the Whigs promised, it would not be a final remedy but would lead only to further demands for additional concessions. In a break with Wellington's disastrous declaration of November 2, Lyndhurst admitted that the Constitution was not "perfect or not liable to objection." But, as a conservative striving to conserve in the tradition of Edmund Burke, he cautioned that "our Constitution is not the work of a day; it has been built by Time, and we have been most fortunate in its construction." He denied that constitutions could be created or transplanted. They are, he declared, the growth of time.

Preaching caution lest the Lords consent to "abandon or even hazard" their system blending the sovereign power, the aristocracy, and democracy, Lyndhurst focused on the object of the bill. The consequence of this version of reform was "to make, not a slight alteration in the most important and influential of the three estates, but to make an entire change in the persons who are to elect, and, consequently, an entire change in the persons elected. The object is to give a greater degree of power and preponderance to one estate — to destroy the nice balance now existing, and in this respect to give us a new Constitution."[17]

Should this precious legacy be altered, the English ran a risk of degenerating into "a fierce democratic assembly . . . whatever name the Government chose to give the Bill, it is in fact and in substance a revolutionary measure." It might endanger the rights and privileges of the monarchy or even bring about a republic. A quasi-republic in the shape of a limited monarchy was one possible consequence of so extreme a change. The potential consequences were limitless. The Protestant Church of Ireland was vulnerable. It would be one of the first targets of the reformers, who had an agenda to carry out once they had constituted a reformed Parliament. Lyndhurst urged his listeners to consider the aims of the reformers, "for they say that they do not ask the reform for the sake of Reform, but for the sake of the consequences." He admonished his fellow peers to consider these implications, which included the abolition of tithes, a reduction in taxation that might undermine the rights of the public creditor, a change in the Corn Laws, and an abandonment of colonial possessions. All of these measures, he argued, would be attacked in a reformed Parliament.

Lyndhurst rebuked the Whig leaders for their pledge that the bill's wide scope would satisfy the demands of reformers and set a seal of finality on the work of England's lawmakers. He singled out Grey, his benefactor, for exhorting his colleagues to "give largely in order that the people may not want more." He characterized this approach as an invitation to additional demands for power. People were driven by their own self-interests, and, once possessed of the means by which to extend their own power — which the bill would surely provide — the herd would not cease to grasp at more power. Lyndhurst declared that the Prime Minister was "ready to throw open the floodgates that will admit the torrent of democratic power." This torrent, he predicted, would rush in and overpower both Whigs and Tories.

In his peroration Lyndhurst alluded to the menacing threats directed at "malignant and rotten-hearted Lords" during the public debate over passage of the bill. In a plea for courage among the peers, he made a rare reference to his own elevation to the peerage: "I cannot boast of an illustrious descent. I have sprung from the people. I am proud of being thus associated with the descendants of those illustrious names which have shed lustre upon the history of our country." However, if he thought the Lords were vulnerable to intimidation from public clamor, he "should be ashamed of this dignity, and take refuge from it in the comparative obscurity of private life, rather than mix with men so unmindful of the obligations imposed upon them by their high station and illustrious birth."[18]

Finally, Lyndhurst reminded his colleagues that they were not placed in Westminster to pass Vestry Acts or Road Bills but to guard the Constitution against the rashness of Ministers. Further, he maintained, these same Ministers were responsible for what he believed was extensive exaggeration of public feeling regarding the bill before them. Mindful that the Lords were placed in what he called a perilous situation, Lyndhurst described it as a proud one as well. The country looked to the peers to do their duty in conserving the vital legacy of the sinews of government. In doing so they would "merit the eternal gratitude of every friend of the Constitution and of the British Empire."[19]

Lyndhurst resumed his place and gave way to Grey. The latter described Lyndhurst's speech as a full condemnation of his government's conduct and added that he regretted the tone and spirit in which this opposition had been offered. In rejecting the severity of the attack, he spoke directly of the "sneers" and "sarcasms" Lyndhurst had aimed at the ministry on the basis of alleged inconsistencies. Bristling with reproach, Grey declared that his Chief Baron, "after his own conduct upon the Catholic question, is the last man in the world who has any right to make an attack upon the King's Government, upon the score of consistency." He went on to question Lyndhurst's own consistency in his views on reform. Grey needled him with the challenge: "Upon this very Question of Parliamentary Reform were his opinions never different from those which he has this night supported?"[20]

After Grey had finished, Lyndhurst replied to one point that troubled him in particular. He referred to Grey's allegation that during an earlier stage of his life, he had held opinions that contradicted his current ones. Lyndhurst assured him that he "is grossly misinformed and utterly mistaken." Grey replied that he understood that Lyndhurst "at one period of his life entertained opinions favourable to the consideration of Parliamentary Reform." The Chief Baron cried out: "Never!"[21] Campbell, present during this exchange, recorded his own colorful and highly partisan version of what followed:

> Lord Denman, who had gone the circuit with Lyndhurst, and full well knew what those opinions had been, was then standing by me. Shaking his fist in a manner which made me afraid that he would draw upon himself the notice of the House, he exclaimed, "Villain! lying villain!" But, in reality, what the noble and learned Lord said was literally true, for at the period of his life alluded to he was not favourable to parliamentary reform, but wished Parliament to be abolished, that a National Convention might be established in its place.[22]

Lyndhurst's boldness in raising the issue of political consistency courted countercharges and simultaneously sent a signal to Whigs and Tories alike. He proclaimed that he was neither the bought goods of the Whigs nor squeamish about taking up the Tory offense. He was, lest any forget, the Tories' foremost oratorical champion. Lady Holland, writing just prior to the second reading debate, had observed, "Much will depend on Ld Lyndhurst, who is now the great card . . . but you know well that he is slippery."[23] After his oratory in the House of Lords, she wrote of "Ld Lyndhurst's sneers & sarcasm" and resolved that "he has lost my warm & cordial friendship."[24] The Chief Baron had erased any doubt of where his loyalties lay.

In the early morning hours of October 8, the government was defeated by a vote of 199 to 158 on the bill's second reading in the House of Lords. Riots at Derby and Nottingham followed from October 8 through 10. More riots broke out in Bristol on October 29 and continued for three days. Greville thought the violence at Bristol might "vie with some of the worst scenes of the French Revolution."[25] On October 12 London witnessed a rampage, as the people demonstrated their outrage over what the Lords had done. While he was in residence, the crowd stoned Wellington's Apsley House for nearly an hour. Stones sailed through his plate-glass windows. One damaged a portrait of Lady Lyndhurst by Wilkie. Another narrowly missed the Duke as he sat at his writing table.

By means of a letter in the *Times* on October 18, Grey pledged to reintroduce a "not less efficient" bill.[26] But Parliament did not reassemble until the first week of December, and many hoped to work out a compromise during the recess. The Earl of Harrowby and Lord Wharncliffe hoped to employ the time to secure a compromise. Wellington wished to use the time to stall in the hope that the upheaval would subside. The Lords' rejection of the bill had a disastrous result because it emboldened the Tories. They were resolved to oppose any reform, and they believed their own rhetoric of institutions imperiled and the dykes of revolution about to burst.

Harrowby and Wharncliffe, working in tandem, resurrected the latter's plan for a modified bill — in effect, a compromise. They informed the Cabinet of their proposal through the Earl of Carlisle. On October 12 Wharncliffe announced his support for a modified bill. Harrowby echoed this conciliatory stand the next day. The two worked for passage of a new bill in exchange for concessions. The waverers had begun their quest to break the crisis. They labored against a disunited Tory camp, an important segment of which, like Wellington, had taken heart over the recent rejection of the bill.

Wharncliffe presented his list of alterations to Grey on November 23. The Cabinet pondered them for three days, rejecting the bulk of them. Wharncliffe met with Grey for a second time and found him so intractable that he suspended the negotiations. A final session on December 10 ended in stalemate. Wharncliffe's unfruitful parleys with an unyielding Grey only strengthened the hard-liners' case for all-out opposition. Thus, the waverers' failure shifted the ground in favor of the ultras. At the same time, the moderates' failed efforts served to reveal to the government the desired concessions that, if granted, would dampen the enthusiasm of some of the opposition forces.

Why had the negotiations failed? The answer lay in the modifications the waverers sought. Dropping the £10 clause, eliminating the proposed London boroughs, abolishing Schedule B (which called for eliminating one Member from forty-six boroughs with populations below four thousand), and separating town householders from those in the counties were changes of such impact that they created an impression that the bill was being drastically altered. Six days after Parliament reassembled, on December 12, Russell introduced a new Reform Bill that made the concession of redrawing the schedules to satisfy Tory moderates. This involved changing the criteria for disfranchisement to a formula based on the number of houses in a borough and the amount of assessed taxes paid. The previous bill had called for disfranchisement based on population. The opposition had argued that population figures could be falsified, whereas the number of houses could not. Six days after its introduction in the House of Commons, the bill passed its second reading in that chamber. The ministry prepared to confront the Lords again.

14
This Fatal Bill

"In one sense that most revolutionary aspect of the Reform crisis of 1831–2 was not the Reform Bill itself," wrote Norman Gash, "but the coercion of the House of Lords."[1] The unsuccessful attempts to reach a compromise prompted the government to reconsider the most drastic weapon in its arsenal: the creation of a large number of new peers. Because this device was so extreme, it had given the Whig leaders pause. Now they examined it anew.

They did so because the Lords' rejection of parliamentary reform by a vote of 199 to 158 had forced them to come to grips with the fact that they were hopelessly outnumbered in the House of Lords as it was presently constituted. Their efforts at righting this imbalance had been as ineffective as they had been hesitant. Nonetheless, their peerage creations had drawn Tory censure as blatant maneuvers to achieve political ends. Twenty-two peerages had been awarded to mark William IV's coronation in September 1831. In all, there were twenty-eight new peers in the first year of Lord Grey's ministry. The early months of 1832 brought eight more creations. Yet these were not enough. The lack of impact underscored the government's need for at least fifty additional peers. The ministry could not escape the necessity of such an invention.

The King was not alone in his reluctance to take this step. Grey himself was hesitant. How many new peers were needed? Fifty might not be enough. How high could he escalate his demand? The Prime Minister believed the necessary number of new peers might be so large as to make the demand unpalatable. Massive creations might shake to their very foundations throne, aristocracy, and Whig ministry. Grey had assured the King that he would not ask for a creation "unless a very small addition would have been effectual for the purpose."[2]

At the end of November 1831, Lords Durham, Brougham, and Holland lobbied Grey to ask the King to create a number of peers sufficient to ensure the passage of the Reform Bill. On January 13, 1832, the Cabinet formally requested a promise from the King to create enough peers to prevent another defeat of the bill. This request characterized the Lords as a body that had set itself against the will of the nation and the House of Commons. The kingdom was carried to the brink of crisis, and the King would now be acting in a legitimate manner to rescue the Constitution from peril. No number was mentioned. Two days later William agreed to a creation in principle but stipulated that no more than three new titles should be created. The rest of the required conscriptees were to be drawn from the eldest sons of existing peers.

Word of the King's promise soon leaked out. There was, however, uncertainty about the extent of his pledge. How many creations would he be willing to endorse? The Bishops had agreed to drop their opposition to a second reading, and, if they were added to those who no longer opposed a favorable division at this stage, their action was expected to reduce the opposition's barrier to twenty peers. The King was under this impression, and Grey encouraged him to expect a number that might "not exceed, or at all events not greatly exceed," twenty-one.[3]

The threat of a creation once again activated Baron Wharncliffe's efforts to head off a confrontation. This was as Grey intended: "The Prime Minister's policy of utilizing the *threat* instead of the *fact* of a creation of peers was based upon his belief that the former would be adequate to assure the second reading in the House of Lords. It was the King's answer to the Cabinet's minute of 13 January that made it possible to use that threat, and so to reopen with better prospects of success the negotiations with the 'Waverers' which had broken down in the previous November."[4] Wharncliffe had offered on January 8 to deliver the support of his friends on a second reading if the ministry would alter the measure on minor points. However, a creation of new peers would inspire the waverers to vote against the bill. Wharncliffe met with the Duke of Wellington on January 19 in an attempt to forge a common front. The Duke was unshakable: no compromise. He carried the political baggage of his past renunciation of reform, and he was not ready to set it down. Wharncliffe, after consulting the Earl of Harrowby, decided to press on in his efforts to reach a compromise. The unproductive interview between Wharncliffe and the Duke underscored the split between waverers and die-hards that divided the Tory camp.

Events moved quickly in the remaining months of parliamentary debate. The third Reform Bill passed through the Commons on March 24.

Two days later it was introduced into the House of Lords. Both Wharncliffe and Harrowby announced that they would give their votes to a second reading. The Bishop of London followed with the same pledge. Wellington had the last word. Charles Greville recorded his promise "that if the Bill went into committee he would give his constant attendance and do all in his power to make it as safe a measure as possible. So finished this important evening much to the satisfaction of the moderate, and to the disgust of the violent party."[5]

The Lords turned their full attention to the second reading debate on the bill on April 9. Lyndhurst had not taken a prominent role in developments since his strong denunciation of the bill the previous October. Following that effort he and Lady Lyndhurst had departed for the sparkle of Paris. After his return his time was taken up with his judicial duties on the circuit. The reopening of the reform debate in the Lords brought him once again to the fore. There was no doubt about his position now. Whig hopes had been dashed by his October stand when, in Lord Holland's words, he had "disappointed and exasperated us."[6] On New Year's Day 1832, Grey declared to Brougham that the language of the Tories was "as violent and confident as ever, and Lyndhurst is becoming more and more an avowed and prominent supporter of their views."[7] Grey had abandoned any illusion that Lyndhurst's appointment as Chief Baron had drawn the latter's political fangs. In the fashion of a warhorse hearing the call to battle, the ex-Chancellor had been inspired by the Reform Bill to reenter the political fray.

Lyndhurst spoke on the fourth evening of the debate, and throughout his address he repeatedly harried the Prime Minister, citing Grey's assurance that the new bill was as efficient as the previous ones. Lyndhurst's words were harsh: "It is as efficient, and, according to my interpretation of its provisions, as mischievous and as flagrant." After all of his "meditations and inquiries," he could see no reason to change his opinion and was resolved to give his negative vote to the second reading. Lyndhurst moved directly to a denunciation of the Ministers for deliberately fanning public feeling as an excuse for proposing so extreme a measure. He averred that in the elections of 1830, parliamentary reform had not even been mentioned initially. The slave trade had been the most prominent issue until the news of revolution in Paris arrived. Only then did the cry for parliamentary reform emerge. Grey's ministry, after only two months in office, had proposed a plan of reform "that astounded every person — that surprised even the party of the Movement" — Lyndhurst's name for the body of radical political sentiment. He attributed the large scale of public agitation as much to the Ministers as to the bill itself.

Lyndhurst also took up the pressure on the government to resort to a creation of new peers to ensure the bill's passage. He warned Grey against any attempt to pack the House of Lords, but he acquitted him of any desire to bring about so outrageous an assault on the peers: "I do not impute to the noble Earl the intention of resorting to such a rash, and desperate, and wicked measure, which would overwhelm him with disgrace, and the country with ruin." But, he cautioned, others were not so hesitant in their desire to tamper with the Constitution.

Whereupon the Chief Baron catalogued the foremost supporters of the bill. The entire Whig party did not approve of the bill so much as they saw it as an avenue to continued political power. The second group was "the whole party of the movement or revolution," which saw the bill as a springboard to more extensive changes in the future. Next came the Dissenters as well as the propertyless. Finally, there was the periodical press, which prospered through agitation and hoped to benefit from an infusion of democracy. This menacing alliance in favor of reform could reconstitute itself, after passage of "this fatal Bill," in assaults against the property of the Church, against the standing army, and against the legislative authority of the House of Lords.

Speaking directly of Grey, Lyndhurst declared that "if it had been the sole object of that noble Earl to crush forever his political opponents, and to perpetuate his own power, he could have adopted no course more effectual." The Tory leader went on to describe the ramifications of the bill, which enfranchised on the one hand while disfranchising on the other. Sixty-four members would be added to the House of Commons and be "thrown into the scale of extreme democracy." In practical terms, Lyndhurst was denouncing the prospect of a flood of new Members who would augment the ranks of the Whig party and oppose the Tory interest at every turn.

Lyndhurst struck out at Grey's pledge that the measure before them would be a permanent solution to the demands for reform. He assured his colleagues that "no person looking at this Bill, at its various provisions, its anomalies, its absurdities, can for a moment imagine that it will be permanent." The Chief Baron reminded the peers of the menacing tone the debate had taken: "My Lords, it is said, if we throw out the Bill, there will be a collision between the two Houses of Parliament on this subject. I cannot believe this. This House is as independent of the House of Commons as that House is of us. We have the same authority to reject the Bill that they had to pass it; and there would be no more disrespect on our parts in now rejecting it than there was upon theirs in sending it up, after our solemn rejection of it, a second time."[8] Lyndhurst had gone to what constituted the core of the issue for him and many others: the very safety, indeed, the very viability of the House of Lords. To cave in to the mounting pressure for passage would be to announce the termination of that chamber's independent state. The aristocratic chamber would set itself on a road to extinction. This Lyndhurst believed, and it was a conviction he expressed when he told Greville that with passage of the reform measure, "there was no chance of the House of Lords surviving ten years."[9]

Lyndhurst had spoken the gospel of conservatism, which requires that people act carefully, with respect for history and institutions. And he had voiced the fear that the Lords would be swept away in the flood of change. Significantly, he had placed himself more deeply within the Tory fold, proving his usefulness as a powerful, even an indispensable weapon in parliamentary debate. Lord Jeffrey, who heard Lyndhurst speak, called his contribution "by far the cleverest and most dangerous" speech in opposition to the Reform Bill.[10]

Grey could not be still: he must respond to the Chief Baron, whose voice neither friendship nor patronage had silenced. He rose for the first time in this debate to defend himself against what he characterized as "the suspicions which have been cast upon me." He noted that Lyndhurst blamed the current Ministers for the agitation for parliamentary reform. Grey rejected this charge, declaring that "the statement is untrue that we caused the present excitement. That excitement existed previously." When he came into office, he had found himself in a situation in which "the necessity of doing something" was generally admitted by most political participants, both Whigs and Tories. Grey directed a question to Lyndhurst that he called upon him to answer "aye or no." The peers listened in silence as the Prime Minister inquired of the ex-Chancellor: "Did you not admit, when you left office that it was absolutely necessary to grant some Reform to carry on the government of the country?" Lord Lyndhurst made no reply. His silence on this occasion needs to be reconciled with his "Never!" on a previous one when Grey had asserted that Lyndhurst favored parliamentary reform early in his life. Now Grey was inquiring specifically about Lyndhurst's views on the need for reform when he left office — a question that carried a different meaning.

Grey pressed on, asserting that recognition of a need for reform "was the opinion of the noble and learned Lord, and of all his colleagues in the Administration, the noble and gallant Duke alone excepted." William IV had told Brougham that all of the retiring Ministers, save Wellington, believed some measure of reform was necessary. Brougham had passed on this information to his chief, who now taunted Lyndhurst with his reported admission. Grey pressed even further in his attempt to portray Lyndhurst as a reformer: "Even the noble and learned Lord, who now at last is a Reformer — who, in the early times of his life, had never heard of, or argued for, or supported Reform — I suppose the noble Lord will not contradict that statement — even the noble Lord who, reluctantly consenting, admits that there is some necessity for Reform." This reference, coupled with the allegation that he was at heart a reluctant reformer, prompted Lyndhurst to interrupt Grey, declaring: "I made no such admission; nothing I said could be construed into it."[11]

Having touched a raw nerve, Grey did not hesitate to discuss the option of a creation of peers sufficient to secure passage of the bill. He cited "all the best constitutional writers" agreeing that although a creation for a particular purpose should rarely be resorted to, cases might arise in which it might be absolutely necessary. Such a case would involve a collision between the two Houses of Parliament with public opinion supporting one branch of the legislature against the other. Grey's quiet words heralded the very real prospect of a mass creation of peers to force the Reform Bill through and permanently hobble the House of Lords.[12]

With Grey's words still echoing in their ears, the peers gave the bill its second reading in the early morning hours of April 14. The vote was 184 to 175, giving the government a majority of nine votes, and the bill went to committee, a new battleground for both opponents and supporters of the measure. The leaders of the Tory opposition gathered on April 17 to plan their strategy. Lords Lyndhurst and Ellenborough represented the diehards at this conference, and Harrowby, Wharncliffe, and Haddington spoke for the waverers. They grappled with the problem of passing the first and second clauses, which called for disfranchising fifty-six and thirty boroughs, respectively. The government had offered to drop these figures, allowing the Tories an opportunity to consent to disfranchisement without committing themselves to specific numbers. The Ministers were firm, however, in their requirement that the disfranchising clauses must be taken up before the enfranchising one.

The Tory caucus of April 17 accepted this plan. Both die-hards and waverers would accept the two disfranchising clauses with figures eliminated. However, there was an immediate stumbling block. When Lyndhurst and Ellenborough met with Wellington, the Earl of Rosslyn, and Bathurst on April 18, their agreement was rejected. Wellington raised an objection that won support. He pointed out that although many of their followers would vote for the omission of fifty-six and thirty boroughs in the two clauses, they would balk at allowing the clauses as amended to pass without a division. Such a division would split the party and alienate some supporters who would stay away for the remainder of the contest, undermining the Tory effort. It was decided to acquaint Lord Harrowby with this potential danger in the hope that he and his allies would vote for the postponement of the two clauses. Then, the committee would support enfranchisement.

Lyndhurst and Ellenborough, go-betweens for the two wings of the party, met with the waverers a second time later that day. Ellenborough recorded in his diary what transpired:

> The reasons for postponing the clauses of disfranchisement were explained and deemed sufficient to require that course. It was felt that the passing of the clauses without a division after the omission of fifty-six and thirty would have placed us in a better position. Still the essential point was to keep the party together for ulterior operations.
>
> It was decided therefore that we should all support the postponement of the clauses and Ld. Lyndhurst should make the motion, declaring at the same time his full adherence to the principle of disfranchisement, now sanctioned by the House, and his disposition to act upon it to some extent.[13]

Lord Lyndhurst was in the thick of it: he would carry his party's lance against "this fatal Bill" in committee. He had established himself as a force who was always at the center of events. Lyndhurst was also committed to undertaking personal political rehabilitation. This effort on his part was meeting with success, as the Tory factions enlisted him as their spokesperson.

Lyndhurst told Wharncliffe to meet with Grey once again in an attempt to learn the ministry's next move. At their April 28 meeting, Wharncliffe advised Grey of the Tory plan to postpone a vote on disfranchisement. Grey refused to accept postponement and asked Wharncliffe to work to have the decision reversed. Wharncliffe promised to try. Now events moved quickly. On May 5 Lyndhurst and Ellenborough secured the waverers' pledge to support postponement. Lyndhurst objected to a suggestion that Grey be notified of this decision. He feared such a warning might further alienate the hard-liners, who had already been put off by Wharncliffe's meeting with Grey. So, at Lyndhurst's insistence, a mantle of secrecy cloaked the group's decision, and the Ministers were unaware of the waverers' agreement to back postponement on disfranchisement. Lyndhurst could detect opportunity, and weakness and uncertainty in others were the harbingers of opportunity for him. He detected the vulnerability of Grey's government. It had been backed into a corner over the bill and would likely resign. He sensed how real the possibility was of toppling the ministry. He had told Ellenborough so on January 26, 1832. He had "said he thought these fellows might be turned out provided it were known that an administration could and would be formed if they went out."[14]

Just as Lyndhurst was attempting to sharpen his image as a loyal Tory, a new scandal involving Lady Lyndhurst battered his public stature. Dolly was reputed to be the mistress of Lord Dudley, who had served for several months as Wellington's Foreign Secretary. Canning had first put Dudley in the Cabinet, and Wellington kept him on. Both Prime Ministers regarded their colleague as an eccentric, not a madman. However, Dudley's mental instability worsened, and he left the Cabinet in May 1828. Harriet Arbuthnot had noted that "Ld. Dudley is as mad as Bedlam, knows nothing of business & is proverbially idle."[15] Both Lyndhursts continued a close relationship with the charming lunatic. Part of his charm stemmed from his generosity. He presented Dolly with a diamond necklace valued at £600 and a pearl necklace worth £400. He wanted her to choose one, but she hesitated for so long in making a choice that he let her keep both. Sir Denis Le Marchant recorded that "all Lord Dudley's friends are furious. They say the poor man's disease has been aggravated by the conduct of the Lyndhursts ... the Lyndhursts, however, have almost identified themselves with him. He drove to their house at 2 in the morning and entreated that a clergyman might be sent for to baptize their 2nd daughter who is near 4 years old, and whom scandal ascribes to him. With difficulty they got him home."[16]

Further difficulties plagued the Lyndhursts' relationship with the hapless Dudley, who became permanently mad in 1832. His family institutionalized him, a step that caused Lady Lyndhurst considerable dismay. Lady Holland noted the cause of Dolly's unhappiness in her diary: "The on dit is that she is very sullen at the sudden restraint upon Ld D. as there was a draft for £5,000 on his table which was destined to her; but the banker had been ordered not to make payments."[17] When Le Marchant recorded this incident, the sum had grown to £6,000. In his account, Dudley had drawn a draft in that amount on Hugh Hammersley, the banker at 69 Pall Mall. The latter's suspicions were aroused, and he deferred payment. The rest of this version casts Dolly in an unfavorable light: "Lady Lyndhurst stormed at Hammersley's squeamishness and the deno[u]ement that rapidly followed left no doubt of her unblushing and unfeminine voracity for money. I have not yet seen a friend of Lord Dudley's that speaks of her with patience. . . . This transaction is a stain on the English aristocracy."[18]

Lyndhurst is reported to have told a visitor who admired the furniture in his house at Richmond that "I leave all these things to my wife and ask no questions."[19] Such a policy, when applied to larger matters, may have lulled his sensibilities at times, but it created an impression of a husband who could not control his wife. Events move along on wheels, both large and small. A public scandal involving his already controversial wife was a matter of some significance for the former Chancellor as he attempted to map out a course for both his party and himself during the crisis of reform. The Dudley scandal may have propelled him to gamble on more dramatic but less cautious behavior.

Lyndhurst dared the government to resign. His gamble was that postponement would bring down the government because Grey would not accept a defeat of this nature. Lyndhurst guessed, too, that the King would not keep his promise to create peers. If those hunches proved correct, Grey was doomed, and the Tories would be back in power to rescue the King with a Reform Bill of their own. Lyndhurst assumed that neither Wellington nor Peel would leave the King without an alternative government and without being at Grey's mercy. The success of his strategy hinged on the willingness of Wellington and Peel to return to office. Whatever the outcome, Lyndhurst's action could be justified as an effort to keep the Tory party in the Lords united as a fighting force.

15
The Most Splendid Moment

On May 7, 1832, the Reform Bill was taken up in committee. Lord Ellenborough described what took place: "Ld Lyndhurst moved the postponement of the 2 first clauses in a quiet, good, argumentative speech, showing the importance of the principle of making disfranchisement follow enfranchisement, & that principle had been acted upon by all former Reformers."[1] Lyndhurst's motion was endorsed by a vote of 151 to 116, a defeat for the ministry by a margin of 35. Denis Le Marchant, Henry Brougham's secretary, noted the government's surprise, confiding to his diary:

> The majority was startling. We had not counted on such determined hostility either from the Waverers or the bishops. The former had latterly professed amicable disposition, whilst the latter had allowed themselves to be called favourable to the principles if not the details of the Bill. He (Grey) did not know that the Archbishop of Canterbury had already assured them privately that the King was resolved not to make peers. This was equivalent to the annihilation of the Government.[2]

The ministry treated its defeat as a rejection of the entire bill. The following afternoon Lords Grey and Brougham set out for Windsor. They laid an ultimatum before the King: they must have a creation of peers, or they would resign. The King asked the number that would be required. When told sixty or even eighty, he observed "that was a very large number indeed."[3] The monarch wanted time to consider this sweeping request. The next day William IV sent his answer: he accepted his government's resignation. Then he sent for Lord Lyndhurst.

The Chief Baron was sitting on the bench of the Court of Exchequer when a message from Sir Herbert Taylor, the King's private secretary, summoned him to Windsor. Lord Campbell called this "the most splendid moment of Lyndhurst's career."[4] The King asked Lyndhurst to sound out any individual he might think willing and able to form a new government. Campbell speculated about what transpired during the interview and its implications. He prefaced his account with a disclaimer: "I never heard him (Lord Lyndhurst) relate the particulars of this audience, and the accounts of it circulated at the time were probably founded rather on conjecture than authentic information."[5] Having made this forthright statement, Campbell proceeded to put detailed speeches into the mouths of the two participants.

In Campbell's fabricated dialogue, the King began by expressing his great confidence in the Chief Baron and his opinion that Lyndhurst was "a very honest man." He went on to explain that he had pledged to grant a liberal measure of parliamentary reform and that although his Ministers had gone too far, he could not go back on his word. He was troubled by reports that Lyndhurst believed that all reform was mischievous and that, therefore, he was unalterably opposed to any innovation whatsoever. If this were true, the King could not enlist his aid in this crisis. Campbell then had Lyndhurst speak a discourse in which he presented his views on reform — a statement that was consonant with his disclaimer in the debates on the bill in the House of Lords.

> Sir, — Your Majesty has been entirely misinformed on this subject. True, I have been always opposed to the wild, democratical, Jacobinical principles which generated the horrors of the French Revolution; but I have long seen the necessity for temporate, well considered reform in our representative system, to bring it back to what it was in the reign of your royal ancestor, Edward I . . . the Reform Bill of your late ministers as it now stands would, in my opinion, be fatal to the monarchy, and for that reason I have been driven very reluctantly to oppose it. But it no doubt contains enactments which may be salutary, and if it could be reasonably modified, it might strengthen the Crown, while it gives contentment to your Majesty's subjects.

The King was delighted to hear these words and replied effusively: "My Lord Chief Baron, my Lord Chief Baron, you are the very man for me: you have hit upon the basis I wish for my new administration." Lyndhurst was in his familiar role of aiding his sovereign in finding a Prime Minister. Campbell went so far as to proclaim that "Lyndhurst seemed now to have the premiership within his grasp."[6]

But Campbell had it wrong. Lyndhurst was content to resume the Chancellorship, which would certainly be his if he were the instrument of the Tories' return to power. His immediate goal was not to be a Prime Minister but to find one. Rumors flew as Lyndhurst carried out his negotiations for the formation of a new ministry. In doing so he looked to Sir Robert Peel. John Wilson Croker, who had been Secretary to the Admiralty for two decades, was present at Apsley House when Peel closed this door. Croker asked Lyndhurst, "Whom do you mean to put at the head?" Lyndhurst waved his hand toward Peel and said, "*That* Peel must answer." In Croker's account, "Peel then said, with a tone of concentrated resolution that he could not and would not have anything to do with the settlement of the Reform Question and that it was evident that it must be settled now, and on the basis, as he understood, of the present Bill." Peel referred to the King's instruction to Lyndhurst that a new ministry must be pledged to bring about "an extensive reform."[7] This, Peel knew, was the object of Lyndhurst's mission.

Peel would have none of it. To him it was Catholic Emancipation all over again. He had been compelled by circumstances to abandon his convictions in the resolution of that impasse, and he refused to adopt once again so distasteful a course. In the presence of Wellington, Lyndhurst, and Croker, he spoke of "the advantage to the country that public men should maintain a character for consistency and disinterestedness, which he would forever forfeit if, a second time, he were on any pretence to act, over again anything like his part in the Catholic Question."[8] This pronouncement carried more significance than that of a rebuke to his colleagues. It spoke the doom of Lyndhurst's efforts. Peel indicated his refusal to participate in a Tory government that would bring in "an extensive reform" on May 10. This declaration dogged all of Lyndhurst's subsequent negotiations. Only the previous day he was "confident of success," by Le Marchant's account, and contemplated a resumption of the Chancellorship: "Lord Lyndhurst openly made his arrangements for returning to the Court of Chancery."[9] Peel's intransigence put his plans on a less certain footing.

Lyndhurst turned to the Duke. On the same day that Peel rejected a role in a new government, Lyndhurst sent a pressing message to Wellington: "The more I consider the subject of our consultations (and I have considered it much), the more I am satisfied that you must consent to be *the minister*, or everything will fail. I am confident we can manage the affair, and the situation of things is such that, at all events, it is *our duty to try.*"[10] After writing this memorandum, Lyndhurst went to Windsor to report his progress to the King. Upon returning to London, he dashed off a second message, which struck a note of urgency: "everything is, I think, well. But I must see you for a few moments; where shall I find you?"[11]

In his first message of May 10, Lyndhurst had used the one approach that was certain to persuade the Duke to serve: the call to duty — "It is our duty to try." The Duke would never turn aside such a plea even though he might have to recant his numerous public declarations reviling reform. His answer to Lyndhurst's entreaty spoke of making "an effort to enable the King to shake off the trammels of his tyrannical Minister." The rest of his reply was a soldier's credo: "I am perfectly ready to do whatever his Majesty may command me. I am as much averse to the Reform as ever I was. No embarrassment of that kind, no private consideration, shall prevent me from making every effort to serve the King."[12]

The Duke might be ready once more to serve his sovereign, but the proponents of reform were prepared to fight him for that privilege. A run on the Bank of England was heralded in placards that appeared around London: "To Stop the Duke Go for Gold." In these ominous circumstances, Lyndhurst calmly sent a detailed memorandum to the Duke, packed with names of possible Cabinet selections, including notations of their strengths and weaknesses. Wetherell was a peculiar character but a most important card. Croker's consent to serve was absolutely necessary. Wharncliffe might be troublesome with us, but he could be troublesome against us. One was an excellent speaker. Another had useful family connections. Yet another had high pretensions but should not be neglected.[13]

It was all for naught. Wellington's colleagues did not share his sense of obligation to serve. Only Henry Hardinge and Sir George Murray pledged their willingness to go with him. Because Peel had refused to form or join a ministry, Henry Goulbourn, Croker, and John Herries declined to come in. Alexander Baring and Manners Sutton also refused to join. This left a serious vacuum on the front bench in the House of Commons. It was becoming apparent that the Commons would not permit the Duke's resumption of the Premiership. Far from being hailed as a perennial hero, he was now being reviled as a villain who insincerely embraced the Reform Bill he had so long denounced.

On May 15 the Duke gave up his attempt to form a government, informing the King of his failure. When Wellington withdrew as a possible Premier, he endorsed an alternative Tory candidate for the post of First Minister: Manners Sutton, Speaker of the House of Commons and a reluctant aspirant to the office. Charles Greville saw Peel's hand in this development. Recalling Pitt's domination of the Addington ministry early in the century, Greville speculated that Peel "thought to make Manners Sutton play the part of Addington, while he was to be another Pitt . . . he resolved that a government should be formed the existence of which should depend upon himself. Manners Sutton was to be his creature . . . and as soon as the fitting moment arrived, he would have dissolved this miserable Ministry and placed himself at the head of affairs."[14]

The confusion engulfed Lyndhurst, and he committed a slip that aggravated the already unsettled situation. When Wellington accepted the King's commission to form a government, it was decided to prorogue Parliament. Lyndhurst was instructed to carry this command to Grey. The effect would have been to deny the followers of the outgoing ministry a parliamentary forum in which to denounce Wellington and the Tory efforts to form a new government. Communicating the King's pleasure in this matter was Lyndhurst's responsibility. Greville explained what happened: "He forgot it! In after times, those who write the history of these days will probably discuss the conduct of the great actors, and it will not fail to be a matter of surprise that such an obvious expedient was not resorted to in order to suspend violent discussions. Among the various reasons that will be imagined and suggested, I doubt if it will occur to anybody that the real reason was that it was *forgotten.*"[15] Lyndhurst's omission was no secret, apparently, and Greville was not the only one to note the Chief Baron's lapse. Ellenborough wrote, "Ld. Lyndhurst omitted to deliver the King's message to Lord Grey . . . which was to adjourn both Houses."[16]

Thus, Parliament continued in session because of Lyndhurst's oversight and took full advantage of its ungagged state. Speaker after speaker lashed out at the Duke for his 180-degree turn on reform in order to regain power. This firestorm of abuse helped to preclude his return to office. Peel also remained firm in his refusal, even after an interview with the King on May 12. His suggestion of Manners Sutton revived some hope, which was reinforced when Alexander Baring, who had declined to serve under the Duke, agreed to be Chancellor of the Exchequer in a Cabinet headed by Sutton. The Speaker, the Tories' last card, was uncertain: he wanted time to make up his mind. Lyndhurst and the Duke met with him at Apsley House, where he inflicted on them a rambling three-hour speech. Lyndhurst, in disgust, "returned home, flung himself into a chair, and said that he could not endure to have any thing to do with such a *damned tiresome old bitch.*"[17]

Sutton wanted until the next morning to make up his mind. When morning came he wanted until evening. Both Lyndhurst and Wellington were put off by Sutton's performance. The next day, May 14, they exchanged notes. Lyndhurst had "a sort of feeling that it cannot succeed" and doubted that their "anti-reforming friends" would "consent to be thus handed over to other hands." He thought it was too late to retreat, and, should Sutton accept, that they must make the best of it. His final thought on the subject was redolent with die-hard resolution: in the event that Sutton declined, "we must assemble some dozen of the best of our young friends in the House of Commons, and ask them whether they will undertake the fight; and if they consent I think we ought not to give the affair up."[18]

Lyndhurst was clutching at straws. The option of a last-ditch fight was past. The time had arrived for Lyndhurst and his "anti-reforming friends" to fold their tents and get out of the way as reform and its proponents preempted the political field. Wellington shared Lyndhurst's uneasiness about Sutton and believed "that many of our friends will not approve of the arrangement." It was clear to him that he "must take steps to reconcile them to it."[19] Both Lyndhurst and Wellington were exasperated at Sutton's delay, but they were mindful of his one great advantage as a candidate for Prime Minister: he was, although an anti-reformer, uncommitted on the bill because of his neutral role as Speaker. He did not carry the baggage of a recent hostile anti-reform stance. He could creditably bring in a Tory measure. But Sutton could not make up his mind. The events that evening in the House of Commons helped him to decide.

The debate was over a petition from the City of London entreating the Commons to refuse to vote supplies until the Reform Bill was enacted. Greville described the scene:

> On that evening ensued the memorable night in the House of Commons, which everybody agrees was such a scene of violence and excitement as never had been exhibited within those walls. Tavistock told me he had never heard any thing at all like it, and to his dying day should not forget it. The House was crammed to suffocation; every violent sentiment and vituperative expression was received with shouts of approbation, yet the violent speakers were listened to with the greatest attention.[20]

The Duke was the particular target for censure, and some moderate men and even a few Tories joined in. When the debate was over, Baring and Sutton went to Apsley House to relate what had occurred to the Duke. Baring conveyed the intensity of what had passed when he declared that he "would face a thousand devils rather than such a House of Commons."[21]

Lyndhurst's "most splendid moment," as Campbell called it, had passed. The next morning the Chief Baron, accompanied by Wellington, waited upon the King and informed him that no administration could be formed. William asked for their advice about what he should do now. They advised him to invite Lord Grey to return, to resume the government, and to carry the bill. When this request was relayed to Grey, he replied that he could give no answer until the full Cabinet had met. What resulted was a firm insistence that the King agree to create enough peers to carry the bill. This crucial passage of the correspondence, written in the third person, was, as Grey knew, a bitter pill for the King to swallow:

> It is most painful to Earl Grey to press upon your Majesty any thing to which he has reason to believe that your Majesty's opinions are adverse, but he is under the necessity of adding, with the unanimous consent of his colleagues, that it appears indispensable, if it should be your Majesty's pleasure to continue them in their present offices, that they should have your Majesty's consent to a creation of Peers, if it should be required to give additional strength to your Majesty's Government in the House of Lords.[22]

The Tories had to deal with a new reality. They were about to be carried, against their will, into a post-reform world. There were many unanswered questions, and Lyndhurst raised one in a message to Wellington on May 17. He inquired, "Suppose the King should make a certain number of Peers — for instance, twenty — how, in such a case, do you understand our engagement?"[23] On the same day that Lyndhurst quizzed the Duke as to their future course, a message was relayed to Wellington by the sovereign's private secretary, Sir Herbert Taylor. The latter announced "that all obstacles . . . will be removed by a declaration in the House of Lords this day from a sufficient number of Peers that, in consequence of the present state of things, they have come to the resolution of dropping their further opposition to the Reform Bill, so that it may pass in its present form."[24]

King William requested that the Duke confer with Lord Lyndhurst on this subject. In reply, Wellington announced that both he and Lyndhurst would not attend any further discussions of the Reform Bill.[25] This intention was not immediately adopted. On the evening of May 17, both the Duke and the Chief Baron rose in the House of Lords to deliver their swan songs in the struggle against "this fatal Bill." Although Wellington had promised the King that he would end his opposition to reform and urge his friends to follow his example, he balked at revealing his pledge in Parliament. The Duke was disgusted with what he regarded as Grey's success at bringing the King to heel. His bitterness permeated his speech, but his expression of his commitment to duty was his own best tribute to himself. He declared with deep emotion, "If I had been capable of refusing my assistance to his Majesty — if I had been capable of saying to his Majesty, 'I cannot assist you in this affair' — I do not think, my Lords, that I could have shown my face in the streets for shame of having done it — for shame of having abandoned my Sovereign under such distressing circumstances."[26]

Then it was Lyndhurst's turn. Greville described his effort: "Lyndhurst was exceedingly able, highly excited, very eloquent, and contrived to make his case a good one. It was a fine display and very short."[27] He traced his steps after the King invited him, as his former Chancellor, to survey those who might be both willing and able to serve him in a new ministry. He had high praise for the Duke, that illustrious individual whose sense of duty had propelled him to make any sacrifice to rescue his sovereign. He added that he had communicated with a few other individuals, nameless but numbering about six, before he reported the findings of his mission to the King. Then his assignment was terminated. It was a sketchy account, and the remainder of his brief address consisted of a spirited defense of his conduct. Lyndhurst declared with fervor that "it is for this, My Lords, of which I have given you a full and faithful narrative, that I have been traduced, maligned, calumniated." He singled out as tormentors both "persons high in station" and "the periodical press, which now reigns paramount throughout the land, unrestrained by Government." He called for the prosecution of the *Times* for degrading the monarchy. Finally, he answered the charge that he had, by heeding the King's command to conduct these transactions, acted inconsistently with his duty as a judge.

This charge had been leveled at him in the House of Commons by Sir Francis Burdett. Lyndhurst pointed out that as a member of the Privy Council, "I am bound, by virtue of my office, to give advice to my Sovereign if he requires it." He replied, too, to a charge that as a judge, he was inappropriately "the leader of a violent and virulent party" in the House of Lords. In answer the Chief Baron gave a review of his conduct since assuming his current judicial post. He submitted, "I will only say, that I never aspired to such a position as leader of a party; it is alike foreign to my inclination and my habits. I have neither the disposition nor the leisure for such a place. Since the noble Earl became a Minister of the Crown, I have seldom attended the House; I have taken no part in its proceedings; I never engaged in any political discussions. At last, when the Reform Bill was introduced, I did come forward." In conclusion, Lyndhurst conceded that "the Reformers are triumphant." He added a note of despair, observing that the barriers had been broken down, that the waters had been let out, and that none could predict their course, let alone the devastation they might cause. He ended by expressing his hope that "my anticipations may prove unfounded, and that the country will not be ruined by the measure which has been forced upon us by the noble Earl."[28]

Neither Lyndhurst nor Wellington had offered the clear pledge Grey had sought — to drop all opposition. Instead, they had made grudging acknowledgments of the inevitable. Grey wrote bluntly to the King of what had occurred in the House of Lords: "The Duke of Wellington and Lord Lyndhurst opened the discussion in two speeches of extreme violence, which seemed to be made less with a view to the explanation of their own conduct, than for the purpose of attacking the conduct of your Majesty's present servants."[29] Grey was particularly offended by the failure of either Wellington or Lyndhurst to make a declaration that he would abstain from any opposition to the Reform Bill as he had expected they would do. In reality, both Wellington and Lyndhurst had simply assured the King that they would not attend further discussions on the bill. Other peers had given similar assurances to the King. William accepted these pledges "as an abandonment of their further opposition to the Bill in the House of Lords, and as an engagement which placed in his hands the option and the means of relieving himself from the necessity of exercising his prerogative in an extensive creation of Peers for the purpose of carrying the Reform Bill."[30] Grey did detect the course his opponents had resolved to follow. He described in a letter to Sir Herbert Taylor the final scene as the Tories exited the chamber: "They got up in a body . . . and left the House; which was, I suppose, intended as a secession, but without any declaration of an intention to let the Bill pass, so that they are at liberty to return in force whenever they may see a favourable opportunity for striking a blow."[31]

But the struggle was over. On May 30 the entire bill breezed through committee. On June 4 the bill was carried on its third reading in the House of Lords by a vote of 106 to 22. Neither the Duke nor Lord Lyndhurst was present. The Royal Assent was given by commission on June 7. Grey had hoped to persuade the King to give his approval in person, but William was determined not to give way in the matter. Grey realized "the strength of His Majesty's feelings on this subject," and he "forebore pressing what appeared to be so repugnant to them."[32] Between thirty and forty members of the Commons came to witness the conclusion of the long contest. Only a handful of peers attended. The opposition was noticeably absent. It all passed quietly, and the absent monarch was accorded the popular sobriquet of "William the Reformer."

When Greville exclaimed that the bill "had procured virtually a complete revolution in this country," Lyndhurst retorted, "aye, much more than that of '88, which merely changed the Dynasty."[33] However, his spirits were not crushed. He had played a large role in the unfolding drama, and he knew that he could lose and yet endure to fight another day. His contempt for his detractors flashed when he hotly declared, in what seemed to be a reference to his wife, "they may wound me, and wound me deeply, too, through connections which are dear to me; but as far as I am myself concerned, I treat them with ineffable scorn."[34] Lyndhurst had attempted to bring the Tories back to power and to earn their gratitude. It was a daring foray into high politics played for high stakes. Benjamin Disraeli's account, under the heading "Lord Lyndhurst's Recollections," may well reveal the Chief Baron's own assessment of what occurred: "The hesitation of M.S. [Sutton] and B. [Baring], and the unwillingness of Peel to act without their adhesion, lost everything. Had the Tories formed their Government it would have had the power of modifying the Reform Bill."[35]

Restoring his party to power became Lyndhurst's larger goal. Yet he also sought a more personal attainment. He set a return to the Woolsack as his reward for both rescuing the King and returning the Tories to power. Despite this reality, Campbell's suggestion that Lyndhurst nearly became Premier echoed in the obituaries that announced the former Chancellor's death more than thirty years later. The *Illustrated London News* declared him "a remarkable political character" who possessed the confidence of William IV "to such an extent that he was once charged by the Sovereign, as Prime Minister, with the formation of a Government, although he did not succeed in his object."[36] The *Spectator* flatly asserted that "he aimed at the Premiership," adding, "when King William set him to form a Ministry in 1832, it was stipulated that he should carry through a full measure of reform."[37] Although Campbell may have believed that Lyndhurst coveted the Premiership, he gave the lie to his own assessment by recording that "Lyndhurst sagaciously predicted that he should ere long be again presiding on the Woolsack."[38] A return to the Woolsack was Lyndhurst's heart's desire, and he did not abandon his wish when his effort to restore the Tories fell to pieces.

16
Dolly's Exit and Peel's Hour

Much of politics is about patronage. No one knew this better than Lord Lyndhurst. The aftermath of the passage of reform underscored this lesson. For him, in a personal sense, the struggle against the Whig-sponsored Reform Bill had been an opportunity to redeem himself in Conservative[1] eyes. He had, by his steady opposition to the bill, erased in most Conservative minds the taint he had acquired by accepting Whig patronage. However, by the same act, he had released Lord Grey from any inclination the latter may have had to promote his welfare. Proof of this alteration in political goodwill was not long in finding expression.

Lord Tenterden died on November 3, 1832, and upon his death the office of Lord Chief Justice of the Court of King's Bench fell vacant. The post was a judicial plum of the first order, and it was reported that Grey had promised this appointment to Lyndhurst should Tenterden retire or die. Charles Greville asserted that "when he was made Chief Baron a regular compact was made, a secret article, that he should succeed on Tenterden's death to the Chief-Justiceship; which bargain was of course canceled by his declaration of war on the Reform question and his consequent breach with Lord Grey."

The appointment went to Sir Thomas Denman, whom some regarded as lacking the judicial weight that had characterized his predecessors. His competitors for the Chief Justiceship had included, besides Lyndhurst, James Scarlett and James Parke. Greville concluded that although the Chief Baron was "by far the fittest man," his political aggressiveness had put him out of the running. The diarist summed up his speculations by declaring, "Lyndhurst will be overwhelmed with anguish and disappointment at finding himself forever excluded from the great object of his ambition and in which his professional claims are so immeasurably superior to those of his successful competitor; nor has he lost it by any sacrifice of interest to honor, but merely from the unfortunate issue of his political speculations."²

Greville was missing a perception of the political horizon that was not lost to Lyndhurst. The Conservatives might regain power, and in that event he wanted to ensure that they would view him as a champion of their principles rather than as an opportunistic renegade who had sold himself to the Whigs. In a real sense, the reform crisis had supplied Lyndhurst with a serviceable bridge over which to return to the party fold. Greville might describe the lost Chief Justiceship as the "great object of his ambition," but the Chancellorship, with its political dimensions, more accurately met Greville's definition. The Woolsack offered an opportunity to be a leading political actor as well as the chief legal personage in the country. Bolstered by a sense that his political standing had been shored up among his fellow partisans, Lyndhurst met Denman and shook hands under Greville's eagle-eyed gaze, which detected "much politeness and grimace."³

The parliamentary session of 1833 found Lyndhurst absent from Westminster and committed to riding the circuit as Chief Baron. He did, however, monitor Parliament's deliberations and communicated his opposition to Henry Brougham's Local Courts Bill in a written declaration. The main object of Brougham's proposal was to permit an inexpensive process for the settlement of small debts. To accomplish this end, he sought the creation of a layer of local courts that would remove these suits from the grip of the centralized legal system. James Beresford Atlay, in *The Victorian Chancellors*, explained the problem:

> During the five years ending in 1827 no fewer than 30,000 out of the 90,000 causes entered annually at Westminster were for sums not exceeding 20l.; the lists at assizes were swollen with cases which to-day would not go beyond the county court registrar; the cost of recovering sums under 50l. was often ludicrously out of proportion to the amount at issue. Many banks and commercial houses systematically submitted to loss and robbery rather than prosecute their claim in a court of law, and large classes of the community were forced to submit to a general denial of justice.⁴

In 1828 Brougham had called for reform in the administration of the law, and in response Lyndhurst appointed a commission to examine the procedures of the Courts of Common Law. Before this group had com-

Coplinda Lindhursta the cook. "I do rule the roast . . . but my spouse is a sad plague to me," 1829. Used by permission of the British Museum.

pleted its findings, Brougham had designed his own bill for the creation of Local District Courts. He submitted this measure in 1830 while the Conservatives were still in power. Upon the dissolution of Parliament, the bill died. The New Year found Brougham in the role of Lord Chancellor, and he lost little time in reviving his plan in the form of the Local Judicature Bill.

Lyndhurst had been urged by the Duke of Wellington in mid-June to respond to Brougham's plan before the Tory Lords threw it out. Proposing a strategy, he recommended that they refrain from rejecting the bill on a second reading, allow it to go into committee, and finish the measure off on its third reading. He believed there would be more support for rejection if this more circuitous path were taken.[5] Wellington voiced the same proposal to the Bishop of Exeter. He restated his recommendation to Lyndhurst that some portion of the debate "should be devoted to the purpose of enlightening the publick mind upon the question." Lyndhurst, as a former Chancellor, was the appropriate spokesperson to respond to a tampering with the judicial branch.[6]

There was no division at the second reading, and Lyndhurst saved his dissent for the committee stage. On June 17 he pointed out that "cheap law does not always mean cheap justice." He criticized the projected use of a decentralized array of barristers whose collective expertise was no match for the existing system of judges, whose continuing interaction was a check on the precision and purity of their performance.[7] Atlay emphasized the widespread objections to the measure:

> The Bill immediately in question was clumsily drawn, the details were bad, and much of it was unintelligible owing to the schedules not being filled in or printed. But Lyndhurst's dislike for it was not grounded merely on the inartistic draftsmanship. The whole principle of local courts was, at that period of his career, distrusted and dreaded by him, and in this he only gave expression to the great volume of professional opinion. For the leaders and leading juniors of the Common Law Bar, as well as for the London attorneys who acted as agency firms, the existing system "was a lucrative monopoly, and it could not be expected that they would regard proposals for scattering the business save with feelings of abhorrence, or that, being so near to the legislative centre, they would forbear to encourage resistance to all

Lyndhurst in his parliamentary robes. Used by permission of the Master and Fellows of Trinity College, Cambridge.

proposals for reform."* And so strong was the feeling that a few days after Brougham's introductory speech a deputation from the chief London agency firms had waited upon the Chief Baron and requested him to undertake the opposition to the Bill.[8]

*Sir Thomas Snagge, *The Evolution of the County Court*, 8.

When the bill reached its third reading in the House of Lords on July 9, 1833, Lord Lyndhurst returned to London from the circuit to pronounce his dissent in person. An eyewitness, Samuel Warren, described the scene in an account that stressed the awe-inspiring presence Lyndhurst brought to any oratorical duel in which he participated:

> Lord Lyndhurst was one of the last that entered. Accustomed as we are to see his noble figure in the flowing costume of the Bench, we hardly recognized him in plain dress. His black surtout, elegant waistcoat, brown curly wig, and ton-ish hat and gloves, give you the idea rather of a colonel of a cavalry regiment, than of a grave law lord. Without an atom of foppery, there is a certain fashionable air about him which surprises one familiar only with the stateliness of the full-bottomed wig, bands, and ermine robe. A few papers peeping out of the breast-pocket of his surtout, together with a certain flush on his features, assured one that he had come prepared for battle. . . . When Lord Lyndhurst rose almost every peer present turned instantly towards him in an attitude of profound attention — of anxious interest — and continued so till he had concluded; as well they might, while listening to one of the most masterly speeches ever delivered in Parliament. There was a manly fervour, a serious energy, in his tone and manner — a severe simplicity of style — a beauty and comprehensiveness of detail — a graceful, good-humoured, but most caustic sarcasm — a convincing strength of argument, which elicited repeated cheering from the House — followed, at its close, by several minutes' applause.[9]

Boldly, Lyndhurst attacked the Local Courts Bill as an attempt simultaneously to curry public favor and to increase the patronage at the command of the Lord Chancellor. Labeling the bill "an enormous job," he spoke of his successor on the Woolsack.

> I am well aware that personally my noble and learned friend on the woolsack has no wish for this unlimited power; my noble and learned friend does not desire this vast patronage, and while exercised by him it would be safe; but the Great Seal may be transferred to another who may be ambitious and desirous of gratifying puffing and sycophantish dependents. My noble and learned friend has candidly told us that he had looked about to see where this formidable patronage could be lodged with less peril, and that, not being successful in his search elsewhere, he had been compelled as a *dernier ressort* to retain it for himself.

The mockery in Lyndhurst's voice increased as he invited his fellow peers

> to contemplate the possibility of a Lord Chancellor, with the commanding eloquence and transcendent abilities of my noble and learned friend, yet not possessed of his moderation and disinterestedness, — on the contrary, anxious to devote the whole of his energies to the purposes of personal aggrandizement, and indisposed to those institutions which may appear to him calculated to check his career. Such a person, conscious of the fleeting nature of popular applause, might wish to establish his power on some substantial foundation, and might find it convenient to surround himself with a band of gladiators arrayed as judges, ready to obey his commands and to deal destruction among his adversaries.[10]

Lord Holland thought Lyndhurst "spoke with great perspicuity and eloquence," adding that the Chief Baron had tried "to conceal, under a calm and suppressed manner, much real bitterness and personal malignity to Brougham."[11] Lyndhurst seemed to enjoy taunting his adversary. Greville found him after his speech, "drinking tea, not a bit tired, elated, chuckling: 'Well, how long will the Chancellor speak, do you think, eh? We shall have some good fun from him. What lies he will tell, and how he will misrepresent everything! Come, let's have done with our tea, that we mayn't miss him, eh?'"[12] On its third reading, Brougham's cherished Local Courts Bill was felled by only five votes. A dozen years would pass before the main provision of the measure, the establishment of county courts, would be realized. In later years, Brougham noted in his memoirs that "to Lyndhurst's mischievous opposition we owed the loss of my Local Courts Bill."[13]

Politics is always hungry for rumors, and Lord Holland recorded "a strange rumour" in his diary shortly after this episode. The speculation was that "Lord Lyndhurst . . . is invited to take the lead of the Conservative party and destined by them to become in case of a change, not Chancellor, but Premier!" Holland added that the idea was so absurd that he would not have recorded it "if some ambiguous phrases that dropped from Lady Lyndhurst did not so far corroborate the suspicion as to shew that preference of a political to a judicial station had trotted through her head very recently."[14] Absurd or not, the report signaled the continuing fact that Lord Lyndhurst was in the political arena and that if he did not stand at the center of it, he stood very close to that center. He was more than a judicial figure — a fact that had been confirmed numerous times. Lyndhurst was a major political actor who possessed remarkable staying power. Whatever motives his supporters or critics might ascribe to him, he would not go away. He had to be reckoned with.

Autumn found thoughts of Paris and its gaiety trotting through Lady Lyndhurst's head. She took up residence in the French capital while the Chief Baron remained at his judicial post. Dolly was a prominent participant in the social regimen that centered around the British Embassy, where Earl and Countess Granville presided. While in Paris, Dolly hosted the children of her husband's sister, Elizabeth Greene. Martha Babcock Amory and John Singleton Copley Greene were visiting from the United States. During the New Year holiday recess from the bench, Lord Lyndhurst joined the group in Paris. He introduced the American visitors to the gastronomic treat of French frog legs and gave his young niece a gift of a white satin frock.

These details were recalled many years later by Martha Amory, who wrote of Lady Lyndhurst: "I thought I had never seen any one half so handsome, and certainly no one more kindly." Her initial impression of Lord Lyndhurst as "older and graver" than she had expected was relieved by his sense of merriment, and he "asked questions about Boston as if he had trod its streets but yesterday."[15] The holiday ended when Lyndhurst had to return to England to resume his judicial duties. Lady Lyndhurst planned to accompany him to London. They set out together, but when they reached Beauvais, Dolly became ill. She returned to Paris with her daughter while her husband continued his journey.

Lady Lyndhurst died suddenly on January 15, 1834, following a miscarriage. A month earlier Harriet Countess Granville, the British Ambassador's wife, had written of Lady Lyndhurst's arrival in Paris and noted her unhappy state: "Dolly arrived, looking sulky, ill and affronted, not with any one in particular, but with public opinion and private feeling." The Countess added that the attention paid to her "does not seem to unruffle Dolly's plumes."[16] Dolly's death sent a shudder through the English community in Paris. Countess Granville reacted to the news: "It has caused great horror, she was at a ball here, well and brilliant, on the Friday before last, and the violence against her makes it more felt."[17] That image of Dolly, "radiant and covered with diamonds" at the Embassy ball, now gave to many "one of those dark, awful impressions that such calamities bring with them."[18]

The shocking news, which took two days to reach Lord Lyndhurst, found him as he was presiding on the bench of the Court of Exchequer. He set out immediately for Paris. Sir Theodore Martin and Lord Campbell, Lyndhurst's opposing biographers, both described his reaction to this unexpected event. Martin declared that "the shock of the death of this beautiful woman, in the flower of her womanhood, — she was only thirty-nine — was very great, and it was long before he gained his usual buoyancy of mind."[19] Campbell recounted the episode in a less sympathetic vein: "He was sitting as Chief Baron in the Court of Exchequer when he received the fatal news. He swallowed a large quantity of laudanum, and set off to see her remains. But his strength of mind soon again fitted him for the duties and pleasures of life."[20] In a footnote, Martin replied to this reference to Lyndhurst's use of laudanum. He pointed out that "had Lord Campbell really known anything of Lord Lyndhurst as a friend, he would have known that he never travelled at night without taking a small phial of laudanum with him mixed with water, to make him sleep. Out of this fact Lord Campbell's fiction was manufactured."[21]

A melancholy scene awaited Lyndhurst in Paris. He had come not only to take his late consort's body back to England but also to claim his motherless daughter, who was inconsolable. Countess Granville wrote that the "poor little girl" was "in a state of misery. We immediately sent my maid with the carriage to bring her here, but Mr. Greene, the nephew, said it was impossible to persuade her to leave the house."[22]

Many observers had regarded the Lyndhursts' marriage as one of convenience, resembling a political partnership more than a loving union. Lord Lyndhurst's reaction to his wife's death was commented upon by several individuals. One week after she received the news, his sister, Mary, declared, "My poor brother is heart-broken."[23] After more than four months had passed, the loyal sister assured their sister in the United States that "his spirits are as good as I can expect, but he feels his loss severely. It is fortunate that his business engrosses so much of his time."[24] Both Earl and Countess Granville received notes of thanks from the widower for all they had done. She observed that "they would have been deeply affecting from any body else, from him they were proper, and I have no doubt he felt much shocked by the rapidity of the last events."[25]

A month later the Countess wrote on the same subject to Lady Carlisle: "I think Lord Lyndhurst behaved most properly. He seemed to feel the shock very strongly, and gratitude to those who had been kind to her. George Anson told me yesterday that though one knew the sort of relation they must have been upon, yet his manner when with her was that of kindness and even fondness."[26] Lady Holland received a letter from Lyndhurst "brimful of feeling about her."[27] Whatever his true sentiments, the unexpected death of his vivacious and beautiful wife was no doubt a shock to Lyndhurst. "Kindness and even fondness" might appear to some to encompass the totality of their relationship. However, a strong bond had united the two in a shared destiny. Greville had pinpointed their relationship as a partnership for political ends. Whatever else it might be, it was truly a joint striving to propel Lyndhurst along the corridors of power.

Although Lyndhurst continued to accord his wife the same respect in death that he had granted to her in life, some found her death an occasion for censure. William Holmes, a Conservative party agent, wrote to the Duke of Wellington without a trace of compassion. He stated that "no person who takes an interest in Lord Lyndhurst's fame or good character can regret the event though we may lament the suddenness of the occurrence."[28] Even kind words from a more loyal quarter were not untinged with censure. Mary Copley extolled her late sister-in-law as "not only a fond mother but a very sensible, clever woman, and extremely well qualified to direct the education of her daughters." Following this praise Mary added a subtle criticism: "Perhaps she had too high an opinion of the attractions of the world, but that can hardly be wondered at in a person in her situation." Finally, she added a gloomy observation: "I have had a lesson which I shall not easily forget. Only ten days from the splendor of a court and the bloom of health to the grave!"[29]

Much of the reaction to Lady Lyndhurst's death emphasized its suddenness. In later years there was some discrepancy in explanations of the cause of her demise. Martin stated that she was "seized with congestion of the lungs, and died not many days afterward."[30] Her niece, Martha Babcock Amory, attributed her aunt's death to heart disease.[31] Both of these explanations were recorded nearly fifty years after the event. Contemporaries of

Lady Lyndhurst knew precisely what had ended her life, and it was not an unusual cause of death in that era. Countess Granville wrote of Dolly, "After ten days of illness she died at five o'clock yesterday. Premature labor, Lord Lyndhurst absent."[32] Wellington received the news that "Lord Lyndhurst was called out of court . . . in consequence of the death of his wife in child bed."[33] On January 18 the *Times* announced "the melancholy intelligence," adding that "Her Ladyship, we believe, died in consequence of a severe attack of illness, immediately following a miscarriage."[34] One previous miscarriage had been recorded when Lord and Lady Lyndhurst had been visiting Wellington at Walmer Castle in August 1829.[35]

The curious could read not only the details of Dolly's death but also those of Lord Lyndhurst's current difficulties. On Friday, January 24, the *Times* brought its readers up to date: "The remains of the late Lady Lyndhurst are expected in town from Paris for interment on Tuesday next, and his Lordship, with such relatives as were staying with her Ladyship at the period of her decease, on Sunday. His Lordship suffered severely from the boisterous state of the weather in his passage across the Channel, which, added to the shock occasioned by his late bereavement, we are sorry to say, has much affected his health."[36]

The funeral was held on Tuesday, February 4, and a distinguished company, led by Lord Lyndhurst and his three daughters, took Sarah Baroness Lyndhurst to her rest. The hearse was followed by two mourning coaches. The rest of the somber procession consisted of the private carriages of Lord Chancellor Brougham, the Earl of Carlisle, Lord Holland, Chief Justice Tinsdale, the Master of the Rolls, Baron Vaughan, Baron Gurney, Judge Anderson, and "other distinguished personages." The coffin, the *Times* assured its readers, "was a very splendid one." At her last opportunity to dazzle her contemporaries, Dolly exited in a coffin "covered with crimson velvet, studded with gilt nails, and having the family armorial escutcheons in silver gilt frames. The inscription plate, which was silver gilt, had the following inscription: — 'Sarah Garay, Baroness Lyndhurst, aged 38 years, died 15th of January, 1834.'"[37] Dolly's remains were deposited in the family vault at St. John's Church in Paddington.

Atlay wrote in praise of Dolly's role: "Lady Lyndhurst had been, in the fullest sense, a helpmeet to her husband; no small part of his political and social success was due to her, and his warm and affectionate disposition felt the bereavement most keenly."[38] This judgment was not shared by many who regarded Dolly as a tireless wire-puller, using secret and unethical influence to work her will. Hers was an elevated destiny but one tinged by an unsettling desperation to get on in the world. Lady Holland pronounced this epitaph: "Poor Lady L., a melancholy finale indeed! It was always my apprehension that she was a condemned person, how I could not say; but her temper and character denoted a fatal catastrophe, as she was always a wretched woman in her most brilliant days."[39]

Dolly's death left a void in Lyndhurst's life — for the time being. He stayed away from the House of Lords and its deliberations for many months. Then a turn in events lifted him to political heights once more. Initially, his role was a passive one. All he had to do was play a waiting game as the Whig ministry, triumphant as the instrument of reform, fell apart. The Whigs' problems were related to the Irish Church. The Cabinet was divided over demands that Church revenues be diverted for secular purposes. When Lord Russell declared in favor of the secularization of Church property, his announcement was followed by a resolution from Henry Ward, Member for St. Albans, calling for the redistribution of Irish Church income. Fearing a loss of Radical support in the House of Commons, the government shrank from rejecting such a proposal outright and opted for the temporizing alternative of creating a commission of inquiry. Even this concession was too much for Lord Stanley, a Whig who had entered Grey's administration as Chief Secretary for Ireland and transferred to the Colonial Office. He resigned from the Cabinet, and three of his associates followed him: Sir James Graham, the Duke of Richmond, and the Earl of Ripon (formerly Viscount Goderich). Graham was a Whig; Richmond and Ripon were not. Stanley never returned to the Whig fold, eventually moving to the Conservative party.

The need to renew the Irish Coercion Act was a second occasion for discord within Grey's ministry. Wellesley, the Irish Lord Lieutenant, had several reservations about some of the clauses in the measure. Daniel O'Connell obtained this information in confidence. Wellesley had the mistaken impression that his dissent would be welcomed. However, when the Cabinet rejected Wellesley's dissent, O'Connell exposed the entire matter in the House of Commons. An uproar over the publication of the relevant correspondence followed and led to the resignation on July 7 of Lord Althorp, the Chancellor of the Exchequer. Earl Grey decided to submit his resignation the following day. This episode had been set in motion behind Grey's back. Therefore, worn and disillusioned by the conflict within his ministry, Grey of the Reform Bill threw up his hands and quit the struggle. The King sent for Lord Melbourne and asked him to attempt to construct a coalition government that would include Wellington, Sir

Robert Peel, and Stanley. Peel wrote a full account of these negotiations to Lyndhurst, who was riding the circuit. Peel did not write to the Chief Baron at the outset of the talks, but he took pains to explain his silence: "Had I thought there could be any doubt as to the course to be pursued, or that there could be the slightest reason for pressing your return to London, I should without scruple have written to you at once."[40]

The projected union was doomed from the outset. It could only have been the brainchild of a monarch who had overlooked the brutal realities separating political forces within his realm. Melbourne had rejected the proposal out of hand, citing the opposition party's stand on both the Irish tithe bill and the Irish Church Commission. The King, however, was persistent. He directed Melbourne to communicate to the Duke, Peel, and Stanley copies of his rejection of the proposal for a united ministry. Peel and Wellington felt it was unnecessary to reply with a detailed explanation of their position and returned only a perfunctory rejection. But the King pressed his former Ministers to reconsider. Peel received another letter from Melbourne informing him of the King's wish that he submit a written reply expressing his thoughts on the proposal.

Peel explained in his letter to Lyndhurst that he had pointed out to King William the real reason for the breakup of Grey's ministry. It had collapsed not as a result of hostile majorities opposed to its measures but as a consequence of dissension among its own members. If individuals who shared principles on public questions could not compromise their differences, how could those who disagreed about the same general principles be expected to unite with honor or advantage to the King's service? This was a question the King could not answer. If the Whigs were disunited among themselves, how could union with the Conservatives rescue the situation? Melbourne had been cold to the idea from the beginning. Peel underscored the fact that it was Melbourne and not he who had refused to advance the King's plan for a coalition. Peel advised Lyndhurst that he had added these words to his memorandum:

> Lord Melbourne justly observes that measures still under discussion or open to review, which he considers vital and essential measures, have lately encountered opposition from those with whom Your Majesty has desired Lord Melbourne to communicate, — and I must therefore express my entire concurrence in the opinion which Lord Melbourne has already expressed to Your Majesty, that there can be no successful result of negotiations, in which, according to his own expression, Lord Mel-

bourne would have everything to demand and nothing to concede.[41]

The Irish Church was the foremost barrier to this royal proposal for political unification. The King had begun his initiative on July 9. Within days he had admitted to Peel that he thought the objections to union were insurmountable. On July 15 Peel informed Lyndhurst of the outcome of the King's statesmanship: "His practical conclusion was, to put the formation of the Government into the hands of Lord Melbourne."[42]

When Melbourne took office as Prime Minister on July 16, he embarked upon an exercise in futility. Lord Althorp returned to the Cabinet, and his leadership on the front bench in the Commons was deemed essential to combining the fractious segments of the Whig party. However, the prospect of his abandoning this post increased as his father's grip on life lessened. With the death of Earl Spencer, Lord Althorp was elevated to the House of Lords, and the ministry found itself bereft of his service in the Commons. Earl Spencer died on November 10, 1834, causing Melbourne to write immediately to the King. His brief message was blunt: "He apprehends the most serious difficulty and embarrassment will be the consequence of this event."[43]

In a second missive the following day, Melbourne informed the King that when the ministry had been formed the previous July, "Visct Althorp informed Visct Melbourne that when the event which has now taken place should arrive, he would take that opportunity of withdrawing from office altogether." The harried Prime Minister added his "hope that a sense of duty and the evident difficulties of the country would be sufficient to overcome this determination." He was not, however, confident of the outcome.[44]

On November 12 Melbourne underscored for the King the precariousness of the situation:

> Yr. My. will recollect that the Govt. in its present form was mainly founded upon the personal weight and influence possessed by Earl Spencer in the H. of Commons, and upon the arrangement wh. placed in his hands the conduct of the business of Govt. in that assembly. That foundation is now withdrawn by the elevation of that nobleman to the H. of Peers and in these new and altered circumstances it is for yr. My. to consider whether it is yr. pleasure to authorize Visct. Melbourne to attempt to make such fresh arrangements as may enable yr. Maj-

esty's present servants to continue to conduct the affairs of the country, or whether yr. Majesty deems it advisable to adopt any other course.⁴⁵

Melbourne had opened the door for his government's departure. The King, although not noted for his sharpness, did not miss the crucial point that Althorp had been the underpinning for the ministry and that now that foundation had been removed. In his reply William declared that "he cannot help feeling also that the Govt exists by the support of that Branch (the House of Commons) only of the Legislature, and therefore that the loss of Visct Althorp's services in that House must be viewed also with reference to that contingency."⁴⁶

On November 14 the King and his First Minister met at Brighton, the royal residence by the sea. Their exchange was the final denouement of Melbourne's government. The Premier informed the King that both Lord Lansdowne and Thomas Spring-Rice had indicated their intentions of retiring from the Cabinet, which was divided over the Irish Church issue. Norman Gash has explained the King's position:

> William's mind was made up. What alarmed him above all was the attitude of the government towards Irish Church reform, further plans for which had been indiscreetly communicated to him by Duncannon. Melbourne's only important proposal — the appointment of Russell as leader of the House of Commons in place of Althorp — seemed proof that his ministers were now firmly committed to the extreme policy which had provoked the resignation of the Stanleyites in the summer.⁴⁷

The King, like the Stanleyites, found intolerable an "extreme policy" that required the secularization of property dedicated to the support of religion. In his own memorandum of his interview with Melbourne, the King noted that he "could not look with confidence or security to the services of a leader of the H. of Commons on the Govt side who was so pledged and he could not help considering Ld. John Russell to be otherwise unequal to the task."⁴⁸

William IV dismissed his Ministers and immediately summoned the Duke of Wellington to Brighton. The King invited the Duke to form a ministry — a mission the practical soldier thought attended with difficulties in view of the large majority that supported the government in the House of Commons. The King, however, had single-handedly toppled the ministry — the last occasion when a British sovereign would do so. Presented with this accomplished state of affairs, Wellington insisted that Peel must head the new Cabinet.

Sir Robert Peel was vacationing in Italy for the winter, and until he could return, the Duke agreed to serve as caretaker. He would act as Peel's proxy, assuming the posts of First Lord of the Treasury and Secretary of State for the Home Department. He took custody of the seals of other secretaryships as well, but the Great Seal was for Lyndhurst — he was to be Lord Chancellor once again. Lady Cowper summed up the situation: "the Duke is a proud conqueror, having as sole colleague Lyndhurst, and giving orders to everyone."[49] A messenger was dispatched to Italy in search of Peel.

Meanwhile, Greville told Lyndhurst that he hoped there would be "no foolish declarations fulminated against Reform . . . and that the old principle of hostility to all reforms must be abandoned." Lyndhurst's reply was a sample of his outlook at this juncture. He believed Peel would "be *flexible*, that if such declarations were made, and such principles announced, they must be upset." He added, however, that the high Tories would be difficult to manage and that they would be up in arms if there were "not a sufficient infusion of their party."[50]

Lyndhurst and Greville agreed that "all the evils of the last four years — the breaking up of their Government, and the Reform Bill that was the consequence of that catastrophe — were attributable to the High Tories." Having assigned blame, Lyndhurst expressed his conviction that these reactionaries must adapt to the new day that had enveloped them all. They must learn to survive, even if they had to sacrifice their own values to do so. Lyndhurst's verdict was starkly pragmatic:

> They can hardly play the same game over again; they must support this Government, even though it shall not act upon the high-flying principles which they so fondly and obstinately cherish. Their salvation and that of all the institutions to which they cling require that they should support the Duke and Peel in carrying on the Government upon those principles on which, from the circumstances of the times and the events which have occurred, an Administration *must* act in order to have a shadow of a chance of being tolerated by the House of Commons and the country.[51]

Here we have the politics of flexibility and of the Tamworth Manifesto, of which this commitment was a harbinger. Lyndhurst was in step with

Peel on this ground, and he could plot a flexible statesmanlike course for both himself and the ultra-Tories with detachment. In a spirit of detachment, too, Lord Lyndhurst always seemed to know who his friends should be, and he knew, therefore, when it was time to convert a foe into an ally. Before Peel reached England, Lyndhurst had, with the help of Greville, made an overture to Thomas Barnes — the editor of the *Times* — whose support he valued for the new government. Greville was acquainted with Barnes and had suggested to Lyndhurst that the new government should attempt to obtain the newspaper's backing. In 1832 Lyndhurst had denounced the journal for insulting the monarchy, and he had censured the press in general for capitalizing on popular unrest and fanning the brushfire of democracy. Now Barnes had been alienated from Brougham and was disposed to wish Peel's new ministry well.

The editor declared the terms on which he would support Peel's efforts: "No mutilation of the Reform Bill, and the adoption of those measures of reform which had been already sanctioned by votes of the House of Commons last session with regard to Church and corporations, and no change in our foreign policy." Greville passed these terms in written form on to Lyndhurst. Charles Greville continued to play the go-between, carrying the Chancellor's written reply to Barnes, who was satisfied and pleased by Lyndhurst's offer to meet with him. Next, Lyndhurst extended the hospitality of his home to the previous target of his scorn. Greville wrote that "Barnes is to dine with Lord Lyndhurst, and a gastronomic ratification will wind up the treaty between these high contracting parties."[52] A symbolic breaking of bread occurred on December 1.

Brougham surrendered the Great Seal to the King on November 22, and that same day it was delivered into the hands of Lord Lyndhurst. Peel returned from Italy on December 9 to assume his place at the helm. A month later Lyndhurst voiced his reservations about his chief when he talked to Greville about the state of affairs. It was becoming clear that the new government would have difficulty surviving. Referring to Peel, the Chancellor put these questions to Greville: "Is he enough of a man of the world? Does he know enough of what is going on in the world?" The two agreed that the new Prime Minister had missed an opportunity to put distance between himself and the old elements in his party. The support of the Tories alone could not sustain the ministry, and they should have been made to understand that their interests depended upon keeping many of them out of the Cabinet.

Lyndhurst seemed to have contemplated some sort of Whig-Tory coalition. He had been comfortable among Whig allies, accepting patronage from a Whig ministry and the frequent hospitality of the Whig citadel, Holland House. Peel emerged as the straight party man on this occasion. The Chancellor confessed that he had not been consulted much and that if he had been, the formation of the government would have proceeded very differently. He would have opted for a small Cabinet, eight or ten at most. He stressed that these would have been new men and that he would have "left out Aberdeen, Goulburn, Herries, and the rest of that description, employing them if possible abroad, or if not, telling them that it was necessary to lay them on the shelf for a time and that he would do what he could for them at a future period." Lyndhurst had pressed Peel to take in Viscount Sandon, a supporter of the Reform Bill, and Lord Carnarvon, but the Premier had demurred and declared that the latter was too young and might be passed over for the present. Lyndhurst, in frustration, had protested, "Why it is the present for which it is necessary to provide, and it is *now* that he might have been made available." Ellenborough displayed some of the same outlook when he declined Peel's invitation to come into the government, citing his belief that he was not popular. Peel declared that Ellenborough's willingness to sacrifice himself made it all the more necessary to include him and insisted that he be brought into the ministry. Lyndhurst spoke to Greville of the moderate men he would have taken in had he been the Cabinet maker. He concluded that "a great mistake had been committed, and that, as it was irreparable, so it would very probably be fatal."[53]

The Cabinet, as Lyndhurst had objected, consisted of a great number of veterans from Wellington's government, including himself. This extensive inclusion of survivors of the Duke's era was not a good omen. When Peel was selecting his Cabinet, he had attempted to persuade Stanley to join the government. Stanley refused, not because he objected to Peel but because he wanted no association with Wellington, whose administration had allied with ultra-Tories. Stanley and his friends considered forming their own party, which might have played a balancing role between the government and its opposition in the House of Commons. Stanley's refusal to join Peel's ministry was a genuine setback, because it limited the new Prime Minister's sources of support.

Campbell observed: "Sir Robert Peel, on returning from Italy, although he acquiesced in Lyndhurst's appointment as Chancellor, reposed little confidence in him, and without consulting him wrote the 'Tamworth

Manifesto,' laying down the principles on which the new Government was to be conducted."⁵⁴ Martin responded to this belittling appraisal: "On Sir Robert Peel reaching London (9th December) he immediately put himself in communication with Lord Lyndhurst, on whose courage and loyal support he knew he could count under all circumstances. The difficulties which he saw ahead made such a colleague of especial value both in council and in action. They acted in concert in all their deliberations."⁵⁵

Lyndhurst was piqued over having been shut out of the decisions that forged a Cabinet. However, his spirits should have been raised by the publication of the Tamworth Manifesto, which stated for the country the principles of the new administration. The document, which had been drafted at a Cabinet meeting at Lyndhurst's home on December 17, was published in the London papers the next day. Barnes, in the wake of his meeting with Lyndhurst, had proposed such a public statement, and the idea took fire with Peel. Upon assuming the Premiership, Peel was required to stand once more for his seat at Tamworth. The statement of purpose was an appropriate gesture as he faced his constituency. The Tamworth Manifesto struck the chord of moderation in policy that Lyndhurst had desired to see embodied in the composition of the Cabinet.

Who was right, Campbell or Martin, in assessing Lyndhurst's impact on Peel's ministry? The Chancellor had complained that he had little influence on the composition of the Cabinet and was unable to counter Peel's insistence on full representation for the old Tories whose support he felt he needed. On the other hand, Lyndhurst fortified Peel's inclination in policy. He endorsed Barnes's suggestion for a public statement of intent. Lyndhurst liked what Barnes was proposing, and he channeled the suggestion to Peel. But Lyndhurst had a mixed influence. Peel used the Tamworth Manifesto to offset the backward-glancing impression created by the composition of his Cabinet. Lyndhurst was more Tamworthian than Peel in the sense that he wanted the Tamworth spirit to be reflected in the administration's personnel. The different approaches of Peel and Lyndhurst on the uniformity of both policy and personnel highlight a common contradiction of politics. Yet both men shared the same goal: to gain acceptance of the Reform Bill.

In the Tamworth Manifesto, Peel publicly embraced the Reform Bill as "a final and irrevocable settlement of a great Constitutional question." If acceptance of that historic measure pledged his ministry to "a careful review of institutions, both civil and ecclesiastical" and to "the correction of proved abuses and the redress of real grievances," then, he declared,

"I can for myself and colleagues undertake to act in such a spirit."[56] Having broadcast these conciliatory words, Peel determined to dissolve Parliament on December 30, 1834, and assemble a new one on February 19, 1835.

The response to Peel's appeal to the nation was mixed. The election produced these results: the government won 290 seats, Radicals 150, Whigs and Stanleyites 218. Much depended on the goodwill of Stanley and the inclination of some Whigs to cross over. The opening salvo of the new Parliament was the election of a Speaker. By a vote of 316 to 306, James Abercromby, a Whig, was chosen over the government-backed candidate, Manners Sutton. A second defeat came when an amendment to the King's address was carried in the House of Commons by a majority of seven. The amendment expressed regret that the progress of reform had been interrupted and threatened by the dissolution of the previous Parliament. A similar amendment was offered by Melbourne in the House of Lords. This development brought Brougham to center stage, where he denounced as unconstitutional the King's dismissal of Melbourne and his Whig colleagues while they still retained the confidence of the Commons. He castigated Peel and his fellow Ministers for accepting office under these circumstances.

Lyndhurst had predicted that in the new Parliament, Brougham would be "the most troublesome fellow that ever existed, and do all the mischief he can."[57] The Chancellor felt the lash of Brougham's censure when the recent occupant of the Woolsack denounced Lyndhurst for changing his views on Catholic Emancipation solely to retain office. Lyndhurst's response was filled with passion. He first refuted Brougham's charge that he had reversed his stand on Catholic relief merely to keep his place.

> The noble and learned Lord has dared to say that I pursued the course I took for the purpose of retaining my possession of office. I deny peremptorily the statement of the noble and learned Lord. I say, if I may make use of the expression, he has uttered an untruth in so expressing himself. So far from that measure being brought forward and supported by us with a view to preserve our places, it must be well known that we hazarded our places by pursuing that course. What right, then, has the noble and learned Lord in his fluent, and, I may say, flippant manner, to attack me as he has dared to do?[58]

Finally, the Chancellor defended the manner in which Melbourne and his colleagues had been dismissed. He declared that he would have acted exactly as the King had done and that he considered himself, as one of the Ministers involved, responsible for what has transpired.[59]

The bombardment of Lyndhurst continued. On February 27 Joseph Hume rose to pose a question that he proceeded to answer himself: "What is Lord Lyndhurst? He is an apostate — a notorious apostate from the principles of his early youth. There are many Honourable Members in the House who can prove it. They remember the time when he was brought from America where he had been educated in republican principles, and where he had imbibed doctrines, which he afterwards openly professed, far more radical than any which I have ever avowed."[60] Lord Lyndhurst was three years old when his family brought him from the New World to the Old World. Just what degree of republican principles or doctrines he was able to "imbibe" at this tender age is unclear.

The Irish Church issue sealed the fate of Peel's ministry. In the Lichfield House Compact adopted on February 18, the day before Parliament convened, O'Connell pledged the support of his followers to the Whig interest in exchange for that party's endorsement of Irish reform. In keeping with this agreement, Lord John Russell moved that no tithe settlement for Ireland should be adopted unless the entire issue of the application of the surplus revenues of the Church of Ireland was considered. This proposal was carried by a vote of 322 to 289, with a majority of 33 against the government. On April 8 Peel resigned.

Thus, for the second time, Lyndhurst descended from the Woolsack. The pension of an ex-Chancellor had been increased from £4,000 to £5,000 annually. The Whigs would not rescue him a second time. But Lyndhurst was never one to look back or lament his fortunes. The year had been a tumultuous one. His partnership with Dolly had ended, and life went on. The uncertain twists and turns of the political wars had brought him the Chancellorship again, and, despite his brief possession of this office, he was back at the center of Conservative affairs. Finally, there was a development that added a new dimension to Lyndhurst's activities: in the summer of 1834, he had met and befriended Benjamin Disraeli.

17
Disraeli's Staunch Friend

During the summer of 1834, young Benjamin Disraeli was attempting to enter Parliament, social climbing, and exaggerating his progress at both of these endeavors. When he met Lord Lyndhurst, he bridged both spheres of his ambition. On July 11 he wrote to his sister, Sarah, of their first encounter: "Yesterday I met Lord Lyndhurst, whom I like very much."[1] The Chief Baron accepted Disraeli's invitation to sleep at Bradenham House, the young man's family home in High Wycombe, the next time he rode the Norfolk circuit. Within months of their first meeting, Disraeli proclaimed with only a little of his customary exaggeration: "The Lord Chancellor is my *staunch friend*, nor is there anyth[in]g for my service w[hi]ch he will not do."[2]

Lyndhurst was sixty-two and Disraeli was twenty-nine when they met. The thirty-three-year gap in their ages was no barrier to their recognition in each other of kindred spirits. The difference in their ages contributed to a mentor-pupil relationship. Lyndhurst became the teacher-patron, the role model for the aspiring younger man. He was the highest-ranking figure to befriend Disraeli up to that point. In a dedicatory preface to his collected works, published seven years after Lyndhurst's death, Disraeli extolled those qualities of his patron that their friendship enabled him to witness: "The world has recognized the political courage, the versatile ability, and the masculine eloquence of Lord Lyndhurst; but his intimates only were acquainted with the tenderness of his disposition, the sweetness of his temper, and the playfulness of his bright and airy spirit."[3] James Beresford Atlay underscored the similarity of their backgrounds: "one of them a Hebrew by descent, the other a North American colonial by birth, they both looked at English party traditions and conventions with a detachment that finds no parallel among their contemporaries. Lyndhurst felt by intuition the extraordinary qualities which lay hidden beneath the bizarre and dandified exterior of his young friend."[4] Cynical, outsiders, and a little beyond the pale, the two had a great deal in common. Not everyone shared Lyndhurst's favorable impression of Disraeli. Much was conveyed in Lady Salisbury's reaction upon first meeting him: "at times his way of speaking reminded me so much of Lord Lyndhurst, I could almost have thought him in the room. He is evidently very clever, but superlatively vulgar."[5]

When Lyndhurst first met Disraeli, the younger man was desperately in love with Lady Henrietta Sykes, a married woman, and it was she who brought the two together. Disraeli recorded his first meeting with Lyndhurst in his "Political Notebook," revealing that he "sat next to him at dinner at Henrietta's."[6] The two lovers united in developing a plan for her to charm the conservative politician in hopes of furthering Disraeli's political career. Her own words proclaimed her intentions: "Lord Lyndhurst arrived in town last night. I can make him do as I like so whatever arrangement you think best *tell me* and I will perform it. . . . Ld Lyndhurst is anxious you should be in Parlt. Seriously he is a most excellent being and I am sure I can make him [do] what I please."[7] Many people believed an unscrupulous Disraeli encouraged Henrietta to form an adulterous relationship with the former Chancellor to further his own ambitions.

In August 1834 Henrietta accepted Lyndhurst's invitation to visit him at St. Leonard's, a popular resort. The following autumn the young woman traveled with Lyndhurst in Europe, and he paid her expenses. His sister and daughters completed the party and served as the smoke screen of chaperons. Lyndhurst's reputation as a womanizer and his own comment on platonic attachments support the conclusion that Henrietta was his mistress. Lady Tankerville once asked Lyndhurst whether he believed in platonic friendships. "After, but not before," was the reply.[8]

Henrietta threw herself into her assignment enthusiastically and declared, "I like Lord L very much. He is good natured and I only wish he had the power to serve us but he is too unambitious and only thinks of driving away care. He has a magnificent house." An important man with a grand house, recently widowed, Lyndhurst was an ideal target for Henrietta's manipulation. She assured Disraeli, "He is a perfect fool where women are concerned."[9] Yet given Lyndhurst's reputation with women, it is doubtful that she could have held this particular fool, perfect or otherwise, at bay for long even if she had tried. Henrietta assured Disraeli that she had influence over his patron, whether she was urging Lyndhurst to raise a subscription for Disraeli at the Carlton Club or pressing him to write to Francis Bonham, the Conservative election agent, on his behalf. There had to be some basis for the attractive woman's influence over the older man, and many contemporaries were certain they knew what it was.

Lyndhurst, Disraeli, and Henrietta set tongues wagging when they visited Bradenham, Disraeli's father's home, in July 1835 and paid an encore visit the following September. Buckinghamshire society did not know what to make of this curious ménage à trois, but it was pleased to think the worst. Nobody knew for certain the true nature of this threesome. One thing was sure: the speculation, coupled with the blatant disregard for public opinion occasioned by the Bradenham visits, did Disraeli no good among many whose goodwill he needed. His friend Sir Philip Rose prepared a memorandum in 1882 that focused on the unconventional triangle. Rose was putting the late Prime Minister's papers in order when he discovered letters tied in bundles and marked "Henrietta." They shed light on an entanglement that had been rumored to that day:

> The positive assertion at the time that Lady Sykes was the mistress both of D. and also of Lord Lyndhurst was evidently true, but by which of the two she was introduced to the other there is no evidence to show. The allegation at the time was that D. had introduced her to Lord L. and made use of the influence she acquired over Lord L. to forward his own advancement. I can well remember the scandal in the county at this connexion and especially at the visit of Lady Sykes to Bradenham accompanied by Lord L. and the indignation aroused in the neighbourhood at D. having introduced his reputed mistress and her Paramour to his *Home* and made them the associates of his *Sister* as well as of his father and mother. It did him much harm at the time and to show how unfavourable impressions linger long afterwards I have had it thrown in my teeth by influential county people within very recent years that this was an act which would never be forgotten and which all D's subsequent career could never obliterate.[10]

There is no doubt about the nature of Henrietta's relationship with Disraeli: they were lovers. Henrietta's complaisant husband, Sir Francis Sykes, seemingly gave his blessing to the match while he found comfort with his own mistress, Clara Bolton. Whether Lyndhurst was Henrietta's "Paramour," as Rose described him, is, although not a certainty, at least a probability. This, at any rate, is what people concluded. Lady Emily Cowper wrote to Princess Lieven in 1834 that "the Chancellor is behaving in a ridiculous manner — there is an odious Lady Sykes living with him in his house, whom he brought back from Paris, a *demi-mondaine* rather after the style of his late wife, and with whom he is so infatuated that he has no brain left."[11] Lady Cowper had her facts wrong. Lyndhurst did not discover Henrietta in Paris; she never lived in his house; nor did his liaison with her consume his brain. In no way did it harm him politically or ruin his reputation. He had no unstained reputation to protect. Lyndhurst's raffish behavior was accepted as part of the total man, a reminder that he was a product of Regency England. Disraeli was the political outsider who should have weighed the damage to his reputation that scandalous behavior might create.

As this three-cornered relationship evolved, Disraeli continued to press his hope of entering Parliament. He was interested in those people or measures that might smooth his way to office. He displayed no attachment to principle, and he was very much like Lyndhurst in this respect. His hunger for office had led him to court the Whigs initially, and he had applied to Lord Durham, Earl Grey's son-in-law. Durham was cool to Disraeli's request for help, merely offering his good wishes should the young man stand for the House of Commons.[12]

When Lyndhurst and Disraeli began their friendship in the summer of 1834, the Conservatives were out of office, and the cynical Disraeli put little stock in the Chief Baron's ability to advance his political fortunes. By December the Conservatives had regained power, and Lyndhurst was Lord Chancellor once again. He received a letter from Disraeli on December 4 that misrepresented Durham's reaction to Disraeli's parliamentary ambitions. Lyndhurst was informed by his new friend that "Lord D. had offered me a seat in the expected Parlt. for the mere legal expenses, and, alarmed as I apprehended by some rumors which have reached him, entreats me in case I decline his proposal not to enter the house, but wait the result of the great experiment, as he is confident it will be all over in six months."[13]

When Lyndhurst received Disraeli's letter, Sir Robert Peel had not yet reached London from Italy. The Duke of Wellington and the Chancellor held lonely sway over political affairs. Lyndhurst loomed much larger than he would when the new Prime Minister took command. Disraeli struck while the iron was hot with this declaration: "I have only to observe that altho' I am myself far from sanguine as to your success, I wd. sooner lose with the Duke and yourself than win with Melbourne and Durham, but win *or* lose I must — I cannot afford to be neutral. How then, my dear Lord, am I to act?"[14]

Benjamin Disraeli, from a drawing by Count d'Orsay, 1834. Used by permission of the British Museum.

The gamble had its desired effect. Lyndhurst believed the story that Durham was prepared to secure for Disraeli a seat in Parliament. The Lord Chancellor told this to Charles Greville, a Whig, when he called on him on December 6. Lyndhurst added that Disraeli was a friend of the Conservative Marquess of Chandos, a champion of the agricultural interest and heir to the ultra-Tory tradition. Greville recorded this appraisal of Disraeli in his journal: "His political principles must, however, be in abeyance, for he [Lyndhurst] said that Durham was doing all he could to get him by the offer of a seat, and so forth, if, therefore, he is undecided and wavering between Chandos and Durham, he must be a mighty impartial personage." Greville summed up a reaction that others shared: "I don't think such a man will do, though just such as Lyndhurst would be connected with."[15]

When Lyndhurst's efforts to find a parliamentary district for his young protégé failed, Disraeli was forced to fall back on a contest in High Wycombe, his home base. He was not optimistic about his chances in a district where the voters had already rejected him twice. He also believed that Peel's government would not survive. Disraeli faced a choice: should he embrace the unpromising Conservatives or run again under a Radical label as he had in the past? He attempted to do both. He ran as a Radical with Conservative backing.

Lyndhurst attempted to pressure Lord Carrington, the local political magnate in High Wycombe, to place his influence behind Disraeli's candidacy. Carrington's son and heir, the Hon. Robert Smith, was the sitting member for Wycombe and a Whig. Also, Carrington did not have a favorable opinion of Disraeli, and he was thought to have encouraged the circulation of a letter, signed by John Runsey, discouraging the young man's candidacy. Runsey was a lawyer in High Wycombe and also a Whig. Lyndhurst brought the letter to Apsley House on December 10, when he and Disraeli attended a banquet there together. He showed it to Wellington, who became enraged when he read it and scathed Carrington: "The Lord C[hancello]r has this moment shown me the enclosed: we both think your conduct incomprehensible. This is an affair in which I am most interested, and I must come to a definite understand[in]g. The Ld C[hancello]r will have the honor of calling on yr L[ordshi]p tomorrow at 4 o'ck hereon, if convenient."[16]

When Lyndhurst assured Disraeli that Carrington would "swallow the leek," he was mistaken. Carrington would not be moved, and Disraeli had to take comfort in his faith that "it is imposs[ib]le for anyone to be warmer than the Duke or Lynd."[17] Wellington wrote a letter to Granville Somerset, chair of the Conservative election committee, urging that if Wycombe could not be secured for Disraeli, another place must be found for him, because "a man of his acquirement and reputation must not be thrown away."[18] Lyndhurst showed the Duke's letter to Disraeli before he sealed and sent it. Lyndhurst also secured £500 for his protégé from the central party war chest. Despite this backing, Disraeli was not sanguine about his chances in the electoral contest, but he declared his faith that "with such zealous friends all will yet go right."[19]

Disraeli was right in believing that he must rely upon "zealous friends" for his salvation, because the electors of High Wycombe rejected him for the third time on January 7, 1835. The final results for the two-member constituency were Robert Smith (Whig) 289, Charles Grey (Whig) 147, and Disraeli (Independent) 128. The contest convinced him that his stance as an independent Radical would never be the key to victory. His defeat stiffened his resolve to embrace the Conservative standard as his own. Lyndhurst would be his patron. Disraeli concluded that he must follow the only man of stature who was enthusiastic about an exotic and unorthodox genius.

By the time Peel's ministry fell in April 1835, Lyndhurst was employing Disraeli as an unofficial private secretary and a political aide-de-camp. Upon Peel's resignation, the possibility of a coalition between Whigs and Conservatives emerged. Caroline Norton, Melbourne's friend and confidante, acted as his representative in these negotiations.[20] Lyndhurst designated Disraeli as his agent. Disraeli had several conferences with Mrs. Norton, "prompted by L.[yndhurst], and paid her visits sometimes of two hours." She stipulated that Melbourne wanted the coalition to be arranged by Lord Lyndhurst and said he was prepared to "throw over Brougham as Chancellor for L." Disraeli emphasized the friendly feelings that existed between Melbourne and Lyndhurst, underscoring that "when all was over M. consulted L. through Mrs. Norton as to putting the Seals in commission" in an effort to dislodge Brougham.[21]

Big things seemed to be in the offing, but within days the dream of a joint effort vanished. Daniel O'Connell and his Irish followers threw their parliamentary support behind Melbourne's ministry in exchange for a less hostile policy toward Ireland. But Disraeli's reward for his efforts appeared to be blooming as well. The Conservatives invited him to be their candidate for Parliament in a by-election. The opportunity materialized when Henry Labouchere, representing Taunton, had to stand for reelection because Melbourne had appointed him Master of the Mint in his administration. Taunton became the next battleground in Disraeli's restless quest for electoral confirmation. The Taunton by-election was a significant turning point for Disraeli: for the first time he sailed forth with the official endorsement of the Conservative party.

Lord Lyndhurst assured the candidate that he had the backing of Francis Bonham, the energetic Conservative election agent. Lyndhurst sent an encouraging message: "I have received a note from Bonham. He and all our friends are most anxious of your success." In the same letter, Lyndhurst reaffirmed his own confidence in his protégé's merit, declaring, "I am sure you will include me in the number and I feel from what I know of you that if you were to be returned for Taunton it would not only give you an opportunity of gaining distinction but be of great importance to the Cause."[22] This endorsement reinforced Disraeli's own faith in his destiny. Lyndhurst arranged for the party headquarters to allocate £300 to Disraeli's campaign. The former Chancellor could offer encouragement and produce funding. However, he could not deliver the votes necessary to make Disraeli a member for Taunton. When the polling ended, the electors had divided 452 for Labouchere and 282 for Disraeli.

Despite this setback, there was much to occupy Disraeli. When Lyndhurst mounted an opposition to the Whig Municipal Corporations Bill in the House of Lords, he enlisted Disraeli's talents as a political writer. Lyndhurst's battles were now Disraeli's fights as well. The younger man wrote outrageous and anonymous articles for the *Morning Post* in support of Lyndhurst. William Monypenny, in his biography of Disraeli, pointed out that "the articles . . . are in the strain of reckless vituperation which was then the fashion even in responsible journals. . . . For argument there is a great deal of the doctrine that the House of Commons is no more representative of the people than is the House of Lords."[23] Disraeli noted his project in his diary: "Write the M.[orning] P.[ost] for L. — three leading articles a day for nearly a month."[24]

Writing "for L." — all was "for L." during these heady days when Disraeli followed the great man around. In early August 1835, Disraeli had a scare that underscored how fully he depended on his mentor for the fulfillment of his political hopes: "nursing brought our friend Ld L quite round, tho' on Saturday I thought him very ill indeed; and the physicians thought he was going to have a fever which frightened me out of my wits, as every thing now entirely depends upon him." As Lyndhurst's role grew, Disraeli proclaimed that "there is every probability of his being Prime Minister."[25]

In the autumn of 1835, Lord Lyndhurst encouraged Disraeli to write a defense of the House of Lords and its rejection of the Municipal Corporations Bill. The work was entitled *Vindication of the English Constitution in a Letter to a Noble and Learned Lord, by Disraeli the Younger*. The "noble and learned Lord" was, of course, Lyndhurst. There is a suggestion that the two men may have collaborated on the *Vindication* in the fact that Disraeli advised two different editors, John Murray and Richard Bentley, to whom he sent the work, to reply to him at "Lord Lyndhurst's, George St., Hanover Sqr."[26]

The *Vindication* argued that the House of Lords was as representative of the people as was the House of Commons, an interpretation Lyndhurst had advanced in the debate on the Reform Bill and again in his fight against reform of the municipal corporations. Disraeli trumpeted the Conservative party as more democratic than the Whig oligarchy. He stressed, too, that the Conservatives were the national party in contrast to the Whigs, who had reached out to extra-national elements to gain and hold power. He drew a parallel between the Parliamentarians, who had united with Scottish Presbyterians against Charles I, and the modern-day Whigs, who clung to power with the backing of Irish Papists and Scottish support. Lyndhurst thought the *Vindication* "admirable."[27]

Disraeli's "Letters of Runnymede" in the *Times*, published from late January through mid-May 1836, represented another of his efforts to create support for Lyndhurst. He exhorted the Lords to follow his mentor's lead and "be bold, be resolute, be still 'the pillars of the state.'"[28] The season was ripe for action, and the peers who read the *Times* were assured that "in spite of the machinations of the anti-English faction, never was your great assembly more elevated in the esteem and affection of your countrymen than at this perilous hour."[29] Disraeli, in supporting Lyndhurst's emphasis on the importance of the House of Lords, was opposing Peel, who downplayed that chamber's role in preference to the House of Commons where he led his party. As an attack on the Lichfield House Compact, "Runnymede" echoed the *Vindication*'s theme of the anti-English party, shoring up Whig rule in return for unpatriotic concessions. After the last of the epistles had appeared, Lyndhurst lamented that "the time is dull without 'Runnymede.'"[30]

Lord Lyndhurst's life, however, was never dull. In the summer of 1836, Daniel O'Connell threatened to reveal just how thrilling it had been. The Irish Radical publicly promised to reveal "with hideous details" the "private life" of Lord Lyndhurst. Disraeli prepared an answer for publication, reflecting the dictum that the best defense is a good attack. He denounced "the manner in which the ruffian speaks of one of the most amiable as well as the most able of our public men; and one not less beloved in domestic life for his active virtues, than he is dreaded by his political opponents for his public services and hated by the rebels whom he keeps in check by his firmness and sagacity."[31] In his original draft, Disraeli described O'Connell as "a creature outside the pale of civilisation" and alluded to "the polluted sanctuary of his domestic life."[32] When the reply appeared in the *Times* on August 29, it had been purged of most of its invective at the insistence of Thomas Barnes, the newspaper's editor. Disraeli informed his readers that "of all public men we believe that Lord Lyndhurst has the least reason to shrink from a 'history of his private life.'" He added, "But what an unredeemed and unredeemable scoundrel is this O'Connell, to make such a threat."[33]

Changes in Lyndhurst's domestic life continued following Dolly's death. His aged mother, Susannah Farnum Copley, died January 11, 1836, at age ninety-one. Disraeli attributed her death to "pure old age. . . . Her appeti[te] quite failed and she expired with[ou]t a struggle."[34] The old woman was buried in the crypt of St. John's Church, Paddington, beside Dolly, who had died just two years earlier. Lyndhurst's three daughters, Sarah, Susan, and Sophia, continued to be cared for by his unmarried sister, Mary. The house on George Street, the shelter of "our circle" — albeit a changing one — was always a refuge for Lyndhurst. From it he made numerous excursions into the fast-paced and cosmopolitan world that awaited a hale and hearty widower in his early sixties. Crowned with a wig of dark curls, the dashing widower would dally in Paris, where some thought his taste in women was none too discriminating. Disraeli commented on Lyndhurst's "susceptibility to the sex, which was notorious" and referred to "gleams of want of refinement from early associations, when the females were not ladies."[35]

Disraeli's association with Henrietta Sykes ended in 1836, when she took a new lover, the lusty and handsome Irish painter, David Maclise, while Lyndhurst enjoyed an extended holiday in Paris. Disraeli feared that in the wake of their soured love affair, Henrietta might attempt to turn Lord Lyndhurst against him. He took a decisive step by writing to Lyndhurst, laying before him his side of the blighted affair. Lyndhurst's reply put Disraeli's fears to rest. He wrote: "The affair with Ly S is merely temporary. She is warm tempered and *proud* (circumstances have made her so). Her heart is the kindest and best that ever animated the frame of woman."[36] Disraeli's sense of relief was great when he received this letter. Two days before Christmas, he wrote to his friend, Count D'Orsay, "I have received the most affectionate letter from L[d]. Lyndhurst. . . . All is right, nothing can be better as far as he is concerned, and I shd. think my letter of today to him will lay all doubts, if any remain as to her influence. She has written to him recently, he says a short note."[37]

When the former Chancellor returned after a long stay in Paris, Disraeli found him "gay and spirited as usual and full of his adventures of four months." The admiring protégé added, "He has seen every one of note and distinction of every party and class, literary and political, Carlist, Constitutional, Republican. He was greatly feted — and enjoyed himself much. But details must be left to conversation."[38] These details that could not be committed to paper may have included his association with a mysterious "Miss G." Lyndhurst had not yet met his future wife, Georgiana Goldsmith. The "Miss G" in question may have been either Giulia or Carlotta Grisi, two cousins whose beauty attracted the attentions of several prominent men.[39] Lyndhurst wrote to Disraeli of the speculation: "This affair of Miss G is ridiculous enough. . . . I have walked with her two or three times in the course of 3 months and given her a Bouquet or two. *Voilà tout!*" Then the old charmer added: "I have been married to 3 or 4 different women already — this is all gossip — but when it gets into print it is beastly."[40]

Disraeli passed this refutation on to his friends, saying that the story about "Miss G" was "not only humbug; it is a hoax." He assured those who might be interested that Lyndhurst "returns unfettered and unscathed."[41] This description applied to both men in regard to Henrietta Sykes, and it applied to their friendship as well. Both Lyndhurst and Disraeli emerged from that curious triangle with their deep regard for one another intact. Lady Blessington wisely perceived the importance of the link between the two men. She wrote to Disraeli on December 26, 1836: "I am glad you have written to Lord L and trust you will never permit anything to make a division between him and you as nothing could have a worse appearance before the public."[42]

In reply, Disraeli wrote of his mentor: "I feel interested in his career, more than in my own; for he is the most amiable of men."[43] This statement seems disingenuous, because it is impossible to believe that Benjamin Disraeli was capable of feeling more interested in anyone's career than in his own. However, his expression of this idea underscores the importance of Lyndhurst to young Disraeli and the enormous political stature of the former Chancellor within Conservative circles.

18
Breathing Life Into the Party

The year 1835 marked a turning point in Lord Lyndhurst's parliamentary career. Benjamin Disraeli chronicled an important new development: "It was in this Session that Lord L. first formed his great plan of stopping the movement. Fixed upon the English Mun[ici]p[al] Ref. Bill as the basis."[1] The Lords glumly anticipated their fate as the unreformed half of a reformed Parliament. Lyndhurst shared this initial pessimism and had equated the passage of the Reform Bill with the destruction of the House of Lords. However, one year later — before the end of the 1833 session — Lyndhurst and others had shaken off their sense of doom and had awakened to the realization that they had survived their great ordeal. Britain's House of Lords was delighted, reinvigorated, and almost giddy in grasping that it had successfully weathered a political hurricane. The House of Commons might have changed, but the Lords had escaped the severest threat: a large creation of peers.

Public opinion was not united against the Lords. Many in the Upper House believed they opposed a government whose mandate had spent itself in the passage of the Reform Bill. The Conservative Lords knew what they must do, and they set about their work. In July 1833, a year after reform's passage, Charles Greville found them "perfectly rabid, and reckless of consequences, regardless of the embarrassment they cause the King, and of the aggravation of a state of things they already think very bad; they care for nothing but the silly vain pleasure of beating the Government, every day affording fresh materials for the assaults that are made upon them by the press, and fresh cause for general odium and contempt."[2]

After Peel resigned, Lyndhurst was no longer Chancellor, nor could he resume his post as Chief Baron. He had a great deal of time to act on his conviction that it was the duty of an opposition to oppose, amend, alter, and crush, if need be. His fertile, mischievous, and detached cast of mind came into full play. Lyndhurst commented on the Duke of Wellington's attempts to amend the Whig proposals, expressing his own distaste for so secondary a role: "I shall attend no more, what's the use of it? The Duke comes down every day, and tries to make the Bills *better*; if I could make them *worse* I would come too."³

The political struggle was moving in a direction that would afford Lyndhurst the role he most desired. Wellington began to lose his grasp on the leadership of the Upper House. Greville perceived the Victor of Waterloo's increasing difficulties: "The Duke of Wellington has no power over them for good purposes and they will only follow him when he will lead them on to some rash and desperate enterprise."⁴ Lyndhurst did not equate an aggressive stand by the peers of England with "some rash and desperate enterprise." He had warned repeatedly during the debates on the Reform Bill that the passage of that revolutionary measure was but the first installment in a succession of reforms. The Whigs would press on to finish the work they had begun, and the development on which everything hinged was the destruction of a House of Lords that was the last bastion of Conservative power.

Greville caught the mood of the restless Lords and pulled away the veil of rhetoric when he declared in August 1834: "One thing is clear to me, that those Tories who are always bellowing 'revolution' and 'spoliation,' and who talk of the gradual subversion of every institution and the imminent peril in which all our establishments are placed, do not really believe one word of what they say, and instead of being oppressed with fear, they are buoyed up with courage."⁵ Lyndhurst recognized this spirit of defiance, and he prepared to marshal the forces eager to reassert the independence of the House of Lords. He signaled his comprehension of this new state of things when he offhandedly said to Greville in the early weeks of 1835, "Well, I think we are safe now; I have no fears . . . we are on a rock — adamant."⁶

Lyndhurst emerged as the best choice to lead the tattered Conservative forces. His hunger to be in the spotlight, to be at the center of events, meshed with the Tory need to follow a leader who could rally the party and at the same time strike fear in Whig hearts. In doing so, Lyndhurst performed an enormous service: he breathed a new spirit into the party, holding it in battle formation, ready to rebound and forge ahead when given an opening. He was keeping the party together.

The Municipal Corporations Bill, destined to be the battleground on which Lyndhurst would lead his Conservative legions, reached the House of Lords near the end of July 1835. The measure was the work of a royal commission that had been appointed to investigate the condition of the municipal corporations. Many local governments were under the control of closed corporations composed of self-elected men who oversaw the properties and income of their towns. Corporation members had exclusively possessed the right to elect Members of Parliament, a right that had been handed down through many generations and that was based on both usage and charter guarantees. The Reform Bill of 1832 ended this privilege in forty-three boroughs in which it existed but did not otherwise tamper with closed corporations. Now, three years later, the recommendation of the commission called for a thoroughgoing alteration in the formation and composition of local government. The proposed bill promised a revolution at the grassroots level. In 183 boroughs it transferred the election of the corporation from the freemen to the ratepaying householders who had been in residence for three years. A municipal council chosen by the ratepayers would in turn elect a mayor and an aldermen. The pecuniary rights of the freemen were preserved, but they lost their monopoly over the parliamentary franchise, and no additional freemen could be created. The freemen were deprived of their exclusive trading privileges as well.

As the bill was being debated in the Commons, Sir Robert Peel had attempted to amend the proposal so that it would not eliminate the existing rights of freemen. He had failed in this effort, but he refrained from opposing the measure, James Beresford Atlay suggested, "partly from disinclination and partly from having pledged himself, in the King's Speech, to deal with the question."[7] The bill sailed through the House of Commons without difficulty. However, it met with a hostile reception from the peers, and Lyndhurst came to the fore to voice Conservative hostility.

Lyndhurst believed the Corporations Bill was "nearly as important as the Reform Bill." In this he was correct, because municipal reform brought an expansion of the political power of the middle class. However, he was mistaken when he told Greville that the change would open the way for the Radicals to seize control of the new councils. He thought, too, that this turn of events would end the independent authority of the House of Lords, leaving only the Commons to exercise power. Lyndhurst perceived the legislation as a bold challenge to aristocratic power in the boroughs because it would supplant traditional authority with elected corporations answerable to the electorate. Faced with this bleak prospect, he pronounced the fate he believed awaited the House of Lords: he saw no chance that it would survive for ten years.[8]

Believing the Municipal Corporations Bill portended the doom of the Lords' constitutional role, Lyndhurst came out fighting with an aggressive oratorical bombardment. He began with an assault that was calculated to raise Whig bile, attacking the Whiggish composition of the commission whose findings had paved the way for this measure. Lyndhurst read the names of the commissioners, emphasizing their political allegiances and concluding that of the twenty members, all, with one exception, were "Whigs or something more."[9] He scorned the royal commission and the fruits of its efforts as nothing more than a ploy to advance the political fortunes of the Whig party. This blunt assault summoned the Whig partisans like a fire bell. Lyndhurst had enormous power to make his opponents wince, and the personal intensity of their counterattack was a measure of his towering strength as a Tory warhorse.

Lord Lansdowne established the pattern of the rebuttal. He responded to Lyndhurst's attack on the partisan nature of the commission by pointing out that "if the circumstance of an individual having been 'a Whig or something more' were to be a disqualification, it would reach to much higher and more eminent characters than those who have been the subject of the noble and learned Lord's insinuations."[10] This was a different point from the previous allegation that Lyndhurst had been a Whig. Lyndhurst replied that he had never intended to make a charge against the commissioners but, rather, against the government that had appointed them. Next he coupled a disavowal of the insinuation against him with a challenge: "I never belonged to any political party till I came into Parliament. I never belonged to any political society. I have been in Parliament sixteen years, and I wish the noble Marquess to point out any speech or act of mine which can justify my being described as a Whig, or something more than a Whig."[11]

No one could point to any speech or act that might prove that Lyndhurst was an apostate Radical. Neither were his adversaries going to abandon the vague, yet compelling charge that Lyndhurst's Tory credentials were flawed by Whig antecedents. Lansdowne had fired the first salvo on August 3. Ten days later Lord Melbourne himself took up the cudgel against the formidable foe who still merited a Prime Minister's personal attack, just as he had in the era of Earl Grey. Melbourne declared that Lyndhurst's "most private friends and companions" shared the opinion that he was at one time a Whig. Then the Premier goaded his adversary by asking for a denial. Before Lyndhurst could answer, Melbourne rushed to add: "No; on the contrary, he admits it." Lyndhurst countered with a passionate reply: "I never — ("Order!") I am perfectly in order. The noble Lord says I admit it. My Lords, I never did admit it. I do not admit it, nor is there the slightest foundation for the statement. I heard of the attack and I repelled it, and it never was renewed til lately. It is a base calumny, and I give it the most unqualified contradiction."[12]

Yet it was a calumny that would not cease. Two weeks later Lord Denman took up the same line of attack. Once before Denman had contradicted Lyndhurst's denial that he was a political apostate. During the course of the Reform Bill debate, when the then Chief Baron had refuted Grey's avowal that Lyndhurst had early in his life endorsed parliamentary reform, Denman was reported by the highly partisan and hostile Lord Campbell to have declared "Villain! lying villain!"[13] Denman had not been present to hear Lyndhurst's angry rejoinder to Melbourne's personal charges against him. Now he, too, adopted the refrain that Lyndhurst had entertained "extreme opinions." He added that such was "the perfect conviction of all who knew him."[14] The Whig forces were resolved to press their accusation and ensnare the Conservative champion on a charge that destroyed his credibility. But Lyndhurst persisted in his aggressive disclaimer. He challenged his accusor to "adduce a single fact in support of his charge." Failing this, he could not respond in specific terms to unspecific charges. In exasperation the former Lord Chancellor concluded that against him who "throws his arrows in the dark, I know not what to combat."[15] The Whigs had entrusted Denman with a mission: to nail down the often repeated charge that Lyndhurst had once possessed liberal opinions. However, Lyndhurst had stood unshaken. He had faced down the charge. Denman was forced to back down, and Brougham apologized for him that same evening. No specific evidence was ever brought forward to substantiate these charges, nor has any evidence ever been discovered. However, the perennial allegation of political apostasy was too useful a cudgel for Lyndhurst's opponents to abandon.

When the Conservative peers gathered at Apsley House on August 3, they heard Lyndhurst prevail upon them to support Lord Carnarvon's amendment that evidence be heard against the bill. Although opposed by Wellington, the Lords followed Lyndhurst's lead, and that evening the debate in the House of Lords "was dashing in the extreme." To this description Disraeli added, "Ld Ls speech was by far the crack one. Most bold and triumphant and received with tumultuous cheering."[16] Lyndhurst attacked the bill as a "party object" calculated to destroy the Conservative party and strengthen the party that brought it in: "The measure was Whig — Whig in its principle, — Whig in its character, and Whig in its object."[17]

Lyndhurst's partisan efforts might inspire Disraeli, but they alarmed Charles Greville, who feared that "these Tory Lords will never rest till they have accomplished the destruction of the House of Lords.... They are resolved to bring about a collision with the House of Commons, and the majority in each House grows every day more rabid and more desperate." Greville questioned, too, Lyndhurst's role at the head of so aggressive a strategy. He confided to his journal that "I am at a loss to comprehend the views by which Lyndhurst, the ablest of the party, is actuated.... I would give much to see the recesses of his mind, and know what he really thinks of all these proceedings, and to what consequences he believes that they will lead."[18]

By Greville's account, the Lords found hearing evidence "the greatest bore" and so tiresome that in short order they were "sick to death of it." Both Brougham and Lyndhurst agreed that *it is all damned nonsense, and they will hear nothing more after Saturday next.*" The inveterate diarist concluded, "So this is the end of all this hubbub, and here are these two great comedians thundering against each other in the House of Lords overnight with all imaginable vehemence and solemnity, only to meet together the next morning and agree that *it is all damned nonsense.*"[19]

Lyndhurst was no comedian, however, and Greville could not see the recesses of his mind. The leader of the Tory Lords was too crafty to give himself over to an enterprise that was "all damned nonsense." On the surface Lyndhurst was attacking the Municipal Corporations Bill as a totally Whig measure and rallying the Conservative party. Beneath this assault he was mounting a challenge to Peel. Peel had said, "We will have a Municipal Corporations Reform Bill." Lyndhurst was saying, "No." An implicit conflict existed between Lyndhurst and Peel during these years, a conflict that was rooted in their different approaches to dealing with the Whigs. Lyndhurst was very skillful at the political game. Therefore, one must search for the political line underlying his rhetoric. He was announcing to Peel that he was prepared to use the House of Lords as a force to stop the Whig program. And should there be any compromise, Lyndhurst wanted to dictate that compromise from the House of Lords rather than allow Peel to dictate it from the House of Commons. At the same time, Lyndhurst was rallying the Conservative party to form its legions and battle anew. He was giving back to the Lords, so recently routed, their amour propre.

Norman Gash, when he wrote in his *Reaction and Reconstruction in English Politics 1832–1852* of "Lyndhurst's wrecking squads," rejected the importance of Lyndhurst's role at this time.[20] Yet the restraint of both Peel and Wellington might have been less effective had not Lyndhurst put some steel into the backs of the Lords. Dismissing what he labeled as "the rhodomontades of Lyndhurst," Gash assigned a negligible role to the former Chancellor, who nonetheless continued to loom as a strong political force on Peel's horizon.[21] Gash ignored the two-pronged policy of simultaneous restraint and aggression that carried the Conservative party through its years of crisis in the 1830s. Lyndhurst was an essential element in that successful approach.

The tedium of hearing evidence ended for the peers on August 9. That same day the Conservative Lords met at Apsley House to plan their next move. Some wanted to reject the bill in a decisive and scornful gesture. Lyndhurst, contemplating a more subtle method of destruction, recommended that the bill be amended until it bore no resemblance to its original Whig shape. This plan was adopted, and Lyndhurst entered the lists as his party's champion. Greville thought the Conservative solon had set himself upon a "desperate course" certain to "bring down all the wrath of the Commons on him and his Conservative majority." He concluded:

> At all events the Lords are playing a desperate game; if it succeed, they who direct the energies of the party are great and wise men; but what if it fail? They seem to have no answer to this but that if they
>
>> Screw their courage to the sticking place,
>> It will *not* fail.[2]

The House of Lords resolved itself into a committee on the Municipal Corporations Bill, and Lyndhurst moved a series of amendments that altered the Whig measure to the point at which it was unrecognizable. Moving his first amendment, he proposed that the rights of current and future freemen and burgesses should be maintained unimpaired, as though the act had not been passed. He argued that these rights, which encompassed common lands, public stock, and the rents and profits derived from them, made the issue one of the sanctity of property. This property belonged to the freemen absolutely, and they could transmit it to their children, their grandchildren, and all other descendants without limitation. The peers responded to this appeal by passing the amendment 130 to 37 — a majority of 93 against the government.[23]

Next Lyndhurst proposed a new qualification for the municipal franchise. Under the provisions of the proposed bill, any person paying even the smallest amount of tax would be eligible to become a member of a municipal council. To preclude this development, Lyndhurst advocated that the ratepayers should be divided into six classes and that the one-sixth who paid the highest rates should be those from whom the councillors would be selected.[24] Lyndhurst declared flatly that his object in proposing this amendment was "the preservation of property" — a goal certain to rally the support of Conservative peers.[25] This amendment was carried 120 to 39. Lord Russell confided to the Duke of Richmond that the Commons would never accept the bill with such an alteration. Richmond, who sided with the government on the measure, thought the "House of Lords was nearly done for" and that the Commons "would adopt some violent course, and then there would be a 'row royal'"[26] Greville speculated that the government had a strategy of its own and that it was "content to exhibit its paltry numbers in the House of Lords, in order that the world may see how essentially it is a Tory body, that it hardly fulfills the conditions of a great independent legislative assembly, but presents the appearance of a dominant party-faction." He also noted, "What astonishes me most in all this is that Lyndhurst, a man of great abilities . . . should urge these desperate courses."[27]

Greville might be astonished and the Whigs furious, but the Tory peers were reinvigorated and eager to follow their new leader for whom they had abandoned the Duke of Wellington. Lyndhurst had more in store for both his opponents and his followers. On August 17 he proposed that one-quarter of the town councils consist of aldermen elected for life. He argued that a check of this nature would merely parallel the check exercised by the House of Lords on the House of Commons, a point hardly likely to allay Whig resentment while, on the other hand, embodying the principle of aristocracy — a necessary element, he contended, to dampen the excesses of democracy.[28] The Lords carried the amendment providing for aldermen for life by a vote of 126 to 39.

Lyndhurst was not finished. He moved on August 25 that the same principle of life tenure should be extended to the town clerks, and this requirement was endorsed 104 to 36.[29] Lyndhurst immediately proposed another clause "to the effect that the power vested in Corporations with respect to Church property should be confined to members of the Established Church." The Bishop of London carried the burden of arguing for the amendment's adoption. While stating that the proportion of members of the Established Church to Dissenters was nine to one in England, a vast exaggeration, the Bishop pointed out that the Dissenters were concentrated in the towns and usually belonged to the very class from which the corporation members would be chosen. He added that the Dissenters behaved not only as a religious sect but also as a political body. He did not have to elaborate. The amendment was carried without a division.[30]

By Disraeli's account, Lyndhurst "literally had to draw every clause himself." He failed to get help from those quarters from which he sought it. After seeking the expertise of Henry Merewether, who had just published his *History of Boroughs and Municipal Corporations*, Lyndhurst put the results of Merewether's labors in the fireplace and called him an "intense fool." He had to research and compose each amendment while managing meetings and hearing the testimony of witnesses from midmorning until midnight. The experience "knocked him up," but he quickly regained his strength and was once again "full of force and spirit." Disraeli, inspired by his chief, concluded, "But for him, all wd. have been lost."[31] Disraeli's high praise for his mentor was balanced with censure for Peel. He believed Lyndhurst's strong opposition to municipal reform was "one of the greatest cards the Tories ever played, and has quite revived the House of Lords." He ridiculed Peel's declaration of support in the House of Commons for the Municipal Reform Bill in principle. With this statement Disraeli thought Peel had thrown the Tories' winning card away, and "but for the boldness of one man, nothing wd. have been done."[32]

Some saw evidence of a rift between the two Conservative leaders in their different responses to the government bill. Greville questioned how Lyndhurst could "fancy that any object is attainable which involves in it a breach or separation between Peel and the great body of the Tories."[33] Peel's cooperative approach stemmed from his view that the government's bill could have been much worse. He did not share the opposition of many Tory Lords to any form of local government reform and had pledged to introduce a measure of his own at the outset of his short ministry. Moreover, unsympathetic to any rejection that might present the Whigs with an excuse to resign, he was adamant about refusing to be lured into a repetition of his ineffective hundred days as Prime Minister. Norman Gash summed up events at this juncture: "While the Tory peers under Lyndhurst's flamboyant leadership tore the government's bill to ribbons, Peel stayed at Drayton."[34] Speculation that the Whigs might fall and that Peel would refuse to resume the reins of government fed reports that Lyndhurst would lead a new ministry. Disraeli, not always a reliable witness, exulted that "there is every probability of his being Prime Minister," adding that "his own disinclination alone stands in the way." Lyndhurst made his own predictions. He confided to Disraeli that "there are only three things certain, that the Tories will be in before we are many moons perhaps weeks older, that Parliamt. will be dissolved and that my (Disraeli's) seat is secured."[35]

Lyndhurst was wrong on all three counts. However, his hostility toward Peel was unmistakable. When Campbell reproached him for mutilating sections of the bill that Peel had endorsed, he answered, "Peel! What is Peel to me? Damn Peel!!!" Campbell qualified his account of this hostile retort by suggesting that "this however, might be only *badinage*, intimating that he would not be slavishly led by Peel, although he might still consider him head of the party."[36] Sir Theodore Martin responded to Campbell's report, taking pains to comment on the ex-Chancellor's relationship with the former Prime Minister. Martin stressed that "however Lyndhurst may have differed on particular questions from Peel, or thought him mistaken, as it is well known he did think him, in not having infused new blood, and a spirit more in consonance with the altered circumstances of the times, into his last Ministry, still he looked steadily to him, as entitled by experience and by his influence in the country, to be the leader of his party." Martin also denied that Lyndhurst had any ambition to lead the nation from 10 Downing Street. In a flat denial, the favorable biographer declared, "Moreover, under no circumstances whatever would he have agreed to become Premier either then or at any other time. His ambition was regulated by knowledge of what he could and what he could not do."[37]

This disavowal contradicted an assertion that appeared in the *Times* on the day of Lyndhurst's death. An obituary, which some believed was written by Disraeli, stated that King William IV, alarmed by Melbourne's uncertain grasp on the helm and baffled by Peel's "sulking at Drayton Manor," looked to Lyndhurst, the perennial refuge of monarchs in distress, "to take the reins if Peel refused." This account continued in a laudatory vein and noted that "the high courage and self-confidence of Lord Lyndhurst could only admit of one answer. He accepted His Majesty's expression of his desire as an injunction, and the terms on which he was to assume the Premiership were as formally arranged as such terms ever are." What followed in the *Times* article was the substance of Disraeli's "Memo of Session 1835."[38] This "Memo" cited a pledge of ten seats in the Commons that would be distributed among ten young men selected by Lyndhurst — apparently a means of introducing his trusted lieutenants into that assembly. Disraeli named himself as one of these men and mentioned two other individuals: Bickham Escott and Frederick Thesiger. In the memoir of Lyndhurst published at his death, the number had grown to twelve, but Disraeli was "the first on the list," followed by Escott and Thesiger. One additional detail was supplied that was lacking in Disraeli's original account: "At the suggestion of the King himself, Lord Lyndhurst was to have an earldom, and with the title of 'Earl Copley' was to have led the ranks of the reaction, and to have dictated the policy which the country was now evidently preparing to receive from a Conservative Ministry."[39] If Disraeli was not the author of the *Times* article, the affirmation of his "Memo" suggests he was the source for the information. Whatever Lyndhurst's ambitions, he had changed the Municipal Corporations Bill completely, and he had led an impressive exercise in flexing Tory muscle.

The question of how the government would respond was answered when Lord Russell announced that the Ministers were prepared to accept some of the Tory amendments while rejecting others, particularly those that assured life tenure for aldermen and town clerks. Peel, in turn, declared his support for some of the amendments, arguing for the right of the House of Lords to exercise an independent judgment. He withheld his endorsement from other amendments, particularly those that called for life tenure for aldermen and those that preserved the property rights of freemen.[40]

Peel declared his belief that the wish of the country was for the bill to pass into law. However, he repeated his demand that the House of Commons "uphold the perfect independence of the House of Lords with the same zeal as they would defend and protect their own privileges."[41] Disraeli described the quick resolution of the crisis: "Peel came up from Drayton and threw him [Lyndhurst] over, and a part of the Lords, led by Wharncliffe frightened at not being supported in the Commons seceded from their engagement at a meeting at Apsley House at the end of August or beginning of September."[42] On September 3 a large Conservative council assembled at Wellington's London home. Some participants, notably the Duke of Cumberland, desired to press the fight and not bend. Lord Harrowby argued that issues other than municipal reform might be better suited in the future as a basis for preserving the independence of the House of Lords. These remarks seemed to attract the support of many of those present. Lyndhurst, reading the tenor of the meeting, did what he was uniquely able to do: "He assumed a curiously detached attitude."[43] He had fought the contest, and the moment had arrived to move on. This behavior is indicative of Lyndhurst's philosophy of compromise. His tactic was to play a high-spirited game all along and in the end, when he had pressed his adversaries to the limit, to show a willingness to compromise. During these years he acted as though he believed his militancy was the key to squeezing reciprocal concessions from the government.

On the following day, September 4, Melbourne opened the discussion in the House of Lords, expressing his faith that the peers would "meet the spirit of accommodation and conciliation" shown by the House of Commons.[44] Lyndhurst followed him and opposed abandoning the amendment that preserved life tenure for a quarter of the aldermen. This provision had been traded for a six-year elected term, something he could not countenance. He accepted the other concessions, secure in his belief that he had fought unstintingly for property rights and had attained enough of his objectives so that now he could be reasonable and could compromise.

Using the same words Melbourne had used, Lyndhurst alluded to a "spirit of conciliation" and closed with a reference to the personal attacks that had been made on him both in and out of Parliament. He stressed that he had not volunteered to lead the opposition to the bill but that many of his colleagues had prevailed upon him to take up the fight. He noted, too, that he had been charged by his opposition with seeking to gratify some personal ambition. He answered this contention with strong words: "I deny it once and for ever; all my ambition has long since been satisfied. I have twice . . . passed that Chair (pointing to the Woolsack) — I have twice . . . had that splendid bauble (pointing to the mace behind the Speaker) before me. Whatever ambitious views I may have had in early life, have all been fulfilled. My ambition has been gratified. I have no wishes unfulfilled."[45] Lyndhurst was probably speaking truthfully — at least for the moment — for he did not cherish illusions, and although he might have always been attuned to the main chance, he was never one to fool himself. He was now sixty-three years old. He had tasted the honors of the world and had been no stranger to power. But there had always been a streak of indolence in Lyndhurst. Disraeli had thought he could have been Prime Minister if he had not lacked the ambition. Henrietta Sykes, too, had despaired at his lack of fervor in this regard.

People speculated about Lyndhurst's real motives because he had acquired the reputation of an arch-intriguer. Many, like Greville, wondered what went on in the secret recesses of his mind. Was he truly plotting to make himself Prime Minister? A. S. Turberville concluded in *The House of Lords in the Age of Reform*:

> There is no mystery about his inducements to action, and no good reason to doubt his sincerity upon this occasion when he

> declared that all his ambitions had long since been satisfied. The simple explanation is that Lyndhurst had an acute mind, a great love of, and capacity for, destructive criticism, and when invited to devise amendments in a Bill which he cordially disliked and to lead the Tory ranks against it he readily agreed, because he thoroughly enjoyed the experience.[46]

By this point in his career, Lyndhurst had probably put aside whatever ambition he might have had to be Prime Minister. He sought instead to be a continuing force that could not be ignored. If he had laid aside a drive to be the King's First Minister, he had not abandoned a greater and more abiding urge to be at the center of events and to participate in determining the direction of those events as they unfolded. This desire, so pervasive throughout his career, was not a dishonorable goal. However, it did not make him a statesman. Neither did it make him a villain.

No less a political adversary than Brougham paid homage to Lyndhurst for his "able and judicious speech."[47] Brougham had been dropped by Melbourne as his Chancellor. Feeling politically adrift, he had found comfort in Lyndhurst's friendship, which transcended political allegiance. Brougham, bearing a deep regard for his colleague that he maintained into old age, declared in his memoirs that Lyndhurst "was a most effective adversary in the Lords. His legal learning and reputation, his former official experience and character, his admirable power of clear condensed statement, far exceeding that of any man I ever knew; his firm courage, his handsome presence, his musical voice, his power of labour, *when he chose*, though generally hating work, — made him a most formidable antagonist."[48]

The Whigs agreed to accept the Lords' amendments, and the royal assent completed the legislative process. The long controversy surrounding passage of the bill had catapulted Lyndhurst to a preeminent place in the leadership of his party. Greville described this development in a censorious tone: "The manner in which the Duke has been ousted from the leadership, and the alacrity with which the Lords have followed Lyndhurst, because he led them into violent courses, is not the least curious part of this business."[49] Some explanation may have lain in the Duke's increasing deafness, which made participation in debate difficult. At the start of the 1835 session, he had told Lyndhurst that he wanted a "quiet life."[50] Added to this consideration was the fact that he had a fierce distaste for the ultra-Tories, who had helped to sack his ministry. At the same time, he had no liking for elected mayors and corporations. His association with Lyndhurst did not suffer because of his former Chancellor's enthusiastic dissection of the Municipal Reform Bill. Lyndhurst's methods may have alarmed Wellington, but he did not find their object of preserving the unelected corporations unpalatable.

In the session of 1836, Disraeli recorded that Lyndhurst "forms another and still more comprehensive plan for arresting the Movement."[51] When Melbourne attempted to extend municipal reform to Ireland, the peers once again looked to Lyndhurst to lead them in opposition to a government measure. The notion of popularly elected local councils in Ireland alarmed Peel as well as Lyndhurst, and the two leaders' unity was reflected in their separate attempts to alter the bill. The common Conservative goal in both chambers was to replace the old municipal governing bodies, as well as sheriffs and magistrates, with appointees of the Crown. Among the several speeches against the Irish Municipal Corporations Bill, the one Lyndhurst delivered on April 26 proved the occasion for a bitter quarrel. Lyndhurst was accused of characterizing His Majesty's Irish subjects as "aliens in blood and language and religion." Daniel O'Connell and Richard Lalor Sheil excoriated the leader of the House of Lords for his alleged statement. Lyndhurst denied the charge the next day, and Sir Theodore Martin stressed that "Hansard will be searched in vain for the phrase, and Lord Lyndhurst always denied that he used it." Martin conceded, however, that "the germ" of the notorious sentence was in Lyndhurst's speech when he stressed the divisions between the two parties, English and Protestant, Irish and Catholic.[52]

Lyndhurst repeated his denial during a speech before the Lords on June 27. Before he broached the subject of the controversy of his infamous remarks, he proclaimed his support for the independence of the House of Lords. He denounced Melbourne for implying that the peers were bound by the judgment of the House of Commons. Lyndhurst, rejecting such thinking, declared in ringing tones: "This House also represents the nation — that we are no less the representative of the nation than the House of Commons, which is stated to represent the people; and I believe at this moment, that we as fully, and no less fairly, represent the opinions, the sentiments, the feelings of the great body of the nation, as their representatives in the other House of Parliament."[53] In this bold defense of the House of Lords, Lyndhurst challenged Melbourne and his Whig ministry to alter in any way the legislative position of the second chamber. He argued from his belief that they would not do so because they lacked sufficient public support to launch and carry through so revolutionary an objective.

From his strong justification for an aristocratic chamber, Lyndhurst moved on to defend himself against the taunts of his detractors. He alluded to the actual description he claimed he had made of the Irish: "Persons of a different and, with regard to the English party to whom I referred, of an alien descent. The sense in which these words were used is quite obvious. They differ to a great extent in manners, language, habits and religion, and they look on us as invaders. I admit that I said they were anxious for a separation, and desirous to drive us from the country. Is this, or is it not, a correct description of the two parties in Ireland?"[54] More than "the germ," which Martin noted, was present in Lyndhurst's language. The words were the same. He had, in the rough and tumble of debate, said the words or something very near to them.

During his speech Lyndhurst attacked O'Connell, his chief accuser, in scorching language for his coarse and scurrilous jests, and he described him as "an apostle of agitation."[55] The Irish leader came into the House of Lords after Lyndhurst had finished speaking. Disraeli, always attuned to the effect created, regretted O'Connell's late arrival and observed, "He *was* there, and it was a grand hit, for everybody believed him to be there." As for the oration itself: "Lyndhurst's speech was a masterpiece. . . . Since Canning there has been nothing like it."[56]

The Lords' protracted discussions of Irish municipal reform produced an amendment that erased the bill's elective principle. The proposal was simply to abolish the boroughs, leaving their inhabitants subject to the ordinary institutions of county government controlled by the magistrates. The House of Commons rejected this amendment, but the Lords were steadfast in their insistence on the change, which they had endorsed 203 to 119. Because neither house would surrender its position, the bill was doomed. O'Connell underscored the contrast between the peers' willingness to reach a compromise on the English Municipal Corporations Bill and their contempt for Irish demands for reform. The recalcitrant Lords poured salt into the Irish wound when, in July 1836, they rejected the appropriations clause of an Irish Tithes Bill. The message was unmistakable: the Conservative Lords were hell-bent on demolishing the handiwork of the Whig House of Commons. Greville summed up this development, which was certain to provoke Whig ire and create Tory satisfaction: "The Lords have been bowling down Bills like ninepins."[57]

The 1836 session ended with Lyndhurst's oratorical fireworks. He chided the ministry for its lack of success in securing passage of its measures, a dilemma of which his listeners recognized he was the chief author.

He wound up his scathing denunciation with a contemptuous exclamation: "And this, my Lords, is a Government!"[58] It was pure Lyndhurst — pouring on scorn, ladling out contempt, and simultaneously cutting down his opponents, an exercise that thrilled his followers as it propelled Melbourne into a vigorous defense of his government. Melbourne's sympathetic biographer, W. P. Torrens, noted that he made "the happiest and ablest speech of his life" in reply to "the subtlest and most powerful of his adversaries."[59] His remarks were an acknowledgment of Lyndhurst's enormous influence in contemporary politics. The annual reviews of the sessions were not important for their content. What is important is the role Lyndhurst took for himself in delivering these speeches. This role underscored his place at the center of politics.

The Whigs never forgave Lyndhurst for employing his brilliance against them. However, begrudging admiration filled some Whig hearts. Greville recorded that his opponents universally admitted that "Lyndhurst's speech was of consummate ability. . . . Lord Holland, who endeavoured to answer it, said he thought Lyndhurst's one of the best speeches he had ever heard in Parliament."[60] Disraeli, writing to his sister, Sarah, noted that the speech "really has made everyone quite mad. You cannot form the most remote idea of it from the dull twaddle of the report in the *Times*. The Chronicle howr. and the other papers in some degree did it as much justice as a report can."[61] The *Morning Chronicle* thought "Lord Lyndhurst outdid himself last night."[62]

Would Lyndhurst continue to outdo himself in the session of 1837? Some expected that he would. Grey, in retirement, shared his thoughts with Princess Lieven: "What the House of Lords will do now, remains to be seen; but I am told that Lord Lyndhurst and his associates are determined to persevere in their opposition."[63] Lyndhurst spent four months, beginning in October 1836, in Paris, his favorite refuge. Before returning to London, he encountered Greville and told him he had "never passed such an agreeable time as the last four months; not a moment of ennui." He then shared his reflections on what had passed in the previous session: "I'm sure I shall not go on in the House of Lords this year as I did the last. I was induced by circumstances and some little excitement to take a more prominent part than usual last session; but I don't see what I got by it except abuse."[64] He had established himself vis-à-vis the Duke as the party's leader in the House of Lords.

Lyndhurst offered this self-analysis in late January of the new year. A month later, on February 23, a scene unfolded that underscored the reservoir of bitter feeling that had carried over from the recent contest. The Irish Municipal Corporations Bill had been reintroduced in the House of Commons on February 9. Lyndhurst was present in that chamber when Richard Lalor Sheil, the Irish Radical, denounced opponents of the measure.

> Lyndhurst was sitting under the gallery, and Sheil, turning to him as he said it, uttered one of his vehement sentences against the celebrated and unlucky expression of "aliens." The attack was direct, and it was taken up by his adherents, already excited by his speech. Then arose a din and tumultuous and vociferous cheering, such as the walls never echoed to before; they stood up, all turning to Lyndhurst, and they hooted and shouted at him with every possible gesture and intonation of insult. It lasted ten minutes, the Speaker in vain endeavouring to moderate the clamour. All this time Lyndhurst sat totally unmoved; he neither attempted to stir, nor changed a muscle of his countenance.[65]

Lyndhurst, who had been an alien early in his life, could not escape such abuse, nor could he escape demands that he once again lead his party in the House of Lords. Shortly after his arrival in Paris in the fall of 1836, the Duke of Wellington wrote his approval of the path along which Lyndhurst had led the party and recommended that "we in the House of Lords must follow the same course as the last year: that is to say, confine ourselves to legislation: to originate nothing on our side of the House, but to allow nothing to pass which shall be thought inconsistent with principle, or with the interests of the country."

Knowing that Lyndhurst planned to spend the winter in Paris, Wellington urged him to return in time for the new parliamentary session early in the year. He declared his conviction that "you have established yourself not only as the first speaker in the House of Lords, but as the first in your profession. . . . I hope that you will not lose sight of this position, so honourable to your character and so important to the country in the circumstances in which it is now placed."[66] The Duke need not have feared a defection; Lyndhurst would not opt for a quiet role in the face of partisan rebuke. Once again he led the Lords in trampling the ministry's Irish Municipal Corporations Bill, warning that "concession, we know, leads to still further concession according to the natural course of events" — a statement that might have been construed as a repudiation of his turnaround in support of Catholic Emancipation.[67] The bill was rejected and met the same fate in the next two sessions. A much altered version passed in 1840, Martin noted, "after it had undergone material modifications in the direction indicated by Lord Lyndhurst."[68]

Many censured Lyndhurst for a wanton mutilation of the government's program and predicted that no other outcome could result than to alienate the House of Lords from the respect and goodwill of the country. They were wrong. It was important for the future role of the Lords that Lyndhurst make the stand he did. In replying to Melbourne, he had declared his views on the independence of a House of Lords as a coequal partner with the Commons in the legislative process. This requirement for independence was of major importance because the years immediately following passage of the Reform Bill were a time of trial for the peers. They had caved in to the demand for that historic measure, unable to hold back the inevitable. Many wondered what the fate of the Upper House would be as Radicals clamored for its extinction, and the more moderate demanded some alteration in its function. However, when the advocates of change divided among themselves and their mandate ran out, they let slip the chance of intimidating the Lords. Time revealed that there was no strong body of opinion in favor of curtailing the power of the Upper House. Norman Gash described how the Lords won their salvation: "The House of Lords had survived the stormy thirties . . . by a show of activity which had been in effect both strong enough to win victories and restrained enough to save it from driving still deeper into peril . . . they had at least survived a testing period with no technical loss of power; and survivors could always live to fight another day."[69]

At the same time, Lyndhurst had made a crucial contribution in ultimately tempering the Lords' rebellion by promoting and securing the acceptance of compromise. To discover this truth we must look beneath his words and monitor his behavior. During this period of his career, he was challenging Peel for the right to dictate the terms of compromise with their Whig opponents. Gash minimized Lyndhurst's importance, as he focused on Peel's emergence as the pivotal figure of these times. His interpretation, like that of several earlier historians, is linked to Campbell's partisan and personal censure.[70] Lyndhurst may rightly be separated from that burden and be recognized as the strong political force he continued to be for so many years.

19

New Queen, New Wife, New Ministry

"We have begun a new reign in England. The P[rivy] Council has proclaimed Victoria Queen and we have taken the oath of allegiance to our new Sovereign."[1] With these words Lord Lyndhurst heralded a new day and a new era, the Victorian Age. As a Privy Councillor Lyndhurst attended Victoria's Accession Council at Kensington Palace. Benjamin Disraeli accompanied him on his journey to and from this convocation and described Lyndhurst's reaction: "He was greatly affected by the unusual scene: a youthful maiden, receiving the homage of her subjects, most of them illustrious, in a palace in a garden, and all with a sweet and natural dignity."[2]

Lyndhurst may or may not have been "greatly affected," as Disraeli observed. However, with his eye on the future, Lyndhurst was turning over in his mind the implications of this change, and he shared his thoughts in a letter to Princess Lieven: "We are all wondering what is to follow. The predictions are various. . . . For myself I think she will for the moment at least go on with the present ministers." He had detected a signal in the speech the new Queen had made to the Privy Council. He noted that she had "intimated her approbation of the *liberal* policy of his late Majesty" and added, "of course this speech was dictated by Melbourne."[3]

Lyndhurst may not have been as enchanted by the scene as Disraeli suggested: "The Queen is not at all pretty!" he observed. "She read her speech rather with a foreign accent" — a shortcoming he blamed on "the manner in which she has been brought up." She had not been allowed, he thought, sufficient interaction with other young persons to balance the companionship of a German mother, a governess, and servants. Lyndhurst did, however, detect some steel: "She is not at all nervous, but conducted herself with much self-possession."[4] If the Queen's lack of beauty and her

German accent were flaws in Lyndhurst's eyes, Victoria had her own reservations about the Tory politician. Her enthusiasm for Lord Melbourne led her to find fault in those who opposed his policies. In this regard, Lyndhurst led the pack. Then, too, a raffish reputation was no recommendation to an eighteen-year-old virgin Queen who had no doubt heard of his liaisons. He was all too like the Queen's uncles, whose reputations for moral laxity she sought to counter.

Always unwilling to hide her feelings, Victoria was determined quickly to establish her independence from her mother. Lyndhurst had extolled the virtues of the Duchess of Kent in the parliamentary debate that ended in her being designated a Regent should Victoria become Queen before reaching her eighteenth birthday. The Princess, however, attained that age shortly before the death of King William IV. A Regency, therefore, was unnecessary, but Victoria had noted Lyndhurst's warm support for her oppressive mother in that role. Thomas Creevey, who was present at the Queen's first reception, claimed that when she spied the former Chancellor, she stiffened as if she had seen a snake.[5] On another occasion, the Queen told Melbourne she disliked Lord Lyndhurst because he was an evil man.[6] At the Queen's coronation, after pledging his fealty to the newly crowned sovereign on bended knee, Lyndhurst failed to back away as royal etiquette required. He absentmindedly turned his back on the Queen and sauntered away.[7]

Susan Penelope, Lyndhurst's middle daughter, died in Paris on May 9, 1837. She was fourteen and the victim of consumption. Princess Lieven met Lyndhurst in Paris a few days before the girl died and noted that "his grief is so deep."[8] Lyndhurst found consolation in an attachment to a younger woman he had met in Paris. His family and friends were astonished when he suddenly married thirty-year-old Georgiana Goldsmith on August 5, 1837, at the British Embassy in Paris. Writing to her sister, Elizabeth, in Boston, Mary Copley announced this new development: "my brother being tired of a single life, has taken to himself a wife. . . . It was almost as unexpected to me as it will be to you. The lady is a very charming person." She added some information about the circumstances that had first drawn Lyndhurst to his future bride. Georgiana had been in Paris during Susan's last illness. Mary Copley attested that "she was so very kind that I hardly know what I should have done without her."[9] Apparently, Lyndhurst turned to Georgiana Goldsmith for comfort.

Disraeli reacted with consternation: "It is a bad business I fear, but he is so lucky, he will fall on his legs."[10] Disraeli's sister, Sarah, shared this unfavorable view of the union, commenting, "The marriage of milord was quite a thunderbolt. . . . As a domestic calamity it is surely unmitigable."[11] Disraeli did not meet Lyndhurst's new wife until the following February at a reception hosted by Lady Salisbury, and he found her to be "an agreeable surprise."

> Without being absolutely pretty, her appearance is highly interesting. She was sitting on the large Ottoman in the centre of the new saloon, and therefore I can scarcely judge of her (height) figure. She is very little, but her appearance is elegant and delicate . . . her features being very small. She was most becomingly dressed, in a white turban of very recherché construction. Her manner calm and assured, yet tinged with a certain degree of reserve not unbecoming.[12]

Yet Georgiana Goldsmith was nothing like her predecessor. She was neither beautiful nor vivacious nor skilled at political wire-pulling. Lady Salisbury gave this appraisal: "There is nothing to object to about her, but one cannot help saying, when she comes into the room, 'Why did he marry her?' She is not handsome, but looks intelligent and got through very well."[13] "Why did he marry her?" was the question on many lips.

Part of the answer lay in the fact that Lyndhurst was providing a mother for his young daughters. "Sarah is quite delighted," Mary Copley wrote, "and little Sophy is all impatience to see her new mamma."[14] Lyndhurst also lacked a male heir. His first marriage had produced one son, John Singleton, in 1824. The child had lived only thirteen months. Lyndhurst was sixty-five in 1837, and his bride was thirty. Lyndhurst was, Disraeli noted, "in high spirits, but if he have not a son, I think he will sink under the disappointment. He talks of nothing else."[15] On May 5, 1838, nine months to the day after their marriage, Lady Lyndhurst presented her husband with a healthy baby — albeit a girl, christened Georgiana Susan after her mother and the daughter whose death had brought her father and his second wife together.

Who was Lyndhurst's second wife? Mary Copley said, "She is English, though born in Paris."[16] Lord Campbell, noting that she was "a beautiful Jewess," had a great deal to say about her father: "Lewis Goldsmith, a Portuguese Jew, once famous as the author of a Jacobinical, or rather regicidal book — 'The Crimes of Cabinets' — and who had been employed privately by all the great governments of Europe."[17] After Campbell's unflattering biography of Lyndhurst appeared in 1869, his claim of a Jewish lineage for Lady Lyndhurst drew a denial in a publication called *Pall Mall*. A brief item under the heading "Occasional Notes" stated that the author "speaks of her as a 'beautiful Jewess' — the truth being that this lady was not a Jewess."[18]

Sir Theodore Martin, the person the second Lady Lyndhurst chose to write her husband's biography, was economical in reporting his subject's remarriage. He devoted only two sentences to the event, submitting that "of this union, it is only necessary to say, that it was one of unbroken happiness."[19] On December 28, 1838, Lyndhurst playfully alluded to his marriage in a letter to his friend, Francis Barlow: "Wetherell has followed my example (in getting married). I hope the precedent will apply throughout, and that in due time fruit will appear. Tell him these things are the consequence of being out of office. Idleness, you know, etc. Is it true that he has got £60,000 with his bride? I did not set him that example."[20] Although she chose a solely domestic life, Georgiana was the keeper of the flame until her death in December 1901. Lyndhurst was served well by the two women he wedded. The first was a political ally, and the second, after providing for him a home marked by domestic contentment, defended his reputation against the handiwork of political detractors who would reach beyond the tomb.

In 1837 Lyndhurst remained very much alive and a towering figure in the House of Lords. He had told Charles Greville that he would not resume the vigorous role of opposition that had earned him so much abuse in the past. Despite this statement, he presented in the Lords his annual review of the session of 1837. Lyndhurst attacked the government for its failure to enact a single important bill. He taunted Melbourne and his colleagues for being powerless, a condition he had done his best to create. In conclusion he noted that "a ray of hope breaks in upon us from another quarter."[21] This was his bow to the little Queen, who disliked him.

During the session of 1838, Lord Lyndhurst confined himself to social legislation and gave his support to legal reforms that benefited women and children, an indication that he believed the agenda of politics had changed or that he wished to change it. His move in a new direction was an anticipation of Disraeli's Young England of the next decade. In staking out this new legislative terrain, Lyndhurst was suggesting that the Whigs were only interested in political reforms. This may have been an attempt to counter traditional Whig claims for a unique commitment to positive goverment.[22] He questioned the government's intentions in connection with the Juvenile Offenders Bill, drawing attention to the treatment of

Drawing of Lyndhurst seated, bearing his signature and the words: Author of "Summary of the Session." Used by permission of the British Museum.

children imprisoned in reformatories. He underscored the negligence, indifference, and even cruelty that sometimes prevailed in these places. Lyndhurst had been a member of a committee that had heard testimony relating to the condition of children confined in reformatories. He brought to the Lords' attention the case of ten-year-old Matilda Seymour, who was serving a sentence of three years for theft she had committed at the instigation of her mother.[23]

Matilda Seymour's sentence, Lyndhurst declared, had been intended not as punishment but as reformation and instruction. The object of the state was to rehabilitate a wayward child, and the current system failed to accomplish this purpose. A different system was called for, one that would liberate all of the Matilda Seymours from being "shut up by herself in a cell not much larger than that table." Lyndhurst related that the child suffered from scrofula, which she had contracted during her confinement. Doctors who had examined her had said that she would not recover as long as she remained confined in her narrow, sunless cell. Consumption had caused the death of Lyndhurst's daughter, Susan, little more than a year earlier. Many among his listeners understood that a heavy heart inspired Lyndhurst to plead for compassion for the youngest inmates of Her Majesty's prisons. The government gave an assurance that the bill would be amended to provide for boards of visitors to inspect the prisons on a regular basis and report their findings.[24]

Lyndhurst, in a similar spirit, brought in a Custody of Infants Bill to change the law that barred a wife separated from her husband from having access to their children unless her husband consented. In this effort he was encouraged by Caroline Norton, whose own child custody fight had inspired her to write "A Plain Letter to the Lord Chancellor on the Law and Custody of Infants." Caroline Norton was separated from her husband, and he had denied her access to her children. The law was on his side. Lyndhurst gave flesh to the bare bones of the law when he cited cases in which loving and respectable mothers had lost their children to cruel or adulterous husbands and been shut out of their children's lives. He stressed, too, the unwillingness of the courts to restore these children to their mothers when these unfortunate women sought legal redress. Yet, in a poorly attended House, eleven of twenty-one peers voted against the bill, and it was lost for the session. Lyndhurst entered a protest against the rejection of the bill, proclaiming that "nature and reason point out the mother as the proper guardian of her infant child."[25]

Some might snicker to hear Lyndhurst denounce an adulterous husband and champion the cause of oppressed women. Yet he was a man who genuinely enjoyed the company of women in either a platonic or a sensual relationship. Lyndhurst's household was made up entirely of women. Before he married Dolly, he had lived with his mother and sister. After his marriage, his parent and sibling continued to make their home with him. Three daughters completed the family circle. After the deaths of Dolly, Mrs. Copley, and Susan, he remarried, and an altered household evolved. A new wife and daughter joined his two remaining daughters. His spinster sister, Mary, continued to be a part of the household, helping to care for the children. Lyndhurst dwelled in a world of women. Small wonder he became their advocate.

An opportunity of a more urgent and intensely political nature arose when Melbourne's government found itself in difficulty in 1839. The ministry had been tainted by the extremism of Daniel O'Connell, and moderate reformers were unenthusiastic about its alliance with so fierce an ally. Its majority of fifty-eight had dropped to thirty-two after the election that followed Victoria's accession. When the government attempted to discipline the rebellious Jamaican colonial Assembly, this number dwindled to five on May 6, 1839. Melbourne went to the Queen the following day and resigned. He advised her to send for the Duke of Wellington, who in turn counseled her to invite Sir Robert Peel to form a ministry. The young Queen's distaste for Peel was compounded by his request that as a sign of her confidence in him, she replace some of her Whig Ladies of the Bedchamber with Tory counterparts. When pressed by Peel, the young and politically inexperienced Queen refused to give up any of her Ladies. For Peel the issue involved a symbolic gesture of confidence.

Peel consulted the Conservative notables who would be his colleagues in a new government. Among them was Lord Lyndhurst. All agreed that because their prospective ministry would face a hostile majority in the House of Commons, a public sign of confidence from the Queen was of fundamental importance. Without this gesture they could not accept office. It was all up to Victoria, and she had discovered that her stubbornness would allow her to work her will all the way around. By insisting that she must keep her Ladies, she would also keep Melbourne, who was counseling her to reject Peel's demand both as contrary to usage and repugnant to her feelings.

Although he did not take a leading role in the bedchamber crisis, Lyndhurst resumed his leadership in the House of Lords and delivered his annual review of the session of Parliament on August 23, 1839. He hit upon the ministry's most embarrassing and culpable conduct, which was its tenacity in retaining office long after it had lost the vigor to rule. Lyndhurst reviewed the recent resignation of the Ministers and charged them with advising the Queen to break off negotiations with Conservative leaders and to restore themselves. The Ministers, Lyndhurst thundered, had lost the confidence of both Parliament and the country.[26]

Lyndhurst's bond with Benjamin Disraeli was strengthened when he served as best man at Disraeli's marriage to Mary Anne Lewis in 1839. The excited prospective groom wrote to his sister, Sarah, of the prenuptial preparations and announced that "Ld. Lyndhurst is to go with me and only he." Disraeli added that he had taken time to attend Lyndhurst's review of the session: "He made the finest speech last night that he ever yet did — far beyond his first and famous summary — I went down there casually, and just managed to hear it — abt. an hour, and great ener[g]y of deliv[er]y for him — and altog[ethe]r more flow and force — indeed very grand and effective."[27]

The fall of 1840 found Lyndhurst with his family at Baden where he sought the healthful effects of the waters. During his stay on the Continent, he learned of his nomination as a candidate for the office of High Steward of the University of Cambridge. He was opposed by Lord Lyttelton, a Whig. This news brought a swift request from Lyndhurst to Francis Barlow to act as his agent and determine the likelihood of his success. Lyndhurst, always attuned to a political pitfall or opportunity, foresaw a potential trap should he be rejected in this contest. He wrote frankly to Barlow that "I will *not* run any risk. It would be very mortifying to me to be *defeated.*" He added, too, a concern for the effect a loss would have on his party: "It would also be, in some degree, a blow to the Conservative cause — at least, it would be so interpreted by the Rad[ica]ls. — Pray consider this well, and don't let me be committed." Finally, he came back to the consideration of what a loss might mean to him personally: "It is fighting at great odds, as the loss to me (in the event of loss) would far exceed any advantage from the appointment."[28]

Lyndhurst was apparently able to overcome his doubts, because on October 30 a letter from him, dated October 24, appeared in the newspapers accepting the nomination. Within days he arrived in England "looking younger than ever." The initial pessimism had lifted, and Disraeli declared him "perfectly safe." He also reported him "in high spirits" and contemptuous of the criticisms of him on moral grounds that Lyttelton's supporters had advanced. He was "anxious to ascertain what was the immoral part of his character, as he always considered himself a pattern."[29] Lyndhurst playfully suggested that he should "present himself on the hustings surrounded by his wife and family."[30]

Lyndhurst now seemed confident of his success, and his appearance at the Senate House at Cambridge to cast his vote was greeted by a twenty-minute ovation. The *Times* reported that he was received by the undergraduates "with the most deafening cheers, that lasted for several more minutes, and were renewed at intervals whilst his Lordship remained."[31] Lyndhurst's candidacy brought an expression of support from Peel as well as a contribution of £50. Peel wrote to Sir John Beckett, chair of Lyndhurst's election committee, declaring that he considered "it a paramount obligation to do all in my power for a man of superior pretensions for the office of Lord Steward, but, above all, for a former colleague and personal friend, with whom in office and out of office I have always been on the most confidential intercourse in public matters."[32]

When the votes were counted, Lyndhurst's majority against Lyttelton was a solid 973 to 488. He acknowledged the large show of support he had received in a printed message that was received by his followers. He wrote of "the gratification and pride which I feel at the result of the contest."[33] He still desired to stand at the center of events, and the anticipated fall of the Melbourne ministry promised his return to the Chancellorship. This long-awaited denouement occurred in August 1841, when, following an election that gave the Conservatives a majority of 76, an amendment was offered on the Queen's speech that expressed a lack of confidence in the ministry. On August 21 Lyndhurst and others met with Peel to discuss this course of action. A vote of 360 to 269 in the Commons gave Melbourne's foes a majority of 91, and on August 30 the resignation of the government was announced. A grim-faced Queen Victoria received Sir Robert Peel at Windsor Castle. The Conservatives' decade of opposition, broken only by Peel's Hundred Days, was over.

On September 6 Lord Lyndhurst resumed both his place on the Woolsack and a seat in Peel's Cabinet. Peel would never have selected Lyndhurst to be his Chancellor on two occasions if he had not valued him in this role. Peel needed a legal authority in the post of Lord Chancellor; Lyndhurst answered that need. Peel was also aware that Lyndhurst possessed considerable political influence. Therefore, it was better to have him inside the Cabinet cooperating than outside making mischief. Any one or a combination of these reasons reflects well on Lyndhurst's ability to make himself a force in politics.

Lyndhurst had proved his staying power as a force within the Conservative party during the lean years on the opposition benches. He had led the fight against further advances by reformers in the wake of their great victory in 1832. He had marshaled the House of Lords in the aftermath of its humiliating surrender over the Reform Bill and, while challenging Peel, had inspired that body to resist and repel threats to trim or abolish its powers. Lyndhurst had rallied the party and emerged once more in his familiar role as a flexible force who could lead the Conservative peers back from a political abyss. He was always moderate in the final accounting. However, his strong leadership had instilled a new spirit in his party when its fortunes were at their lowest ebb. He had held together the party that Peel would lead into a new decade. At the same time, when Lyndhurst took issue with Peel over municipal reform, he signaled that the independence of the House of Lords was even more important to him than the cohesion of the party.

20
His Last Chancellorship

In the year before he resumed the burden of office, Lord Lyndhurst made a commitment that symbolized his desire to escape from care — he signed a fourteen-year lease on Turville Park, a sixty-acre estate in Buckinghamshire. Quiet isolation and rural seclusion were not the customary yearnings of Lord Lyndhurst. However, the constant moving about with his family each autumn had palled on him. His new estate was, by his sister's account, "eleven miles from a railway station, which makes it very convenient [to Lyndhurst's London home], as we can go from one house to the other within three hours."[1] The nearest neighbor was between two and three miles away, and visitors agreed that in summer the house had a beautiful setting. Lyndhurst's farm was small. "One hundred sheep, four cows, and above eighty head of poultry" completed the bucolic existence at Turville Park.[2] Yet some were not enraptured by the rural charm of Lyndhurst's retreat. Benjamin Disraeli, after passing a weekend there, gave his verdict: "Turville is indeed a great bore."[3]

Turville Park was an attempt by Lyndhurst to alter the rhythm of his life as he approached its eighth decade. Some observers thought they detected signs of a loss of vigor in his behavior. When Lyndhurst took his place on the Woolsack for the first time after the formation of Sir Robert Peel's second ministry, Lord Campbell thought he was "excessively nervous, and, looking bewildered, did not seem at all to recollect the forms with which he had so long been familiar." Lord Melbourne was present and, according to Campbell, said "in a loud whisper, 'Who would think that this is the same impudent dog who bullied us so unconscionably in his Reviews of the Session?'" Campbell added that "Lyndhurst was soon himself again, laughing at everybody and everything, and especially delighting in a jest against any of his colleagues."[4] Campbell was not alone in detecting signs of infirmity in Lyndhurst. When the Cabinet assembled at Windsor Castle for a meeting of the Privy Council, Charles Greville noted that "the

Chancellor was there, looking very ill and broken, but evidently wishing to be thought strong and capable. He not only affected to be very merry, but very active, and actually began a sort of dancing movement in the drawing room . . . seventy years of age, ten years of idleness, and a young wife will not do for the labor of the Great Seal."[5]

Appearances aside, Lyndhurst was embarking on his longest Chancellorship, during which he devoted much of his time to measures of legal reform. Some of these he introduced himself; others were the work of his colleagues. Sir William Holdsworth, in *A History of English Law*, declared that "Lyndhurst was willing to promote all reforms which could be reasonable."[6] He submitted that "the best evidence of this fact is the number of reforming statutes passed between 1841 and 1845 during his last Chancellorship."

> Important reforms were made in the land law — the mode of conveyancing was improved, feoffments ceased to have a tortious operation, the enfranchisement of copyholds was facilitated, the law of copyright was reformed. The incapacity of witnesses on account of the commission of crime or on account of interest was abolished. The Factory Act was extended; and the formation of joint stock companies was facilitated and regulated by Act, which in effect begins the modern history of company law. Extensive reforms were made in the judicial machinery of the state. Reforms were made in the offices of many of the courts. The equitable jurisdiction of the Court of Exchequer was transferred to the Court of Chancery. The practice and procedure of the Judicial Committee were reformed. Lyndhurst supported Campbell's Act for the amendment of the criminal law of libel.[7]

Lyndhurst was diligent in his attempts to mend or block poorly conceived changes, and, as a consequence, Campbell frequently felt the sting of his verbal lash. Campbell had been the Lord Chancellor of Ireland for only a few weeks when Melbourne's ministry resigned. Although a newcomer to the House of Lords, he had attempted to provoke opposition to the new government. He chafed at the treatment he received, complaining that "Lyndhurst, notwithstanding our long and familiar intimacy, was disposed to treat me very cavalierly, and, with Brougham's help, to crush me as speedily as possible."[8] In the session of 1842, Campbell submitted three bills to the House of Lords. One sought to create a permanent Chief

Judge in the Court of Chancery. The second proposed to abolish the Judicial Committee of the Privy Council. The third sought to designate the House of Lords, presided over by the Chancellor, as the only court of last resort for appeals from England, Scotland, Ireland, or the colonies in civil, criminal, and ecclesiastical matters. Campbell contrasted his own "very modest and deferential manner" on this occasion with the "very sneering countenance and mocking tone" of Lord Lyndhurst.[9] Sir Theodore Martin pointed to Henry Brougham's ardor for legal reform and cited his concurrence with Lyndhurst in opposition to Campbell's proposals as evidence that the measures were lacking in merit.

If Campbell felt "the heavy hand of Brougham with sledgehammer force," he suffered more intensely from Lyndhurst's subtle contempt.[10] In reality, although craving Lyndhurst's approval and intimacy, he was never able to secure signs of approbation. More than politics separated the two men. Lyndhurst felt no respect for Campbell, and, although he was usually commended for his kindness, he made no attempt to hide his conviction that Campbell's pretensions made him a figure of fun. Yet Campbell, wrestling with ambivalent emotions toward Lyndhurst, could occasionally find cause to praise his sneering hero. In the session of 1843, Campbell found Lyndhurst behaving "very laudably" in helping to amend the libel law. Campbell cited Peel's approval of the bill but added that he had "no reason to suppose that Lyndhurst's support of this measure did not spontaneously flow from his own conviction; for, when without an interested motive to the contrary, he was always for progress."[11] Campbell's appraisal on this latter point was not far from the mark. Lyndhurst combined a sense of self-interest with a sense of detachment. In the years that lay ahead, he would increasingly embrace "progress." The hallmark of Lyndhurst's career was his ability to move with the tide and not be left behind by events. As he entered the final phase of his career, both the satisfaction of his ambition and his advancing age proved to be liberating forces.

Campbell wanted Lyndhurst's approval, but failing to achieve it, he nursed a grudge that he would have happily abandoned in exchange for a pat on the head from this leading figure in contemporary politics. Campbell fairly glowed in the pages of his book when he related that he and Lyndhurst labored at the same oar in the passage of a series of three "excellent bills" that touched upon religious issues. He proclaimed that he

> had now great satisfaction in fighting under the Lyndhurst banner, to which I had so often been opposed —

> — in this glorious and well fought field
> We kept together in our chivalry.

When the measures were securely framed in law, Campbell savored the fact that Lyndhurst "thanked me very handsomely, both in private and public, for the aid I had afforded him."[12]

Generally, however, Campbell met with only scorn. Pompous and vain, he was frequently a target for ridicule in Westminster. "But of all his legal prosecutors," noted one observer, "Lord Lyndhurst was the most merciless and disdainful. The bare mention of Jock Campbell's name would call a mirthful smile on the visage of Lyndhurst, who delighted to play on his weaknesses and render him ludicrous."[13] Campbell made a point of explaining that when Lyndhurst introduced the "three very excellent bills" in the session of 1844, he did so at Peel's direction. The first measure recognized the validity of marriages performed in Ireland by clergy outside of the Established Church. The second proposal abolished praemunire (the penalty for resorting to the authority of the Pope), which was almost never enforced, and other penalties against Roman Catholics. The third bill entitled Unitarian congregations in both England and Ireland to have access to the endowments attached to their places of worship after a waiting period of twenty-five years, even though these endowments had been established by Trinitarian or Calvinistic patrons for the support of their own sects.

During his final Chancellorship, one case above all others tested Lyndhurst's capacity to preserve the dignity of the law. A writ of error against the original indictment in the case of *O'Connell v. the Queen* was appealed to the House of Lords in 1844.[14] The Irish leader had been convicted the previous year of high treason on a charge arising out of his "Monster Meetings" held throughout Ireland at which he advocated in burning words the repeal of the Union. *Monster Meeting* was a term that expressed Victorian hyperbole. The repeal movement had grown to ominous proportions, and it brought demands for the prosecution of Daniel O'Connell. The government acted after placards appeared that summoned the attendance of "Repeal Cavalry" at a final Monster Meeting. Although O'Connell repudiated the threat of force the words carried, he and six of his cohorts were arrested on October 13, 1843, for conspiracy to commit treason.

O'Connell was convicted, and his appeal before the House of Lords was loaded with political import. Could the Irish agitator gain a fair hearing before an assembly of peers, most of whom were intensely hostile toward him as well as toward his policies? Could O'Connell secure justice from a tribunal presided over by Lyndhurst, frequently the target of his venom? On September 4, 1844, in a passionless speech, Lyndhurst moved that O'Connell's conviction be affirmed. He earned high praise from Campbell for his bearing on this occasion: "The demeanour of the Chancellor, who had hitherto been the most violent against O'Connell, was that of a dignified magistrate, whose only object was to arrive at a right conclusion, and do justice between the Crown and the subject."[15] After the Chancellor had moved the affirmation of O'Connell's conviction, Brougham concurred in his judgment, whereas Lords Denman, Cottenham, and Campbell — all loyal Whigs — united to reverse the conviction.

Many of the peers on the Conservative benches, eager to see O'Connell brought low, wanted his conviction upheld. Their hostility found an opportunity for expression when Lyndhurst posed a question from the Woolsack that stated the traditional formula: "Is it your Lordships' pleasure that the judgment of the Court below be reversed? As many of your Lordships as are of that opinion will say 'Content.'" Denman, Cottenham, and Campbell answered in the affirmative. Then Lyndhurst posed the alternative question: "As many as are of an opposite opinion will say 'Not Content.'" Brougham said, "Not content." Simultaneously, the rage of several Tory Lords leapt from their lips. "Not Content," they thundered.[16] James Beresford Atlay recounted the drama and the significance of this demonstration of hatred for the man who would smash the Union:

> It was a grave crisis: the character of the supreme tribunal for impartiality, indeed its very existence as a court of law was at stake. The distinction between law lords and lay lords was theoretically unknown to their lordships' House; there was nothing to prevent any member taking part in its judicial proceedings, and there were cases of comparatively recent date in which lay lords had exercised the right of dividing on the hearing of appeals. But if these admitted exceptions were to be followed, the authority of the House of Lords as a court of justice and as the fountain of precedent would not only be impaired but ruined. Lord Wharncliffe, the President of the Council, implored his brother peers not to break through the honourable tradition; he was followed by Brougham and Campbell. And, last of all, Lyndhurst, whose influence in the assembly was of a different order from that exercised by his learned brethren, threw his weight into the scale.[17]

Lyndhurst's simple appeal to the Lords restored an atmosphere of calm and impartiality when he declared, "I think those noble Lords who have not heard the arguments will decline voting if I put the question again." The Chancellor's words smoothed what might have developed into an awkward and potentially harmful impasse. Atlay's tribute to Lyndhurst's nobility on this occasion summed up what many were thinking: "Few members of the House had been more truculently assailed by O'Connell than Lyndhurst, and he must have been more than human not to rejoice at this opportunity of heaping coals of fire upon the head of his enemy."[18]

Lyndhurst, although not "more than human," was no fool. He could not embrace a victory that would injure the House of Lords, damage the Conservative party, undermine his own reputation as an impartial jurist, and exalt O'Connell as a martyr to English trickery. He recognized and opted for the best course among his limited alternatives. The manner in which his angry colleagues deferred to his wise counsel indicated their respect for his astuteness. They accepted, too, as they had in the past, his signal for moderation and reined in their desire for O'Connell's downfall. The Irish leader, denied a martyr's fate, continued to turn his energies to agitating the frustrated masses throughout his unhappy homeland. He toured the length and breadth of Ireland preaching repeal of the Union at re-creations of the infamous Monster Meetings, which had become synonymous with his name. These meetings were supplemented by the formation of quasi-military brigades whose midnight drilling exercises posed a threat that fighting words might soon be backed up by bullets. Ultimately, O'Connell suffered a mental and physical breakdown near the end of his life and died on a pilgrimage to Rome.

Ireland was aflame, and Sir Edward Sugden, the Lord Chancellor of Ireland, took action. He expelled from the Commission of the Peace those Irish justices who had made known their support for the repeal meetings by either summoning or attending them. Notable among them was Lord French (Ffrench on the document), who had conspicuously attached his name to a proclamation that convened one of these meetings. On account of his decisive action, Sugden was denounced by Irish partisans both in and out of Parliament. Lord Clanricarde proposed a motion of censure against Sugden for his dismissal of the justices. During the debate on Clanricarde's censure motion on July 14, 1845, Lord Lyndhurst vigorously defended Ireland's Chancellor, declaring that he would have adopted the same course. He sketched in vivid tones the enormity of the movement that was being set in motion to rupture Ireland's Union with England. He argued that the Monster Meetings were no mere exercises in the right to petition Parliament for a redress of grievances. The single-minded objective of what he called "this foul conspiracy" was the repeal of the Union.

An Irish House of Commons created by universal suffrage, a reconstituted Irish peerage, the disestablishment of the Protestant Church of Ireland, including confiscation of its property, and finally, the transfer of property from the landlords to the tenants — all of these objects were being dangled before the excited masses by demagogues who were embroiled in a conspiracy that would wreck more than the Union. Lyndhurst urged his fellow peers to grasp the implication of the state of affairs in Ireland where the Repeal Association had moved far its excursion toward mayhem. Lyndhurst's conclusion was simple but sobering: "No person can for a moment doubt that the repeal of the Union must necessarily be followed by the dismemberment of the Empire."[19] Lord Clanricarde's motion to censure was supported by twenty-nine peers, whereas sixty-nine colleagues heeded Lyndhurst's plea to reject the expression of disapproval. Lyndhurst had held out the olive branch to Ireland when he had reversed his stand on Emancipation. In the intervening years, he had come to recognize that this concession had failed to dampen the passion that shook Ireland. His harsh words announced his disillusionment with a policy of accommodation.

Peel's second ministry spanned five years, beginning in 1841. Before its second year was over, Lord Lyndhurst was talking about relinquishing the Seals of Office. The first hint that he might retire came in the spring of 1843 when Mary Copley advised her sister, Elizabeth: "How you would be delighted to see him Chancellor! Do, pray, come, but it must be soon, for he says he will not retain the office long, and indeed he sighs for repose from his labours."[20] One year later Mary repeated the message in another letter to her sister. She reported that Lyndhurst "has been and is remarkably well, sometimes tired with the hard work of office, which he does not intend to hold much longer."[21] These remarks were natural regarding an old man and may not have reflected a serious intention to resign. However, there were soon indications that the end of Peel's government might be in the offing.

The summer rains of 1845 had rotted Ireland's potato crop and aggravated a fungus condition that destroyed the main staple of the Irish diet. The misery that followed shocked Peel and convinced him to take a decisive step. He would call for the repeal of the Corn Laws, which protected agricultural interests by keeping the price of food high and prohibiting the importation of lower-priced corn. Peel temporarily suspended the Corn Laws. When his Cabinet was divided on the issue, he resigned on December 6, paving the way for Lord John Russell to bring in a similar measure. Russell stumbled when Lord Grey, the son of the former Premier, refused to serve as Colonial Secretary while Lord Palmerston headed the Foreign Office. Unable to break this impasse in his efforts at Cabinet making, Russell acknowledged that he was unable to form a government. This stalemate brought back Peel minus Lord Stanley, the Colonial Secretary who opposed free trade. William Gladstone, who had left the Cabinet the previous year over the Maynooth Grant that subsidized Roman Catholic seminaries in Ireland, now replaced Stanley and gave his support to repeal.

Lyndhurst, too, was back with the Cabinet, which would press an end to protection. He had anticipated during the previous year that the Corn Laws would become the central issue on England's political agenda. Therefore, he had requested that Gladstone "lend me something very full, but at the same time concise, upon the subject of the Corn Laws — the cream, if you please."[22] Whether Gladstone accommodated the request is unknown. But when the issue came to the center of the political arena, Lyndhurst was a firm supporter of his chief.

Protection for the agricultural interest through retention of the Corn Laws was a major tenet of the Conservative credo. Peel's decision to abandon this commitment unleashed one of the most traumatic episodes in British politics during the nineteenth century. Lyndhurst had no significant role in the formation of this divisive policy, which split the Conservative party and led to the fall of the government. But when the issue came to the center of the political arena, he was a firm, unhesitating supporter of Peel's new policy. Campbell reported him exclaiming "in a loud voice, 'Campbell! I find the Corn Laws are all a humbug. I used to suppose that the prosperity of our agriculture and of our commerce all depended upon *Protection*; but I tell you *Protection* is a *humbug*. There is nothing for it now but Free Trade.'" Campbell added that Lyndhurst confided that "he himself, and all the other members of the Cabinet, had resolved to sacrifice themselves for the good of the country."[23] Lyndhurst did not side with Disraeli in his searing attack on the Prime Minister. He stood with the man who had placed him in the Chancellorship on two occasions.

The Whigs were keen on supporting Peel in his efforts to repeal the Corn Laws, a move that divided the Conservative party. However, once that measure was enacted, they combined with the Protectionists to expel the innovative Prime Minister and his colleagues. Amid a climate of impending doom, Lyndhurst moved the second reading of the Charitable Trusts Bill, a proposal that had won the endorsement of the Lords the previous year but failed to pass the Commons before that body ended its deliberations. On May 18, the same evening the Corn Importation Bill received its first reading in the House of Lords, Lyndhurst urged the peers to once again endorse the bill they had supported in the last session. Many incidents involving misappropriations of funds attached to charitable trusts had arisen over the years. Few charities could afford the great expense incurred when bringing a case before the Court of Chancery, the only tribunal in the country that had any jurisdiction over charitable trusts. Small charities in particular were at a disadvantage. The remedy proposed in the bill was the creation of an independent tribunal for administration of charitable trusts. A panel of three Crown appointees was to exercise summary jurisdiction over charities in the interest of dispensing justice without the numerous steps and delays of a formal trial.[24]

Lyndhurst did not save the Charitable Trusts Bill. The Whigs, who had opposed the bill all along, were aided by the Protectionist peers in rejecting this measure that Lyndhurst had labored to see enacted in two sessions. Campbell described the significance of the bill's defeat and what followed: "The loss of the 'Charitable Trusts Bill' was the death-warrant of Sir Robert Peel's administration; but it did not receive the coup de grâce till the division in the House of Commons upon the 'Irish Coercion Bill,' when there was a similar coalition with a similar result, and this proved instantly fatal."[25] The end came on June 26, 1846, when the antigovernment forces, swollen by a Protectionist thirst for revenge, defeated the Coercion Bill by a majority of seventy-eight votes. Peel's resignation allowed Lyndhurst to lay down the cares of office.

For Lyndhurst the loss of office was bittersweet. Mary Copley's letter to her sister conveyed this feeling: "We bear our defeat with great philosophy. To be sure my brother had made up his mind some time since to retire from the fatigues of office upon the first convenient opportunity; still it would have been more agreeable to have left the other members of government behind."[26] Lyndhurst later wrote to his sister in Boston of his retirement: "this tranquil sort of life is a great relief and a great pleasure to me, after the constant dull routine of office, and of public life for so many years."[27]

Yet before he could settle into a "tranquil sort of life," Lord Lyndhurst became embroiled in a public row that stemmed from his attempt to play the role of peacemaker between the alienated wings of the Conservative party. He was a natural person to assume this task of party healing between

Peel and Disraeli, who had thrown himself so enthusiastically into the effort to bring down the government. Lyndhurst was reported to have proposed a reunion in opposition to a bill permitting the free importation of foreign sugar, regardless of whether it was produced by free or slave labor. He sought to conciliate the Protectionists by curbing the Peelites' commitment to free trade. Lyndhurst was moving closer to the Protectionists. Lacking a majority by eighty or ninety seats, the Whig government was weak. It clung to office with the backing of the Protectionists, who sought to banish Peel permanently from Whitehall. The Peelites wanted Russell to remain in office to prevent Stanley from taking his place.

Lyndhurst did not go directly to Peel. First he met with several associates to sound them out as to their views. Peel, in a subsequent letter to Lyndhurst, reviewed what had transpired at their interview: "You informed me of a fact of which I was previously unaware, that you had been in communication with some members of my late Government and of the party which supported me . . . that before you went further you had resolved to speak to me." Peel's response to Lyndhurst's initiative was a disappointment: "My answer was that I must decline being any party to this proceeding, that I said . . . that the return to office was as little in my contemplation as it was in yours — and that I was not prepared to enter into any party combination with that aim."[28]

Rebuffed by Peel, Lyndhurst continued to sound out the leaders of the party. He met with Lord Stanley, who, although giving encouragement, said he had to leave London. His departure removed him from the negotiations and caused Lyndhurst to contact Lord George Bentinck, who led the Protectionist faction in the House of Commons. Lyndhurst later stated that he was "personally unacquainted" with Bentinck and consequently approached him through an emissary.[29] Bentinck rebuffed the overture, saying that because both Stanley and Lyndhurst sat in the House of Lords, it would be more suitable for all communication to pass between these two peers. This response caused Lyndhurst to conclude that "he had found so much bitterness of feeling and personal hostility that he abandoned the task and took no further steps."[30]

Sir James Graham, a Peelite and a recent Cabinet colleague of the former Chancellor, employed the term *intrigue* in a letter to Peel to describe Lyndhurst's attempt.[31] Lyndhurst's initiative was suspect in many quarters. For all of his talk of retirement, he retained a cast of mind that saw opportunity in chaos. Lord Bentinck was among those who viewed Lyndhurst with a jaundiced eye. Bentinck had emerged as a leader of the

Protectionist ranks, although some regarded him as a sullen and erratic figure. His enthusiasm for racing and horse breeding had led some wags to sneer that he had a stable mind. Stable or unstable, Bentinck had set his mind against both the gesture for reunion and Lyndhurst himself. On August 18, 1846, Lord Bentinck attacked Lyndhurst in a slashing speech in the House of Commons. The basis for his verbal assault was Lyndhurst's role in an alleged "nefarious job" that was totally unrelated to the Tory solon's efforts at fence-mending. Martin described the alleged wrongdoing as "of a complicated kind" and supplied these details:

> Sir Henry Roper, Chief Justice of Bombay, on the eve of the Peel Ministry going out of office, had been superseded, and Mr. David Pollock, one of the Chief Commissioners in London for the Relief of Insolvent Debters, had been appointed in his stead, the appointment having been "pressed upon him by the Lord Chancellor." The motive invented by Lord George Bentinck for this was to make a place for Mr. Phillips, the Commissioner of the Bankruptcy Court of Liverpool, in order that the vacancy thus created might be given to Mr. Perry, one of the Lord Chancellor's secretaries. Nor was this all. The appointment of the Chief Justice of India rested not with the Chancellor, but with the President of the Board of Control (Lord Ripon), and his consent to the transaction, Lord George Bentinck alleged, had been bought by the Chancellor appointing a nominee of Lord Ripon's to the living of Nocton.[32]

Bentinck's denunciation of Lyndhurst put Disraeli in an awkward situation. Bentinck and he had allied to bring down Peel. Bentinck was Disraeli's new friend, but Lyndhurst was his old friend. The Commons listened with anticipation when he spoke following Bentinck. Disraeli left no doubt about his esteem for his mentor when he made this public tribute: "No one intimately acquainted with (Lord Lyndhurst) could suppose him influenced by selfish purposes. On the contrary, I believe there never has been a public man animated by more generous impulses." Disraeli shared his recollection of a conversation in which Lyndhurst had declared to him that during his long career, he had been influenced by three considerations: the first his duty to the public, the second his duty to his party, and the third his duty to his friends. Some might have argued the accuracy of this ordering, but none could have mistaken Disraeli's conviction when he affirmed his belief that these were "the principles which animated Lord Lyndhurst," and he added his faith that "if this question were investigated, the conduct of the noble and learned Lord would come out perfectly immaculate."[33]

Lyndhurst no doubt took satisfaction from having his friend come to his defense. But he was a man who could speak for himself, and on August 20 his wrath rained down on Bentinck. Greville marveled at the force of his reply: "Lyndhurst came down to the House of Lords, and in a towering passion delivered a tremendous philippic against George Bentinck for his personal attack on him. It was extraordinarily powerful and eloquent, but language so bitter was hardly ever heard in the House of Lords."[34] Lyndhurst began by establishing the seriousness of what Bentinck had done, citing the "grave character" of his charges. He pledged to "state fully and plainly, and in detail, all the circumstances of the transaction." He would let the facts speak for themselves.[35] Lyndhurst ran through the chain of appointments in which Bentinck had detected some malignant plan. Finally, Lyndhurst came to what he termed "the most grave part" of Bentinck's charges. This allegation affirmed that Pollock's appointment as Chief Justice of India had been made by Lord Ripon, in his capacity as President of the Board of Control, as the consequence of a bargain whereby Lyndhurst as Lord Chancellor had appointed a clergyman to a post that carried an income, in a manner calculated to please Ripon. Lyndhurst proceeded to censure Bentinck as a man "who makes charges without investigation . . . he scatters about his attacks without in the least considering how they operate, and whom they may affect and injure."[36]

Lyndhurst denounced Bentinck, declaring that his behavior "shows him to be utterly unfit for any public situation." He declared that his critic's character was "not only weak, low, and silly; but its weakness, lowness, and silliness only are equalled by its folly and baseness."[37] He asked the Lords to consider whether Bentinck thought that

> everything is fair in party politics — that to blacken and traduce the character of political opponents, by means however base or foul, is perfectly justifiable. The noble Lord may perhaps have acted upon that principle, or perhaps from his early associations and his early habits he may have been led to form so low an opinion of the principles on which mankind acts, as to suppose that every man in his transactions of life be directed by some base, selfish, sordid motives.

Lyndhurst dismissed Bentinck as a mere man of the turf with political pretensions. In closing, Lyndhurst protested that "although refuted, these attacks are not harmless; they have a public effect, sometimes a lasting effect. Persons remember the attack — they do not always remember the defence."[38]

Lyndhurst's slashing rebuttal inspired Bentinck to respond the following day. Greville recorded the curious scene:

> George Bentinck, who has a sort of bulldog resolution that nothing daunts or silences, made a reply to Lyndhurst's terrific attack on him the previous night. He reiterated the charges and attempted to make them out . . . but not very successfully. The most curious part of his speech was a strange story he told of Lyndhurst having sent his secretary and an eminent merchant on the morning of the 10th of July, with a proposition to join Lyndhurst in the formation of a Government. As the speech is reported it does not appear very clearly how, or by whom, or with what object this Government was to be formed. This revelation, however, adds to the interest of the squabble, and will probably elicit something more from Lyndhurst or somebody.[39]

Bentinck's reply forced Lyndhurst's previous attempt at peacemaking into the open. Lyndhurst reviewed his efforts and the circumstances that had led him to approach the Protectionist leader. He submitted the testimony of the messenger he had employed to contact Bentinck, and he read from Peel's letter, which reviewed their meeting during which Peel declined to be a party to a reunion and renounced further political ambition as well. In his first reply to Bentinck, Lyndhurst had said, "To me, my Lords, it is most humiliating, at the close of my public life, and at the close, I may say, almost of my natural life, to be called upon to repel accusations of this kind."[40] Now, in his second answer to Bentinck, he returned to the same theme in rebutting the insinuation that he had used intrigue to regain office. He told the peers that "every one knows that I am no longer a candidate for office; that in consequence of a severe illness the holding of office during the past Session has been a painful and irksome task for me, and that I am desirous of passing the short remainder of my days among my family and my friends; and nothing even on this occasion should have drawn me forth, but the virulent personal attack made on me."[41] These sentiments illuminate Lord Lyndhurst in transition. The man who had sought and clung to office through the exigencies of political conflict had been reaching for retirement during the greater part of his last Chancellorship. He had set himself upon a new path, one that would lead him from an active partisan role to that of an elder statesman.

21
A Living Link

A sage has said that if you live long enough, everything happens to you, and some fairly remarkable things happened to Lord Lyndhurst during the last years of his life. His final accomplishments were to achieve length of days and to emerge as a national institution. But before Lyndhurst could assume that elevated role, he had to conquer a few longings for the palmy days of office. The administration of Lord Russell had a shaky grasp on power, and Lyndhurst dreamed of a return to the Woolsack. Benjamin Disraeli observed that "Lord Lyndhurst . . . is in great force, & seems to think he is going to be Chancellor again. Such are the gay illusions of perpetual youth."[1]

Lyndhurst's illusions may have been fed by expressions of regard Lord Stanley conveyed in a letter dated December 9, 1846, a little more than two weeks before Disraeli made his observation. Stanley's tone seemed to confirm the importance of Lyndhurst's cooperation, indeed, of Lyndhurst himself, in any future developments. Stanley may also have desired to smooth any ruffled feathers resulting from Lyndhurst's unsuccessful attempt to play peacemaker and the bitter aftermath of that initiative the previous summer. The Conservative elder, in retirement at Turville Park, must have savored this endorsement of his continuing importance in contemporary politics:

> I hope that we shall meet in London, and that, notwithstanding the breach made in the Conservative party by the events of last year, and all that took place latterly, personally unpleasant to yourself, we may be able to act cordially together and co-operate in maintaining a defensive and Conservative policy, watching, but not unnecessarily assailing the Government, and seeking to reunite the scattered fragments of the great Conservative party. This is the object at which I intend to aim as far as I can exercise any influence. I cannot of course answer for all; but I trust

that in our house, at least, the difficulties will be comparatively small. Your co-operation would infinitely reduce them.²

Such words, although not a pledge of a future Chancellorship, might have been sufficient to put Lyndhurst "in great force," as Disraeli concluded. Stanley had also expressed his wish "to reunite . . . the great Conservative party." His objective was akin to Lyndhurst's: both sought to preserve their party. Stanley had resigned from Peel's government in 1845. Robert Stewart wrote in *The Foundation of the Conservative Party 1830–1867* that Stanley did not do so "because he was a protectionist . . . he argued only that repeal was irrelevant to the Irish famine and that the government had, therefore, no case to introduce it on a plea of necessity." Stewart concluded that "Stanley resigned to preserve his reputation for political consistency, not to fight for the Corn Laws against a Conservative government."³ Stanley's position changed as the repeal crisis intensified and he decided that the schism in the Conservative party would never be healed under Peel. In the aftermath of that rupture, Stanley sought contact with Peelites such as Lyndhurst in the hope of a reunion. Both men underestimated the depth of the conflict that separated the two wings of the party. The Protectionists would not accept free trade as a settled issue, and their intransigence precluded the fulfillment of any desire they may have had for reconciliation.

Meanwhile, Lord John Russell, the Whig Prime Minister, was struggling in the political mire of Ireland. Mounting violence confronted an indecisive ministry that by November 1847 was forced to introduce a Coercion Bill. Before doing so, the government had attempted to create public employment through the construction of roads and bridges, which already existed in plentiful supply. It had spurned a proposal from Lord Bentinck through which the same purpose might have been achieved by the construction of railroads, which were in a rudimentary stage of development. With the ministry's dubious spending program in mind, Lyndhurst posed a question: "How can Ministers justify month after month spending such large sums of the public money without calling Parliament together to sanction it?"⁴

Although Lyndhurst's interest in parliamentary developments continued, there was to be no return to the Woolsack. The life of retirement he had so desired during his last years in office stretched before him. Now he had time to look after Turville Park, where he tended his garden and kept livestock. He improved roads in the parish and laid out a new road to the parish church. Lyndhurst was, however, no recluse of Turville Park. He continued to commute to London. George Street was a social magnet for the elite, whether Lyndhurst was in or out of office. Even after Lyndhurst retired, his home was the scene of lavish dinners and receptions. The marriage of his eldest daughter, Sarah, to Henry Selwin in 1853 was an occasion of deep personal significance as well as social celebration.

These years were politically quiet for Lyndhurst. Lord Campbell described his sojourn at Turville Park in disparaging words: "here he pretended to devote himself to improved methods for the raising of flowers, corn, and cattle; but his time was spent in reading the newspapers, in sauntering about his grounds, in corresponding with Lord Brougham, from whom he almost daily received a letter, and in quiet chat with a few friends who paid short visits to him."[5] Brougham was a daily caller when Lyndhurst stayed in London. Despite their earlier roles as antagonists in parliamentary debate, Lyndhurst and Brougham settled into an easy intimacy in their advancing years.

The years at Turville Park were interrupted by Lyndhurst's return to the House of Lords on June 19, 1849, to speak for the first time since the controversy with Bentinck. Lyndhurst's increasing blindness seemed to preclude any future resumption of his past service as a trumpet of his party. Consequently, his reappearance in the House of Lords after a long absence elicited surprise on both sides of the floor. He had come to speak in support of Brougham's motion to withhold the royal assent from an Act passed by the Canadian legislature granting compensation to those who had suffered losses in the suppression of the rebellion in 1837 and 1838. He argued that the measure would open the way for some who had fomented the rebellion to receive compensation for losses they might have suffered in its suppression. In effect, they would profit from the consequences of their own lawlessness. On the other hand, the issue of full self-government in Canada was involved. Lord Elgin, the Governor General, had formed a colonial government whose Ministers were from Canada's majority party. The compensation bill was a consequence of this spirit of self-government and promised equal treatment for both French Catholic Lower Canada and Protestant Upper Canada. It was opposed by many who, like Lyndhurst, supported a strong imperial discipline. Many among those present were struck by Lyndhurst's changed appearance, which bore the marks of decline. He communicated a degree of pathos when he expressed regret that he had felt compelled to depart from his self-imposed silence by addressing the Lords. Then he added, "And perhaps it is the last time I shall ever do so."[6]

During 1849 Lyndhurst experienced increasing blindness. Mary Copley informed her nephew, John Singleton Copley Greene, on February 19, 1850, that "my brother has been afflicted during the last seven months with a gradual decay of sight." Then she added a cause for optimism: "we are hoping that he will be ready for an operation before the season will be too far advanced, as we are told that it must be performed before the end of May or not until the autumn." Lyndhurst was being treated by an oculist named Dalrymple, who expressed confidence that the operation for removal of cataracts would prove a success. For the time being, by his sister's account, Lyndhurst could not "see either to read or to write."[7]

Two months later Mary could report that her brother bore "his deprivation with patience, looking forward to a speedy cure." She pointed out that the weather played a determining role in deciding when the operation could be performed. The surgery had been scheduled for mid-April, but "a change from warm to cold" had caused a postponement. The same letter contained a brief reference to the surgical procedure and an assurance that "there is no harm in the removal of the cataract, and it is over in fifteen seconds, but I understand that it will be a month before he will be allowed to use his eyes as before." Lyndhurst was afflicted with lameness as well, and "for the last two months he could not even walk without some one to take care of him, and now he is perfectly helpless."[8]

The weather continued in an unsettled state, so it was June 21 before the watchful sister could announce to her counterpart in Boston that "the cataract has been removed successfully from my brother's eye, and . . . he now sees."[9] Six weeks after the cataract was removed, Lyndhurst was able to pen a letter to his sister in the United States. He described his progress, declaring that "the result has been in the highest degree favourable for all the ordinary purposes of life. The sight is sufficient, and when I am allowed to use glasses, for which I must wait a few weeks longer, I shall see as perfectly as at any period of my life." Lyndhurst had high praise for Mr. Dalrymple, who had accomplished the hoped-for result without, by Lyndhurst's account, any pain or suffering.[10]

By October the patriarch was playing backgammon and whist with members of his household, although he was able to read only by daylight. When twilight descended, the ever faithful Mary, who seemed to live only to serve her brother and his family, would read to him, sometimes sharing this duty with Sophy, his second daughter. Lyndhurst added a line to one of

Mary Copley's missives, declaring that his postscript was "the best proof of the success of the operation which has restored to me the blessing of sight, the full value of which those only can justly appreciate who have had the misfortune to be deprived of it."[11]

In early 1851 Lyndhurst was strong enough to resume his attendance in the House of Lords. With his return he launched himself upon a decade that increased his stature in the eyes of his countrymen. Lyndhurst the careerist, Lyndhurst the mischief maker gave way to the venerable peer whose wise counsel people could regard as untainted by ambition. Although Lyndhurst did not tower in the national consciousness to the degree Wellington did, after the Iron Duke's death in 1852 he helped to satisfy the nation's desire for an elder whose advanced years made him a living link between a romanticized past and an uncertain future.

There was irony in the next development that touched the retired Conservative statesman. Lyndhurst received a summons to duty involving the one thing he shunned at this time: a return to an active role in politics. The invitation came from Lord Stanley, who, after the death of his father, had become Lord Derby. As leader of the Conservative party, he anticipated the fall of Lord Russell's weak Whig ministry at any moment. When Russell resigned in 1851, Derby attempted to form a government. Although his failure to do so gave Russell's ministry a new lease on life, many believed the lease would be a short one. Despite his unsuccessful attempt at Cabinet making, Derby anticipated that a second opportunity would present itself with little delay. Therefore, he devoted his attention and energies to preparing the groundwork for that enterprise. Significantly, he turned in Lyndhurst's direction.

Derby's overture came by a circuitous route. He wrote to Lady Lyndhurst because he was "unwilling to make a proposition to Lord Lyndhurst, which a sense of public duty might lead him to accept, without ascertaining from [Lady Lyndhurst] that he might do so without injury to his health or comfort." He declared that Lyndhurst's "co-operation, given officially, even if it were for a short period, would very much strengthen my position." He proposed that Lyndhurst take a seat in a future Cabinet "with high station, but involving no very heavy amount of labour." Derby did not envision a fourth call to the Woolsack for Lyndhurst but thought of the much less arduous office of President of the Council. Few real duties were attached to this position other than overseeing the work of the Committee of the Council on Education. If Lyndhurst would agree to accept this offer, Derby declared that "my Cabinet would be complete." Derby sweetened his

Lyndhurst. Used by permission of the Master and Fellows of Trinity College, Cambridge.

proposal by announcing that "the acceptance of this high office would probably render it desirable that it should be accompanied by an elevation in rank of the Peerage, which on other grounds would be well merited, and which, however little weight it might have with Lord Lyndhurst himself, might not be unacceptable as it might affect his Daughters."[12]

Sir Theodore Martin related that "Lady Lyndhurst disliked the idea, and thinking that in any case it would be time enough to deal with the question of office when it actually arose, the matter was left in abeyance."[13] Not for long. Russell's ministry succumbed on a vote over its Militia Bill. Lord Derby began his efforts to form a ministry, and in the course of his labors he called on Lord Lyndhurst to join his Cabinet. Derby offered "many thanks for your private hints, on which I have acted," hints involving the Foreign Office for the Earl of Malmesbury and a peerage for Charles Canning, the son of the late Prime Minister. Then Derby came to the point: "I have undertaken the task, but it is heavy work. You would greatly aid my Cabinet by consenting to become a member of it."[14] He had apparently been offered objections that included both the precarious state of Lyndhurst's eyesight and the equally unstable state of his finances. Derby addressed both of these difficulties when he declared that "even if your eyes did not allow you to undertake the duties of President of the Council, the Privy Seal would involve no labour or expense, and I should be happy to recommend Her Majesty to add an Earldom to it . . . which might neutralize some of my Lady's objections."[15]

Lady Lyndhurst was unmoved by the prospect of becoming a Countess. Lyndhurst promised Derby that he would "act in concert with your Government as far as my strength will permit. But you must allow me to decline office, for, to tell you frankly, I cannot afford it."[16] Derby was persistent, stressing that "we *must* have you in the Cabinet, even *without* an office — but *with* the Earldom, which I am authorized to offer you as the accompaniment."[17] The reason the Earl of Derby was so persistent in his attempts to bring Lyndhurst into his Cabinet lay in the relative anonymity of many of his new Ministers. Disraeli, the Chancellor of the Exchequer–designate, was known by most, but the others were so obscure that the aged and deaf Duke of Wellington repeatedly inquired "Who? Who?" in a loud whisper as their names were read in the House of Lords. This brought both embarrassment and the label of the "Who? Who? Ministry." Mary Copley wrote that "Lord Derby was very anxious to get my brother to be a member of his cabinet. He offered him the presidency of the council with an earldom; then the privy seal; and lastly, a seat in the cabinet, without any office." Mary bluntly explained to her sister that "the reason of his refusal is because he cannot afford the expense. It would cost about £800 to be made an earl, and if he were in the cabinet, he must spend at least a thousand a year more, and, having a pension, he cannot receive any addition."[18]

The pension of an ex-Chancellor had been raised from the sum of £4,000, which it had been when Lyndhurst first left the Woolsack in 1830. He now received £5,000 annually. As his sister pointed out, he would receive no additional remuneration by accepting a Cabinet position. Instead, he would incur new expenses. Money had always been Lyndhurst's special need because he never had enough of it. Political advancement had made him powerful; it had not made him rich. Neither of his two marriages had brought him a fortune. Lyndhurst had always maintained an expensive lifestyle. Now he was living a long life, and he had to consider the expenses of his final years and the welfare of a younger wife. Mary Copley observed to her sister that "under these circumstances, you will think, with him, that he has judged wisely."[19]

Lady Lyndhurst may have objected to her husband's return to office because of the cost it involved. However, she had another reason for opposing his return to a more active political role: a recurrence of his blindness now afflicted his other eye. He resolved to have this eye operated on in June, but it was the end of July before his sister could report that he had undergone the procedure with success.[20] A slow convalescence ensued. He had to "be *very* careful. He is still kept in a dark room, and is not to use glasses for three months, and is not to read for six."[21] Lyndhurst's dutiful sister returned to her role of reading Acts of Parliament aloud. Not until October could she report that "the sight of my brother's eye . . . is quite restored."[22]

By the middle of 1853, Lyndhurst had recovered his sight sufficiently to return to Parliament. He had suffered a "fit of the gout," which caused Mary to comment that "if it were not for his lameness, he would be quite a young man (and this at eighty-one)."[23] Lord Campbell agreed, and he described Lyndhurst's vigorous address when he moved for a select committee to consider the claims of Baron de Bode for compensation out of the funds France paid to the English government pursuant to a treaty in 1815.

> His voice was strong, articulate, and musical, his arrangement lucid, his reasoning ingenious and plausible, and he displayed a power of memory which at any age would have appeared almost miraculous. He had to narrate very complicated proceedings, extending over a very long period of time, and to specify numerous dates and sums of money forming items in voluminous accounts, and the names of many foreign places and persons — yet in a speech of two hours he never was at fault, he never hesitated, looked at a note, and he never made a mistake. This was the most wonderful effort of a public speaker I ever witnessed.[24]

At age eighty-one Lyndhurst could still amaze his admirers and confound his critics.

About this time, a low rail was placed before Lyndhurst's seat in the House of Lords to assist him in rising to his feet. In 1853 he returned to the chamber without a Cabinet portfolio but with increased stature as the elder statesman of his party. Campbell detected a new role for the ex-Chancellor when he explained that "Lyndhurst showed that he had no object of personal ambition to gain, further than the glory of being the unofficial protector of the new Government. Refusing to become President of the Council, he crossed over to the ministerial side of the House, and was at all times prepared to extend his aegis over the head of the Premier, saying by his looks, — 'I am content he shall reign: but I'll be Protector over him.'"[25]

In his golden days, Lyndhurst lifted both his voice and his aged body to exhort the nation from behind his little rail in the House of Lords. He also struck out in a direction that demonstrated his independence from Derby's policies. Corporation offices but not seats in Parliament had been opened to Jews during Peel's second ministry. Lyndhurst's support for the admission of Jews into Parliament in May 1853 put him in opposition to the Conservative Prime Minister, who opposed any change in this direction. Before taking a seat in Parliament, an individual had to take three oaths: one of allegiance, expressing the duty of the subject to the sovereign; another of supremacy, directed at Roman Catholics, which they were no longer required to take; and finally, an oath of abjuration, renouncing all allegiance to the descendants of James II. Lyndhurst moved the second reading of a bill to consolidate the pledges into a single oath that Jewish subjects could take in good conscience.

Lyndhurst skillfully traced the development of these oaths, which he demonstrated had been adopted to keep not Jews but Roman Catholics out of Parliament. He declared that "it is utterly against the principle of the constitution to exclude the Jews from Parliament on any such ground." Then he expressed his conviction that this principle "is the mainspring of our glorious constitution, that no British subject, no natural-born subject of the Queen, ought to be deprived of the rights enjoyed by his fellow subjects unless he has committed some crime, or unless he is excluded by some positive enactment of the Legislature directed against him or against the class to which he belongs."[26] The bill gained a second reading in the Lords but perished on a motion to send it into committee.

Lyndhurst used his independence from Derby's ministry to challenge what he regarded as the government's vacillating response to the challenge of a Russian policy for expansion. An early critic of what he viewed as a Russian threat, on July 12, 1853, he pressed for answers regarding a recent Russian denunciation of English policy and Russia's demand for the withdrawal of British naval forces from Turkish waters. Czar Nicholas's attempt to dominate the Sultan of Turkey required, in Lyndhurst's opinion, a strong response from England. An ultimatum had pledged that until the crumbling Ottoman Empire satisfied its demands for hegemony in the Bosphorus and the British fleet had been swept from Turkish waters, Russia would not abandon its occupation of the principalities along the banks of the Danube. Lyndhurst believed Russian ambitions and British reluctance to confront them at an early stage would inevitably result in war.[27]

Within a year Lyndhurst's projections had proved correct. The Czar sent troops into the Turkish-Rumanian provinces after the Sultan rejected a list of demands that included the right to protect Orthodox Christians in the Turkish Empire. The British and the French dispatched a combined naval force to the Dardanelles to forestall any aggression against Constantinople. When the Sultan declared war against Russia in October 1853, the Russians destroyed the Turkish fleet at Sinope on the Black Sea. British and French naval forces were sent to the Black Sea, and war was declared in March 1854. By this time Derby's ministry was gone, and Russell was Prime Minister.

Lyndhurst challenged the new government to prosecute more vigorously the Crimean War, which the disintegration of the Ottoman Empire had thrust upon an unready ministry. He rose on June 19, 1854, to denounce a return to the status quo antebellum as unsatisfactory to public opinion and as insufficient to secure the territorial integrity of Central Europe. Lyndhurst declared that England was not fighting for so tame an end. He insisted that Russia's cession of territory at the mouth of the

Danube was necessary to ensure the free navigation of that river.[28] Did Lyndhurst's warning have a bearing on the outcome of peace negotiations after the war? Lord Clarendon, the Foreign Minister, insisted on Russia's concession of Bessarabia, which the Czar resisted. However, Clarendon was firm, and he won the point. Lyndhurst had advocated a cession of territory by Russia as a guarantee for the security of Central Europe, and his advice had been heeded. He had settled into his role as an elder statesman, exhorting the nation and continuing to serve in the public forum.

22
The Nestor of His Party

Lord Lyndhurst suffered from gout in 1854. At the end of that year, his second daughter, Sophia, married Hamilton Beckett, and Mary Copley, in writing an account of the wedding, referred to her brother's affliction: "My brother was able to go to church. He has been confined for eight weeks with a very severe fit of the gout. It has now left him, though he is still rather lame."[1] Lyndhurst was past eighty, and his advanced age was a factor in his decision not to renew his lease on Turville Park in 1855, thus ending his fourteen-year rental of the property. Instead, he spent several months in Paris, long one of his favorite haunts. He was lionized in that city as a grand old man, and the Emperor Napoleon III received him at the Tuileries. Sir Theodore Martin explained their previous association: "Lord Lyndhurst had often met the Prince Louis Napoleon in London, at Lady Blessington's. He had no particular liking for the Prince, and indeed he knew him only as one knows those one meets at a friend's house."[2] Lyndhurst arrived at the palace accompanied by his wife and youngest daughter and later described the encounter: "I was presented with Lady Lyndhurst and Georgie, to the Emperor and Empress in private. We remained in active conversation, no other person present, for more than an hour."[3]

Upon his return from Paris, Lyndhurst appeared in the House of Lords to denounce a plan for creating life peerages. The government's proposal was designed to inject some prestige into the judiciary by elevating some judges to the upper chamber for the duration of their lives. Baron Parke had been designated as the initial recipient of this embellishment with the style of Lord Wensleydale. The Conservatives decided to press a resolution to deny Wensleydale the right to sit in Parliament as a peer. Lord Campbell supported the Conservative resolution and was delighted to join forces with Lyndhurst. He recorded that the eighty-three-year-old former Chancellor "showed marvelous energy and talent." His praise was hyperbolic.

He believed Lyndhurst's speech was "the most wonderful ever delivered in a deliberative assembly." As if that were not enough, Campbell declared that "Lyndhurst on this occasion, if a man of 35, would have excited unbounded astonishment, by his retentive memory, his deep research, his powers of reasoning, and his strokes of sarcasm."[4]

Lyndhurst raised the question of whether the time-honored hereditary character of the House of Lords would continue or whether it would be periodically remolded by the government of the day. He then cited the political consequences of the proposed change. He spoke of "unscrupulous Ministers" who might seize upon the precedent of creating a few jurists peers for the remainder of their careers and extend it solely for the achievement of their own political ends.[5] Lyndhurst closed with a warning and a reaffirmation of his allegiance to the hereditary principle, which he found "entwined in every part of our Constitution." He cited the commonality between peers and the monarchy in their enjoyment of hereditary rights. Each assisted the other "to form a barrier and defence to protect both those branches of the Constitution against any by whom they may be assailed." Then came the words of warning: "Break in upon that principle — destroy that outwork — and he must be a bold man indeed who will venture to say he can foresee all the consequences that will arise."[6]

Lyndhurst offered a motion to refer Lord Wensleydale's patent to the Committee for Privileges. The motion carried, and the committee heard evidence under the supervision of Lord Lyndhurst. In the end it supported Lyndhurst's motion that it recommend that Wensleydale's patent did not entitle him to sit in Parliament. Despite the government's opposition, the committee's report was endorsed in the House of Lords by a majority of thirty-five. As a consequence, the ministry withdrew the initial patent, and, subsequently, Baron Parke was raised to the peerage as Lord Wensleydale in the usual way.

During this Indian summer of his life, Lyndhurst took up a cause that showed him to be in advance of many of his contemporaries. He promoted changes in the manner of obtaining a divorce, advocating a proposal to place women on an equal footing with men in this area that was bounded by a double standard. Lyndhurst had voiced the same outlook when he fought for an increase in a mother's rights in the debate over the Custody of Infants Bill, which was passed in 1839. Lyndhurst — whose household was totally composed of females and who was a dutiful son and brother, a doting father, a respectful and conspiratorial husband to Dolly, an attentive and generous husband to Georgiana, and a connoisseur of a variety of women all his life — was a loyal advocate for womankind.

Campbell heralded Lyndhurst's commitment to women's rights in his own curious way: "the Russian War being over, foreign affairs had lost much of their interest, and Lyndhurst thought that he should gain more distinction by devoting himself to social questions which were now agitating the public. So he proclaimed himself 'Champion of the Rights of Women.'" Campbell added his own speculation: "To this course he was impelled partly by the fascination of the accomplished, witty, and still beautiful Mrs. Norton, who had acquired no small literary fame by her poems, as well as by several pamphlets she had written on the wrongs of her sex."[7] Campbell may have been partly right in describing Lyndhurst's motives. Lyndhurst had collaborated with Caroline Norton when he worked for the passage of the Custody of Infants Bill.

Caroline Norton and her husband lived apart. He had asserted his legal rights to deny her contact with her children and to keep the money she had earned from her writings. In 1855 Mrs. Norton published a pamphlet entitled "A Letter to the Queen on Lord Chancellor Cranworth's Marriage and Divorce Bill." She underscored the irony of a nation in which a woman reigned but women could not bring a divorce action because they had no right to do so in the eyes of the law. The pamphlet aroused public reaction, and it impressed Lord Lyndhurst.[8]

Lord Chancellor Cranworth had introduced a Divorce Bill in 1854 that moved the power to grant divorces from ecclesiastical courts to civil courts. This simplified procedure would have replaced the three steps involved in gaining a divorce: attaining a finding of criminal conversation from a law court, securing a divorce from an ecclesiastical court, and finally, obtaining a divorce by a special Act of Parliament. Cranworth's bill reaffirmed the practice of restricting the right of bringing divorce actions to husbands alone. This bill was not enacted, and Cranworth reintroduced it in May 1856.

At age eighty-four Lyndhurst took over the government's bill and pressed for a reform in the legal status of married women.[9] He outlined the plight of a woman legally separated from her husband. She had no right to sue for divorce, and her husband retained all rights to her property and earnings. Lyndhurst attacked the law of criminal conversation whereby a husband could sue his wife's alleged lover for damages. An accused wife could not appear in court to defend herself, but her reputation was destroyed regardless of whether the case was proved. Lyndhurst denounced the government's bill for preserving a situation that involved unequal grounds for divorce. The bill would permit a wife to gain a divorce only on the grounds of a husband's incestuous adultery, grounds Lyndhurst argued were so narrow as to afford women no grounds at all. He declared that "in principle there ought to be no distinction made between the adultery of the husband and that of the wife."[10] He sought to give wives additional grounds, such as adultery combined with cruelty, incest, bigamy, rape, desertion, transportation, four years' penal servitude, or a mistress in the shared residence of a married couple. Lyndhurst, revealing that he had received many letters from women abandoned by their husbands, assured his listeners that he could not describe "how strongly their recitals of the wretchedness of their condition are calculated to wring the heart."[11]

The government's bill was sent to a select committee after its second reading. Lyndhurst, as a member of this group, was successful in persuading the committee to endorse property rights for a separated or deserted wife. However, his plea for equal grounds for bringing a divorce action was rejected by both the committee and the House of Lords. A compromise allowed only incest, bigamy, adultery with cruelty, or four years' desertion as legitimate grounds for a wife's divorce petition. This was a considerable advance in Lyndhurst's direction. Lyndhurst's efforts to bring an end to suits for criminal conversation damages were rejected by the committee, accepted in the House of Lords, and, ultimately, rejected in the House of Commons. After the bill gained a third reading on June 23, 1857, Lyndhurst filed a formal protest in the Upper House declaring his opposition to the unequal grounds for divorce.[12] The attempt to equalize the grounds for divorce had raised the related issue of married women's property. Lyndhurst secured adoption of an amendment that provided that any woman who received a decree of judicial separation was to have sole control over her property.

Lyndhurst next became embroiled in a controversy over pornography. Martin noted that "his action on this occasion has often been misrepresented." He added that "for this misrepresentation Lord Campbell is chiefly to blame."[13] Campbell was alarmed by the increasing number of trials involving obscene books and prints. Therefore, he introduced a bill that empowered a magistrate to issue a warrant to search for, carry away, and destroy such materials. Campbell recounted that "Lyndhurst violently opposed this measure, and on the second reading he delivered a most elaborate, witty, unfair . . . and profligate speech against the bill."[14] The issue was the still contemporary one of freedom of expression versus pornography.

Lyndhurst spoke of the difficulty of defining of what is "obscene," and he regaled the Lords with hypothetical examples involving art, sculpture, and poetry. He spoke of prints that reproduced the works of the celebrated masters of Europe. He cited Correggio's *Jupiter and Antiope,* which he described as "the picture of a woman stark naked, lying down, and a satyr standing by her with an expression on his face which shows most distinctly what his feelings are and what is his object." It was, as well, a picture that hung in the Louvre, "right opposite an ottoman, on which are seated daily ladies of the first rank from all countries of Europe" who had come to study the works of art in that great gallery. A print of the famous painting might be confiscated and the shopkeeper who put it on sale prosecuted under the provisions of what Lyndhurst scornfully labeled "Lord Campbell's Act."

Lyndhurst cited another print of a famous painting that related the story of Danae. He invited the peers to imagine "a naked woman lifting her eyes to heaven, but standing in a very strange attitude, the shower of gold descending upon her, a little cupid peeping over her shoulder pointing with his dart, and other circumstances which I shall not describe." Lyndhurst moved on to sketch the studio of a sculptor, populated by "figures of nymphs, fauns, satyrs, all perfectly naked, some of them in attitudes which I do not choose to describe." All of these statues might be seized under "Lord Campbell's Act."

Finally, Lyndhurst entered the realm of the poets. The works of ancient satirists, of the dramatists of the Restoration, of innumerable French novelists — all of these would be committed to the bonfire by the operation of "Lord Campbell's Act." Whatever might be regarded as immodest, unchaste, or contributing to lewd ideas would be purged by the provisions of "Lord Campbell's Act." Lyndhurst moved that no action be taken until "this Day Six Months."[15] Campbell reported that Lyndhurst's "motion, was rejected."[16] Actually, Lyndhurst withdrew his motion and the bill was given a second reading.[17] Lyndhurst suggested amendments that he believed would prevent unsubstantiated charges from being brought. As the bill was originally written, a warrant for arrest could be issued when any person made an affidavit that he or she had reason to suspect that there were proscribed publications in a particular place. Lyndhurst provided an amendment that required that the plaintiff state to a magistrate the reasons that led to that belief. He stressed that his most important amendment required that the accusor must state what the publications were and that, if published, the party responsible would be guilty of a misdemeanor. The magistrate had to be satisfied that the case was a proper one for prosecution.[18]

Campbell, smarting from the ridicule the octogenarian ex-Chancellor had heaped upon him, let slip "some words so offensive that they are not reported in Hansard." This was Martin's description, and he made much of this incident, maintaining that Campbell uttered his words "in a tone so low that, while others heard them, Lord Lyndhurst, being slightly deaf, did not do so. They were so discreditable that when Campbell sat down, Lord Wensleydale told him he should inform Lord Lyndhurst of what he had said. Knowing this, Lord Campbell called at Lord Lyndhurst's house to apologise, but Lord Lyndhurst refused to see him."[19] After this rebuff, Lord Campbell used the third reading of the bill to make a public apology to Lyndhurst. He announced that he had "been understood to make use of an expression of an insulting and offensive character to (Lord Lyndhurst)." If this had been the case, he had no intention of giving offense, and if he did inadvertently "let fall anything which might possibly be so construed," he begged "most fully and entirely to retract it, and to express regret that I had said anything which might bear such a construction." A contrite Lord Campbell acknowledged that Lyndhurst "has done no more than his duty, and he has since then rendered material assistance in amending the Bill, and for that I beg leave to return thanks to my noble and learned Friend."[20]

Lyndhurst accepted Campbell's apology and simultaneously administered a rebuke. The venerable statesman acknowledged that Campbell had atoned for "what I considered to be the most offensive words which he uttered with regard to myself on the second reading of this Bill." He explained that "I did not hear those words myself, because I have the misfortune to labour under physical infirmity, but they were reported to me by different friends, upon whose accuracy I most completely rely, and certainly they were of a most offensive nature." As Lyndhurst warmed to his subject, he shared with the Lords his contempt for Campbell's literary efforts. He noted "a publication which [Campbell] recently gave to the world." *The Lives of the Chief Justices of England* was a work in which Campbell had made some allusions to Lyndhurst. The former Chancellor described this development scornfully, declaring that Campbell had "inserted two or three paragraphs of a nature by no means complimentary to myself, and having done so, he selects the particular volume containing those paragraphs from the whole set and sends it to me as a present, with the author's compliments."[21]

The exchange between Lyndhurst and Campbell resulted in an estrangement. The relationship between the two jurists had always been civil even though they had frequently been political adversaries. This rupture lasted several months, but it was burdensome for men who were in constant contact. Martin noted that "peace was restored between them, and they remained in friendly correspondence down to Campbell's death in 1861."[22] Martin might have more accurately emphasized that the reconciliation restored the civility that Lyndhurst and Campbell extended to one another. His reference to a "friendly correspondence" is misleading.

Toward the very end of his life, Campbell achieved his last great ambition — to be Lord Chancellor — but he did so with Lyndhurst's help. After the Liberals gained office in June 1859, Lord Palmerston, the new Prime Minister, sought Lyndhurst's advice as to a suitable occupant of the Woolsack. The aged statesman recommended Lord Campbell. According to Martin, Lyndhurst said that "Campbell . . . had always belonged to the Liberal party, he had claims upon the office by seniority, which made it impossible that other candidates should object to his appointment, he was a sound lawyer, and would do no discredit to the Woolsack."[23] Lyndhurst's suggestion was adopted. The evening before Campbell was installed as Chancellor, he dined with a large segment of the legal community. Lyndhurst was present and offered a gracious toast to his colleague. He repeated the praise he had given Campbell in the House of Lords when, on July 1, he congratulated him "on his elevation — on his having attained all that he has ever looked forward to. We may say of him in the words of the poet — 'Thou has it now, King, Cawdor, Glamis, all / As the weird sisters promised.'"[24] When Lyndhurst spoke these not exactly flattering words, Campbell had already penned the damning prose that would be published as the *Lives of Lord Lyndhurst and Lord Brougham* after the biography's author and subjects were dead.[25]

In one passage of this manuscript, Campbell declared that "Lyndhurst was now in hopes that he was about to earn the permanent enjoyment of the title of 'Liberator of the Jews,' conferred upon him when he passed the bill permitting Jews to hold all offices in municipal corporations."[26] This was a reference to the opening of corporation offices to Jews during Peel's second ministry when Lyndhurst was Lord Chancellor. The issue of Jewish disabilities was reopened after Lionel de Rothschild had been elected to the House of Commons six times. After each election he had been denied his seat because he had insisted that he be sworn in by an oath that conformed to his Jewish faith. After Rothschild's seventh election, a bill permitting Jews to sit in Parliament had been endorsed in the House of Commons by a strong majority. Lyndhurst spoke in support of this measure in the House of Lords on July 10, 1857. He castigated his fellow peers with this charge: "You are endeavouring to deprive the Jews of their rights by a side wind — by the voice of one branch of the Legislature only, and that not the representative — or, at least, not the direct representative — of the people."[27] Lyndhurst was criticizing the House of Lords for depriving the Jews of their rights after the House of Commons had made a decision to emancipate them. His words contradicted his previous position as an obstructionist in the Upper House against the Reform Bill and subsequent proposals for reform. Lyndhurst had also separated himself from Lord Derby's leadership by championing Jewish Emancipation. He had moved away from the position of the Conservative party and toward that of Disraeli. Although Derby had voted for Jewish relief in 1830 and 1833, this action did not signify a strong commitment. As leader of the Conservative party, he abandoned his former support for the Jews. Disraeli, however, did not sidestep the issue. He spoke out in support of each Jewish Emancipation Bill that came before Parliament, even though this behavior displeased the philosophical heirs of the ultra-Tories in his party.

A year after Lyndhurst made his declaration, the House of Lords reversed its previous opposition to the admission of non-Christians to either House of Parliament and approved a measure permitting each House to modify the oath for its members. This action resulted from a bill introduced by Lord Lucan, who had ordered the Light Brigade to make its disastrous charge at Balaclava in 1854. Campbell claimed that "Lyndhurst was much hurt by the notion of a cavalry officer carrying off the glory of being 'Liberator of the Jews.'"[28] On July 26, 1858, Baron Lionel de Rothschild took his seat as a Member for the City of London.[29]

A liberated Lyndhurst spoke to the House of Lords in these last years of his life. He was a man freed from a need to advance his career or keep his place. He had survived those decades during which he upheld the party line and harangued the party's legions. Now he could speak to the nation from a place elevated above the political arena, and he could lecture his contemporaries as to the proper role of the aristocratic chamber within the constitutional framework. With this mission before him, Lord Lyndhurst could assure his audience that he had "always considered the duty of this House to be to mature all plans of sound legislation — to serve as a check against the rash, hasty, and unwise proceedings of the other House, and to give time for consideration, and even for the abandonment of improper measures." The House of Lords could speak for the people, and in that role it could challenge the House of Commons. Lyndhurst added a disavowal: "I have never thought, however, that this House ought to be a perpetual barrier against sound and progressive legislation."[30] This statement contrasted with Lyndhurst's position twenty years before when he enabled the Lords to regain their amour propre.

Foreign policy issues commanded Lord Lyndhurst's attention. He believed the France of Napoleon III posed a serious threat to England. In January 1858 an Italian named Felice Orsini had unsuccessfully attempted to assassinate the Emperor. French indignation welled up when it was revealed that Orsini had prepared his plot in London. The following year war broke out in Italy when Piedmont, supported by France, attempted to win independence from Austria. Lyndhurst was alarmed by the spread of French influence on the Continent and the speed with which French forces were mobilized and deployed during the Italian campaign.

With these considerations in mind, Lord Lyndhurst rose on the evening of July 5, 1859, "to call the attention of the House to the Military and Naval Defences of the Country." The eighty-seven-year-old statesman leaned heavily on the small rail that had been installed before his seat. His body was bent with age, his eyes were dimmed by the years, and his face had a faded look that contrasted with the black wig he wore. His voice, however, was clear and strong, and the passage of time had not blunted the incisive logic of his argument. He stressed the great difference between England's present and former positions of military and naval preparedness. A great change had arisen because of the application of steam power to naval warfare. Lyndhurst feared England's traditional edge in sea power had evaporated as a consequence of this significant alteration.[31] He advocated both a Channel fleet to protect England's shores and a Mediterranean fleet to protect England's access to its colonies, particularly India. He recognized that many might dismiss his warnings against France and Russia because Britain was in alliance with the former and was on terms of friendship with the latter. His answer to such protests was "short and simple": "I will not consent to live in dependence on the friendship or the forbearance of any country."[32]

Lyndhurst emphasized his principal goal: that England have a military force sufficient to cope with any power or combination of powers that might be brought against it. Some might object to the expense incurred by such a project, but he urged them to consider that a French army of six hundred thousand soldiers lay within a few hours' sail of England's shores. France was the great power that England must be prepared to confront. Framed within this context, Lyndhurst's question was in the nature of a challenge. He asked, "Are we to sit supine on our own shores, and not to prepare the means necessary in case of war to resist that Power?"[33]

Lyndhurst's message was dismissed by one member of the House of Commons as the meanderings of an old man. The former Chancellor acknowledged that one part of this charge was true. He noted that it had been stated that he was an "old man" or an "aged man" or an "old Peer." He was sorry to say that he was compelled to plead guilty to this characterization. However, he objected to another part of the charge, which accused him of advocating doctrines unsuited "to the present day, and to the present enlightened state of society." He explained that he had merely reminded the Lords that in the past, England had enjoyed perfect security because of the superiority of its navy. However, as a result of the advent of steam power, naval warfare had assumed a new shape, which made it impossible to be certain that England could rely upon this previous state of security. He called upon the government to do everything within its power to put the country's military and naval defenses into a state that would restore the security that had ebbed away.[34]

Lord Lyndhurst returned once more to the subject of naval defenses before a full year had passed. On May 1, 1860, he called the attention of the Lords to the state of the Naval Reserve, asking for an account of its present condition and probable future progress. He began by noting that he was old enough to remember the wars with both revolutionary France and the first Napoleon's empire. England's splendid victories in that era had always been galling to the French. Under Louis Napoleon, the navy of France had been completely reorganized and transformed into a formidable fleet of steam vessels. France had also adopted a training system in which a crew was ready to be put aboard any ship the moment it was launched. By contrast, the lack of trained seamen forced British ships in commission to wait months before they were sent to sea. Lyndhurst, reiterating the demand he had made ten months earlier, called for "a Channel fleet equal to that of France, with the means of replacing it in case of disasters." He added that "we also require a Mediterranean fleet and a fleet of observation for the protection of our distant possessions."[35]

A Commission of Inquiry had recommended in February 1859 that a Naval Reserve of thirty thousand men be raised immediately. Lyndhurst revealed that only eight hundred men had been recruited in a period of three months. At this rate, he declared, it would take about ten years to raise the whole thirty thousand. He blamed the delay on the regulations issued from the Admiralty. These regulations, by which the seamen who enrolled in the Naval Reserve were asked to abide, consisted of 159 clauses. Lyndhurst submitted that "sailors are, as a rule, very simple-minded men and do not like entering into complicated terms of engagement." Lyndhurst labeled the regulations absurd and exhorted the peers "to bear in mind that all your machinery is of no use, and might as well be thrown to the bottom of the sea, unless you have a number of seamen sufficient to man your fleet."[36]

The press amplified the aged statesman's warning. One report suggested that "a national reverse would deprive Lord LYNDHURST of but a very short period of dignity and comfort. Whatever happens, he will leave a great name."[37] The eighty-eight-year-old solon's words excited comment and drew praise:

> Lord LYNDHURST has done good service to the public by calling attention to the question of our naval reserves. The intellect of the venerable ex-Chancellor is still as clear and as strong as ever. He is still as capable as ever of mastering alike the principles and the details of every public question to which he chooses to apply himself. We still admire his unequalled powers of narrative, his vigorous reasoning, and his happy illustrations. Of him it may be truly said that whatever he touches he adorns. And more than this, it may be said of him that whatever he touches he exhausts.[38]

Lyndhurst gained the sobriquet of "The Nestor of His Party" in the closing years of his career. Nestor, the wisest and oldest of the legendary Greeks during the Trojan War, had counseled caution to his companions. Lyndhurst's apotheosis in the popular imagination was celebrated in the pages of *Punch*. On May 12 a cartoon appeared in that publication portraying him as Nestor surrounded by the leading statesmen of the day, all clad in Greek dress. He is pointing to the ruins of the once formidable British navy.[39]

Twenty days after he had called for a rejuvenation of the naval forces, Lyndhurst joined the opposition to a Bill for the Abolition of the Paper Duties. William Gladstone, Chancellor of the Exchequer, had proposed this measure, whose adoption was expected to increase the number of inexpensive publications. Lyndhurst would have opposed the change purely on this ground in the 1820s. Now he argued that this source of revenue was essential at a time when England faced both a large deficit and a need for increased spending for defense. Lyndhurst asked his fellow peers if they would consent to give up "not for the present year only, but permanently, a sum of nearly a million and a half?"[40] Lyndhurst devoted the remainder of his remarks on this occasion to the concurrent issue of whether the House of Lords' rejection of a Money Bill passed by the Commons was an invasion of the privileges of that House. The former Chancellor did not dispute the fact that the Lords had no right to amend a Money Bill. However, that principle did not apply to the rejection of Money Bills.[41] Lyndhurst's appearance on this occasion left a strong impression. Noting the patriarch's increasing lameness, Martin described the scene: "Lord Lyndhurst, — now so weak upon his limbs that he had, on entering the House, to be assisted to his place by a brother peer — grasping the little handrail in front of his seat, raised himself with difficulty to his feet."[42]

The Earl of Derby called attention to the venerable lawmaker's eighty-eighth birthday, declaring that Lyndhurst had "signalized the close on this day of the eighty-eighth year of his honoured life by a speech combining the utmost clearness and power of statement, with a knowledge the most complete of the details of constitutional law and practice."[43] Lord Lyndhurst spoke in the House of Lords only one more time. On May 7, 1861, he voiced his support for a bill to secure the validity of wills.[44] The speech was not particularly remarkable, and its subject was not stirring. Thereafter, Lyndhurst attended the House of Lords occasionally, but his voice was never heard again in its deliberations.

23
Ever Resilient

If Lord Lyndhurst had died in 1830, he would be remembered as the Duke of Wellington's Chancellor who shared his chief's about-face on the issue of Catholic Emancipation. If he had died in 1840, he would be recalled as the great obstructionist who opposed the Reform Bill in 1832 and then captained the forces that forestalled further enactment of the reform agenda. A demise postponed until 1850 would have added little luster to his memory. However, in living into the seventh decade of the century, Lyndhurst added a final fillip to his career. Freed from the burden of seeking and holding on to office, he elevated himself as a force far different from what he had exerted in previous decades.

Lyndhurst had the good fortune to retain his intellect unimpaired even though time had taxed his body. An account of a banquet Lord Lyndhurst attended on June 20, 1860, illustrates the surprising twists that sometimes punctuated his life. The party, hosted by Lord Campbell at Strathedon House, was a gathering of the leading lawyers of the realm. Nearing the close of his ninth decade, Lyndhurst "was too infirm to walk upstairs; but going straight into the dining-room the rest of the company joined him there, and he delighted them all with his wit and good humour."[1] James Moncreiff, Lord Advocate at the time, was also at the party and recalled:

> It was a very remarkable party, from the distinction and age of many of those present, and the vivacity and interest of the conversation. I remember well that Lord Lyndhurst was unusually lively and agreeable. That which dwells on my memory is his leave-taking. He rose to leave the room before the rest of the party — but all the rest rose too — and there was something like a cheer from the others as he went out. I thought the old man was fatigued and was retiring early, but it turned out he was going on to a party at Apsley House.[2]

Several individuals who had the opportunity to visit with Lyndhurst as he approached the age of ninety remarked on his lucid mind and his eagerness to acquire new information. In August 1861 he visited James Nasmyth, a well-known astronomer, at his observatory at Penshurst. Nasmyth showed Lyndhurst his drawings of the moon's surface, which he had based on what he had observed through his powerful telescope. The astronomer was charmed by his distinguished visitor and left an account of their meeting:

> The cogency of the questions that Lord Lyndhurst put to me, as I laid before him these accurate, detailed, graphic representations of what the telescope had revealed to me, was a treat to me beyond expression. His questions followed each other in so clear and systematic a manner as to show that I had a wonderfully intelligent and apt listener. . . . I may also add that when I pointed out to him that the marvellously distinct details of the lunar surface, which a powerful telescope reveals to us, are of an antiquity that infinitely transcends those of the earth's crust's oldest formations, he caught up this special part of the subject as one that to him exceeded all the others in profound interest.
>
> What above all I was most impressed with was his wonderful aptitude to grasp at once the details of a subject that to most others would require a long course of special study.[3]

Many friends called on Lyndhurst at his home on George Street where he lived surrounded by his wife, three daughters, and his ever devoted sister, Mary, who trailed him in age by only two years. Some visitors left accounts of the time they passed in Lyndhurst's company. Lord George Granville, in a letter to Lady Lyndhurst written twenty years after her husband's death, lauded the patriarch for the counsel he received from the elderly man even though they had different party loyalties. Granville, who had been Lord President of the Council in Lord Palmerston's ministry, reminisced that

> during Lord Lyndhurst's dignified and serene old age . . . his kindness and friendship to me was without limit. I have often said with truth, that even in my political career I never received more encouragement from any one of my own party than I did from your husband; and on several occasions, with the knowledge of my chiefs, I consulted him, and always received excellent advice.

> You are aware how often he admitted me to his house, and I need not remind you how charming was his conversation, so natural and cheerful, so pointed, and yet entirely free from personal vanity. It often reminded me of that of Lord Melbourne — both apt to hit the nail on the head without any regard for the commonplace and conventional view of a subject.[4]

William Gladstone spent an hour with Lyndhurst in November 1862 and described the nonagenarian in a letter to his wife. "He is much *older* than when I saw him last," Gladstone wrote, "but still has pith and life in him as well as that astonishing freshness of mind which gives him a charm in its way quite unrivalled. He is very kind, and what is more, he showed, I think, a seriousness of tone which has been missed before."[5] In 1883, when Sir Theodore Martin was gathering material for his biography, which was intended to erase Campbell's calumnies, he asked the widowed Lady Lyndhurst to solicit reminiscences of her husband from his colleagues. She received many testimonials, including one from Gladstone. He recounted an exchange between Lyndhurst and Lord Brougham in which the latter sought out the former to gain advice for untangling a complex legal question. Lyndhurst "expounded the matter in the most luminous way." Brougham "went into raptures" and, referring to his colleague's lameness, made the following declaration: "I tell you what, Lyndhurst, I wish I could make an exchange with you. I would give you some of my walking power, and you should give me some of your brains."[6]

Benjamin Disraeli sometimes passed an hour or two in his old friend's company. The two had continued their earlier association, and they had exchanged intermittent letters over the years. Now Disraeli was Chancellor of the Exchequer, and he did not neglect his first friend in high places. After one of his calls Disraeli wrote, "My visit to Lyndhurst after 90 & recovering from a considerable illness; quite unchanged — easy as 1/2 a century before."[7] Disraeli also recalled an occasion when the conversation turned to George Canning, the first Prime Minister to raise Lyndhurst to the Chancellorship. "After some time, & several interesting details, Lyndhurst asked how old Canning was when he died. Answer 57. '57' Lyndhurst exclaimed — 'a mere boy!'"[8]

Lyndhurst's American niece, Martha Amory, wrote in later years of discovering her uncle laboring over an enormous law book. She remarked that she supposed that this variety of literature was his favorite. Producing a small volume from beneath the legal tome, he replied, "I like this far better; so well, I wish you would read it; it reminds me of my boyhood." The book was *Tom Brown's School Days at Rugby*.[9] In his final years, Lord Lyndhurst was confined to a wheelchair, and he passed much of his time in what had been his father's "painting room." In this old studio, crowded with the associations of his youth, he was surrounded by paintings and sketches, the handiwork of his talented father. In her memoirs, Lyndhurst's niece described his daily routine: "Rising about eight o'clock in the morning, after minute attention to the duties of the toilet, about which he had always been most scrupulous, and partaking a morning meal of almost abstemious frugality, he was glad to receive the various friends who sought his society for pleasure or advice."[10]

In October 1861 Lord Lyndhurst began to keep a diary. Its entries span only a three-week period, October 20 through November 12. Although Lyndhurst occasionally recalled past associations fondly, his last years were no retreat into reverie. His brief journal reveals a keen interest in contemporary developments. Events in Italy made him think about the Pope's refusal to give up the patrimony of St. Peter. He wondered, too, how Prussia could acknowledge the independence of the Italian kingdom, a territory France had claimed by divine right. Prussia's apparent repudiation of that ancient doctrine led him to speculate about the legitimacy of the French Emperor: "As to right divine does it extend to Nap^n 3. chosen by universal suffrage? Vox populi vox Dei."[11]

Reports of floods in the Nile Delta, the discovery of gold in New Zealand, and the "nearly naked" public bathing in Japan caught Lyndhurst's attention. He noted that in the latter nation, "women when young" were "tolerably good looking." He observed that universal suffrage in Australia was working very badly. The death of the Emperor of China interested him, and he recorded details of the six-member Regency Council that had been appointed to rule for the minor who had succeeded his father despite the fact that he was not the eldest son. Lyndhurst considered the prospects of trade with China and noted that Peking was now a city open to foreigners. During the three-week period he documented in his account, Lyndhurst paid another visit to James Nasmyth, who had revealed his findings about the moon's surface to him the previous August. This time the "very agreeable and unaffected scientific person" explained his method for deciphering writing copied from a Babylonian tile. Lyndhurst recorded that he was "very weak with diarrhea" at the time. A Dr. Hawksly called on two occasions, treating him with nitrate of silver and opium. He "gradually recovered" and found the doctor "full of good sense, no fussiness."[12]

Lyndhurst showed an interest in Lord Edward Stanley's ideas on education. Stanley had served in the Cabinet of his father, Lord Derby, as Secretary of State for India. He had pointed out that the children of the laboring class withdrew from school at ten years of age. They could not afford to stay longer because they could earn up to £12 a year to supplement family incomes. Lyndhurst's brief notes outlined the problem and his own observations: "Little learnt — that little soon forgot. Evening schools important. . . . It is said cannot teach ignorant men science. That is not so. Many matters of science objects of sight. Form of earth and its orbit. In mechanics — lever screw — so in other branches." Lyndhurst's interests embraced both the lowliest and the highest in the kingdom. He learned from a visitor, who had just left the Prince of Wales, that the young heir to the throne had pleasant manners and a good memory. However, the learned ex-Chancellor underscored one ominous detail about the future Edward VII: "Prince *never reads.*"[13] On October 26 Lyndhurst, the sturdy survivor of British politics, received "news of the death of Sir James Graham one of my former colleagues — age 69 able and industrious administrator cautious and somewhat timid statesman. Always spoke with weight in the House."[14]

Lyndhurst's notes during the few weeks that he kept his journal reveal an interest in events in the United States, where the spectacle of a divided union held the attention of all observers. As hostilities broke out in their native land, Lyndhurst wrote to his sister, Elizabeth Greene, living in Boston: "How strange that you and I should live to witness two revolutions in the same country."[15] Lyndhurst's diary contains only fleeting observations about the Civil War.[16] However, he gave a more extensive account of his views in letters he addressed to James Amory, the husband of his niece in Boston.[17] Lyndhurst endorsed a neutral course for England, proclaiming, "The conduct of our government will be one of absolute non-interference." He added one stricture: "It is hoped you will not treat the Southern seceders as rebels, in your conduct of the war, but as a *de facto* government, entitled to the ordinary belligerent rights."[18]

Lyndhurst raised the issue of neutrality once more in a letter he wrote to James Amory on June 6, 1861. He acknowledged that "the *Northern States,* perhaps I *shd* say the *Ud* States, are apparently displeased with us. Our policy is, I think, very straightforward and correct. Absolute neutrality in the first place: non-interference in this sad contest. But it cannot be denied that, according to the usual doctrines of international law, the seceding states from their numbers, their strength, and organization, are to be regarded as a belligerent power, and should be treated as such." In closing, the American-born Lyndhurst claimed that "the almost universal feeling is in favor of the Northern states and that the secession is at variance with the principles of the Constitution, and not justified by any of the alleged grievances."[19] This view differed, however, from that which prevailed among the British upper class generally.

Lyndhurst's neutral outlook and that of other British subjects was tested by the *Trent Affair,* which resulted when Captain Charles Wilkes boarded the British steamer *Trent* and forcibly removed James Mason and John Slidell, Confederate commissioners en route to England. News of this seizure inflamed public opinion in England, and there was talk of war. An open conflict was averted on December 26, 1861, when Secretary of State Seward ordered the release of Mason and Slidell. He rationalized that the two commissioners were "personal contraband," and, therefore, Wilkes had been in error in not seizing the ship as well as its passengers. This pretext ended the crisis. However, when Lord Lyndhurst sent New Year's greetings to his American sister, he was unaware of the new development. He wrote: "We are waiting with some anxiety, for the answer to our application for the surrender of the two prisoners. I hope there will be a ready compliance with our demand. The conduct of Captain Wilkes being a flagrant violation of international law, there is but one opinion in Europe upon the subject. To do what justice requires cannot, among reasonable men, be construed into an act of degradation . . . a refusal will be immediately followed by war."[20]

Despite the amicable resolution of this crisis, the two countries seemed to draw closer to war. When Lyndhurst penned a plea for moderation in the spring of 1862, he observed that the relationship between the two nations had become "very uncomfortable, not to say alarming." He regretted that "the seizure of our Vessels bound to neutral ports has produced, as its effect, great and general irritation and led to violent speeches in Parliament and abusive articles in our newspapers short only of the tone of some declaimers in Congress — in public meetings and papers on your side of the Atlantic." Then he expressed his concern lest the situation deteriorate beyond repair: "I anxiously hope that the moderation of our respective governments may be such as to allay this ferment, and to keep us out of the calamity of war."[21]

A continuing theme in Lyndhurst's correspondence that dealt with the U.S. Civil War was his sense of frustration at Northern dissatisfaction with Great Britain's policy of neutrality. In the late summer of 1862, he confessed that "there is one thing which surprises me in all communications from the U. States. That is their constant complaints and irritation against this Country. . . . Now what has been the conduct of our Gov't in this terrible conflict? Perfect and disinterested neutrality!" Lyndhurst expressed his conviction that this was a neutrality "far more advantageous to the North than to the South." He spoke, too, of the impact of this policy on the British people, among whom some were "suffering the severest privations, almost without murmuring." He maintained that both the government and Parliament were committed to a neutral stance and that the North should respond only to that policy and not to "the sometimes provocative opinions of private individuals."[22]

The last letter that contained Lyndhurst's reflections on the conflict across the Atlantic was written on September 9, 1863, a little more than a month before he died. Lyndhurst was pessimistic about future developments. He suggested that as soon as the Union had conquered the South, it would make war on England. The seizure of Montreal might be an initial step. Lyndhurst noted the improved outlook for Northern success and declared, "Your prospects of overrunning the South and of exterminating the Natives, for that is said to be your declared intention — are evidently advancing. You seem inclined to overrun it upon the same principle & in the same spirit, in which the Goths overran the Empire of Rome, establishing yourselves and your armies in the conquered provinces."[23]

The U.S. Civil War was one of Lyndhurst's great interests in his final years. Another of his interests during this period was religion. Martin maintained that "during the latter years of his life the subject of religion occupied much of Lord Lyndhurst's thoughts, and he made an earnest study of the evidences of Christianity . . . the result of these studies was a firm conviction that in the Bible were contained the issues of Divine revelation, and a humble faith in the great articles of the Christian faith."[24] When Lyndhurst was past ninety, Disraeli commented on Lady Lyndhurst's concern over her husband's religious beliefs. He reported that "Lady Lyndhurst, who persecutes him on the subject, has a religious gentleman, of very low views, constantly with him, & I observed on his table, volumes of the Prophecies, & all that. . . . Lady Lyndhurst seems satisfied with his spiritual condition, & I am told he listens with much edification to the gentleman." Disraeli took a cynical view of this development, declaring that "the truth is Lord Lyndhurst now loves nothing so much as conversation, & he must have somebody to talk to him, no matter what the subject."[25] After Lyndhurst's death a statement of his religious beliefs, written in Lady Lyndhurst's hand, was found in a drawer in his library. Subsequently referred to as "Lord Lyndhurst's Creed," it was a conventional rendering of contemporary Christian belief.

Disraeli paid a final visit in the last months of Lyndhurst's life and wrote of the old man: "Lord Lyndhurst's voice at 91 is tremulous, but his conversation is as good, I would say as youthful, as ever; it was always a mixture of playfulness & sound sense. No one more weighty when serious, but shrinking from arguments in conversation — & with the art of apparently touching lightly on subjects, though really with force."[26] Voice tremulous, body lame, Lord Lyndhurst was carried in a litter to St. George's Church in Hanover Square, close to his house, to witness the marriage of his youngest daughter, Georgiana, to Charles DuCanne on June 17, 1863. In the fall Lyndhurst retired to Tunbridge Wells for rest and renewal. On September 28 he fell ill and returned immediately to London. He lay in his large dining room, which had been turned into a bedroom for him, surrounded by his father's paintings. Prominent among them was *The Family Picture* in which Lyndhurst, as a three-year-old boy, was portrayed gazing up into his mother's face while seated on her lap. Calling his daughter to his bedside, he pointed to the family grouping and said, "See, my dear, the difference between me *here* and *there!*"[27]

The reports from Lyndhurst's sickbed told of a steady decline. Yet his mind remained alert, and he received several visitors who reported the tranquility of his final days. When asked if he were happy, he whispered, "Happy? Yes, happy!" Then he added in a stronger voice, "Supremely happy!"[28] In the early morning hours of October 12, 1863, Lord Lyndhurst died at age ninety-one. As the news of his death spread, bells tolled, flags were lowered, and tributes poured forth. The nation mourned an elder whose length of service was itself a distinction. Queen Victoria, who as a young woman had thought him a bad man, now hastened to declare that "Lord Lyndhurst served the Crown so long and faithfully, and was such an authority in the country, that his Sovereign . . . must deeply deplore his loss and cherish his memory." She extolled him as "valued" and "highly-gifted." The Queen's invocation of Prince Albert's sacred memory set a seal of sincerity on her tribute, which included an assurance that "my beloved husband had great admiration for Lord Lyndhurst."[29]

The *Saturday Review* emphasized that "extraordinary longevity, unattended by decay, always commands a certain tenderness and respect."[30] The image of a mellowed Lyndhurst held the attention of many who heard the news of his death. The *Times* devoted a full page, running six columns

Bust of Lyndhurst. A subscription fund was raised to support Lyndhurst's candidacy as High Steward of the University of Cambridge in 1840. The surplus funds were used to commission the sculptor Behnes to produce a bust of Lord Lyndhurst. This bust was presented to Lady Lyndhurst, who presented it to Trinity College, Cambridge, in July 1876. It now stands by the entrance to the Wren Library. Used by permission of the Master and Fellows of Trinity College, Cambridge.

across, to its announcement of Lyndhurst's death and a review of his career. Disraeli was believed to have been the author of Lyndhurst's obituary in the *Times*, even though it appeared anonymously, as was the invariable custom. The best evidence in support of this claim is a memorandum Disraeli prepared on October 13, 1863, beginning with the news: "Lord Lyndhurst died this morning." Disraeli's notations contained parallels to the *Times* obituary in both subject matter and language. Both mentioned Lyndhurst's lackluster role in the House of Commons and contrasted it with his meteoric rise in the House of Lords. Both tributes referred to him as a pleader rather than an orator. Both described his brow as that of "Olympian Jove" while noting the weakness of his lower facial features, indicating deficiencies in his character.[31] Perhaps the most telling clue that the *Times* obituary was penned by Disraeli was its recounting of William IV's desire to make Lyndhurst his Prime Minister in place of Melbourne. The new "Earl Copley" was to have had twelve seats placed at his disposal in the Commons for ambitious young men, and "the first on the list was Mr. Disraeli, then a young man not yet recognized by the public as a statesman."[32]

In his private recording of his mentor's passing, Disraeli was more analytical. He acknowledged that Lyndhurst "rarely originated, but his apprehension was very quick & he mastered the suggestions of others & made them clearer & more strong." Incisively, the future Prime Minister judged Lyndhurst as "deficient in imagination," an individual who "adapted himself to circumstances in a moment though he could not create, or even considerably control them."[33] It was this instinct for adaptability that so repelled his enemies and pleased his adherents. Lyndhurst was, above all things, a practical man who sought to follow a pragmatic course. His commitment to survival made him a bellwether among his contemporaries, who knew he would follow his instinct for self-preservation.

An unsigned personal account of Lyndhurst's lying in state in the family home in George Street was penned by his middle daughter, Sophia. Lyndhurst had died on a Monday morning, and she recounted that on Tuesday evening the widow, all of the family, and the servants gathered for prayers read by the Rev. Henry Howarth, the rector of St. George's. "He lay in the coffin covered in white satin & white roses, & looking like himself — white, calm, & peaceful & with a smile on his parted lips." The funeral was held on Saturday, October 17. Sophia went "for the last time to the room where he lay — but he was no more to be seen — only the coffin with wreaths of immortelles on it. It was like a church — solemn

& holy. I kissed the coffin. I saw it carried down the stairs & I watched it till the bier moved slowly out of sight."[34]

The *Observer* carried an account of the final ceremonies under the heading "Funeral of the Late Lord Lyndhurst." The cortege left the family home at 25 George Street at 9:30 on Saturday morning. Although the funeral was a private occasion and not ostentatious by contemporary standards, a large crowd had gathered before the house and along the route leading to Highgate Cemetery. The hearse was of a new design. It consisted of a light, open bier, fringed and draped in black velvet and drawn by four horses. The *Observer* suggested that "this had a tasty and unique appearance, and not only in that respect, but in a sanitary point of view, is a vast improvement on the old-fashioned hearse." On the sides of the bier were oval escutcheons displaying the coronet, crest, and initials of the late Baron. The onlookers could see the coffin, which was partly visible through openings in the sides of the hearse. It was covered with black silk velvet and medieval ornaments. On a large shield on its lid was engraved the following inscription:

>The Right Honourable
>John Singleton Copley,
>Baron Lyndhurst,
>P.C., F.R.S., D.C.L.,
>Died 12th Oct., 1863, in his 92d year

Lord Lyndhurst's coat of arms decorated the coffin lid as well.

Four mourning carriages containing relatives, friends, and servants followed the hearse. Lord Lyndhurst's carriage and three others of the family, outfitted with mourning appointments, completed the funeral cortege. A long line of carriages belonging to the nobility and the gentry followed. The procession reached the cemetery at 11:15. At the entrance of the Mortuary Chapel, the coffin was met by the Rev. Howarth and the Rev. Arthur Scholefield, the chaplain of the cemetery. Dr. Howarth read the funeral service, and Dr. Scholefield read the lessons and collects. At the conclusion of the service, the coffin was brought out of the chapel, and a procession followed it to the grave. A chaplet covered the coffin, and each pallbearer carried an immortelle, which he placed on the lid of the coffin. The newspaper account noted that "this part of the ceremony was very affecting." Lyndhurst's grave was a large brick vault near the southeastern entrance to the cemetery. Here he rested for two years until his remains were moved to another plot nearby at the direction of Lady Lyndhurst.

The funeral won the approbation of the *Observer*, which concluded its report with this judgment: "The proceedings throughout, notwithstanding the concourse of persons assembled within the cemetery and along the line of route, were altogether conducted with the greatest propriety and solemnity." The obsequies were attended by a number of pickpockets who attempted to profit from the large crowd that had gathered.[35] On the day following the burial, a Sunday, Dr. Howarth preached a funeral sermon after the morning service in St. George's.

Lyndhurst's burial in Highgate Cemetery was an appropriate conclusion to an unusual life. His funeral followed the correct religious rites and included an appropriate number of the aristocracy's coaches. But the choice of Highgate Cemetery was unconventional, indeed odd. Highgate was a civic rather than an ecclesiastical cemetary. England's governing elite found rest in parish churchyards or church crypts. Peel was buried in the parish church of Drayton, Wellington in St. Paul's, Disraeli in the Hughenden parish churchyard, and Gladstone in Westminster Abbey. All were enfolded for eternity in the Established Church. Not so Lyndhurst. There was something not totally respectable, something a bit beyond the pale about Highgate, and something appropriate in its symbolism for his exceptional life.

Part of the significance of Lyndhurst's life lies in his political rise. His story underscores the opportunities available to an ambitious outsider who would, in the words of Lyndhurst's protégé, "climb the greasy pole" of nineteenth-century English politics. He stood at the center, or very near the center, of high politics during a very long and distinguished career marked by idiosyncrasies. He was born in the British colony of Massachusetts, and revolution brought him to England. His talent as a defense attorney for a Luddite and other opponents of the established order caught the notice of the Tories, and they took him into their ranks. The combination of his legal ability and his political flexibility carried him rapidly to the Chancellorship and then made him a perennial occupant of that office. Lyndhurst was a self-made man whose convictions, at least at the beginning of his career, seemed loosely held. But his flexibility contributed to his usefulness. He played an important part in the constitutional crises of the period 1828–1832. Subsequently, he rallied his Tory colleagues and restored to the House of Lords a sense of self-worth. Later he contributed to the transformation of the Tory party into the Conservative party.

Because he was a self-made man, Lyndhurst sought always to attain and retain the prize of high office. His flexibility and frequent support of concessions were linked to his own self-interest in holding on to office or, in the language of his contemporaries, "keeping his place." Yet a compelling case for Lyndhurst as a moderate can be based on his response to the successive constitutional crises of the 1820s and 1830s. Ever resilient, Lyndhurst was able to rally his party at a time when its fortunes were low. He inspired the Conservative peers to grasp that they had survived the trauma of the Great Reform Act. He kept the Tory party alive as a fighting force in the Lords. When he had successfully marshaled his party's forces, he tempered their rebellion with his innate sense of moderation and endorsed the option of compromise. It is important to understand that Lyndhurst's flamboyant defense of the House of Lords did not undermine Peel's political maneuverings. It was an essential part of a two-pronged policy of simultaneous restraint and aggression, which helped the Conservative party navigate through the uncharted waters of the post-reform political world. Peel supplied the restraint, and Lyndhurst provided the aggression — two different elements in a remarkable strategy.

Lyndhurst's career encompassed a succession of steps that not only reveal his climb but shed light on the mechanics of contemporary politics as well. The turning point for him occurred when his ability as a lawyer caught the attention of the government. It rewarded him with a rotten borough and, ultimately, a peerage. From the time of his entry into Parliament, his fate was tied up with the fate of the Tory government. He consistently argued a course of action that kept both his faction and himself in office. Whatever political winds blew, Lyndhurst weathered the storm. He acquired a political wife, and together they assaulted the citadels of power, entertaining lavishly and following a shared instinct for making useful friendships. Dependent on office for his income, Lyndhurst accepted Whig patronage when the Tories lost power. Kings frequently sent for Lord Lyndhurst, and more than once he found himself in the familiar role of helping his sovereign find a Prime Minister. On at least one occasion, it was reported that he himself was to be Prime Minister. Season after political season, Lyndhurst continued in his role as a major political actor who possessed remarkable staying power. His career encompassed both obstructionism and acceptance of compromise. All in all, he revealed himself to be a flexible force, a man whose modest origins and difficult rise had tutored him in adaptation to change. Along the way he became the patron of other ambitious men, notably Disraeli.

All of this comes together as the story of the making of Lord Lyndhurst. His life is an account of an individual whose feet were firmly planted in Regency England — a place that was not far removed from the eighteenth-century political world described by Sir Lewis Namier.[36] Lyndhurst's belief that political office was a prize that should bring financial gain is part of the outlook of that age. Even his sexual libertinism evokes that era. Ironically, Lyndhurst the Regency man lived so long that he came to be judged, after his death and the publication of Campbell's book, by Victorian standards about principle and propriety — standards that were emerging during the twilight of his life.

In his final years Lyndhurst was able to win a new role and a place in people's affections. He lent his energies to important work such as the divorce bill and exhorted the nation to shore up its defenses. A fundamental issue throughout Lyndhurst's career was his lack of consistency on matters of principle. He was never one to nail his colors to the mast and stand unyielding. Yet he deserves reevaluation as a man who was part of Britain's governing elite when it grappled with demands for change during the second quarter of the nineteenth century. As one who counseled Kings and their Ministers, he merits understanding as a person of judgment if not of principle. On his role as an important figure who stood at the center of British politics during many decades must rest Lord Lyndhurst's claim for recognition and reassessment.

Notes

Introduction

1. John Lord Campbell, *Lives of Lord Lyndhurst and Lord Brougham* (London: John Murray, 1869). This was the title of the tenth and final volume in Campbell's series, *Lives of the Lord Chancellors*. The first volume began with a discussion of the Chancellors under the Anglo-Saxon Kings, and the ninth volume concluded with Lord Eldon, Lyndhurst's predecessor as Lord Chancellor. The tenth volume was devoted entirely to separate biographies of Lyndhurst and Henry Brougham, who followed him as Lord Chancellor in 1830, serving until 1834.
2. Sir Theodore Martin, *A Life of Lord Lyndhurst* (London: John Murray, 1884). Martin established his reputation as a eulogizer of deceased husbands when he was enlisted by Queen Victoria, the preeminent widow in her realm, to prepare a biography of Prince Albert, her late consort, in 1880.
3. Ibid., 247.
4. Ibid., 233.
5. Ibid., 514.
6. Campbell, *Lives*, 2.
7. Martha Babcock Amory, ed., *The Domestic and Artistic Life of John Singleton Copley, R.A. With Notices of His Works and Reminiscences of His Son, Lord Lyndhurst, Lord High Chancellor of Great Britain* (Boston: Houghton, Mifflin & Co., 1882).
8. Mrs. Hardcastle, ed., *Life of John Lord Campbell* (London: John Murray, 1881), 1:389.
9. Campbell, *Lives*, 2.
10. Ibid., 11.
11. Ibid., 71.
12. Ibid., 209.
13. Wendy Hinde, *George Canning* (New York: St. Martin's Press, 1973), 445.
14. Philip Ziegler, *Melbourne* (New York: Alfred A. Knopf, 1976), 277.
15. A.A.W. Ramsay, *Sir Robert Peel* (London: Constable & Co., 1928), 202.
16. Ibid., 104.
17. Norman Gash, *Sir Robert Peel* (Totowa, New Jersey: Rowman & Littlefield, 1972), 139.
18. Ibid., 161.
19. Ibid., 621.
20. Hansard, *Parliamentary Debates*, 3rd ser., vol. 30 (August 27, 1835), col. 1042.

21. *Ibid.*(August 13, 1835), col. 439.
22. *Ibid.* (August 27, 1835), cols. 1042–1049, *passim*.
23. Walter Bagehot, *Biographical Studies* (London: Longmans, Green & Co., 1881), 326.
24. *Ibid.*, 326–327.
25. *Ibid.*, 328.
26. Herbert Butterfield, *The Whig Interpretation of History* (New York: Charles Scribner's Sons, 1959), Butterfield examined the tendency to write history from the perspective of the present "and to produce a story which is the ratification, if not the glorification of the present."
27. James J. Sack, *From Jacobite to Conservative* (Cambridge: Cambridge University Press, 1993), 103. Sack states, "There is little doubt that the Jacobin disturbances of the 1790s had engendered a healthy fear within the English governing class of clubs and associations. One almost ubiquitous characteristic of the English Right in the early nineteenth century was its conviction that a revolution was imminent" (p. 103). Sack submits a list of individuals who shared this view. It includes Peel, Charles Arbuthnot, Wellington, and Wordsworth. It concludes with Queen Adelaide, who in 1834 thought she would share the fate of Marie Antoinette.
28. Peter Mandler, *Aristocratic Government in the Age of Reform* (Oxford: Clarendon Press, 1990), 194. Mandler notes that the onset of Chartism "had the effect of suppressing middle-class support for political radicalism — no one talked of House of Lords reform after 1837" (p. 194).
29. Philip Whitwell Wilson, ed., *The Greville Diary* (Garden City, New York: Doubleday, Page & Co., 1927), 1:94. February 25, 1827.
30. Henry Reeve, ed., *The Greville Memoirs, A Journal of the Reigns of King George IV and King William IV* (London: Longmans, Green & Co., 1874), 1:92. December 14, 1830.
31. *Ibid.*, 95. January 19, 1831.
32. The Lyndhurst Papers, Trinity College, Cambridge University, 0.16.38. 18, 1–2.

Chapter 1

1. Lyndhurst Collection, Glamorgan Record Office, Cardiff, D/D Ly 10/5i.
2. Benjamin Woods Labaree, *The Boston Tea Party* (Boston: Northeastern University Press, 1964), 50.
3. *Ibid.*, 67.
4. *Ibid.*, 107.
5. *Ibid.*, 112. Quoted from "Boston Newsletter," November 11, 1773.
6. Martin, *Lyndhurst*, 3–4.
7. Lyndhurst Collection, Glamorgan, D/D Ly 10/5i.

8. John Singleton Copley to Susannah Copley, October 26, 1774, Amory, *Artistic Life*, 37.
9. *Ibid*.
10. John Singleton Copley to Susannah Copley, December 4, 1774, *ibid.*, 43.
11. One child, a boy, was too frail to make the journey and was left behind in the care of Copley's mother. He died shortly after.
12. John Singleton Copley to Susannah Copley, July 2, 1775, Amory, *Artistic Life*, 57–58.
13. John Singleton Copley to Susannah Copley, July 22, 1775, *ibid.*, 62.
14. John Singleton Copley to Susannah Copley, July 28, 1775, *ibid.*, 63.
15. Martin, *Lyndhurst*, 13–14.
16. Amory, *Artistic Life*, 111. See also, Martin, 18.
17. Lyndhurst Collection, Glamorgan, D/D Ly 10/5iii.
18. Amory, *Artistic Life*, 112.
19. *Ibid*.
20. Dr. Horne to Mr. Charlewood, November 23, 1789, Martin, *Lyndhurst*, 18.
21. John Singleton Copley, Jr., to John Singleton Copley, Sr., May 25, 1794, Lyndhurst Collection, Glamorgan, D/D Ly 1/7a.
22. John Singleton Copley, Jr., to Susannah Copley, February 26, 1791, *ibid.*, D/D Ly 1/4a.
23. John Singleton Copley, Jr., to Susannah Copley, November 10, 1791, *ibid.*, D/D Ly 1/5a.
24. Rev. T. Jones to John Singleton Copley, Sr., January 24, 1794, *ibid.*, D/D Ly 1/9.
25. Lyndhurst Papers, Cambridge, 0.16.38. 18, 22.
26. *Ibid.*, 24–25.
27. *Ibid.*, 9.
28. *Ibid.*, 31.
29. *Ibid.*, 34.
30. John Singleton Copley, Jr., to John Singleton Copley, Sr., May 24, 1794, Lyndhurst Collection, Glamorgan, D/D Ly 1/7a.
31. Rev. T. Jones to John Singleton Copley, Sr., October 1, 1795, Amory, *Artistic Life*, 123–124.

Chapter 2

1. John Singleton Copley, Jr., to Susannah Copley, 1795, Lyndhurst Collection, Glamorgan, D/D Ly 1/14.

274   Notes

2. John Singleton Copley, Jr., to John Singleton Copley, Sr., January 2, 1796, Amory, *Artistic Life*, 135–136.
3. John Singleton Copley, Jr., to John Singleton Copley, Sr., February 27, 1796, ibid., 141.
4. Ibid., 142.
5. *Ibid.*, 142–143.
6. John Singleton Copley, Jr., to Elizabeth and Mary Copley, January 21, 1796, *ibid.*, 136.
7. *Ibid.*, 136–141, *passim.*
8. *Ibid.*, 140.
9. John Singleton Copley, Jr., to Susannah Copley, April 20, 1796, *ibid.*, 145.
10. *Ibid.*
11. John Singleton Copley, Jr., Traveling Bachelor Letters, Cambridge University Library, 0o6.95.12. These letters, written in Latin, were translated by William Heath Bennet and published in his *Select Biographical Sketches* in 1867. They also appear in Amory, *Artistic Life*, 155–169.
12. John Singleton Copley, Jr., to the Rev. Richard Bellward, D.D., Amory, *Artistic Life*, 157.
13. *Ibid.*, 159.
14. *Ibid.*, 160.
15. *Ibid.*, 168.
16. John Singleton Copley, Jr., to Susannah Copley, December 2, 1796, Lyndhurst Collection, Glamorgan, D/D Ly 1/18a.
17. *Ibid.*
18. *Ibid.*
19. John Singleton Copley, Jr., to Susannah Copley, November 22, 1796, *ibid.*, D/D Ly 1/17a.
20. *Ibid.*
21. John Singleton Copley, Jr., to Mrs. Charles Startin, July 20, 1797, Amory, *Artistic Life*, 170.

Chapter 3

1. James Beresford Atlay, *The Victorian Chancellors* (London: Smith, Elder & Co., 1906), 7–8.
2. Martin, *Lyndhurst*, 67.

3. John Singleton Copley, Jr., to Gardiner Greene, May 30, 1804, Amory, *Artistic Life*, 254–255.
4. Lyndhurst Collection, Glamorgan, D/D Ly 30/8.
5. Campbell, *Lives*, 13–14.
6. Susannah Copley to Elizabeth Greene, March 15, 1805, Amory, *Artistic Life*, 269.
7. Susannah Copley to Elizabeth Greene, November 5, 1805, *ibid.*, 274.
8. Susannah Copley to Elizabeth Greene, May 13, 1806, *ibid.*, 280.
9. Mary Copley to Elizabeth Greene, January 28, 1807, *ibid.*, 283.
10. John Singleton Copley, Sr., to Gardiner Greene, September 12, 1805, *ibid.*, 274.
11. Mary Copley to Elizabeth Greene, May 1, 1806, *ibid.*, 279.
12. Mary Copley to Elizabeth Greene, April 29, 1807, *ibid.*, 285.
13. Susannah Copley to Elizabeth Greene, July 28, 1804, *ibid.*, 258.
14. Mary Copley to Elizabeth Greene, April 5, 1806, *ibid.*, 279.
15. E. P. Thompson, *The Making of the English Working Class* (New York: Alfred A. Knopf, 1963), 543.
16. *Ibid.*, 584.
17. Martin, *Lyndhurst*, 116.
18. *Ibid.*, 117.
19. Susannah Copley to Elizabeth Greene, August 16, 1813, Amory, *Artistic Life*, 308.
20. John Singleton Copley, Sr., to Gardiner Greene, March 4, 1812, *ibid.*, 304.
21. Susannah Copley to Gardiner Greene, February 1, 1816, *ibid.*, 316.
22. Susannah Copley to Elizabeth Greene, February 20, 1807, *ibid.*, 284–285.
23. Susannah Copley to Elizabeth Greene, July 2, 1808, *ibid.*, 290.
24. Susannah Copley to Elizabeth Greene, August 10, 1810, *ibid.*, 300.
25. Susannah Copley to Elizabeth Greene, November 14, 1818, *ibid.*, 332.
26. Susannah Copley to Elizabeth Greene, August 23, 1809, *ibid.*, 295.
27. Susannah Copley to Elizabeth Greene, September 23, 1811, *ibid.*, 303.
28. Mary Copley to Elizabeth Greene, February 16, 1819, *ibid.*, 334.
29. Campbell, *Lives*, 14.
30. John Singleton Copley, Jr., to Gardiner Greene, June 4, 1804, Amory, *Artistic Life*, 256.
31. John Singleton Copley, Jr., to Elizabeth Greene, July 28, 1803, *ibid.*, 242–243.
32. Campbell, *Lives*, 15.

276   Notes

33. A barrister trying to establish a career usually couldn't be too particular about the cases he accepted. One cannot conclude that Copley was a Radical in his youth based on the cases he took. Charles Wetherell is a good example of this point. He sat in Parliament as a Tory beginning in 1813 and was a noted reactionary.

34. Martin, *Lyndhurst*, 127.

35. The *Times*, London, June 10–14, 1817, *passim*.

36. T. B. Howell, *State Trials* (London: Longman, 1824), vol. 32, col. 500.

37. *Ibid.*, col. 505.

38. *Ibid.*, col. 506.

39. *Ibid.*, col. 532.

40. *Ibid.*, col. 534.

41. *Ibid.*, col. 535.

42. *Ibid.*, col. 513.

43. *Ibid.*, col. 536.

44. Campbell, *Lives*, 16.

45. *Ibid.*, 15.

46. *Ibid.*, 19.

Chapter 4

1. Howell, *State Trials*, vol. 32, col. 1061.

2. *Ibid.*

3. Campbell, *Lives*, 15.

4. Bagehot, *Biographical Studies*, 327.

5. *Ibid.*, 329.

6. Howell, *State Trials*, vol. 32, col. 1394.

7. Martin, *Lyndhurst*, 143.

8. *Ibid.*

9. R. G. Thorne, *The History of Parliament, The House of Commons, 1790–1820* (London: Secker & Warburg, 1986), 2:195–196.

10. Campbell, *Lives*, 20.

11. Susannah Copley to Elizabeth Greene, November 14, 1818, Amory, *Artistic Life*, 332–333.

12. Campbell, *Lives*, 20.

13. *Hansard*, 1st ser., vol. 38 (May 4, 1818), col. 510.
14. Campbell, *Lives*, 21.
15. *Hansard*, 1st ser., vol. 38 (May 19, 1818), col. 821.
16. Ibid.
17. Ibid., col. 822.
18. Ibid., cols. 822–823.
19. Thorne, *History of Parliament*, 2:101.
20. From "Criticisms on the Bar," published in 1819. Quoted in William Sidney Gibson, *Lord Lyndhurst, In Memoriam* (London: n.p., 1865), 12.
21. Susannah Copley to Elizabeth Greene, November 14, 1818, Amory, *Artistic Life*, 332–333.
22. Susannah Copley to Elizabeth Greene, February 11, 1819, *ibid.*, 333.
23. Campbell, *Lives*, 19.
24. Susannah Copley to Elizabeth Greene, July 8, 1807, Amory, *Artistic Life*, 287.
25. Susannah Copley to Elizabeth Greene, August 10, 1810, *ibid.*, 300.
26. Susannah Copley to Elizabeth Greene, June 27, 1815, *ibid.*, 310.
27. Mary Copley to Elizabeth Greene, February 3, 1816, *ibid.*, 317.
28. Susannah Copley to Elizabeth Greene, March 25, 1819, *ibid.*, 334.
29. Campbell, *Lives*, 25.
30. Atlay, *Victorian Chancellors*, 29.
31. *Hansard*, 1st ser., vol. 41 (December 2, 1819), col. 598.
32. *Ibid.*, col. 600.
33. *Ibid.*, col. 599.
34. *Ibid.*, col. 600.
35. *Ibid.*, col. 605.
36. *Ibid.*, col. 607.
37. *Ibid.* (December 20, 1819), col. 1356.
38. *Ibid.* (December 21, 1819), col. 1438.
39. *Ibid.*, col. 1440.
40. Quoted in Atlay, *Victorian Chancellors*, 24.
41. *Ibid.*

Chapter 5

1. Martin, *Lyndhurst*, 173.
2. Howell, *State Trials*, vol. 33, col. 915.
3. *Ibid.*, col. 918.
4. *Ibid.*, col. 1296.
5. *Ibid.*, col. 1303.
6. *Ibid.*, col. 1304.
7. *Ibid.*, col. 1300.
8. *Ibid.*, col. 1304.
9. Leonore Davidoff and Catherine Hall, *Family Fortunes: Men and Women of the English Middle Class, 1780–1850* (Chicago: University of Chicago Press, 1987). Davidoff and Hall described the trial as "an important moment in radical politics with the royal divorce proceedings symbolizing the corruption of the political system." 151.
10. *Hansard*, 2nd ser., vol. 2 (September 7, 1820), col. 1363.
11. *Ibid.*, col. 1364.
12. *Ibid.*, col. 1374.
13. *Ibid.*, vol. 3 (October 28, 1820), cols. 1354–1357, *passim*.
14. *Ibid.*, cols. 1375–1376.
15. *Ibid.*, (October 9, 1820), cols. 452–456, *passim*. See also, Martin, *Lyndhurst*, 187.
16. *Hansard*, 2nd ser., vol. 3 (October 30, 1820), col. 1428.
17. *Ibid.* (November 6, 1820), cols. 1698–1701; (November 10, 1820), col. 1744–1746.
18. British Library, Add. MSS. 69730, ff. 18–20.
19. Lord Russell of Liverpool, *Caroline the Unhappy Queen* (London: Robert Hale, 1967), 159; see also, Roger Fulford, *The Trial of Queen Caroline* (New York: Stein & Day, 1968), 243.
20. *Ibid.*
21. *Standard*, October 13, 1863.
22. Gibson, *Lord Lyndhurst, In Memoriam*, 13.
23. Susannah Copley to Elizabeth Greene, March 22, 1821, Amory, *Artistic Life*, 338.
24. Susannah Copley to Elizabeth Greene, January 10, 1824, *ibid.*, 340.
25. Susannah Copley to Elizabeth Greene, January 11, 1826, *ibid.*, 341.
26. Mary Copley to Elizabeth Greene, May 26, 1826, *ibid.*, 342.
27. Campbell, *Lives*, 43.
28. Martin, *Lyndhurst*, 207.

29. *Hansard*, 2nd ser., vol. 16 (March 6, 1827), col. 909.
30. *Ibid.*, col. 925.
31. *Ibid.*, col. 927.
32. *Ibid.*, cols. 993–1008, *passim*.
33. The coat of arms of the new Baron Lyndhurst was a silver shield emblazoned with a sable cross paty and encompassed with an azure border on which were scattered eight silver escallops. The shield was surmounted by a baron's coronet, and above the coronet was an arm holding a sword aloft. The shield was flanked by two phoenix birds. A streamer spanning below the shield bore the motto Ultra Pergere. Lyndhurst's crest appears in stained glass in a window in the Hall at Trinity College, Cambridge.
34. Susannah Copley to Elizabeth Greene, April 21, 1827, Amory, *Artistic Life*, 343.
35. Susannah Copley to Elizabeth Greene, October 25, 1827, *ibid.*, 344.
36. Martin, *Lyndhurst*, 218.
37. Campbell, *Lives*, 49.
38. *Standard*, October 13, 1863, Lyndhurst Collection, Glamorgan, D/D Ly 29/6.
39. Lord Lyndhurst to Lord Eldon, April 26, 1827, Horace Twiss, *The Public and Private Life of Lord Chancellor Eldon, With Selections From His Correspondence* (London: John Murray, 1846), 2:171.
40. Campbell, *Lives*, 52.
41. Reeve, *Greville Memoirs*, 1:135. June 29, 1828.
42. *Ibid.*

Chapter 6

1. The reference "Protestants" is to Protestants opposed to Catholic Emancipation, whereas "Catholics" refers to Protestants in favor of Emancipation — rather than to actual Protestants and Catholics. Of course, everyone in the government had to adhere to the Protestant religion.
2. Earl Grey to Lord Lansdowne, April 16, 1827. Quoted in P.J.V. Rolo, *George Canning* (London: Macmillan & Co., 1965), 150, n. 4.
3. Hinde, *Canning*, 450–451.
4. *Hansard*, 2nd ser., vol. 17 (June 26, 1827), cols. 1421–1422.
5. "A Sketch of the Reign of Elizabeth," Lyndhurst Papers, Cambridge, 0.16.38. 7, 2.
6. *Ibid.*, 17.
7. "A Dissertation Upon the Character and Memory of William III," Lyndhurst Papers, Cambridge, 0.16.38. 18, 31.
8. Martin, *Lyndhurst*, 224.

280 Notes

9. Viscount Goderich to George IV, December 11, 1827, A. Aspinall, ed., *The Letters of King George IV, 1812–1830* (Cambridge: Cambridge University Press, 1938), 3:344–346.
10. George IV to Viscount Goderich, December 12, 1827, *ibid.*, 347.
11. William Huskisson to Viscount Goderich, December 13, 1827, British Library, Add. MSS. 38752, ff. 222. Quoted in A. Aspinall, "The Coalition Ministries of 1827, Part II, The Goderich Ministry," *English Historical Review* 42 (October 1927): 549.
12. Aspinall, Letters of King George IV, 3:347, n. 1, British Library, Add. MSS. 38752, ff. 240.
13. George IV to Sir William Knighton, December 16, 1827, *ibid.*, 351.
14. Lord Lyndhurst to Sir William Knighton, December 20, 1827, *ibid.*, 352–353.
15. E. A. Smith, *Lord Grey 1764–1845* (Oxford: Clarendon Press, 1990), 246–247.
16. Aspinall, "Coalition Ministries, II," 554.
17. Lord Lyndhurst to Sir William Knighton, December 31, 1827, Aspinall, *Letters of King George IV*, 3:356.
18. The Duke of Wellington to Harriet Arbuthnot, January 9, 1828, Gerald Wellesley, the seventh Duke of Wellington, ed., *Wellington and His Friends* (London: Macmillan & Co., 1965), 80.
19. Ibid., 81.
20. The Duke of Wellington to Sir Robert Peel, January 9, 1828, Charles Stuart Parker, ed., *Sir Robert Peel, From His Private Papers* (London: John Murray, 1899), 2:27.
21. George Macaulay Trevelyan, *Lord Grey of the Reform Bill* (London: Longmans, Green & Co., 1920), 197.
22. Lord Lyndhurst to Sir William Knighton, January 11, 1828, Aspinall, *Letters of King George IV*, 3:362–363.
23. *Ibid.*, 263.
24. *Ibid.*
25. The Duke of Wellington to Harriet Arbuthnot, January 9, 1828, Wellesley, *Wellington and His Friends*, 81.
26. The Duke of Wellington to Sir Robert Peel, January 9, 1828, Parker, *Peel, From His Private Papers*, 2:27.

Chapter 7

1. *Hansard*, 2nd ser., vol. 19 (April 25, 1828), col. 116.
2. *Ibid.*, col. 118.

3. G.I.T. Machin, *The Catholic Question in English Politics, 1820 to 1830* (Oxford: Oxford University Press, 1964), 117.
4. Martin, *Lyndhurst*, 248.
5. *Hansard*, 2nd ser., vol. 19 (June 10, 1828), col. 1252.
6. *Ibid.*, col. 1258.
7. Machin makes this point in *Catholic Question*, 122–123.
8. July 3, 1828, Lord Colchester, ed., *Earl of Ellenborough: Political Diary, 1828–30* (London: Richard Bentley & Son, 1881), 1:124.
9. The Duke of Wellington to George IV, August 1, 1828, Wellington Papers, Southampton University, WP1/950/1.
10. The Duke of Wellington to Harriet Arbuthnot, August 10, 1828, Wellesley, *Wellington and His Friends*, 83–84.
11. J. H. Hexter, "The Protestant Revival and the Catholic Question in England, 1778–1829," *Journal of Modern History* 8, no. 3 (September 1936), 302.
12. Wilson, *Greville Diary*, 1:134. November 20, 1829.
13. George IV to the Duke of Wellington, August 3, 1828, Wellington Papers, Southampton, WP1/946/4.
14. The Duke of Wellington to Lord Lyndhurst, August 8, 1828, *ibid.*, WP1/950/20.
15. The Duke of Wellington to Sir Robert Peel, August 9, 1828, *ibid.*, WP1/950/23.
16. Sir Robert Peel to the Duke of Wellington, August 11, 1828, Lord Stanhope and Edward Cardwell, *Memoirs of Sir Robert Peel* (London: John Murray, 1856), 1:194–197, *passim*.
17. Lyndhurst's role in the resolution of the Catholic issue has been disputed by his two principal biographers, Lord Campbell and Sir Theodore Martin. Campbell declared, "I do not think the Chancellor was at all consulted, before the measure of Catholic Emancipation was finally determined upon by the Duke of Wellington and Sir Robert Peel." Campbell, *Lives*, 60. Martin retorted that "in all the deliberations between the Duke and Mr. Peel, the Lord Chancellor had taken an active part, and his advice had helped to mold the measure, with which they finally resolved to dispose of the question on the meeting of Parliament." Martin, *Lyndhurst*, 254.
18. The Duke of Cumberland to Sir William Knighton, October 11, 1828, Aspinall, *Letters of King George IV*, 3:438–439.
19. The Duke of Wellington to Charles Arbuthnot, September 23, 1828, Wellesley, *Wellington and His Friends*, 84.
20. Colchester, *Ellenborough: Diary*, 1:286. December 27, 1828.

Chapter 8

1. Colchester, *Ellenborough: Diary*, 1:308–309. January 21, 1829.
2. *Ibid.*, 313–317, *passim*. January 23, 1829.
3. *Ibid.*, 325. January 28, 1829.
4. *Hansard*, 2nd ser., vol. 19 (February 5, 1829), col. 4.
5. *Ibid.*, cols. 4–5.
6. Colchester, *Ellenborough: Diary*, 1:336. February 5, 1829.
7. E. J. Littleton, *Diary*, February 5, 1829, Hatherton Papers; Machin, *Catholic Question*, 163.
8. G. M. Willis, *Ernest Augustus, Duke of Cumberland and King of Hanover* (London: Arthur Barker, 1954), 177.
9. *Ibid.*
10. *Ibid.*, 186.
11. *Ibid.*, 190.
12. Colchester, *Ellenborough: Diary*, 1:376–377. March 4, 1829.
13. Cited in Norman Gash, *Mr. Secretary Peel* (Cambridge: Harvard University Press, 1961), 569.
14. *Hansard*, 2nd ser., vol. 20 (February 19, 1829), col. 387.
15. *Ibid.*, col. 386.
16. *Ibid.* (March 18, 1829), col. 1264.
17. Gash, *Mr. Secretary Peel*, 578.
18. Colchester, *Ellenborough: Diary*, 1:399. March 19, 1829.
19. *Ibid.*, 401. March 20, 1829.
20. *Hansard*, 2nd ser., vol. 21 (April 3, 1829), col. 190.
21. *Ibid.*, cols. 193–194.
22. *Ibid.*, col. 195.
23. *Ibid.*, cols. 203–204.
24. *Ibid.*, col. 215.
25. *Ibid.*, col. 216.
26. *Ibid.*
27. *Ibid.*, col. 219.
28. *Ibid.*, col. 220.
29. Atlay, *Victorian Chancellors*, 65.

30. M. Dorothy George, *Catalogue of Political and Personal Satires* (London: Trustees of the British Museum, 1954), 15705.
31. *Hansard*, 2nd ser., vol. 21 (April 4, 1829), col. 390.
32. Ibid., col. 58.
33. Ibid., col. 391.
34. Reeve, *Greville Memoirs*, 1:198–199. April 4, 1829.
35. F. Bamford and the Duke of Wellington, eds., *The Journal of Mrs. Arbuthnot, 1830–32* (London: Macmillan & Co., 1950), 2:264. April 6, 1829.
36. Thomas Grenville to the Duke of Buckingham, April 14, 1829, the second Duke of Buckingham, ed., *Memoirs of the Court of George IV, 1820–30* (London: Hurst & Blackett, 1959), 2:295.
37. *Age*, April 19, 1829, 124.
38. Ibid., March 15, 1829, 84.

Chapter 9

1. *Age*, April 5, 1829, 110.
2. Ibid., April 12, 1829, 117.
3. George, *Political and Personal Satires*, 17090.
4. Ibid., 17293.
5. Carola Oman, ed., *The Gascoigne Heiress* (London: Holder & Stoughton, 1968), 198.
6. Bamford and Wellington, *Journal of Mrs. Arbuthnot*, 2:127. June 17, 1827.
7. Colchester, *Ellenborough: Diary*, 2:50. June 11, 1829.
8. Ibid., 53. June 20, 1829.
9. *Morning Journal*, June 26, 1829, 3.
10. Ibid., June 9, 1829, 2.
11. Ibid., June 11, 1829, 2.
12. *Age*, June 7, 1829, 181.
13. Wilson, *Greville Diary*, 1:96. July 21, 1830.
14. A. Aspinal, ed., *Three Early Nineteenth Century Diaries* (London: Williams & Norgate, 1952), 225. Le Marchant, April 10, 1832.
15. There were few houses, even Whig houses, where Lady Holland was received. She had been a divorcée when Lord Holland had married her.
16. Lady Holland to Henry Fox, October 15, 1827, Sixth Earl of Ilchester, ed., *Lady Holland to Her Son, 1821–45* (London: John Murray, 1946), 70.

17. Lady Holland to Henry Fox, December 8, 1828, *ibid.*, 91.
18. Lady Holland to Henry Fox, April 9, 1832, *ibid.*, 132.
19. Wilson, *Greville Diary*, 1:96. December 15, 1830.
20. *Ibid.*, 338–339. December 12, 1830.
21. *Ibid.*, 96. August 8, 1829.
22. *Age*, August 2, 1829, 244.
23. Willis, *Duke of Cumberland*, 189.
24. Wilson, *Greville Diary*, 1:97. August 18, 1829.
25. Bamford and Wellington, *Journal of Mrs. Arbuthnot*, 2:301. August 28, 1829.
26. British Library, Add. MSS. 47350, fols. 102–104.
27. Wilson, *Greville Diary*, 1:99. August 18, 1829.
28. Reeve, *Greville Memoirs*, 1:223. August 18, 1829.
29. *Ibid.*, 224. August 18, 1829.
30. Wilson, *Greville Diary*, 1:99. August 25, 1829.
31. Princess Lieven to Earl Grey, August 11, 1829, Guy Le Strange, ed., *Correspondence of Princess Lieven and Earl Grey* (London: Richard Bentley & Son, 1890), 1:266.
32. Earl Grey to Princess Lieven, August 14, 1829, *ibid.*, 272.
33. Princess Lieven to Earl Grey, August 23, 1829, *ibid.*, 278.
34. Earl Grey to Princess Lieven, August 26, 1829, *ibid.*, 280–281.
35. Reeve, *Greville Memoirs*, 1:227. August 22, 1829.
36. John Gore, ed., *Creevey's Life and Times* (London: John Murray, 1934), 307–308. September 22, 1829.
37. Princess Lieven to Earl Grey, August 29, 1829, Le Strange, *Correspondence of Princess Lieven and Earl Grey*, 1:284.
38. The Duke of Wellington to Harriet Arbuthnot, August 27, 1829, the seventh Duke of Wellington, *Wellington and His Friends*, 88.
39. The King of Hanover to Lord Lyndhurst, October 6, 1845, Lyndhurst Collection, Glamorgan, D/D/ Ly 16/23.

Chapter 10

1. In his novel *Bleak House*, Charles Dickens wrote of the case of Jarndyce and Jarndyce, which dragged on in the Court of Chancery for many years, incurring huge expenses that ultimately absorbed the entire inheritance at issue. It has been suggested that Dickens based the Lord Chancellor in his book on Lord Lyndhurst, having observed

him many times while reporting cases in his court. See Susan Shatto, *The Companion to Bleak House* (London: Unwin Hyman, 1988), 20.
2. J. H. Baker, *An Introduction to English Legal History* (London: Butterworths, 1979), 96.
3. Ibid., 97.
4. *Hansard*, 2nd ser., vol. 15 (May 18, 1826), cols. 1207–1209.
5. The terms of the Chancery Court are named for feast days in the Church of England's religious calendar. Michaelmas term takes its name from the feast of St. Michael on September 29. It is the autumn term and falls between October and December. The next term is Hilary (Lent), beginning in January. It is followed by the Easter and Trinity terms. The Long Vacation separates the Trinity and Michaelmas terms.
6. *Hansard*, 2nd ser., vol. 15 (May 18, 1826), cols. 1225–1236.
7. Ibid., col. 1228.
8. Ibid.
9. Ibid., cols. 1229–1230.
10. Ibid., vol. 16 (February 27, 1827), col. 701.
11. Ibid., col. 702.
12. Ibid., col. 703.
13. Ibid., cols. 708–714, *passim*.
14. Ibid., vol. 21 (May 12, 1829), cols. 1280–1284, *passim*.
15. Ibid. (May 21, 1829), cols. 1492–1501, *passim*.
16. Ibid., vol. 23 (March 22, 1830), cols. 674–681, *passim*.
17. Ibid., vol. 25 (June 10, 1830), cols. 211–216, *passim*. See also *ibid.*, 1st ser., vol. 24 (February 11, 1813), cols. 491–494, *passim*.

Chapter 11

1. Bamford and Wellington, *Journal of Mrs. Arbuthnot*, 2:356. May 12, 1830.
2. Reeve, *Greville Memoirs*, 2:93. December 15, 1830.
3. Princess Lieven to Earl Grey, September 28, 1830, Le Strange, *Correspondence of Princess Lieven and Earl Grey*, 2:97.
4. Earl Grey to Princess Lieven, October 6, 1830, *ibid.*, 102.
5. Princess Lieven to Lady Cowper, September 27, 1830, Lord Sudley, ed., *The Lieven-Palmerston Correspondence, 1828–1856* (London: John Murray, 1943), 18.
6. Princess Lieven to Alexander Lieven, September 24, 1830, Lionel G. Robinson, ed., *Letters of Dorothea, Princess Lieven, During Her Residence in London 1812–1834* (London: Longmans, Green & Co., 1902), 244.

7. Reeve, *Greville Memoirs*, 2:15. July 26, 1830.
8. Princess Lieven to Lady Cowper, September 27, 1830, Sudley, *Lieven-Palmerston Correspondence*, 18.
9. *Hansard*, 3rd ser., vol. 1 (November 2, 1830), cols. 52–53, *passim*.
10. Martin, *Lyndhurst*, 272.
11. Colchester, *Ellenborough: Diary*, 2:419–420. November 7, 1830.
12. Ibid., 420. November 7, 1830.
13. Ibid., 438. November 19, 1830.

Chapter 12

1. Lady Carlisle to the Duke of Devonshire, November 14, 1830, F. Leveson Gower, ed., *Letters of Harriet Countess Granville 1810–1845* (London: Longmans, Green & Co., 1894), 2:68.
2. The Duke of Devonshire to Lady Carlisle, December 21, 1830, Aspinall, *Three Early Nineteenth Century Diaries*, 4, n. 2.
3. The Duke of Wellington remarked to the Duke of Cumberland in 1828; *ibid*.
4. Ibid., 4–5. Le Marchant, November (?) 1830.
5. Mrs. Hardcastle, *Life of John Lord Campbell*, 1:498.
6. John Croker to Lord Hertford, November 16, 1830, Louis J. Jennings, ed., *The Croker Papers* (London: John Murray, 1885), 2:76.
7. Aspinall, *Three Early Nineteenth Century Diaries*, 5, n. 1.
8. Lady Carlisle to the Duke of Devonshire, November 11, 1830, Gower, *Letters of Harriet Countess Granville*, 2:67.
9. Ronald K. Huch, *Henry, Lord Brougham: The Later Years, 1830–1868: The Great Actor* (Lewiston, New York: Edwin Mellen Press, 1993). Huch makes several references to the relationship between Lyndhurst and Brougham: "The association between Brougham and Lyndhurst is not always an easy one to understand. They represented opposite political views, and by the late 1820s there were reports of 'great enmity.' It was, if anything, a political enmity, not a personal one." 53. "Neither seemed to take the other's comments as a personal attack, no matter how personal the comments were." 97. "There were times, to be sure, when Lyndhurst encountered the wrath of Brougham, but he never considered these verbal attacks as a personal assault. In his company, Lyndhurst, as so many others, found Brougham warm and charming." 177.
10. Campbell, *Lives*, 69.
11. John Croker to Lord Hertford, November 18, 1830, Jennings, *Croker Papers*, 2:77.
12. Reeve, *Greville Memoirs*, 2:89. December 12, 1830.
13. Wilson, *Greville Diary*, 1:338. December 5, 1830.

14. Campbell, *Lives*, 70.
15. Wilson, *Greville Diary*, 1:343. November 22, 1830.
16. Lord Lyndhurst to Lady Lyndhurst, Lyndhurst Papers, Cambridge, 0.16.38. 65.
17. Jennings, *Croker Papers*, 2:193. November 5, 1832.
18. Reeve, *Greville Memoirs*, 2:92. December 14, 1830.
19. The Duke of Wellington to Lord Lyndhurst, December 8, 1830, Lyndhurst Papers, Cambridge, 0.16.38. 40.
20. Sir Robert Peel to Lord Lyndhurst, December 9, 1830, Lyndhurst Collection, Glamorgan, D/D Ly 18/1.
21. Lord Aberdeen to Lord Lyndhurst, December 9, 1830, Lyndhurst Papers, Cambridge, 0.16.38. 66.
22. Reeve, *Greville Memoirs*, 2:92. December 14, 1830.
23. Lord Grey to Lady Lyndhurst, no date, Lyndhurst Papers, Cambridge, 0.16.38. 64.
24. Lord Durham to Lady Lyndhurst, no date, *ibid.*, 0.16.38. 67.
25. Wilson, *Greville Diary*, 1:96. December 15, 1830.
26. Reeve, *Greville Memoirs*, 2:92. December 14, 1830.
27. Sir William Alexander to Earl Grey, January 12, 1831, Lyndhurst Papers, Cambridge, 0.16.38. 68.
28. Earl Grey to Lord Lyndhurst, January 12, 1831, *ibid.*, 0.16.38. 69.
29. Martin, *Lyndhurst*, 276. See Huch, *Brougham*, 53–54. Huch points out that the office of Chief Baron was in the patronage of the Lord Chancellor, and, although cooperative in Grey's request, Brougham reminded him of this fact.
30. Martin, *Lyndhurst*, 276.
31. Lord Tenterden was Chief Justice of King's Bench. Wilson, *Greville Diary*, 1:343. December 15, 1830.
32. Reeve, *Greville Memoirs*, 2:89. December 12, 1830.
33. Aspinall, *Three Early Nineteenth Century Diaries*, 33. Ellenborough, December 11, 1830.
34. Reeve, *Greville Memoirs*, 2:92. December 14, 1830.
35. A. H. Manchester, *Modern Legal History* (London: Butterworths, 1980), 128–129.
36. Quoted in *ibid.*, 277.
37. *Ibid.*
38. Description of Lord Lyndhurst presiding at Anglesea Assizes at Beaumaris in 1832. Compiled November 30, 1880. Lyndhurst Collection, Glamorgan, D/D Ly 31/6.
39. Campbell, *Lives*, 71–72.
40. *Small v. Attwood, English Reports* 159:1051–1104, *passim*.

41. Martin, *Lyndhurst*, 284–285.
42. Campbell, *Lives*, 73.
43. *Hansard*, 3rd ser., vol. 2 (February 25, 1831), cols. 934–941, *passim*.
44. *Ibid*.
45. Reeve, *Greville Memoirs*, 2:94. December 15, 1830. Greville quoting Lyndhurst.
46. *Ibid.*, 75–76. November 25, 1830.
47. *Ibid.*, 94. December 15, 1830.

Chapter 13

1. Trevelyan, *Lord Grey of the Reform Bill*, 262.
2. Earl Grey to Princess Lieven, January 31, 1831, Le Strange, *Correspondence of Princess Lieven and Earl Grey*, 2:151.
3. Earl Grey to Princess Lieven, January 22, 1831, ibid., 2:141.
4. Henry Lord Brougham, *The Life and Times of Henry Lord Brougham* (London: W. Blackwood & Sons, 1871), 3:146.
5. *Hansard*, 3rd ser., vol. 3 (March 28, 1831), col. 993.
6. The Duke of Wellington to Lord Lyndhurst, March 25, 1831, Wellington Papers, Southampton, WP1/1180/14.
7. Lord Lyndhurst to the Duke of Wellington, *ibid.*, WP1/1179/10.
8. Michael Brock, *The Great Reform Act* (London: Hutchinson Library Press, 1973), 191.
9. Sir Henry Hardinge to the Duke of Wellington, May 28, 1831, Wellington Papers, Southampton, WP1/1185/32.
10. Wilson, *Greville Diary*, 1:344. September 22, 1831.
11. Abraham D. Kriegel, ed., *The Holland House Diaries, 1831–1840* (London: Routledge & Kegan Paul, 1977), 58. September 21, 1831.
12. Wilson, *Greville Diary*, 1:344. September 24, 1831.
13. Lord Lyndhurst to the Duke of Wellington, September 20, 1831, Wellington Papers, Southampton, WP1/1195/35.
14. The Duke of Wellington to the Marquess of Bath, September 22, 1831, the second Duke of Wellington, ed., *Despatches, Correspondence, and Memoranda of Field Marshall Arthur Duke of Wellington, K. G.* (London: John Murray, 1878), 7:531–532.
15. The Duke of Wellington to the Marquess of Londonderry, October 15, 1831, *ibid.*, 563.
16. *Hansard*, 3rd ser., vol. 8 (October 7, 1831), col. 283.
17. *Ibid.*, cols. 287–288.

18. *Ibid.*, col. 298.
19. *Ibid.*, cols. 298–299.
20. *Ibid.*, cols. 311–316, *passim*.
21. *Ibid.*, col. 340.
22. Campbell, *Lives*, 78.
23. Lady Holland to Henry Fox, September 23, 1831, Ilchester, *Lady Holland to Her Son*, 118.
24. Lady Holland to Henry Fox, October 9, 1831, *ibid.*, 120.
25. Henry Reeve, *Greville Memoirs* (New York: D. Appleton & Co., 1887), 2:19. November 11, 1831.
26. The *Times*, October 18, 1831, 3.

Chapter 14

1. Norman Gash, *Reaction and Reconstruction in English Politics 1832–1852* (Oxford: Clarendon Press, 1965), 30.
2. Earl Grey to Sir Herbert Taylor, October 8, 1831, Henry Earl Grey, ed., *The Reform Act, 1832: Correspondence of Earl Grey with King William IV and With Sir Herbert Taylor* (London: John Murray, 1867), 1:366.
3. Earl Grey to King William IV, January 16, 1832, *ibid.*, 2:120.
4. A. S. Turberville, *The House of Lords in the Age of Reform* (London: Faber & Faber, 1958), 282.
5. Reeve, *Greville Memoirs*, 2:273. March 27, 1832.
6. Kriegel, *Holland House Diaries*, 67. October 12, 1831.
7. Earl Grey to Lord Brougham, January 1, 1832, Brougham, *Life and Times*, 3:166.
8. *Hansard*, 3rd ser., vol. 12 (April 13, 1832), cols. 429–439, *passim*.
9. Wilson, *Greville Diary*, 1:518.
10. Henry Lord Cockburn, *Life of Francis Jeffrey* (Edinburgh: A. & C. Black, 1872), 1:323.
11. *Hansard*, 3rd ser., vol. 12 (April 13, 1832), cols. 440–446, *passim*.
12. *Ibid.*, col. 452.
13. Protocol no. 3, Ellenborough MSS., Public Record Office, 30/12/20/6. Cited in Brock, *Reform Act*, 283.
14. *Ibid.*, 288.
15. Bamford and Wellington, *Journal of Mrs. Arbuthnot*, 2:152. December 16, 1827.

290   Notes

16. Aspinall, *Three Early Nineteenth Century Diaries*, 225–226. Le Marchant, April 10, 1832.
17. Lady Holland to Henry Fox, April 9, 1832, Ilchester, *Lady Holland to Her Son*, 132.
18. Aspinall, *Three Early Nineteenth Century Diaries*, 226. Le Marchant, April 10, 1832.
19. *Ibid.*

Chapter 15

1. Aspinall, *Three Early Nineteenth Century Diaries*, 238. Ellenborough, May 7, 1832.
2. *Ibid.*, 241. Le Marchant, May 7, 1832.
3. Brougham, *Life and Times*, 3:193.
4. Campbell, *Lives*, 81.
5. *Ibid.*, 82.
6. *Ibid.*, 82–83.
7. Croker, *Croker Papers*, 2:155. May 10, 1832.
8. *Ibid.*
9. Aspinall, *Three Early Nineteenth Century Diaries*, 247. Le Marchant, May 9, 1832.
10. Lord Lyndhurst to the Duke of Wellington, May 10, 1832, the second Duke of Wellington, *Despatches, Correspondence, and Memoranda*, 8:303–304.
11. Lord Lyndhurst to the Duke of Wellington, May 10, 1832, *ibid.*, 304.
12. The Duke of Wellington to Lord Lyndhurst, May 10, 1832, *ibid.*
13. Lord Lyndhurst to the Duke of Wellington, May 12, 1832, *ibid.*, 307.
14. Wilson, *Greville Diary*, 1:393–394. October 26, 1832.
15. *Ibid.*, 395. January 8, 1834.
16. Aspinall, *Three Early Nineteenth Century Diaries*, 248. Ellenborough, May 11, 1832.
17. Reeve, *Greville Memoirs*, 2:299. May 17, 1832.
18. Lord Lyndhurst to the Duke of Wellington, May 14, 1832, the second Duke of Wellington, *Despatches, Correspondence, and Memoranda*, 8:316.
19. The Duke of Wellington to Lord Lyndhurst, May 14, 1832, *ibid.*
20. Reeve, *Greville Memoirs*, 2:299. May 17, 1832.
21. *Ibid.*, 300. May 17, 1832.
22. Earl Grey to King William IV, May 15, 1832, Grey, *Correspondence of Earl Grey With King William IV*, 2:411.

23. Lord Lyndhurst to the Duke of Wellington, May 17, 1832, the second Duke of Wellington, *Despatches, Correspondence, and Memoranda,* 8:331.
24. Sir Herbert Taylor to the Duke of Wellington, May 17, 1832, *ibid.,* 332.
25. The Duke of Wellington to Sir Herbert Taylor, May 17, 1832, *ibid.*
26. *Hansard,* 3rd ser., vol. 12 (May 17, 1832), col. 997.
27. Reeve, *Greville Memoirs,* 2:303. May 19, 1832.
28. *Hansard,* 3rd ser., vol. 12 (May 17, 1832), cols. 999–1002, *passim.*
29. Earl Grey to King William IV, May 17, 1832, Grey, *Correspondence of Earl Grey With King William IV,* 2:422.
30. King William IV to the Earl of Mansfield, May 18, 1832, *ibid.,* 428.
31. Earl Grey to Sir Herbert Taylor, May 17, 1832, *ibid.,* 424.
32. Earl Grey to Sir Herbert Taylor, June 8, 1832, *ibid.,* 467.
33. Wilson, *Greville Diary,* 1:415.
34. *Hansard,* 3rd ser., vol. 12 (May 17, 1832), col. 1000.
35. William Monypenny, *The Life of Benjamin Disraeli* (New York: Macmillan & Co., 1913), 1:388.
36. *Illustrated London News,* October 24, 1863, 417.
37. *Spectator,* October 17, 1863, 2623.
38. Campbell, *Lives,* 88.

Chapter 16

1. The appellation *Conservative* spread quickly as a consequence of the reform crisis. It signified the party that stood for the conservation of the important traditional institutions. It lacked the negative sound of *anti-reformer* and the reactionary connotation of the term *Tory.*
2. Reeve, *Greville Memoirs,* 2:330. November 7, 1832.
3. *Ibid.,* 331. November 15, 1832.
4. Atlay, *Victorian Chancellors,* 101.
5. The Duke of Wellington to Lord Lyndhurst, June 15, 1833, John Brooke and Julia Gandy, eds., *The Prime Ministers' Papers: Wellington, Political Correspondence, 1833–November 1834* (London: Her Majesty's Stationery Office, 1975), 1:235.
6. The Duke of Wellington to the Bishop of Exeter, June 16, 1833, *ibid.,* 261.
7. *Hansard,* 3rd ser., vol. 18 (June 17, 1833), cols. 869–871, *passim.*
8. Atlay, *Victorian Chancellors,* 102–103.

292 Notes

9. Samuel Warren. Quoted in Martin, *Lyndhurst*, 311–312.
10. *Hansard*, 3rd ser., vol. 19 (July 19, 1833), cols. 313–314.
11. Kriegel, *Holland House Diaries*, 224. June 24–30, 1833.
12. Reeve, *Greville Memoirs*, 3:7. July 12, 1833.
13. Brougham, *Life and Times*, 3:439.
14. Kriegel, *Holland House Diaries*, 235. July 26, 1833.
15. Amory, *Artistic Life*, 360.
16. Harriet Countess Granville to the Duke of Devonshire, December 12, 1833, Gower, *Letters of Harriet Countess Granville*, 2:145.
17. Countess Granville to the Duke of Devonshire, January 16, 1834, ibid., 149.
18. Countess Granville to Lady Carlisle, February 1834, *ibid.*, 151.
19. Martin, *Lyndhurst*, 314.
20. Campbell, *Lives*, 94.
21. Martin, *Lyndhurst*, 314, n. 1.
22. Countess Granville to the Duke of Devonshire, January 16, 1834, Gower, *Letters of Harriet Countess Granville*, 2:149.
23. Mary Copley to Elizabeth Greene, January 24, 1834, Amory, *Artistic Life*, 351.
24. Mary Copley to Elizabeth Greene, June 1, 1834, *ibid.*
25. Countess Granville to the Duke of Devonshire, January 23, 1834, Gower, *Letters of Harriet Countess Granville*, 2:149.
26. Countess Granville to Lady Carlisle, February 27, 1834, *ibid.*, 152.
27. Lady Holland to Lady Augusta Fox, February 4, 1834, Ilchester, *Lady Holland to Her Son*, 143–144.
28. William Holmes to the Duke of Wellington, January 19, 1834, Brooke and Gandy, *Prime Ministers' Papers*, 1:425.
29. Mary Copley to Elizabeth Greene, June 1, 1834, Amory, *Artistic Life*, 351.
30. Martin, *Lyndhurst*, 314.
31. Amory, *Artistic Life*, 360.
32. Countess Granville to the Duke of Devonshire, January 16, 1834, Gower, *Letters of Harriet Countess Granville*, 2:149.
33. Williams Holmes to the Duke of Wellington, January 17, 1834, Brooke and Gandy, *Prime Ministers' Papers*, 1:423.
34. The *Times*, January 18, 1834, 2.
35. The Duke of Wellington to Harriet Arbuthnot, August 27, 1829, the seventh Duke of Wellington, *Wellington and His Friends*, 88.

36. The *Times*, January 24, 1834, 2.
37. Ibid., February 5, 1834, 4.
38. Atlay, *Victorian Chancellors*, 108.
39. Lady Holland to (?), January 28, 1834, Ilchester, *Lady Holland to Her Son*, 143, n. 3.
40. Sir Robert Peel to Lord Lyndhurst, July 15, 1834, Lyndhurst Papers, Cambridge, 0.16.38. 76.
41. Ibid.
42. Ibid.
43. Viscount Melbourne to King William IV, November 10, 1834, ibid., 0.16.38. 77.
44. Viscount Melbourne to King William IV, November 11, 1834, ibid., 0.16.38. 79.
45. Viscount Melbourne to King William IV, November 12, 1834, ibid., 0.16.38. 81.
46. King William IV to Viscount Melbourne, November 12, 1834, ibid., 0.16.38. 82.
47. Gash, *Sir Robert Peel*, 79.
48. King William IV to Viscount Melbourne, November 14, 1834, Lyndhurst Papers, Cambridge, 0.16.38. 85.
49. Lady Cowper to Princess Lieven, December 4, 1834, Lord Sudley, *Lieven-Palmerston Correspondence*, 67.
50. Reeve, *Greville Memoirs*, 3:152. November 17, 1834.
51. Ibid., 154. November 17, 1834.
52. Ibid., 155–159, *passim*. November 19–26, 1834.
53. Ibid., 189–190. January 8, 1835.
54. Campbell, *Lives*, 95.
55. Martin, *Lyndhurst*, 325.
56. The *Times*, December 18, 1834, 2.
57. Reeve, *Greville Memoirs*, 3:152–153. November 17, 1834.
58. *Hansard*, 3rd ser., vol. 26 (February 24, 1835), col. 127.
59. Ibid., cols. 128–135, passim.
60. Ibid. (February 27, 1835), col. 432.

Chapter 17

1. Benjamin Disraeli to Sarah Disraeli, July 11, 1834, J.A.W. Gunn, John Matthews, Donald M. Schurman, and M. G. Wiebe, eds., *Benjamin Disraeli Letters: 1815–1834* (Toronto: University of Toronto Press, 1982), 1:338.

2. Benjamin Disraeli to Sarah Disraeli, November 24, 1834, *ibid.*, 435.
3. Monypenny, *Disraeli*, 1:337.
4. Atlay, *Victorian Chancellors*, 112.
5. Oman, *Heiress*, 248.
6. Political Notebook II, MEMS. 1834, Gunn et al., *Benjamin Disraeli Letters: 1835–1837*, 2:426.
7. Henrietta Sykes to Benjamin Disraeli (undated), Hughenden Papers, Box 13, A/IV/H/85.
8. Helen M. Swartz and Marvin Swartz, eds., *Disraeli's Reminiscences* (New York: Stein & Day, 1975), 120.
9. Henrietta Sykes to Benjamin Disraeli, September 25, 1834, *Hughenden Papers*, Box 13, A/IV/H/23.
10. *Hughenden Papers*, Box 27, A/XI/A/8.
11. Lady Cowper to Princess Lieven, December 1834, Sudley, *Lieven-Palmerston Correspondence*, 68.
12. See Robert Blake, *Disraeli* (New York: St. Martin's Press, 1967), 120.
13. Benjamin Disraeli to Lord Lyndhurst, December 4, 1834, Gunn et al., *Disraeli Letters*, 1:436.
14. Ibid.
15. Reeve, *Greville Memoirs*, 3:170. December 6, 1834.
16. Quoted in Benjamin Disraeli to Sarah Disraeli, December 11, 1834, Gunn et al., *Disraeli Letters*, 1:438.
17. Ibid., 439.
18. Benjamin Disraeli to Sarah Disraeli, December 8, 1834, *ibid.*, 437.
19. Benjamin Disraeli to Sarah Disraeli, December 11, 1834, *ibid.*, 439.
20. Caroline Norton's estranged husband, George Norton, brought a suit for criminal conversation against Lord Melbourne. The trial on June 22, 1836, resulted in an acquittal.
21. Memorandum of 1836, Monypenny, *Life of Benjamin Disraeli*, 279.
22. Lord Lyndhurst to Benjamin Disraeli, April 21, 1835, Hughenden Papers, B/XXI/L/438.
23. Monypenny, *Life of Benjamin Disraeli*, 305.
24. The Mutilated Diary, Gunn et al., *Disraeli Letters*, 2:415.
25. Benjamin Disraeli to Sarah Disraeli, August 11, 1835, *ibid.*, 87.
26. Benjamin Disraeli to John Murray, November 19, 1835, and Benjamin Disraeli to Richard Bentley, November 22, 1835, *ibid.*, 104–105.

27. Benjamin Disraeli to Isaac D'Israeli, November 24, 1835, *ibid.*, 106.
28. The Letters of Runnymede, Letter XVI to the House of Lords, April 18, 1836, *ibid.*, 399.
29. The Letters of Runnymede, Letter XVII to the House of Lords, April 23, 1836, *ibid.*, 401.
30. Lord Lyndhurst to Benjamin Disraeli, Hughenden Papers, B/XXI/L/457.
31. Hughenden Papers, B/XXI/O/2.
32. *Ibid.*
33. The *Times*, August 29, 1836, 2.
34. Benjamin Disraeli to Sarah Disraeli, January 12, 1836, Gunn et al., *Disraeli Letters*, 2:133.
35. Quoted in Swartz and Swartz, *Reminiscences*, 119–120.
36. Lord Lyndhurst to Benjamin Disraeli (undated), *Hughenden Papers*, B/XXI/L/458.
37. Benjamin Disraeli to Count D'Orsay, December 23?, 1836, Gunn et al., *Disraeli Letters*, 2:203.
38. Benjamin Disraeli to Sarah Disraeli, January 27, 1837, *ibid.*, 220.
39. *Ibid.*, 207, n. 2.
40. Lord Lyndhurst to Benjamin Disraeli, January 6, 1837, *Hughenden Papers*, B/XXI/L/458.
41. Benjamin Disraeli to William Pyne, January 8, 1837, Gunn et al., *Disraeli Letters*, 2:207.
42. Lady Blessington to Benjamin Disraeli, December 26, 1836, *Hughenden Papers*, B/XXI/B/580.
43. Benjamin Disraeli to Lady Blessington, January 12, 1837, Gunn et al., *Disraeli Letters*, 2:211.

Chapter 18
1. Memo of the Session 1835, Gunn et al., *Disraeli Letters*, 2:422.
2. Reeve, *Greville Memoirs*, 3:16. July 26, 1833.
3. *Ibid.*, 23. August 20, 1833.
4. *Ibid.*, 16. July 26, 1833.
5. *Ibid.*, 118. August 12, 1834.
6. *Ibid.*, 198. January 23, 1835.
7. Atlay, *Victorian Chancellors*, 118.

8. Reeve, *Greville Memoirs*, 3:313. September 9, 1835.
9. *Hansard*, 3rd ser., vol. 29 (August 3, 1835), cols. 1390–1391.
10. *Ibid.*, col. 1412.
11. *Ibid.*, col. 1415.
12. *Ibid.*, vol. 30 (August 13, 1835), col. 439.
13. Campbell, *Lives*, 78.
14. *Hansard*, 3rd ser., vol. 30 (August 27, 1835), col. 1042.
15. *Ibid.*, cols. 1048–1049.
16. Benjamin Disraeli to Sarah Disraeli, August 4, 1835, Gunn et al., *Disraeli Letters*, 2:73.
17. *Hansard*, 3rd ser., vol. 29 (August 3, 1835), col. 1389.
18. Reeve, *Greville Memoirs*, 3:284. August 4, 1835.
19. *Ibid.*, 285. August 6, 1835.
20. Gash, *Reaction and Reconstruction*, 35.
21. *Ibid.*, 42.
22. Reeve, *Greville Memoirs*, 3:288–289. August 15, 1835.
23. *Hansard*, 3rd ser., vol. 30 (August 13, 1835), cols. 435–438, *passim*.
24. *Ibid.* (August 14, 1835), col. 483.
25. *Ibid.*, col. 496.
26. Reeve, *Greville Memoirs*, 3:287–288. August 15, 1835.
27. *Ibid.*
28. *Hansard*, 3rd ser., vol. 30 (August 17, 1835), col. 584.
29. *Ibid.* (August 25, 1835), cols. 965–966.
30. *Ibid.*, cols. 971–975, *passim*.
31. Benjamin Disraeli to Sarah Disraeli, August 11, 1835, Gunn et al., *Disraeli Letters*, 2:88.
32. Benjamin Disraeli to Sarah Disraeli, August 17, 1835, *ibid.*, 90.
33. Reeve, *Greville Memoirs*, 3:284. August 4, 1835.
34. Gash, *Sir Robert Peel*, 134–135.
35. Benjamin Disraeli to Sarah Disraeli, August 11, 1835, Gunn et al., *Disraeli Letters*, 2:87.
36. Campbell, *Lives*, 109.
37. Martin, *Lyndhurst*, 343.
38. Memo of Session 1835, Gunn et al., *Disraeli Letters*, 2:422.

39. The *Times*, October 13, 1863, 7.
40. *Hansard*, 3rd ser., vol. 30 (August 31, 1835), cols. 1145–1156, *passim*.
41. *Ibid.*, col. 1156.
42. Memo of Session 1835, Gunn et al., *Disraeli Letters*, 2:422.
43. Turberville, *House of Lords in the Age of Reform*, 357–358. Based on an account of this meeting in a letter from Lord Fitzgerald to Sir Robert Peel. British Museum Add. MSS. 40323, ff. 318–322.
44. *Hansard*, 3rd ser., vol. 30 (September 4, 1835), col. 1336.
45. *Ibid.*, cols. 1341–1352, *passim*.
46. Turberville, *House of Lords in the Age of Reform*, 358–359.
47. *Hansard*, 3rd ser., vol. 30 (September 4, 1835), col. 1352.
48. Brougham, *Memoirs*, 3:436.
49. Reeve, *Greville Memoirs*, 3:305. September 1, 1835.
50. The Duke of Wellington to Lord Lyndhurst, May 13, 1835, Wellington MSS. Quoted in Elizabeth Longford, *Wellington: Pillar of State* (London: Weidenfeld & Nicholson, 1972), 311.
51. Session of 1836, Gunn et al., *Disraeli Letters*, 2:423.
52. Martin, *Lyndhurst*, 346.
53. *Hansard*, 3rd ser., vol. 34 (June 27, 1836), col. 888.
54. *Ibid.*, cols. 892–894.
55. *Ibid.*, col. 889.
56. Benjamin Disraeli to Sarah Disraeli, July 1, 1836, Gunn et al., *Disraeli Letters*, 2:172.
57. Reeve, *Greville Memoirs*, 3:361. August 13, 1836.
58. *Hansard*, 3rd ser., vol. 35 (August 18, 1836), cols. 1282–1295, *passim*.
59. W. P. Torrens, *Memoirs of Viscount Melbourne* (London: Macmillan & Co., 1878), 2:194–195.
60. Reeve, *Greville Memoirs*, 3:362. August 21, 1836.
61. Benjamin Disraeli to Sarah Disraeli, August 20, 1836, Gunn et al., *Disraeli Letters*, 2:180.
62. *Ibid.*, n. 2.
63. Earl Grey to Princess Lieven, February 27, 1837, Le Strange, *Correspondence of Lieven and Grey*, 3:227.
64. Reeve, *Greville Memoirs*, 3:378. January 19, 1837.
65. *Ibid.*, 389. February 25, 1837.

66. The Duke of Wellington to Lord Lyndhurst, October 15, 1836, Lyndhurst Papers, Cambridge, 0.16.38. 44.
67. *Hansard*, 3rd ser., vol. 38 (June 9, 1837), col. 1315.
68. Martin, *Lyndhurst*, 378.
69. Gash, *Reaction and Reconstruction*, 58–59.
70. See Introduction for a discussion of Lyndhurst's treatment by Gash and other authors.

Chapter 19

1. Lord Lyndhurst to Princess Lieven, June 20, 1837, British Library Add. MSS. 47376, f. 131.
2. General Preface to the Novels, 1870. Quoted in Monypenny, *Life of Benjamin Disraeli*, 371.
3. Lord Lyndhurst to Princess Lieven, June 20, 1837, British Library Add. MSS. 47376, f. 131.
4. *Ibid.*
5. Quoted in Atlay, *Victorian Chancellors*, 134.
6. Cited in David Cecil, *Melbourne* (Indianapolis: Bobbs-Merrill Co., 1939), 321.
7. Benjamin Disraeli to Sarah Disraeli, July 2, 1838, M. G. Wiebe, J. B. Conacher, John Matthews, and Mary S. Millar, eds., *Benjamin Disraeli Letters: 1838–1841* (Toronto: University of Toronto Press, 1987), 3:71.
8. Harriet Countess Granville to Lady Carlisle, May 5, 1837, Gower, *Letters of Harriet Countess Granville*, 2:229.
9. Mary Copley to Elizabeth Greene, August 12, 1837, Amory, *Artistic Life*, 375.
10. Benjamin Disraeli to Sarah Disraeli, August 8, 1837, Gunn et al., *Disraeli Letters*, 2:290.
11. Sarah Disraeli to Benjamin Disraeli, no date. Quoted in *ibid.*, 295, n. 4. Source is Hughenden Papers, A/I/B/605.
12. Benjamin Disraeli to Sarah Disraeli, February 19, 1838, Wiebe et al., *Disraeli Letters*, 3:25.
13. Oman, *Heiress*, 272.
14. Mary Copley to Elizabeth Greene, August 12, 1837, Amory, *Artistic Life*, 376.
15. Benjamin Disraeli to Sarah Disraeli, February 19, 1838, Wiebe et al., *Disraeli Letters*, 3:25.
16. Mary Copley to Elizabeth Greene, August 12, 1837, Amory, *Artistic Life*, 376.
17. Campbell, *Lives*, 120–121.

18. Pall Mall, 1869, Lyndhurst Collection, Glamorgan, D/D Ly 28/6.
19. Martin, *Lyndhurst*, 379–380.
20. Lord Lyndhurst to Francis Barlow, December 28, 1838, Lyndhurst Collection, Glamorgan, D/D Ly 20/11.
21. *Hansard*, 3rd ser., vol. 38 (June 23, 1837), col. 1568.
22. See Mandler, *Aristocratic Government*, 221. Mandler focuses on the Whig party's "long tradition of putting the rights of man above the rights of property." However, he notes that "a new mood of humanitarianism was evident in the Conservative party of the early 1840s." 204.
23. *Hansard*, 3rd Ser., vol. 44 (July 30, 1838), col. 764.
24. Ibid., col. 770.
25. Ibid., col. 791.
26. Ibid., vol. 50 (August 23, 1839), cols. 499–504.
27. Benjamin Disraeli to Sarah Disraeli, August 24, 1839, Wiebe et al., *Disraeli Letters*, 3:213–214.
28. Lord Lyndhurst to Francis Barlow, October 22, 1840, Lyndhurst Papers, Cambridge, 0.16.38. 94.
29. Benjamin Disraeli to Sarah Disraeli, November 2, 1840, Wiebe et al., *Disraeli Letters*, 3:305.
30. Benjamin Disraeli to Sarah Disraeli, November 9, 1840, *ibid.*, 306.
31. The *Times*, November 12, 1840, 5.
32. Martin, *Lyndhurst*, 238–239.
33. Printed Circular from Lord Lyndhurst, no date, Lyndhurst Papers, Cambridge, 0.16.38. 97.

Chapter 20

1. Mary Copley to Elizabeth Greene, February 28, 1841, Amory, *Artistic Life*, 380.
2. Mary Copley to Elizabeth Greene, September 28, 1841, *ibid.*, 382.
3. Benjamin Disraeli to Sarah Disraeli, November 30, 1840, Wiebe et al., *Disraeli Letters*, 3:313.
4. Campbell, *Lives*, 132.
5. Henry Reeve, ed., *The Greville Memoirs, A Journal of the Reign of Queen Victoria From 1837 to 1852* (New York: D. Appleton & Co., 1885), 1:444. November 2, 1842.
6. Sir William Holdsworth, *A History of English Law* (London: Methuen & Co., 1966), 16:19.

300   Notes

7. *Ibid.*, 19–20.
8. Campbell, *Lives*, 148.
9. *Ibid.*
10. Martin, *Lyndhurst*, 400.
11. Campbell, *Lives*, 150.
12. *Ibid.*, 152.
13. *Athenaeum*, January 30, 1869, 166.
14. O'Connell v. Regina, *English Reports* (Edinburgh: William Green & Sons, 1901), 8:1061–1063.
15. Campbell, *Lives*, 144.
16. *Ibid.*
17. Atlay, *Victorian Chancellors*, 145.
18. *Ibid.* See also *English Reports*, 8:1162.
19. *Hansard*, 3rd ser., vol. 70 (July 14, 1845), cols. 1178–1184, *passim*.
20. Mary Copley to Elizabeth Greene, April 3, 1843, Amory, *Artistic Life*, 384.
21. Mary Copley to Elizabeth Greene, April 2, 1844, *ibid.*
22. Lord Lyndhurst to William Gladstone, May 14, 1845. Quoted in Martin, *Lyndhurst*, 407.
23. Campbell, *Lives*, 159.
24. *Hansard*, 3rd ser., vol. 86 (May 18, 1846), cols. 733–741, *passim*.
25. Campbell, *Lives*, 160.
26. Mary Copley to Elizabeth Greene, July 3, 1846, Amory, *Artistic Life*, 390.
27. Lord Lyndhurst to Elizabeth Greene, December 30, 1846, *ibid.*, 391.
28. Sir Robert Peel to Lord Lyndhurst, no date, British Library Add. MSS. 40442, f. 335.
29. Martin, *Lyndhurst*, 421.
30. Atlay, *Victorian Chancellors*, 150. See *Hansard*, 3rd ser., vol. 88 (August 22, 1846), col. 951.
31. Sir James Graham to Sir Robert Peel, August 31, 1846, British Library Add. MSS. 40452, f. 155.
32. Martin, *Lyndhurst*, 423.
33. *Hansard*, 3rd ser., vol. 88 (August 18, 1846), col. 870.
34. Reeve, *Greville Memoirs* (Reign of Queen Victoria), 2:135–137. August 20, 1846.
35. *Hansard*, 3rd ser., vol. 88 (August 20, 1846), col. 894.

36. *Ibid.*, col. 898.
37. *Ibid.*, col. 902.
38. *Ibid.*, col. 904.
39. Reeve, *Greville Memoirs* (Victoria), 2:137. August 23, 1846.
40. *Hansard*, 3rd ser., vol. 88 (August 20, 1846), col. 904.
41. *Ibid.* (August 22, 1846), col. 951.

Chapter 21

1. Benjamin Disraeli to Lady Londonderry, December 26, 1846, M. G. Wiebe, J. B. Conacher, John Matthews, and Mary S. Millar, eds., *Benjamin Disraeli Letters: 1842–1847* (Toronto: University of Toronto Press, 1989), 4:268.
2. Lord Stanley to Lord Lyndhurst, December 9, 1846, Lyndhurst Papers, Cambridge, 0.16.38. 127.
3. Robert Stewart, *The Foundation of the Conservative Party 1830–1867* (London: Longman, 1978), 224.
4. Lord Lyndhurst to Lord Stanley, December 16, 1846, Martin, *Lyndhurst*, 428.
5. Campbell, *Lives*, 168.
6. *Hansard*, 3rd ser., vol. 106 (June 19, 1849), col. 514.
7. Mary Copley to John Singleton Copley Greene, February 19, 1850, Amory, *Artistic Life*, 397.
8. Mary Copley to Elizabeth Greene, April 19, 1850, *ibid.*, 398.
9. Mary Copley to Elizabeth Greene, June 21, 1850, *ibid.*, 399.
10. Lord Lyndhurst to Elizabeth Greene, July 29, 1850, *ibid.*, 400.
11. Lord Lyndhurst to Elizabeth Greene, October 3, 1850, *ibid.*, 401.
12. Lord Derby to Lady Lyndhurst, May 5, 1851, Lyndhurst Papers, Cambridge, 0.16.38. 129.
13. Martin, *Lyndhurst*, 445.
14. Lord Derby to Lord Lyndhurst, February 22, 1852, Lyndhurst Papers, Cambridge, 0.16.38. 128.
15. *Ibid.*
16. Lord Lyndhurst to Lord Derby (undated), Martin, *Lyndhurst*, 446.
17. Lord Derby to Lord Lyndhurst, February 23, 1852, Lyndhurst Papers, Cambridge, 0.16.38. 112.
18. Mary Copley to Elizabeth Greene, March 3, 1852, Amory, *Artistic Life*, 405–406.

19. Mary Copley to Elizabeth Greene, March 3, 1852, *ibid.*
20. Mary Copley to Elizabeth Greene, July 30, 1852, *ibid.*, 408.
21. Mary Copley to Elizabeth Greene, August 12, 1852, *ibid.*
22. Mary Copley to Elizabeth Greene, October 14, 1852, *ibid.*, 408–409.
23. Mary Copley to Elizabeth Greene, July 7, 1853, *ibid.*, 409.
24. Campbell, *Lives*, 176–177.
25. *Ibid.*, 175.
26. *Hansard*, 3rd ser., vol. 127 (May 31, 1853), col. 847.
27. *Ibid.*, vol. 129 (July 12, 1853), cols. 89–92, *passim*.
28. *Ibid.*, vol. 134 (June 19, 1854), cols. 307–311, *passim*.

Chapter 22

1. Mary Copley to Elizabeth Greene, December 22, 1854, Amory, *Artistic Life*, 412.
2. Martin, *Lyndhurst*, 460.
3. Lord Lyndhurst to Francis Barlow, December 3, 1855, Lyndhurst Collection, Glamorgan, D/D Ly 20/27a,b.
4. Campbell, *Lives*, 192–193.
5. *Hansard*, 3rd ser., vol. 140 (February 7, 1856), cols. 274–275.
6. *Ibid.*, cols. 279–280.
7. Campbell, *Lives*, 194.
8. Dorothy M. Stetson, *A Woman's Issue, The Politics of Family Law Reform in England* (Westport, Connecticut: Greenwood Press, 1982), 35.
9. See Mary Lyndon Shanley, *Feminism, Marriage, and the Law in Victorian England* (Princeton: Princeton University Press, 1989), 35–48. *passim*. Shanley writes, "Lord Lyndhurst was the staunchest supporter in either house of equalizing the grounds of divorce for men and women." 40.
10. *Hansard*, 3rd ser., vol. 142 (May 20, 1856), col. 416.
11. *Ibid.*, vol. 144 (March 3, 1857), cols. 1694–1695.
12. Allen Horstman, *Victorian Divorce* (New York: St. Martin's Press, 1985), 78.
13. Martin, *Lyndhurst*, 471.
14. Campbell, *Lives*, 201.
15. *Hansard*, 3rd ser., vol. 146 (June 25, 1857), cols. 331–333, *passim*.
16. Campbell, *Lives*, 201.

17. *Hansard*, 3rd ser., vol. 146 (June 25, 1857), col. 338.
18. *Ibid.* (July 13, 1857), col. 1360.
19. Martin, *Lyndhurst*, 474.
20. *Hansard*, 3rd ser., vol. 146 (July 13, 1857), cols. 1356–1357.
21. *Ibid.*, cols. 1357–1361, *passim*. Campbell, *The Lives of the Chief Justices of England*. This work in three volumes was first published in the years 1849–1857. In Volume 3 Campbell referred to Lyndhurst's rapid rise and gave an account in which Lord Castlereagh heard the then Sergeant Copley defend Dr. James Watson at his trial for treason. Campbell noted that "Lord Castlereagh was sitting on the Bench during the trial, and expressing great admiration of his Whig-Radical eloquence, is said to have added, 'I will set my rat-trap for him — baited with Cheshire cheese.'" 3:221. This was a reference to Copley's subsequent appointment as Chief Justice of Chester. In another reference Campbell described Lyndhurst as "still in dreadful apprehension of the Pope, although on the verge of a sudden conversion to Catholic Emancipation." 3:314.
22. Martin, *Lyndhurst*, 476–477.
23. *Ibid.*, 480.
24. *Hansard*, 3rd ser., vol. 154 (July 1, 1859), col. 509.
25. Campbell, *Lives*, v. Campbell concluded his writing on Lyndhurst in 1858.
26. *Ibid.*, 199.
27. *Hansard*, 3rd ser., vol. 146 (July 10, 1857), col. 1240.
28. Campbell, *Lives*, 205.
29. *Hansard*, 3rd ser., vol. 151 (July 26, 1858), cols. 2105–2115, *passim*.
30. *Ibid.*, vol. 146 (July 10, 1857), col. 1248. In revising his earlier stand, Lyndhurst anticipated Walter Bagehot's description of the House of Lords in *The English Constitution*, published in 1867. Bagehot concluded that "the House has ceased to be one of latent directors, and has become one of temporary rejectors and palpable alterers." He added, "The House must yield to the people if the people is [sic] determined." Walter Bagehot, *The English Constitution* (Cambridge: John Wilson & Son, 1867), 164–168, *passim*.
31. *Hansard*, 3rd ser., vol. 154 (July 5, 1859), cols. 617–618.
32. *Ibid.*, col. 625.
33. *Ibid.*, col. 626.
34. *Ibid.*, vol. 155 (July 25, 1859), cols. 347–348.
35. *Ibid.*, vol. 158 (May 1, 1860), cols. 427–428.
36. *Ibid.*, cols. 433–434.
37. Miscellaneous press cuttings, Lyndhurst Collection, Glamorgan, D/D Ly 27/10.
38. *Ibid.*, D/D Ly 27/9.

304   Notes

39. *Punch*, May 12, 1860, 193.
40. *Hansard*, 3rd ser., vol. 158 (May 21, 1860), col. 1472.
41. *Ibid.*, col. 1465.
42. Martin, *Lyndhurst*, 494.
43. *Hansard*, 3rd ser., vol. 158 (May 21, 1860), col. 1525.
44. *Ibid.*, vol. 162 (May 7, 1861), col. 1642.

Chapter 23

1. Excerpt from a letter from James Moncreiff. Cited in Campbell, *Lives*, 211–212.
2. *Ibid.*
3. James Nasmyth to Lady Lyndhurst, October 8, 1883, Lyndhurst Papers, Cambridge, 0.16.38. 154.
4. Lord Granville to Lady Lyndhurst, October 8, 1883, *ibid.*, 148.
5. John Morley, *The Life of William Ewart Gladstone* (New York: Macmillan & Co., 1903), 2:96.
6. William E. Gladstone to Lady Lyndhurst, August 31, 1883, Lyndhurst Papers, Cambridge, 0.16.38. 151.
7. Swartz and Swartz, *Disraeli's Reminiscences*, 90.
8. *Ibid.*, 63.
9. Amory, *Artistic Life*, 433.
10. *Ibid.*
11. Lord Lyndhurst's Diary, Lyndhurst Collection, Glamorgan, D/D Ly 27/37. October 20 and 23, 1861.
12. *Ibid.* October 23 and 26, 1861; November 1, 1861; October 27, 1861; and October 20, 1861.
13. *Ibid.* October 23, 1861, and October 20, 1861.
14. *Ibid.* October 26, 1861.
15. Original letter lost. Cited by Martha Amory from memory. Amory, *Artistic Life*, 430.
16. Lyndhurst's Diary, Lyndhurst Collection, Glamorgan, D/D Ly 27/37. October 26 and 27, 1861, and November 1, 4, 6, 9, and 12, 1861.
17. In his biography of Lyndhurst, Sir Theodore Martin devoted a great amount of space to these letters, quoting them in full. He did so to contradict the profession of Sir Henry Holland, a prominent physician, who in his memoirs declared that Lyndhurst "was deeply interested in the events of the Civil War . . . and, though born in Massa-

chusetts, [was] a warm partisan of the South." Martin, *Lyndhurst*, 499. See Holland, *Recollections*, 202.
18. Lord Lyndhurst to James S. Amory, May 15, 1861, Lyndhurst Collection, Glamorgan, D/D Ly 24/1.
19. Lord Lyndhurst to James S. Amory, June 6, 1861, *ibid*.
20. Lord Lyndhurst to Elizabeth Greene, January 2, 1862, Amory, *Artistic Life*, 429.
21. Lord Lyndhurst to James S. Amory, April 24, 1862, Lyndhurst Collection, Glamorgan, D/D Ly 24/1.
22. Lord Lyndhurst to James S. Amory, August 8, 1862, *ibid*.
23. Lord Lyndhurst to James S. Amory, September 9, 1863, *ibid*.
24. Martin, *Lyndhurst*, 511–512.
25. Swartz and Swartz, *Disraeli's Reminiscences*, 95.
26. *Ibid.*, 96.
27. Martin, Lyndhurst, 512. See also, Amory, *Artistic Life*, 438.
28. Martin, *Lyndhurst*, 513. Martin's description of this deathbed scene conformed to the conventions of Victorian biography.
29. Queen Victoria to Lady Lyndhurst, October 16, 1863, Lyndhurst Papers, Cambridge, 0.16.38. 1.
30. *Saturday Review*, October 17, 1863, 513.
31. Monypenny, *Disraeli*, 1:331.
32. The *Times*, October 13, 1863, 7.
33. Monypenny, *Disraeli*, 1:330.
34. An account of Lord Lyndhurst's last illness and death by his daughter, Sophia Beckett, 1863, Lyndhurst Collection, Glamorgan, D/D Ly 10/4v.
35. *Observer*, October 10, 1863; *ibid.*, D/D Ly 29/8.
36. Sir Lewis Namier, *The Structure of Politics at the Accession of George III* (London: Macmillan & Co., 1961), and *England in the Age of the American Revolution* (London: Macmillan & Co., 1963).

Bibliography

Manuscript Sources
British Library Additional Manuscripts
    Aberdeen Papers
    Bonham Papers
    Gladstone Papers
    Graham Papers
    Huskisson Papers
    Melbourne Papers
    Peel Papers
    Wellington Papers
Hughenden Papers
Lyndhurst Collection, Glamorgan Record Office, Cardiff
The Lyndhurst Papers, Trinity College, Cambridge University
The Wellington Papers, Southampton University

Public Records
English Reports
Hansard, Parliamentary Debates
Howell, T. B. *State Trials*

Newspapers
Age
Athenaeum
Evening Gazette
Illustrated London News
Morning Journal
Observer
Pall Mall
Punch
Saturday Review
Spectator
Standard
Times

Published Sources

Amory, Martha Babcock. *The Domestic and Artistic Life of John Singleton Copley, R.A. With Notices of His Works and Reminiscences of His Son, Lord Lyndhurst, Lord High Chancellor of Great Britain.* Boston: Houghton, Mifflin & Co., 1882.

Anglesey, the Marquess of. *One-Leg, The Life and Letters of Henry William Paget, First Marquess of Anglesy.* London: Jonathan Cape, 1961.

Aspinall, A. "The Coalition Ministries of 1827, Part I, Canning's Ministry." *English Historical Review.* vol. 42 (April 1927).

———. "The Coalition Ministries of 1827, Part II, The Goderich Ministry." *The English Historical Review.* vol. 42 (October 1927).

———, ed. *The Letters of King George IV, 1812–1830.* 3 vols. Cambridge: Cambridge University Press, 1938.

———, ed. *Three Early Nineteenth Century Diaries.* London: Williams & Norgate, 1952.

Atlay, James Beresford. *The Victorian Chancellors.* London: Smith, Elder & Co., 1906.

Bagehot, Walter. *The English Constitution.* Cambridge: John Wilson & Son, 1867.

———. *Biographical Studies.* London: Longmans, Green & Co., 1881.

Baker, J. H. *An Introduction to English Legal History.* London: Butterworths, 1979.

Bamford, F., and the Duke of Wellington, eds. *The Journal of Mrs. Arbuthnot, 1830–32.* 2 vols. London: Macmillan & Co., 1950.

Blake, Robert. *Disraeli.* New York: St. Martin's Press, 1967.

Bradford, Sarah. *Disraeli.* London: Weidenfeld & Nicolson, 1982.

Brock, Michael. *The Great Reform Act.* London: Hutchinson Library Press, 1973.

Brooke, John, and Julia Gandy, eds. *The Prime Ministers' Papers: Wellington, Political Correspondence, 1833–November 1834.* London: Her Majesty's Stationery Office, 1975.

Brougham, Henry Lord. *The Life and Times of Henry Lord Brougham.* 3 vols. London: W. Blackwood & Sons, 1871.

Buckingham, the second Duke of, ed. *Memoirs of the Court of George IV, 1820–30.* 2 vols. London: Hurst & Blackett, 1959.

Butler, Lord, Norman Gash, Donald Southgate, David Dilks, and John Ramsden. *The Conservatives, A History From Their Origins to 1965.* London: George Allen & Unwin, 1977.

Butterfield, Herbert. *The Whig Interpretation of History.* New York: Charles Scribner's Sons, 1959.

Campbell, John Lord. *Lives of Lord Lyndhurst and Lord Brougham.* London: John Murray, 1869.

———. *The Lives of the Chief Justices of England.* 3 vols. Freeport, New York: Books for Libraries Press, 1971.

Cecil, David. *Melbourne.* Indianapolis: Bobbs-Merrill Co., 1939.

Chamberlain, Muriel E. *Lord Aberdeen, A Political Biography.* London: Longman, 1983.

Cockburn, Henry Lord. *Life of Francis Jeffrey.* 2 vols. Edinburgh: A. & C. Black, 1872.

Colchester, Lord, ed. *Earl of Ellenborough: Political Diary, 1828–30.* London: Richard Bentley & Son, 1881.

Cookson, J. E. *Lord Liverpool's Administration: The Crucial Years, 1815–1822.* Archon Books, 1975.

Davidoff, Leonore, and Catherine Hall. *Family Fortunes: Men and Women of the English Middle Class, 1780–1850.* Chicago: University of Chicago Press, 1987.

Derry, John W. *Reaction and Reform, England in the Early Nineteenth Century.* Bungay, Suffolk: Richard Clay, 1963.

Faber, Richard. *Young England.* London: Faber & Faber, 1987.

Foss, Edward. *The Judges of England.* 9 vols. London: John Murray, 1864.

Fulford, Roger. *The Trial of Queen Caroline.* New York: Stein & Day, 1968.

Gash, Norman. "English Reform and French Revolution in the General Election of 1830," in Richard Pares, ed., *Essays Presented to Sir Lewis Namier.* New York: St. Martin's Press, 1956.

———. *Mr. Secretary Peel.* Cambridge: Harvard University Press, 1961.

———. *Reaction and Reconstruction in English Politics 1832–1852.* Oxford: Clarendon Press, 1965.

———. *Sir Robert Peel.* Totowa, New Jersey: Rowman & Littlefield, 1972.

———. *Aristocracy and People, Britain 1815–1865.* Cambridge: Harvard University Press, 1979.

———, ed. *The Age of Peel.* London: Edward Arnold, 1968.

George, M. Dorothy. *Catalogue of Political and Personal Satires.* London: Trustees of the British Museum, 1954.

Gibson, William Sidney. *Lord Lyndhurst, In Memoriam.* London: n.p., 1865.

Gore, John, ed. *Creevey's Life and Times.* London: John Murray, 1934.

Gower, F. Leveson, ed. *Letters of Harriet Countess Granville 1810–1845.* 2 vols. London: Longmans, Green & Co., 1894.

Grey, Henry Earl, ed. *The Reform Act, 1832: Correspondence of Earl Grey With King William IV and With Sir Herbert Taylor.* 2 vols. London: John Murray, 1867.

Gunn, J.A.W., John Matthews, Donald M. Schurman, and M. G. Wiebe, eds. *Benjamin Disraeli Letters: 1815–1834.* 4 vols. Toronto: University of Toronto Press, 1982.

Guttsman, W. L. *The British Political Elite.* London: MacGibson & Kee, 1965.

Hardcastle, Mrs., ed. *Life of John Lord Campbell.* 2 vols. London: John Murray, 1881.

Hexter, J. H. "The Protestant Revival and the Catholic Question in England, 1778–1829," *Journal of Modern History.* vol. 8, no. 3 (September 1936).

Hinde, Wendy. *George Canning.* New York: St. Martin's Press, 1973.

Holdsworth, Sir William. *A History of English Law.* 16 vols. London: Methuen & Co., 1966.

Horstman, Allen. *Victorian Divorce.* New York: St. Martin's Press, 1985.

Houghton, Walter E. *The Victorian Frame of Mind, 1830–1870.* New Haven: Yale University Press, 1957.

310   Bibliography

Howell, T. B. *State Trials*. London: Longman, 1824.

Huch, Ronald K. *Henry, Lord Brougham: The Later Years, 1830–1868: The Great Actor*. Lewiston, New York: Edwin Mellen Press, 1993.

Ilchester, the sixth Earl of, ed. *Lady Holland to Her Son, 1821–45*. London: John Murray, 1946.

Jennings, Louis J., ed. *The Croker Papers*. 3 vols. London: John Murray, 1885.

Jerman, B. R. *The Young Disraeli*. Princeton: Princeton University Press, 1960.

Kitson Clark, George. *Peel and the Conservative Party*. London: G. Bell & Sons, 1929.

Kriegel, Abraham D., ed. *The Holland House Diaries, 1831–1840*. London: Routledge & Kegan Paul, 1977.

Labaree, Benjamin Woods. *The Boston Tea Party*. Boston: Northeastern University Press, 1964.

Le Strange, Guy, ed. *Correspondence of Princess Lieven and Earl Grey*. 3 vols. London: Richard Bentley & Son, 1890.

Longford, Elizabeth. *Wellington: Pillar of State*. London: Weidenfeld & Nicolson, 1972.

Machin, G.I.T. "The No-Popery Movement in Britain in 1828–1829." *Historical Journal*. vol. 6, no. 2 (1936).

———. *The Catholic Question in English Politics, 1820 to 1830*. Oxford: Oxford University Press, 1964.

Manchester, A. H. *Modern Legal History*. London: Butterworths, 1980.

Mandler, Peter. *Aristocratic Government in the Age of Reform*. Oxford: Clarendon Press, 1990.

Martin, Sir Theodore. *A Life of Lord Lyndhurst*. London: John Murray, 1884.

Monypenny, William. *The Life of Benjamin Disraeli*. 6 vols. New York: Macmillan & Co., 1913.

Morley, John. *The Life of William Ewart Gladstone*. 3 vols. New York: Macmillan & Co., 1903.

Namier, Sir Lewis. *The Structure of Politics at the Accession of George III*. London: Macmillan & Co., 1961.

———. *England in the Age of the American Revolution*. London: Macmillan & Co., 1963.

Oman, Carola. *The Gascoigne Heiress*. London: Holder & Stoughton, 1968.

Parker, Charles Stuart, ed. *Sir Robert Peel, From His Private Papers*. 3 vols. London: John Murray, 1899.

Petrie, Sir Charles. *Wellington, A Reassessment*. London: James Barrie, 1956.

Porritt, Edward. *The Unreformed House of Commons*. 2 vols. Cambridge: Cambridge University Press, 1909.

Ramsay, A.A.W. *Sir Robert Peel*. London: Constable & Co., 1928.

Reeve, Henry, ed. *The Greville Memoirs, A Journal of the Reigns of King George IV and King William IV*. 3 vols. London: Longmans, Green & Co., 1874.

———, ed. *The Greville Memoirs, A Journal of the Reign of Queen Victoria From 1837 to 1852*. 3 vols. New York: D. Appleton & Co., 1885.

———, ed. *Greville Memoirs*. 2 vols. New York: D. Appleton & Co., 1887.

Richardson, Joanna. *The Disastrous Marriage, A Study of George IV and Caroline of Brunswick*. London: Jonathan Cape, 1960.

———. *Creevey and Greville*. London: Longmans, Green & Co., 1967.

Robinson, Lionel G., ed. *Letters of Dorothea, Princess Lieven, During Her Residence in London 1812–1834*. London: Longmans, Green & Co., 1902.

Rolo, P.J.V. *George Canning*. London: Macmillan & Co., 1965.

Russell of Liverpool, Lord. *Caroline the Unhappy Queen*. London: Robert Hale, 1967.

Sack, James J. *From Jacobite to Conservative*. Cambridge: Cambridge University Press, 1993.

Shanley, Mary Lyndon. *Feminism, Marriage, and the Law in Victorian England*. Princeton: Princeton University Press, 1989.

Shatto, Susan. *The Companion to Bleak House*. London: Unwin Hyman, 1988.

Smith, E. A. *Lord Grey 1765–1845*. Oxford: Clarendon Press, 1990.

Stanhope, Lord, and Edward Cardwell. *Memoirs of Sir Robert Peel*. London: John Murray, 1856.

Stetson, Dorothy M. *A Woman's Issue, The Politics of Family Law Reform in England*. Westport: Greenwood Press, 1982.

Stewart, Robert. *The Foundation of the Conservative Party 1830–1867*. London: Longman, 1978.

Sudley, Lord, ed. *The Lieven-Palmerston Correspondence, 1828–1856*. London: John Murray, 1943.

Sugden, Edward Burtenshaw. *Misrepresentations in Campbell's Lives of Lyndhurst and Brougham*. London: John Murray, 1869.

Swartz, Helen M., and Marvin Swartz, eds. *Disraeli's Reminiscences*. New York: Stein & Day, 1975.

Thomis, Malcolm I. *The Luddites*. London: David & Charles, 1970.

Thompson, E. P. *The Making of the English Working Class*. New York: Alfred A. Knopf, 1963.

Thorne, R. G. *The History of Parliament, The House of Commons, 1790–1820*. 2 vols. London: Secker & Warburg, 1986.

Torrens, W. P. *Memoirs of Viscount Melbourne*. 2 vols. London: Macmillan & Co., 1878.

Trevelyan, George Macauly. *Lord Grey of the Reform Bill*. London: Longmans, Green & Co., 1920.

Turberville, A. S. *The House of Lords in the Age of Reform*. London: Faber & Faber, 1958.

Twiss, Horace. *The Public and Private Life of Lord Chancellor Eldon, With Selections From His Correspondence*. 2 vols. London: John Murray, 1846.

Ward, J. T. *Sir James Graham*. New York: St. Martin's Press, 1967.

Wellington, the second Duke of, ed. *Despatches, Correspondence, and Memoranda of Field Marshall Arthur Duke of Wellington*, K.G. 8 vols. London: John Murray, 1878.

Wellington, the seventh Duke of, ed. *Wellington and His Friends*. London: Macmillan & Co., 1965.

Wiebe, M. G., J. B. Conacher, John Matthews, and Mary S. Millar, eds. *Benjamin Disraeli Letters: 1838–1841*. 4 vols. Toronto: University of Toronto Press, 1987.

———, eds. *Benjamin Disraeli Letters: 1842–1847*. 4 vols. Toronto: University of Toronto Press, 1989.

Willis, G. M. *Ernest Augustus, Duke of Cumberland and King of Hanover*. London: Arthur Barker, 1954.

Wilson, Philip Whitwell, ed. *The Greville Diary*. 2 vols. Garden City, New York: Doubleday, Page & Co., 1927.

Ziegler, Philip. *Melbourne*. New York: Alfred A. Knopf, 1976.

Ziegler, William. *King William IV*. London: Collins, 1971.

Index

Abercromby, James, 179
Aberdeen, Lord, 120
Adams, John, 22
Adams, Samuel, 15–16
Alexander, Sir William, 120–22
Alexandrina Victoria, Princess, 126
Alien Bill (1793), 38
Althorpe, Viscount, 64, 173
American Revolution, 1–4, 6–7
Amory, Martha Babcock, x, 167, 170, 260–61
Arbuthnot, Harriet, 87, 92, 100, 111, 122
Aspinall, Arthur, 64
Atlay, James Beresford, 23, 45, 161, 163, 165, 170–71, 181, 194, 225–26
Attorney General, office of, 54

Bagehot, Walter, xii–xiii, 36–37, 305n.30
Bankes, George, 54–55
Baring, Alexander, 153, 155
Barnes, Thomas, 176
Bathurst, Lord, 127
Bell, Robert, 93
Bennet, Henry Grey, 44–45
Bentinck, Lord George, 230, 231, 233–34
Bexley, Lord, 63
Bill for the Abolition of the Paper Duties, 256–57
Biographical Studies (Bagehot), xii–xiii, 36–37
Biographies, of Lyndhurst: image of Lyndhurst in, ix–xi. *See also* Bagehot, Walter; Campbell, Lord; Martin, Sir Theodore
Bleak House (Dickens), 104, 286–87n.1
Blessington, Lady, 191
Bonham, Francis, 188
Boston, Massachusetts: Copley family and, 1–4; Lyndhurst's description of, 13–14, 15
Boston tea party, 1–4
Brandeth, Jeremiah, xv, 35–37
Brougham, Henry, 118, 122, 124, 126, 149–50, 163, 166–67, 179, 197, 204, 237, 260, 288n.9

Brunsden, Sarah Garay (wife). *See* Lyndhurst, Lady
Brunswick Clubs, 75
Brunt, John, 49
Burdett, Sir Francis, 55, 157

Cambridge University: Lyndhurst as High Steward of, 218–19. *See also* Trinity College
Campbell, Lord (biographer): conflict with Lyndhurst, 251–52; image of Lyndhurst, ix, x–xi; as Lord Chancellor of Ireland, 222–24; on Lyndhurst and Catholic Emancipation, 283n.17, 305n.21; on Lyndhurst's class origins, 92; on Lyndhurst's entry into politics, 36, 40; on Lyndhurst and Grey government, 117; on Lyndhurst's last term as Chancellor, 221–22; on Lyndhurst's legal career, 26, 29–30, 125, 305n.21; on Lyndhurst's oratory, 246–47; on Lyndhurst and parliamentary reform, 137, 150, 159, 201; on Lyndhurst's retirement, 237, 243; on second Lady Lyndhurst, 213–14; on Tamworth Manifesto, 178
Canada, self-government in, 237
Canning, George, 55–56, 60–62
Carlisle, Lady, 117
Caroline of Brunswick, 50–53
Carrington, Lord, 186
Castle, John, 33
Castlereagh, Lord, 34, 40
Catawba tribe, 19
Catholic Emancipation, as political issue, 54–56, 67–68, 69–76, 77–88, 283n.17, 305n.21
The Catholic Question in English Politics, 1820 to 1830 (Machin), 71
Catholic Relief Bill, 82, 87–88
Cato Street conspiracy, xv
Chancery courts, reform of, 104–10, 287n.5
Chandos, Marquess of, 185–86
Charitable Trusts Bill, 229

314   Index

Chief Baron of the Exchequer, 120–26
Chief Justice of Chester, 40
Children: Lyndhurst and social reform, 216–17. *See also* Family
Chilton, Mary, 1
Church of England: Lyndhurst's conservatism, xiv, xv. *See also* Religion
Civil War, U.S., 262–64, 306–307n.17
Clanricarde, Lord, 226–27
Clarke, Jonathan (uncle), 3
Clarke, Richard (maternal grandfather), 1–4, 6, 7
Coercive Acts (1774), 4
Common law, 104, 105
Conservatism: Lyndhurst on parliamentary reform, 144; political role of Lyndhurst, xiv–xv
Conservative party: controversy between Lyndhurst and Bentinck, 230–34; humanitarianism of, 301n.22; Lyndhurst's leadership of, 220; Lyndhurst and parliamentary reform, 192–210; use of term, 293n.1
Constitution, English: Lyndhurst's conservatism, xiv, xv; Lyndhurst's opposition to parliamentary reform, 134–35
Constitution, U.S., 16
Conyngham, Lady, 81
Copley, Elizabeth (sister), 18, 24
Copley, John Singleton (father), 1, 4, 5–8, 9, 20–21, 24, 28
Copley, John Singleton, Jr. *See* Lyndhurst, Baron
Copley, Mary (sister), 40, 169, 212, 213, 227, 229, 238, 242, 246
Copley, Richard (paternal grandfather), 1
Copley, Sarah (daughter), 237
Copley, Sophia (daughter), 246, 267–68
Copley, Susan Penelope (daughter), 212
Copley, Susannah (mother), 1, 5, 6–8, 28–29, 37, 39–40, 40–41, 54, 190
Corn Laws, 228–29
Corruption, political, 92–103
Court of Exchequer, 109, 122, 124–26
Courts, reform of, 104–10, 122, 124–26, 161, 163, 165–67
Cowper, Lady Emily, 101, 175, 184
Cranworth, Lord Chancellor, 248
Creevey, Thomas, 102
Crimean War, 244–45
Criminal law, reform of, 109
Croker, John Wilson, 117, 118, 120, 151

Cumberland, Duke of, 75, 79–81, 97–103, 202
Custody of Infants Bill, 216–17, 247

Davidson, William, 49
Democratic-Republican party (U.S.), 17–18, 22
Denman, Lord, xii, 160, 196
Derby, Lord, 239, 241, 257
Dickens, Charles, 104, 286–87n.1
Disraeli, Benjamin, *185:* Bentinck's denunciation of Lyndhurst, 231–32; Jewish Emancipation, 253; on Lyndhurst as elder statesman, 235–36; on Lyndhurst's final years, 260; on Lyndhurst's interest in religion, 264–65; Lyndhurst as mentor of, 181–91; on Lyndhurst and Municipal Corporations Bill, 192, 197, 200, 201, 202, 205, 207; Lyndhurst's obituary, 267; on Lyndhurst's second marriage, 213; marriage to Mary Anne Lewis, 218
Dissenters, Protestant, 61, 69–70, 200
Divorce reform, 247, 248–49, 304n.9
Dudley, Lord, 96, 147–48
Durham, Lord, 121, 131, 184

East India Company, 2, 4
Education, of Lyndhurst, 9–12
Edward VII, 262
Eldon, Lord, 54, 55, 58, 70, 84, 104–105, 106, 107, 108
Elgin, Lord, 237
Ellenborough, Lord, 81, 83, 93, 115, 122, 133, 145, 146, 149, 177
The English Constitution (Bagehot, 1857), 305n.30
Escott, Bickham, 202

Falmouth, Earl of, 85–86
Family: birth of Lyndhurst's children, 53–54; changes in Lyndhurst's following death of Lady Lyndhurst, 190; childhood of Lyndhurst, 8–9, 10; Lyndhurst's relationships with women, 217
Federalism (U.S.), 16
Fitzgerald, William Vesey, 72
Flinn, Lieutenant John, 51–52
The Foundation of the Conservative Party 1830–1867 (Stewart), 236

France: U.S. relations with, 21
French Revolution, xiii, 38, 43, 274n.27.
    See also Revolution
Fretley, Thomas, 89, 91

Gascoyne, General Isaac, 131
Gash, Norman, xi, 140, 174, 198, 200–201, 209–10
George III, 47, 67, 73
George IV, 50, 58, 60, 73–74, 78–82, 87
Gifford, Sir Robert, 40, 48
Gladstone, William, 228, 256, 260
Goderich, Viscount, 62–65
Goldsmith, Georgiana (wife). *See* Lyndhurst, Lady
Goldsmith, Lewis (father-in-law), 213–14
Graham, Sir James, 231
Granville, Countess, 168, 169, 170
Granville, Lord George, 259–60
Greene, Gardiner, 24–25
Grenville, Thomas, 87
Greville, Charles: characterization of Lyndhurst, xv, 127; on conflict between Bentinck and Lyndhurst, 233; on Disraeli, 186; on Lady Lyndhurst, 97, 132; on Lyndhurst's appointment to Chancellorship, 58–59; on Lyndhurst and court reform, 166; on Lyndhurst and Grey government, 118, 122; on Lyndhurst's last term as Chancellor, 222; on Lyndhurst's oratory, 87; on parliamentary reform, 137, 142, 153, 154–55, 156, 158, 175, 192, 193, 197, 199, 200, 204–205, 207; on political scandal involving Lady Lyndhurst, 100–101, 102
Grey, Lord: on Canning's appointment of Lyndhurst, 61; Goderich government, 64; Ireland and government of, 171–72; Lyndhurst and government of, 117–27; on Lyndhurst and Whigs, 207; parliamentary reform and government of, 114, 128–39, 140–47, 149–50, 157–58; relationship with George IV, 66, 111–12; relationship with Lady Lyndhurst, 97, 101–102; on Wellington and William IV, 112–13

Haddington, Lord, 145
Harding, Sir Henry, 132, 152

Harrowby, Lord, 47, 138, 142, 145, 202–203
Herries, John, 63, 64
Hexter, J. H., 73–74
History: image of Lyndhurst, xi, xiii
History of Boroughs and Municipal Corporations (Merewether), 200
History of English Law, A (Holdworth), 222
Holdworth, Sir William, 222
Holland, Lady, 117, 148
Holland, Lord, 62–63, 96–97, 137, 166, 167, 171
Holmes, Leonard Thomas Worsley, 37
Holmes, William, 169
House of Lords: Bagehot's description of, 305n.30; Lyndhurst as Chief Baron of Exchequer, 125–26; Lyndhurst as elder statesman, 243–45, 257; parliamentary reform and, 133, 140–47, 192–210
House of Lords in the Age of Reform (Turberville), 203
Hume, Joseph, 180
Hunt, Henry, 41
Huskisson, William, 63, 64, 66, 70
Hutchinson, Thomas, 2, 4

Ingham, John, 27–28
Ings, James, 49
Ireland: Catholic Emancipation and affairs in, 67, 70, 71–73, 75, 77–88; famine of 1845, 228; municipal reform and, 205–207; political and religious reform in, 226–27; proposals for political unification of, 171–73; Russell government and, 236
Irish Coercion Act, 171, 229

Jay Treaty (1794), 16–18, 21
Jefferson, Thomas, 21–22
Jeffrey, Lord, 144
Jewish Emancipation, 243–44, 252–53
Juvenile Offenders Bill, 216

Knatchbull, Sir Edward, 130
Knighthood, of Lyndhurst, 41
Knighton, Sir William, 63, 64, 81

Ladies of the Bedchamber, 217
Landsdowne, Lord, 66, 174

Lawrence, Thomas, 41
Legal reform, 222–23
Le Marchant, Sir Denis, 117, 147, 148, 149, 151
Libel, prosecutions for, 93–94
Lichfield House Compact, 180
Lieven, Princess, 101, 112
Life of Lord Lyndhurst, A (Martin, 1884), ix–x
Lincoln's Inn Society, 28
Liverpool, Lord, 60
Lives of the Chief Justices of England (Campbell, 1849–1857), 251–52, 305n.21
Lives of Lord Lyndhurst and Lord Brougham (Campbell, 1869), ix, x–xi
Local Courts Bill, 161, 163, 165–67
Lord Chancellor, position of, 56–59, 118, 175–80
Lucan, Lord, 253
Luddites, 27–28
Ludlam, Isaac, 35–37
Lyndhurst, Baron (John Singleton Copley, Jr.), *57, 164, 215, 240, 266:* Brougham and, 288n.9; Canning government, 60–62; Catholic Emancipation, 54–56, 77–88, 283n.17; charges of political corruption, 92–103; childhood of, 1–12; coat of arms, 281n.33; coronation of Victoria, 211–12; court reform, 104–10, 161, 163, 165–67; and Disraeli, 181–91; as elder statesmen, 235–45; family life of, 53–54; final years, 258–69; Goderich government, 62–65; Grey government, 117–27, 128–39; as High Steward of University of Cambridge, 218–19; as Lord High Chancellor, 56–59; image of in biographies, ix–xi; image of in histories, xi; legal career and entry into politics, 35–46; legal training and early career of, 23–34; marriage to Georgiana Goldsmith, 212–14; parliamentary reform, 128–39, 140–47, 149–59, 192–210; Peel government, 175–80, 219–20, 221–29; political activism during retirement, 229–34; political caricatures of, *86, 90,* 91–92, *95, 119, 123, 162;* political image of, xi–xvi; social reform, 214, 216–17; political significance of life of, 269–71; Thistlewood plot, 47–49; tour of U.S., 13–22; trial of Queen Caroline, 50–53; Wellington government, 65–68, 69–76, 77–88, 111–16
Lyndhurst, Lady (first wife), *42:* charges of political corruption, 92–103; death of, 167–71; description of, 124; marriage to Lyndhurst, 40–41; political activities of, xv, 132; relationship with Dudley, 147–48; relationship with Grey, 118, 121;
Lyndhurst, Lady (second wife): biography of Lyndhurst and, 260; and Lyndhurst's religious beliefs, 264; Lyndhurst's retirement from politics, 241, 242; marriage to Lyndhurst, 212–14

Machin, G.I.T., 71
Martin, Sir Theodore (biographer): on conflict between Bentinck and Lyndhurst, 231; on death of Lady Lyndhurst, 169–70; image of Lyndhurst, ix–x; on Lyndhurst and Catholic Emancipation, 283n.17; Lyndhurst and court reform, 124; Lyndhurst's early legal career, 23; on Lyndhurst as elder statesman, 257; Lyndhurst's entry into politics, 37; on Lyndhurst interest in U.S. Civil War, 306–307n.17; on Lyndhurst and legal reform, 223; Lyndhurst and Napoleon III, 246; Lyndhurst and parliamentary reform, 201; Lyndhurst and religion, 264; on Lyndhurst's remarriage, 214; on Lyndhurst's retirement, 241; on portrait of Copley family, 8; on Tamworth Manifesto, 178
Mastership of the Rolls, 54, 107
Melbourne, Lord, xii, 172–74, 179, 195–96, 203, 207
Merewether, Henry, 200
Military, 254–56
Monarchy, constitutional, 113
Moncreiff, James, 258–59
Money Bills, 257
Monster Meetings, 224–27
Municipal Corporations Bill, 188–89, 192–210
Murray, Sir George, 152
Murray, John, 117–18

Namier, Sir Lewis, 271
Napoleon, 29–30
Napoleon III, 246
Nasmyth, James, 259
Native Americans, 19–20
Naval Reserves, 255–56
Nicholas, Czar, 244
Norton, Caroline, 187, 248

O'Connell, Daniel, 67, 72, 79, 171, 187, 189–90, 205, 206, 224–27
O'Connell v. the Queen, 224–27
Orsini, Felice, 254
Ottoman Empire, 244–45

Palmerston, Lord, 54–55, 252
Parliament: Grey government and reform of, 128–39; Lyndhurst's entry into politics, 37–46; Lyndhurst and reform of, 140–47, 149–59, 192–210; William IV's resistance to reform, 113–14
Peel, Sir Robert: formation of government, 175–80, 219–20; Lyndhurst and Grey government, 120; Lyndhurst's last term as Chancellor, 221–29; on Lyndhurst as Lord Steward of Cambridge University, 219; parliamentary reform and, 130, 151, 197–98, 200–201, 202; Queen Victoria and, 217; reform of criminal law, 109; Wellington government and Catholic question, 66, 69, 73, 75, 77, 82, 83, 91
Peerage: creations and parliamentary reform, 140–41, 149–50, 155–56; Lyndhurst's elevation to, 56–59; Lyndhurst on life peerages, 246–47
Pelham, Peter, 5
Pentridge Rising, 35–37
Pergami, Bartolomeo, 50–52
Pinckney, Charles Cotesworth, 21
Pitt, William, 67
Political caricatures, of Lyndhurst, *86, 90*, 91–92, *95, 119, 123, 162*
Politics: Catholic Emancipation, 54–56; image of Lyndhurst, xi–xvi; Lyndhurst's observations on American, 16–18, 21–22. *See also* Conservative party; Lord High Chancellor; Lyndhurst, Lord; Parliament; Tory party; Whig party
Pornography, 249–51

Preston, Richard, 39
Prime Minister: Lyndhurst and office of, 127, 203, 204
Prison reform, 216
Property rights, 198–99

Reaction and Reconstruction in English Politics 1832–1852 (Gash), 198
Religion: Lyndhurst and legal reform, 224; Lyndhurst's views on, 61–62, 264–65. *See also* Catholic Emancipation; Dissenters; Jewish Emancipation; Unitarians
Republicanism, xi–xii
Revolution: Pentridge Rising as, 35–37; preoccupation with in Regency England, 50, 127; riots over parliamentary reform, 137; Spa Fields riots as, 31–34; Thistlewood plot as, 47–49. *See also* French Revolution; Treason
Reynolds, Sir Joshua, 5, 9
Richmond, Duke of, 199
Ripon, Lord, 232
Romilly, Sir Samuel, 106
Rose, Sir Philip, 183
Rothschild, Lionel de, 252–53
Russia, policy for expansion, 244–45
Russell, Lord John, 70, 128–29, 133, 138, 180, 199, 202, 228, 235, 236, 239, 241

Salisbury, Lady, 92, 182, 213
Scarlett, James, 45
Scotland, court system, 109
Seditious Meetings Bill, 44
Sergeant-at-Law, 28
Sheil, Richard Lalor, 205
Singleton, Mary (paternal grandmother), 1
Six Acts, 41–44
Small v. Attwood, 125–26
Social reform: Lyndhurst's support of, 214, 216–17
Somerset, Lady Fitzroy, 96
Spa Fields riots, 31–34
Spence, Thomas, 34
Spencer, Earl, 173
Spring-Rice, Thomas, 174
Stanley, Lord, 171, 177, 228, 235–36, 262
Stewart, Robert, 236
Sugden, Sir Edward, 226
Sutton, Manners, 153–54
Sykes, Lady Henrietta, 182–84, 190–91

Tamworth Manifesto, 176, 178–79
Tankerville, Lady, 182
Taylor, M. A., 107
Tea Act (May 1773), 2–3
Tenterden, Lord, 121
Test and Corporation Acts, repeal of, 70
Thesiger, Frederick, 202
Thistlewood, Arthur, xv, 31, 47–49
Thompson, E. P., 27
Tidd, Richard, 49
Torrens, W. P., 207
Tory party, 63–64, 66–67, 120, 129–30, 134, 145–46, 177
Townshend Act (1768), 2
Treason, 31–34, 47–49. *See also* Revolution
Treaty of Paris (1783), 16–17
Trent Affair, 263
Trinity College, 9–12, 23. *See also* Cambridge University
Tuberville, A. S., 204
Turner, William, 35–37

Unitarians, 61, 224
United States: Copley family and American Revolution, 1–4, 6–7; Lyndhurst's interest in events in, 262–64; Lyndhurst's tour of, 13–22

Victoria, Queen: coronation of, 211–12; on Lyndhurst's death, 265; relationship with Peel, 217
The Victorian Chancellors (Atlay), 45
Vindication of the English Constitution in a Letter to a Noble and Learned Lord (Disraeli), 188–89
Vyvyan, Sir Richard, 130
Voting: qualifications for and parliamentary reform, 129, 194

Wales, court system, 109
Ward, Henry, 171
Warren, Samuel, 165
Washington, D. C., Lyndhurst's description of, 18
Washington, George, 19, 21
Waterford, Marquis of, 68
Watson, Dr. James, xiv, 31–34, 305n.21
Weightman, George, 35–37
Wellington, Duke of: Catholic Emancipation, 77–88; court reform, 163; formation of Peel government, 174–75; Goderich government, 62–63; government of, 65–68, 69–76; Lyndhurst and Grey government, 120; parliamentary reform, 138, 141, 146, 152–53, 156, 157, 193, 208–209; on scandal involving Lady Lyndhurst, 100; social unrest and decline of government, 111–16
West, Benjamin, 5, 20
Wetherell, Sir Charles, 83, 109, 130, 278n.33
Wharncliffe, Baron, 130–31, 133, 138, 141, 142, 145, 146–47
Whigs: formation of Peel government, 177; interpretation of history, xiii; Ireland and political unification, 172–74; Lyndhurst and Grey government, 117–27; parliamentary reform, 131–32, 135, 140–47, 195, 207; property versus human rights, 301n.22
Wilkes, Captain Charles, 263
William IV: formation of Peel government, 174–75; parliamentary reform and, 111, 112–13, 129, 131, 133, 140–41, 149–51, 155–56
Williams, John, 106–107
Winchilsea, Earl of (George Finch-Hatton), 82
Women's rights, 247–49, 304n.9

....
.... of his past role as a trumpet of his party
.... in the House of Lords after a long absence
.... both sides of the floor. He had come to speak in support
of Brougham's motion to withhold the royal assent from an Act passed by
the Canadian legislature granting compensation to those who had suffered
losses in the suppression of the rebellion in 1837 and 1838. He argued that
the measure would open the way for some who had fomented the rebellion
to receive compensation for losses they might have suffered in its suppression. In effect, they would profit from the consequences of their own lawlessness. On the other hand, the issue of full self-government in Canada
.... the Governor General, had formed a colonial
.... majority party. The com-
.... ernment and
.... Canada and